Crimes, Constables, and Courts
Order and Transgression in a Canadian City, 1816–1970

D1586420

Blending narrative and social history in this fascinating study of crime in a Canadian community, John Weaver describes both the patterns of crime and the evolution of the Canadian criminal justice system over 150 years.

Using Hamilton, Ontario, as his model, Weaver makes extensive use of newspaper accounts and police, court, and jail records in a revealing exploration of individual crime cases and overall trends in crime. In tracing the origin and evolution of courts, juries, police, and punishments, Weaver takes into account various social and cultural issues. For example, he shows how increasing centralization and professionalization of the criminal justice system and police have deprived communities of input, and how the legal system has been male dominated and biased against newcomers, strangers, and marginalized social groups. Often critical of the 'state,' Weaver paints a sympathetic view of police constables, who play an ambiguous role in the community while being saddled with an expanding array of onerous duties.

Crimes, Constables, and Courts is history at its best – informative, entertaining, and accessible with a lively human element woven throughout.

JOHN C. WEAVER is professor of history, McMaster University.

Crimes, Constables, and Courts

*Order and Transgression
in a Canadian City, 1816–1970*

JOHN C. WEAVER

McGill-Queen's University Press
Montreal & Kingston • London • Buffalo

© McGill-Queen's University Press 1995
ISBN 0-7735-1274-8 (cloth)
ISBN 0-7735-1275-6 (paper)

Legal deposit second quarter 1995
Bibliothèque nationale du Québec

Printed in Canada on acid-free paper

This book has been published with the help of grants from the Social
Science Federation of Canada, using funds provided by the Social
Sciences and Humanities Research Council of Canada, and from
McMaster University.

McGill-Queen's University Press is grateful to the Canada Council for
support of its publishing program.

Canadian Cataloguing in Publication Data

Weaver, John C.
   Crimes, constables, and courts: order and transgression in a Canadian
   city, 1816–1970
   Includes bibliographical references and index.
   ISBN 0-7735-1274-8 (bound) –
   ISBN 0-7735-1275-6 (pbk.)
   1. Crime analysis – Ontario – Hamilton – History. 2. Criminal justice,
   Administration of – Ontario – Hamilton – History. 3. Police – Ontario
   – Hamilton – History. 4. Hamilton (Ont.) – Social conditions. 1. Title.
   HV6810.H34W42 1995   363.2'09713'52   C94-900938-5

This book was typeset by Typo Litho Composition Inc. in
10/12 Baskerville.

All illustrations, with the exception of the picture of the radio
dispatcher which is the property of Philip Sworden, are taken from Special
Collections, Hamilton Public Library, and are published with
permission.

Contents

Figures and Tables   vii

Acknowledgments   xi

Illustrations   xiii

Introduction   3

1 Criminal Justice and the Waning of the Old Regime   23

2 Expeditious Courts and Muscular Mercenaries   64

3 Human Agents of Civic Order   108

4 Forced Liberalization and Technological
   Enthusiasms   147

5 The Meaning of Trends in Crime Rates   188

6 The Enduring Circumstances of Violence and
   Theft   225

Conclusion   263

Notes   277

Index   317

Figures and Tables

FIGURES

1.1 The Evolution of Criminal Courts in the Hamilton
Area   30

1.2 Gore District Incarcerations: Crimes against Person,
1832–51   44

1.3 Gore District Incarcerations: Crimes against Property,
1832–51   45

1.4 Gore District Incarcerations: Moral Order Offences,
1832–51   47

2.1 Vagrancy, Vice, and Moral Order Charges, Hamilton,
1859–1959   78

3.1 Moral Order Prosecutions per Constable, Hamilton,
1897–1959   114

3.2 Turnover in the Hamilton Police Force, Men Leaving
and Hired, 1900–45   125

3.3 Annual Wages for Selected Ranks, 1872–1919   126

3.4 Growth of the Hamilton Police Force, 1900–45   127

3.5 Background of New Constables, Former Occupations,
1900–45   131

4.1 Relationship of Size of Police Force to Population of
     Hamilton, 1900–45   166

4.2 By-Law Summonses per 1000 Inhabitants,
     1886–1952   173

4.3 Violent Deaths: Homicides and Automobile Accidents,
     1870–1970   177

5.1 Larcenies per 1000 Inhabitants, Boston, 1849–1949   192

5.2 Assaults per 1000 Inhabitants, Boston, 1849–1949   193

5.3 Offences against Property without Violence, England,
     1860–1910   194

5.4 Court Appearances for Assault, England,
     1860–1910   195

5.5 Theft Rates in Hamilton: Court Appearances,
     1859–1970   205

5.6 Theft Rates in Hamilton: Public Reports and Court
     Appearances, 1859–1970   210

5.7 Trend of Assaults per 1000 Inhabitants, Hamilton, Five-Year
     Intervals   212

5.8 Homicides in Hamilton, 1870–1970   218

6.1 Major Groupings of Theft Occurrences, Hamilton,
     1934–5 and 1942   246

6.2 Value of Items Stolen, Hamilton, 1934–5 and 1942   249

6.3 Articles Most Frequently Reported As Stolen, 1934–5 and
     1942   251

6.4 Most Frequently Cited Places for Thefts in Hamilton,
     1934–5 and 1942   255

TABLES

1.1 Examples of the More Active Justices of the Peace in the
     Gore District, 1833–51   41

2.1 Sex of Complainants before Police Magistrate's Court
     according to Selected Crimes and Groups of Crimes,
     1859–1918   75

2.2 Disposition of Cases before Police Magistrate's Court,
     Hamilton, 1859–1918   79

3.1 Source of Complaints to Police Magistrate's Court
     according to Selected Crimes and Groups of Crimes,
     1859–1918   132

Acknowledgments

I am deeply grateful for the assistance this work has received from the Social Sciences and Humanities Research Council of Canada and the McMaster University Arts Research Board, and for the support extended by family, friends, and students.

I am indebted to several generations of librarians, in Hamilton and elsewhere, who had the wisdom to preserve the records of our past. For my students and myself, public libraries have been indispensable.

In this regard, I especially wish to thank the custodians of the special collections of the Hamilton Public Library, who are maintaining and building an important collection of historical resources for the Hamilton-Wentworth region.

The Hamilton and Wentworth Regional Police Department granted access to records and a place to work when reviewing them. At the department, Cathy Giudice took an active interest and assisted with locating material. The Hamilton Law Association permitted access to its library.

Carolyn Gray of the Archives of Ontario directly initiated this project with a telephone call, during which she described the contents of boxes of material unearthed while preparing a finding aid on Hamilton's civic records. She would have written a better book. My search for directions in the expanding field of criminal justice history was helped by David Philips of the University of Melbourne. As Messecar visiting professor of history at McMaster University in the fall of 1991, David saved me from many errors and inspired by example. A superb teacher, he coaxed reflection and posed a new set of questions that had not occurred to me. Greg Marquis, who read an early draft of the manuscript, greatly improved it. He has brought intelligent commentary and thorough research to the topic of Canadian policing. The lively and critical members of the legal history group organized by Jim Phillips in the faculty of law at the University of Toronto read and commented on an earlier version of chapter 5. For their corrections and generous sharing of ideas and sources, the anonymous readers for McGill-Queen's University Press and the Social Science Federation of Canada have my thanks.

A few friends eased the task of digesting a considerable volume of raw information. More than a decade ago, Helen Carson assisted with the research on the Gore District jail records. More recently, I was fortunate in having as summer research assistants Robert Perrins, Josh Spinner, and William Carter. Jay White contributed to the analysis of the data. It is a rare pleasure to see that all four are becoming scholars in their own right. Students in my crime and criminal justice course have furnished information and insights; some of their papers are cited in the footnotes. By her uncanny ability to detect nonsense, injustice, and authoritarianism Joan Tamorria Weaver has always influenced what I have written and done. Brian Raychaba gave the manuscript careful and critical attention. An early draft was read by Phillip Sworden. Philip Cercone of McGill-Queen's University Press encouraged important revisions without suggesting how I should write this book. Curtis Fahey, a thorough and diplomatic editor, compelled me often to clarify thoughts and prose. I accept sole responsibility for the contents of the book.

My interest in the topics covered in this book grew out of a longstanding curiosity about all aspects of life in the city, and particularly about issues of order and authority. However, the deeper motivation for the book originated in a personal nightmare. The murder of a colleague concentrated attention on crime and the criminal justice system in a terrible way. I dedicate this book to the memory of a distinguished scholar and office neighbour, Edith Wightman.

An artist's conception of the Gore District courthouse in Hamilton, 1818–29. Three days after his trial, on 5 September 1828, Michael Vincent stepped through the arched window and onto a gallows platform.

The Georgian courthouse, c. 1875. Built in 1827–9, the courthouse was later expanded to accommodate new facilities (including a jail yard). This photograph shows how the complex would have appeared when Michael McConnell was convicted of murder and hanged. A street behind the courthouse and jail was named Tyburn Lane, an allusion to Tyburn Tree, the notorious seventeenth- and eighteenth-century gallows site in London.

An unidentified but typically sturdy Hamilton
constable, *c.* 1890.

Another sturdy constable, a war veteran, undertaking a relatively new duty, c. 1925. The task of directing traffic at the intersection of King and James streets was one of many chores added to police work by the automobile revolution.

The 'Castle,' Barton Street Jail, *c.* 1890. Opened in 1877, it remained in service until 1978. Shortly before its demolition, the public was invited to visit its dank cells and to sense briefly the misery experienced by generations of suspects and prisoners.

The imposing third courthouse was constructed in the Second Empire style, a form popular for North American public buildings and one that well expressed the affluence and confidence of the city and county.

This crude and rare photograph, *c.* 1885, shows a constable escorting three prisoners – perhaps vagrants – from the police lock-up into the police magistrate's courtroom on the second floor of the police station. Prisoners walked across what was known as 'the bridge of sighs,' a satirical allusion to the bridge in Venice over which prisoners were led for trial in the ducal palace.

Ready to hear complainants, give advice, and prepare summonses: a contemporary of Toronto's more famous police magistrate, Colonel George T. Denison, George F. Jelfs likewise operated with enormous confidence in his own judgment. For years, the two men ran the busiest courts in the province (*c.* 1920).

Always on the look-out for cost-saving devices, Hamilton council authorized the purchase of this motorized wagon in 1912. Along with the telephone, motorized vehicles assured quicker response to emergencies and trouble. Technological innovations helped revolutionize police work. Constables were no longer merely called upon to deliver summonses; they could intervene during or soon after an incident (*c.* 1915).

Inside the ornate courthouse, courtroom number 1, with high ceilings and a massive carved dais and throne, provided a proper Victorian setting for the pomp of the assize and a counterpoint to accommodations at the jail (*c.* 1890).

Motorcycles were widely used first in the 1920s to patrol the suburbs, which were not covered by beats. In this scene, *c.* 1945, they appear in front of the nearly new police headquarters. The door at the left centre of the picture led to the juvenile court, which had been separated physically from the police magistrate's courtroom by 1937.

Miss Muriel Bostwick, secretary, during a warm morning at the crown attorney's office in the courthouse, *c.* 1956. The worn and mixed furnishings indicate that the back-office operations of the criminal justice system were managed economically, with none of the symbolic display of the major courtrooms.

The link between the police force and militarism was evinced and sustained by high enlistment rates during two world wars. For most constables, patriotism and organized religion were the unquestioned foundations of civic peace. They are seen here participating in a Sunday church parade, some wearing service decorations. Yet the composition of the force was changing and new ideals, such as education and specialization, were influencing hiring and promotions (c. 1955).

This jury room in the third courthouse had a striking similarity with that depicted in the American movie 'Twelve Angry Men.' The similarities between an American courthouse and that in a Canadian jurisdiction were more than a matter of appearances. In both countries, the jury was praised as a cornerstone of democracy; however, alterations in the court system of Ontario, from the 1870s to the 1970s, increasingly diminished the role of the jury.

The all-male jury that found Evelyn Dick not guilty of murdering her husband poses at the side entrance to the courthouse, February 1947.

A common courthouse scene, *c.* 1947. The justice of the peace – in this instance deputy police magistrate Harry Burville – supervises the preparation of bail documents. The suspect was Evelyn Dick's boyfriend, Bill Bohozuk.

A garrulous group of professional debaters, members of the Hamilton Law Association must have felt inhibited in their library in the courthouse (*c.* 1956).

A meeting of Hamilton's sombre patriarchs of law and order, the Hamilton Police Commission, *c.* 1962: police chief Len Lawrence, county judge Allan Ambrose, magistrate Walter Tuchtie, Mayor Lloyd Jackson, clerk James Berry. The mural of the city market provided an appropriate backdrop, because some of the police work of the pioneer village involved enforcing regulations at an early market on the same site as the one depicted.

One of the first grand juries to include women undertakes the traditional tour of the courthouse, ostensibly as part of its historic responsibility to inspect public buildings (*c.* 1958). Appearances suggest that jury service was an occasion for citizens to assert their respectability and civic pride, though they may have found the duty inconvenient. The days of the grand jury were numbered.

The Hamilton force had started to train constables in classroom settings in the 1930s. Mock trials were a part of their education by the 1960s. Here constables rehearse in the police magistrate's court in 1961. This room had changed little since the late 1930s when a new police headquarters building provided a fresh venue. Spartan fixtures were a reminder that it was the lowest court. The royal coat of arms may say as much about loyalist myths in Hamilton as about the traditionalism of the legal establishment.

Constable Jessie Meiklejohn, 1962. Many publicity pictures during the 1950s and 1960s implied that the police force had opened its ranks to women. In reality, the force had set a limit on the number of female constables and on the range of positions they could hold. By the 1970s only eight of more than 500 constables were women. 'I can just see a woman in a tap room handling a 250–pound man' was the reaction within the force to provincial pressure to hire more women. Typically, women dealt with traffic safety, juveniles, and clerical duties.

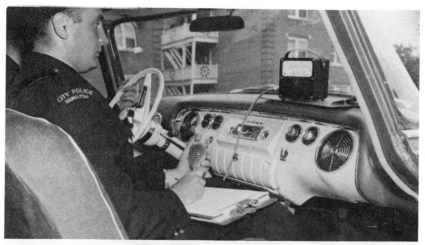

Radar joined assorted technological aids – such as radio and photography – in regulating the city's life in the 1950s. This photograph was taken around 1956.

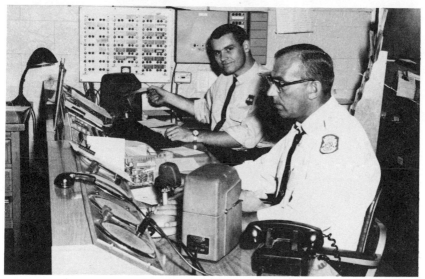

The presence of a radio dispatcher underscored the importance of communications in the regulated city. The Hamilton force refused to hire civilians for this duty, maintaining that only a constable should direct other constables into potentially life-threatening situations. In this respect, as in several others, old attitudes about the fraternal and quasi-military nature of police work intersected with technology. Left to right, Roger Geary and Philip Sworden, 1965.

The new police headquarters, *c.* 1975, suggests the administrative offices of a corporation. The police force was seeking a new image in the community.

Crimes, Constables, and Courts

Introduction

It is a rainy day in November 1992. The entrance to the glazed-brick building on King William Street leads directly into a spacious reception hall, where a pair of women at a long counter answer public inquiries. Behind them stand about twenty desks, each with a computer terminal. A radio plays; the lyrics of 'Heart of Gold' are barely audible above the hum of a pin printer. Women staffing the area wear casual attire. Cheerful and busy, chatting and at ease, commenting on the weather, they give the impression that the office belongs to a modern firm with a pleasantly relaxed atmosphere. The arrival of a uniformed constable to collect a computerized record of a young offender with prior offences jars the mood but helps establish that this is the regional police headquarters. The equipment proclaims the era of records and information, the ascendancy of bureaucracy, while the openness and casualness reflect recent policies to shed certain barriers between police and community.

Six blocks away to the north, on a bleak patch of land lying at the margins of the city's declining industrial district, stands another relatively new and distinctively designed building, the Hamilton-Wentworth Regional Detention Centre. Built in 1978, it replaced 'the castle,' a century-old jail whose stone walls unequivocally reminded passersby that it had been built to punish. From external appearances, the new facility, like the police building, simulates corporate offices.

It is a short walk southwest from the police headquarters to the regional courthouse. Built in 1957 to meet demands for more courtrooms, it soon proved inadequate. Additional courtrooms now are located in two other buildings in the city's core. As the setting for the city and county's more serious criminal trials, the spotless courthouse has retained the decorum, stature, and many of the traditions of the English criminal justice system. Exterior panels depict events from the region's past. The courthouse embodies history.

The three buildings – police station, jail, and courthouse – suggest a few superficial things about the contemporary system of law and order in this city. In recent decades, it has been reasonably well funded, organized into specialized branches, and fashioned to make symbolic statements. The architecture of the criminal justice institutions declares that liberal symbolic statements were recently prepared. But what actually occurs or has occurred behind the walls of police stations, courts, and jails? Where and how did these institutions originate? To answer these questions and learn more about law and order in a community, it is necessary keep in mind the fact that behind new façades and contemporary trends are a thousand years of English history. Claiming distinctive needs, branch societies spreading from the English trunk occasionally deviated from the original institutional models and guiding principles. The history of English justice, therefore, is trebly important: it explains many features of the Canadian system of law; it assists with the identification of innovations; and it highlights ideals against which to measure the consequences of innovation.

The tandem evolution of the law and the state in England during the last millennium produced institutions and practices unlike those on the continent of Europe. Exported through colonization, English institutions and practices, though formed in an insular kingdom, provided the basis for law and order in many new societies.[1] Yet local circumstances in settlement colonies favoured modifications to the English common law, while colonial responsibility for domestic affairs and the impossibility of direct administration from London allowed innovation. Unfettered by most of the old country's social and legal complexities, including its aristocratic particularities, colonial governments modified some features of the law in advance of the English parliament. This was certainly the case in Canada West/Ontario from the 1840s to the 1870s. However, as legal historian Paul Romney has suggested – with reference to the establishment of county crown attorneys – Canadian law reforms were occasionally inspired by British inquiries that had highlighted issues but not achieved actual change at home.[2] It is possible, therefore, to treat the history of criminal law in Canada as a branch of imperial or commonwealth history, as part of an international exchange of ideas. That frames a part of the following story.

Drawing on Romney's analysis one may argue that, owing to the conservatism of the governing élite of Upper Canada, the colony lagged behind England in the reformation of criminal justice. The old regime lingered awhile in Upper Canada because of an imperious 'family compact' which resisted even those moderate changes that England had adopted. What next occurred, from the 1840s to the 1870s, was a series of innovations (crown attorneys, police commissions, trials without juries) made feasible by mid-century social changes that unsettled élites, by the province's attraction to expedient measures that promised economy, efficiency, and convenience, and by inquiries into criminal justice systems in the United States and the United Kingdom. The Upper Canadian or Ontario measures almost invariably elevated professional training or otherwise sought to insulate the criminal justice system from popular participation. The old regime's reliance on local amateurs was in retreat. Local politics and social conditions as well as transatlantic exchanges in ideas affected the shifts in the institutional arrangements of criminal justice; however, what transpired with respect to the law in modern England and its colonies also belongs to a wider pattern in the recent history of social organization.

For at least the last two hundred years in western Europe and its fragments in the New World, the growth in the power of the nation state and the force of technology – not just devices but the idea of technology itself – have eroded localism and amateurism. This erosion of localism and amateurism provides one of the organizing concepts for this book. Indeed, while many features of disorder and crime have persisted over the decades, the pursuit of order and justice has nevertheless promoted change in the institutions dealing with disorder and crime. These changes say less about the actual crimes committed in the community than they do about how community élites defined social problems and then set out to adapt to local circumstances the ideas about safety and control that obsessed the transatlantic world in the nineteenth century. One point of this observation is to stress the significance of institutional history for a social and cultural history of modern times. A 150-year study of criminal justice institutions provides the perspective required in order to see how modifications to institutions reveal the outlines of a culture in nearly constant transition. In fact, the creation of an ongoing law reform commission in Ontario in 1964 – a body that is still at work today – means that this jurisdiction sought to institutionalize change itself. Change was alien to the criminal justice authorities in colonial Upper Canada. The élites of the United Kingdom had attempted to replicate here the fundamentals of the old regime of the whig ascendancy with its balancing of royal and aristocratic, central and local, authority. The criminal justice institutions were meant to convey, in a variety of ways, the perpetuity of a social and moral hierarchy. In modern times, the many inquiries into the criminal justice system emphatically projected the modern state's homage to efficiency. Just what has been improved – the quest for justice or order – is a topic that will be considered.

Over a decade ago, Timothy Curtis advanced convincing and quite practical reasons for historians to pay close attention to institutions and the law when what many social historians wanted to study was crime.[3] Few things could be more difficult than studying crime divorced from the criminal justice system, although crime does exist apart from that system. Modern studies of victims and of criminals, for example, have yielded data suggesting that the real crime rate is far greater than the rate generated by the criminal justice system. Yet any attempt to study crimes in isolation from their legal consequences poses insurmountable research challenges: first, no means exists for deriving statistically valid samples when all crimes are not known; second, criminals tend to be either fairly tight-lipped or unreliable informants; third, it verges on the illogical to declare that a crime has been committed when no one has been tried and found guilty in law. But that raises a dilemma. If crimes exist only when parties have been tried and found guilty, historians would brand as criminals some individuals whom élites may have victimized through their influence over the apparatus of criminal justice. This complicity in injustice raises questions about the system itself. Is it neutral? Have élites manipulated it? If so, how profoundly have they manipulated it? Have broader community standards in any way made an impression upon it? Portions of this book treat these issues.

Let us return to the significance of criminal justice institutions for a study of culture and society. Not only must the institutions be understood in order to appreciate the data generated by the criminal justice apparatus and debated by historians and criminologists, but shifts in the institutions themselves illuminate community values and anxieties. Contemporary communities function as highly regulated places where people seek professional expertise and where professionalism is generally held in high regard. In fact, in contemporary North American communities the basis of legitimate power – that is, the basis of authority – rests in large measure on a trust in experts, on individuals trained for specific tasks. In the Canadian criminal justice system, reforms in the mid-nineteenth century concentrated on requiring legal training for the judges on the benches of the lowest city courts and, within several decades, other reforms brought rudimentary training to the work of constables. From the late nineteenth century onward, various forms of specialization – such as social welfare – were introduced. As Dorothy

Chunn has convincingly argued regarding the evolution of family courts, newer professions such as social work helped to establish 'socialized justice' in Ontario.[4]

Once, not all that long ago, professional management and trained officials staffing regulatory bodies were extremely rare: voluntarism prevailed in both civil and military matters. A narrative and analytical account of the transition to 'modern' ways of social organization could focus on aspects of health care, welfare, warfare, industrial organization, education, and countless other subjects. The topics central to this study – criminal justice, policing, and crime – readily illustrate the theme of professionalization. Fearful urban élites and utilitarian reformers, disatisfied with traditional methods of providing personal safety and security for property, initiated trends toward greater specialization and training. Though unevenly implemented, the changes introduced have become prime features of the modern era. That makes criminal justice history a compelling subject, but there are other reasons for looking at criminal justice. Not only is it a mine field of contemporary controversies, but there is another darker aspect too. Many themes encountered in criminal justice history have dramatic and visceral impact. A brush with a crime or a court appearance can shake the soul. The subject has a disturbing fascination.

This book traces, from settlement to recent times, the institutional developments and underlying values affecting law and order in and around Hamilton. At times, the location of the city and certain trends in its economic and demographic history play a part in the narrative. Hamilton originated in 1816 largely because of a need for a courthouse to serve the growing settlements at the western end of Lake Ontario. The resulting village centred on a courthouse square. Initially, community and courthouse were closely connected because, following the British model, the justices of the peace who attended to local law and order managed village and district government. Boom growth occasioned by immigration, public works, and land speculation helped alter that constitution in the 1830s. Hamilton secured a town charter in 1832. During the next twenty years, as it grew from 1500 to 20,000, fears about newcomers – and especially transients – sped the local adoption of changes in the criminal justice system. At mid-century, Hamilton, a prosperous lakeport, also became a railway centre, a hub on an international rail system. The building of the railway and its rolling stock drew metallurgical industries to the city.

Always closely associated with the Great Lakes cities of the United States, Hamilton had developed especially strong business and labour ties with the republic by the early 1900s. After the turn-of-the-century, the proliferation of new factories, particularly branch plants, attracted

British, Canadian, and American migrants; the city also drew southern and central European immigrants. With its population increasing from just under 37,000 in 1881 to more than 100,000 during the First World War, Hamilton experienced many growing pains in the concentrated years of boom growth from 1905 to 1912. For example, immigrant workers confronted the more conservative members of the city establishment, both on labour questions and on matters of public morality. The police department figured in the complicated social issues faced by a new type of Canadian city, a city struggling to deal with order, health, welfare, and civic efficiency.

From the early 1900s until the early 1980s, Hamilton had reason to pride itself on being Canada's representative 'lunch bucket city.' Gradually the foundries and factories were overtaken in importance by steel making; Hamilton at mid-century became synonymous with steel. After the Second World War, the city once more experienced an industrial and suburban boom, and again became home to thousands of immigrants. Slowly, the formal properties of the criminal justice system adapted to growth and social change. Although the Hamilton-Wentworth region has continued to grow, the population within the city boundaries peaked at around 310,000 in the mid-1970s. That is when this study ends. The introduction of regional government and the beginning of economic deline present a convenient point to conclude. After the mid-1970s, the deindustrialization of Hamilton, the contraction of the steel industry, and a sequence of recessions have created pessimism, misery, and despair.[5] Doubtless, an examination of the police-occurrence books or jail records of the last fifteen years will someday divulge a great deal about this new time of stress.

The history of the city is of some importance to a chronicle of crime and criminal justice. During the several boom periods just mentioned, an anxiety-ridden and conservative élite encountered a changed city; habitually, some of the tension was dealt with by the criminal justice system, principally by the police and the city's lowest court. True the scale and concentration of Hamilton's industrial working class and immigrant communities meant that civic, judicial, and police officials – most certainly constables on the beat – avoided the moral fervour seen at times in neighbouring Toronto. Yet the nuances of local history have little bearing on the major themes of this book. If anything, the conclusions endorse the idea that – judged by the evolution of the criminal justice system – the local community has lost its importance. It has been displaced by the province and, to a lesser extent, by federal measures and international affiliations.

In its descriptive features, the book offers only a general historical guide to Canadian institutions of law and order. Anything more – a comprehensive review of common law and statutes, of the shifts in and additions to crimes, courts, and enforcement agencies – would create a ponderous and tedious reference work. Apart from its intellectual sterility, apart too from its likely failure to make sense of the whole, such an approach would ignore the way things have actually been done. If there is one thing that criminal-justice historians agree upon, it is that statute books and manuals present an orderly picture of processes that in practice are often directed by circumstances. When an attempt is made to see how the local apparatus churned along over a long period of time in one jurisdiction, important though subtle innovations come to light. An example is the history of the preliminary hearing. It originated in England as a hearing before two or more justices of the peace who had to determine whether a complainant's accusation had sufficient merit to require a trial. Today, its ostensible purpose remains, but now the hearing is before a single judge. Moreover, during the last one hundred years it has become a place where a defence lawyer questioning prosecution witnesses works to discover the details of the crown attorney's case against a client. The development of the preliminary hearing depicts portentous changes: the demise of the justice of the peace, the growth of the legal profession, and the rise of the criminal defence lawyer. A study of provincial statutes would not have disclosed the significance of changes to this procedure.

For reasons of compression and clarity, then, what follows must be a selective review. There are further explanations for this approach. Far too little systematic writing has been done on the history of the justice of the peace in Canada, on the lower and intermediate courts, and on the jury. As well, the fragmentary nature of the primary sources compels selectivity. The survival of numerous – though broken – series of police, court, and jail records is a wonder to be appreciated; however, at times, the gaps leave no choice but to construct a narrative out of scraps of information. The following chapters have little to say about changes to many specific legal processes and concepts, the precise set of crimes dealt with by any one court at any one point, and other concerns. Yet the basic structure of the court system, the justice of the peace, the police magistrate, the evolution of policing, and the crown attorney receive ample attention. They typify the theme of evolving professionalization and centralization.

In a federal state where details about criminal justice stray across jurisdictional boundaries, it would be folly to attempt in one volume a description of developments for the entire country. As Desmond Brown has demonstrated in *The Genesis of the Canadian Criminal Code of 1892*, the post-Confederation parliament of Canada began immediately to try to create uniform criminal laws for the new country. The legislative history of that endeavour is complicated enough, but Brown reports a further difficulty. 'If there was a large measure of uniformity in the penal law across the dominion twenty-five years after Confederation, there was still little or none in the institutions that applied it.'[6] For example, Upper Canada/Ontario maintained three levels of courts, while most other provinces supported only two. As a practical matter, therefore, a community-based study offers the appropriate scale for blending law and society, even though this seemingly simplified setting introduces a jurisdictional mare's nest. The third courthouse that served the city and county from 1878 to 1956 sat on land deeded to the crown, had been built with city and county money, and was managed by a joint committee of these local governments. In a courtroom festooned with royal symbols, provincially appointed judges heard cases dealing with federal criminal acts. Cases were prosecuted by county crown attorneys, provincially appointed crown counsels, or both.[7] City, village, and township officials, of different sorts in different eras, selected the panels of jurors. In short, all levels of government participated; indeed, by the late nineteenth century, international aspects to the maintenance of law and order had developed and these professional bridges across borders proliferated in the twentieth century.

Though the several layers of locale cannot be ignored, the evolution of Hamilton's criminal justice system was not unique. Between the early 1830s and the early 1850s, for instance, major changes in punishment, summary justice, public order, and policing occurred in Hamilton as they did in most transatlantic communities. Local authorities introduced some of the new measures in response to specific episodes and general fears attending massive migrations. The communal and coercive controls on old-world landed estates had dissolved and set loose hundreds of thousands of people who became wage workers. Many of them – young males – crowded into rowdy labour camps thrown up around canal and railway construction sites or else they migrated into towns and cities where their recreations, protests, penchant for violence and manipulation by ambitious men alarmed local élites. Michael Cross's justly famous account of how Peter Aylen and a band of roughly 200 Irishmen terrorized Bytown from 1835 to 1837 provides an example of the disturbances that local magistrates could not curb.[8] A host of revisions to the system of law and order soon followed throughout the colony.

As interesting as the individual juridical checks on troublesome migrants and newcomers were, the whole system of law and order in this era as in others articulated forms of sovereign authority, patterns of subordination, and expressions of social power.[9] In common with many European or colonial jurisdictions, the institutions of law and order that originally applied to settlers in the vicinity of modern Hamilton expressed monarchical and aristocratic forms typical of what proved to be a passing old regime. This fading regime insisted on a moral and social hierarchy in which crown, aristocracy, and gentry managed the country and checked 'the passions of the lower orders.' The criminal justice system expressed this hierarchical arrangement, though the twilight of the old order already extended over much of colonized North America just as British authorities, intent on preserving the old regime in a largely unsettled portion of the continent, put into place the instruments of law and order in Upper Canada. In the old regime, sovereignty was personified – focused in the person of the monarch – and so was local justice; the crown issued the commissions of the peace empowering magistrates, some of whom gathered quarterly in the courthouse to deal with law, order, and local government. Justices of the peace and other local notables, usually lacking a scrap of legal training, mediated between crown and commoners. With their aid, commoners drafted petitions in which they approached the crown for redress – an exercise that underlined the respective places of the two groups in the social hierarchy. It is not surprising that Chief Justice John Beverley Robinson – a defender of the old regime – ruled in a decision that the right of English subjects to petition the king was a privilege designed to allow freedom of action and to maintain the common good.[10] The sovereign was not just the sole symbol of justice; the crown was to have a direct link with its subjects.

Just as reform altered the Old World institutions of law and order in the early nineteenth century, so did it affect institutions in this district of a colonial society. Nearly ceaseless innovation followed the initial burst of reform, bringing the administration of law and order to its contemporary position in a complicated federal arrangement that has permitted a diminishing measure of local autonomy and is managed by professionals and bureaucrats. The courthouse, symbolically placed on a central square, lost its exclusive position to a city hall and police stations; the appointed justices and judges had to share authority with elected representatives – the city councillors – and uniformed mercenaries – the local police. By the late twentieth century, demands on a court system that branched out into specialized jurisdictions required a dispersal of courtrooms in ordinary buildings around the city. The parchment commissions with bulky wax seals or the deferential petitions to the crown had been displaced by impersonal forms of standard size and records management, conducted with computers whose capacity for storing and retrieving personal information declared the intrusive ways of the modern state.

The development of the modern state provides a conspicuous

theme for a study of criminal justice. Upper Canada's old regime – like old regimes across Europe – had arbitrary features and a capacity for brutality and repression. Yet the state and its institutions were weak.[11] The modern criminal justice system has shed some arbitrary characteristics and the extreme legal violence of executions; however, the state has concurrently gained strength, and with that strength comes the potential for greater repression. State encroachment on privacy and individualism can be followed through the development of policing, prosecutorial offices, modes of punishment, and the kinds of laws enforced by the criminal justice system. This process requires close analysis, not only to expose the assembling of a 'colonial leviathan,' but to illuminate the state in a way that acknowledges progress in spite of well-founded concerns about its power.[12] It would be a serious misunderstanding of history to pine for an earlier, simpler, and presumably happier time. Aspects of the criminal justice system – or at least a few of the persons who exercised its authority – have been capricious, biased, and cruel.

The English common law that entered Upper Canada in 1792 differed in many ways from continental European law. Its most distinguishing feature, expressed by many particulars, centred on a traditional avoidance of direct state prosecution of a number of felonies. There is no space here to recount how state prosecution gradually was insinuated into the criminal justice system of England and the Anglo-colonial world. Yet the following chapters will reveal how the old-country restraints on state prosecution surfaced in Upper Canada/ Ontario and how, through the appearance of the crown attorney and the police, state prosecution actually arose in the second half of the nineteenth century. There will be an account too of how this epochal shift – achieved by colonial legislators – was countered by the rise of defence lawyers and restrained by the courts. The law itself, as E.P. Thompson argued persuasively in a famous passage in *Whigs and Hunters*, is not solely an instrument to be manipulated by an élite.[13]

The state increased its power mightily in the Victorian era, but the common law and uncommon jurists sometimes checked it. Over the centuries, the common law has expressed principles that have sustained the protection of the rights of the accused. Furthering the protection of individuals against the state has been an achievement of the courts and the defence lawyers. Professionalization and specialization have served individual rights as well the state. In certain situations, law schools, law societies, lawyers, and judges counterbalanced the state; they have been able to do so because of the law. Even the acceptance of the concept that trials represent an adversarial process has provided

a grounding for the preservation of rights in the absence of a constitutional bill of rights. When, during the nineteenth century, jurisdictions
throughout the transatlantic world elevated the rule of law, they gave
themselves greater authority, but paradoxically they also confirmed the
basis for resistance.

A great deal has changed and the state or crown in the Canadian
community under review has not been the unique beneficiary of
change. Legal professionalism, for example, ministered to more than
the needs of a state; it stimulated the vigilance of a legal profession
which could draw upon the riches of the common law and that stream
of the western intellectual tradition that has defended an individual's
rights. This fact alone leads to the obvious conclusion that the legal system ought to be studied historically. The operation of today's mechanisms of law and order are best described by a discussion that starts at
the beginning and proceeds historically, considering the dialectical
process of state innovations and attempts by jurists to uphold what they
perceive to be the traditions of the common law. Commentaries on the
law by legal authorities seldom display such a sense of evolution. They
dissect topics methodically according to stages in a contemporary process or by principles and concepts. Chronology and social forces have
had no major place in law texts. Indeed, the study of law has stripped
the law of connections with the economy and culture in an effort to establish itself as a self-contained discipline. More the pity, for the following pages illustrate that the study of law and history belong together.
More important, history can warn against facile claims that arise in contemporary debates about crimes, constables, and courts.

Like many North American jurisdictions, Hamilton owed much to
British common and statute law. Yet, in the realm of civil law, the early
jurists of Upper Canada had to determine exactly how much of English
law would be received into the colony. In so doing, they remade the
law. The British features of law and order introduced in 1792 underwent modification owing to local requirements and the limits encountered in a society with modest resources. There was nothing unusual in
this. Law and order systems, though sharing fundamental features,
have underscored peculiarities about the communities in which they
have functioned. Michael Hindus's exploration of criminal justice in
ante-bellum Massachusetts and South Carolina concluded that factory
and slave economies tended to generate quite distinct criminal justice
systems: the former fostered adherence to codes and a commitment to
reformation; the latter promoted local discretion and retained the old
regime's arsenal of shaming and physical punishments. The criminal
justice system of Upper Canada acquired a few unique attributes of its

own, including the penalty of banishment and a magistracy drawn from merchants, an expedient arising from the absence of an aristocracy or gentry.

One mild contrast between the pattern of law and order in the United Kingdom and Hamilton, or the old country and Canada more generally, pertains to the municipal focus of policing and the civic control over public order offences; central-government action attempted more in the United Kingdom than in this colony.[14] Local government remained important in both societies, but successive British home secretaries managed to increase central control through legislation setting uniform standards and to promote compliance through conditional grants.[15] Colonial reformers and local élites in Canada held fast to the idea of strong municipal governments. In this sense, Canada had features in common with the United States by mid-century. In both, there was a fragmentation of authority. In Ontario, the provincial government has been asserting central authority since the end of the Second World War. For many years, however, the identification of the police with a local community had implications for relations between the police and the citizens, the recruitment of police constables, and the very nature of police work itself.

The North American pattern of law and order was at root a municipally based one. No powerful enduring national gendarmerie emerged here in the nineteenth century, although the North-West Mounted Police and its successor – the Royal Canadian Mounted Police – came close. Nevertheless, twentieth-century innovations in communication, criminal identification, police training, and much else have caused a gravitation in policing toward the central state. One aspect of municipal policing somewhat distinguishes the Canada West/ Ontario pattern from that of the United States. The long-term control of policing by a commission – a measure designed in 1858 to take law and order out of the hands of elected politicians – contrasts with the political quality of American urban policing in the nineteenth century. It is true that New York experimented with police commissions and this may have influenced the innovation in Canada West; however, the police in the great American cities of the nineteenth century had very overt party connections.[16] It is also worth noting that the commission system in Canada West did not spread immediately to other British North American colonies; that fact reaffirms the theme of initial fragmentation and particularism. Yet the particular forms of policing were not concocted in isolation. Police forces of the nineteenth century mixed ideas copied from other jurisdictions, all of which continuously sought more effective means of managing their citizens.

Features of the British system are readily evident in Hamilton, but so are American influences and indigenous tinkering. In law and order as in so much else, Ontario communities have had a complicated and hybrid quality that one might not have expected from a relatively young community. The simple explanation is that the law and the court system – civil and criminal – preoccupied legislators. And legislators travelled, investigated, and read reports from other jurisdictions. They worked in a transatlantic community. As movers and shakers who worried about revolutionary and demographic upheavals, as promoters who turned to state power to effect economic projects, they acted swiftly to increase the repressive powers of the state.

Despite persistent tinkering, the features and practices of the English system persisted to such an extent that the institutions which Lawrence Friedman and Robert Percival described in Alameda County, California, between 1870 and 1910 are nearly identical to those in Wentworth County, Ontario, during the same era.[17] The two jurisdictions separated by two thousand miles and eight states possessed similar sets of law enforcers and investigators; they also had in common, among many other things, a sheriff and coroners, a three-tiered court system, and grand and petit juries. (So striking are the parallels, including the contexts of crimes, that references to similarities will be made at several points in the following chapters.) Not only were these two counties far apart, but their criminal justice institutions constantly and prominently displayed contrasting symbols of sovereignty, republican and monarchical. By the late nineteenth century, therefore, different national myths supported similar criminal justice systems. Lawyers acting as legislators and jurists, had managed to establish the rule of law – the English common law – as an inherent good that transcended particular political arrangements. Nevertheless, they clashed among themselves about such things as the role of grand and trial juries and the need to streamline the courts.

Systems of law and order consist of more than institutions. Attitudes propel and steer them, especially in matters of morality where the lack of victims – though one could argue that neglected children are victims of 'immorality' – and thus of injured complainants opened the way for considerable discretion by fearful local authorities. These authorities exercised the power to prosecute in order to control recreation and transiency. They branded assorted individuals as dangerous outsiders: vagrants, tramps, hobos, and bums. There is something beyond simple humour in the nickname for Hamilton's former railway, the TH&B (Toronto, Hamilton, and Buffalo). Because the railways represented transiency and that implied strangers and minorities, the TH&B was known locally as 'tramps, hobos, and bums.' At times, Hamilton civic authorities tagged visible minorities and southern and eastern European immigrants as prone to certain sets of crimes; the Chinese were branded as gamblers, dope peddlars, and white slavers, the Gypsies as thieves and con artists, the Italians as hot-blooded gunmen or mobsters. On several occasions in the Hamilton area, the anxieties and stereotypes held by an established faction in the community affected the law and how it was enforced. But the issue of criminal stereotyping is complicated by the subcultures of specific immigrant-male groups. Rabid blind intolerance expressed by the powerful is one thing; fear based on the magnified significance of actual episodes is slightly different.

Were the suspicions of influential people in relation to newcomers and the toiling masses unmitigated? The answer is contingent upon several factors. A great deal depended on the composition of the authorities controlling the law and order apparatus, as well as their ability to reach agreement on questions of civil and moral order. It also depended on the background, outlook, and diligence of the law enforcement officers, whether composed of the appointed amateurs who made up the magistracy and constabulary or the paid professionals staffing the modern police department. The fact that the Hamilton police force began to hire constables from European ethnic minorities only after the Second World War indicates something about likely biases on the force, although in terms of class background – rather than ethnicity – the force had more in common with the people on the beat than with the city establishment.

Socially exclusive institutions such as the court of quarter sessions comprised of the appointed justices of the peace displayed pronounced biases. Similarly, fanatic and arrogant police officials – rare but not absent – precipitated interludes of repression that struck primarily at popular recreation and groups stereotyped as criminal. The pressure of special interest groups – often dealt with perfunctorily because of the inertia of the police – presents another complication. Yet, as the political life of the community allowed more participation and as the institutions of law and order recruited people from assorted social groups, the influence of a small ruling élite of amateurs shrivelled and pressure from civic politicians and provincial governments obliged the police to liberalize – in some areas.

Against this confusing background of influences and interests, policing and public order laws inched away from blatant repression and from the monarchical and personalized forms of the old regime. Over time, courts, policing, and public order laws constituted an increasingly bureaucratic web of power that helped mediate social relations in the city. In another sense, however, the web of power in fact became more entangling, more pervasive, and more astutely and credibly cloaked as a public good. It garnered new authority. In the liberal state of the nineteenth century, the overarching motif in criminal justice ceased being the power of the person of the sovereign and became that of the rule of law. At the summit of authority, the rule of law replaced the rule of the king or queen.

The practical impact of the shift in authority could be seen on two sides of the same coin: the demise of amateur notables who locally represented the crown and the ascendancy of professional enforcers and interpreters of the law. As the state adopted rational and utilitarian projects in matters of law and order, it insisted on education and professional training. At first, the legal profession benefitted and certain offices became by statute the domain of members of the bar. However, in the late Victorian era, scientists and pseudo-scientists staked claims to certain fields of criminal justice. Often, science supplemented the more general trend toward professionalism; yet men of science also spoke out to challenge the jurists in bids to entrench their own professions. Notions about criminal 'types', punishment, and the insanity plea are examples of where science vied with the law. Science also affected criminal detection and identification.

The steps from monarchical, to legal, to scientific authority stand out clearly when reading accounts of selected major trials in the nineteenth and twentieth centuries. A few courtroom dramas will convey this point in the following narrative. The transition is also evident in the history of policing, although here the blurred and imprecise steps are found mostly in the twentieth century, because in the nineteenth century the police force often behaved as a vestige of the old regime. Even in the mid-twentieth century it had to suffer the galling reproach of a judge who said that the police had behaved like 'a village constabulary.'[18] The civic élites and the politicians of the bourgeois state expected the rule of law in the courts, but on the streets they continued to look to intimidation and, on occasion, coercion. All the same, Victorian administrators of the police force struggled to mould it into a professional body, though never quite succeeding. The constables themselves exercised discretion with respect to the enforcement of many laws. For doing so, they risked official punishment; for not doing so, they risked public abuse.

The policeman's lot certainly was not a happy one. Understandably, constables maintained morale with a pride in brawn and uniform. With a fair proportion of recruits from the United Kingdom and many evincing a militaristic bent, the Hamilton police force in the nineteenth century was a visible manifestation of the imperial tie. These sources of its mystique and the enduring use of physical force to control situations made difficult the introduction of training in technical skills, advancement by merit, and the meshing of criminal investigation with the strict requirements of the courts.

The police force in Hamilton perpetuated old practices and attitudes; it long remained a bastion of physical force and persisted for a century as a purely male domain where advancements came to brawny lodge brothers who served the force faithfully for decades. Like contemporary skilled crafts, the Victorian police in this city felt the push of efficiency campaigns and the alteration of tasks by technology. Still, old regime values and habits persisted: discretion, street wisdom, insubordination, and stereotyping. Perhaps the First World War demonstrated to governments the weakness of maintaining order by amateurism and muscle, for during and after that conflict the force turned more resolutely to technology and education. Of course, too, the automobile heaped new regulatory responsibilities upon the police, while the processing of information and related exertions to improve criminal identification inspired rounds of innovation. By the mid-twentieth century, the force routinely provided courses and sent officers on courses that dealt with legal procedure and scientific methods of investigation. Patriotism, fraternal connections, and seniority counted less in advancement than training in a particular technical area of police work. Specialization and an official encouragement of expertise ultimately modified policing.

Professionalization even influenced the way in which the police dealt with the poor and transients. In Hamilton the police retained a direct role in poor relief well into the twentieth century. By the 1930s, they no longer dealt with the poor as they once did when they rounded up great numbers of transients as vagrants or when they ran a hostel and dispensed relief; other agencies claiming greater specialized understanding had taken over the sheltering of the destitute, and both rough treatment and discretionary assistance diminished. Yet the police retained a modified role as a social agency, concerning themselves with specialized handling of juveniles, sexual assaults, and wife beating. The authorities of law and order also enforced a more codified approach to the supervision of labour disputes. The point here is not to condemn or to applaud the institutions of law and order, but to see them as a perpetual ingredient in an increasingly regulated and now profoundly regulated city. The front-line regulators belatedly followed a universal trend of specialization and training.

Like any schematic representation, one alleging that three steps characterized the evolution of criminal justice in Upper Canada/Ontario suffers from the persistence of prior forms into supposedly new epochs. Obviously, the rule of law and the engagement of science in criminal justice did not reach into police stations as swiftly as the higher courts. And even in the courts, the evidence collected for trials in the late twentieth century includes an abundance of traditional material – witnesses statements. Moreover, while the courts furthered the rule of law, they burnished fragments of the old regime. The élites of Ontario promoted myths about the province's anti-republican origins, and the province's first jurists held passionately to old regime forms. This tradition has continued. A monument to the United Empire Loyalists has greeted visitors to the Wentworth County courthouse in Hamilton since 1929, and, on a wider stage, oaths to the crown, titles, robes, and symbols of the crown have had one sure home – the courtrooms of Ontario. An admiration for the trappings of the old regime cannot be wholly attributed to the conservative nature of jurists or a wish to keep the public mystified; other common law communities in the New World changed more quickly than Ontario did. Local history must have played a part in the timing and precise character of change, for that was certainly the case in Hamilton.

Despite the many examples of a monarchical tradition, the rule of law did effectively replace the rule of the crown. Yet many jurists in Upper Canada/Ontario would have maintained that there could be no distinction between the crown and the law. Crowns – current courthouse argot for the crown attorneys – hold a special place in Ontario criminal justice. By the fiction of the crown attorney's neutrality and the crown label, the state likely conferred upon itself advantages in prosecuting suspects. The state, then, promoted traditions and symbols that contributed to the legitimacy of its actions. In recent decades, the state and churches have even discovered a traditional European ceremony – the red mass – for the opening of the high courts. The essence of the old regime – the actual sense of royal justice – no longer exists; however, the forms have endured and, for a while, gathered symbolic value useful to the state. Of course, the precarious standing of royalty in Canada may well impel changes to the rituals and symbols of criminal justice at some future date.

More than persistence of mere trappings of the old regime will blur the stages of a model that has proposed monarchical, legal, and scientific phases in the development of criminal justice. At least as late as the 1920s, in the province's lowest courts, police magistrates meted out swift justice that did not always adhere to legal formalism. Having examined procedures at Toronto's police magistrate's court during the tenure of George T. Denison, Gene Homel concluded that Denison's prejudices and biases undermine notions that legal formalism and bureaucratic administration penetrated the actual dispensing of justice in the lowest court of the city.[19] The same was true of Hamilton. As always in the study of crime and criminal justice, established procedures and codes were often at variance with reality, especially in the lowest courts. American sociologist Joseph Tropea has pursued a similar line of reasoning in criticizing the Weberian model of an historical progression from 'primitive' conciliatory proceedings toward a rational-legal and bureaucratic form of justice.[20]

Tropea alleges that the 'negotiated transactions' of traditional regimes of order have endured. Even as governments in the nineteenth century reformed the criminal justice system in an attempt to rationalize and codify it, the new agents of law and order that they created had to negotiate with people and be responsive to local interests. In the modern system, Tropea points out, the police play a significant part in the 'negotiated transactions,' but unlike prior systems, the new rational one has had to hide or disguise these transactions. Were the transactions made public and deemed important, criminal justice proceedings would seem idiosyncratic rather than guided by firm rational rules; this would strike at the core of the modern legal order. Tropea's argument has merit. In Hamilton the police have taken over many of the mediating functions once performed by the justices of the peace and through informal practices they have in many respects perpetuated negotiation and community involvement. To consider the practices that rubbed against the grain of bureaucracy and the rational legal order, the following account makes extensive use of police and lower court material.

Law and order in one community will be explored through two intertwined narratives: one follows the institutions and the other analyses broadly who was arrested and discharged or convicted and punished. The concepts to keep in mind when considering the institutional developments have just been reviewed: sovereignty and the criminal justice system, the balancing of international trends with local history, and the interplay of professionalization and bureaucratization with the persistence of localism and discretion. The second narrative strand, involving statistics, offers riches of its own. But it also presents perils. Many historians and social scientists who have turned to the data collected from the criminal justice system in the nineteenth and twentieth centuries have interpreted trends as evidence for profound cultural change: that is, the community in question has become either more or less violent. This study takes a different approach. It rests on the view that data has meaning only when associated with the history of the institutions of law and order, and that changes in institutions signal cultural transitions at least as well as trend lines in data. In determining who applied for aid from the institutions of law and order and why, and how the institutions themselves have operated, the following analysis rejects the assumption that terms, practices, and attitudes found today likely prevailed in the past. In several important regards, they did not.

This work also uses statistical data as a way of understanding individual behaviour and the nature of community. Even peripheral information about crimes can tell a great deal about everyday life. For one thing, if court and police records provide a sample of the violence that has transpired in the city, then the poor appear to have been the principal victims and perpetrators. The overwhelming number of reported transgressors harmed their friends, their families, and members of their own ethnic communities; rarely did they hurt strangers. They hardly constituted a dangerous class of outsiders which threatened the whole community, although authorities habitually professed a different philosophy. Excluding carnage by autos, the streets of the city remained fairly safe, which is more than can be said about taverns, hotels, and housing in the poorer areas of the city. It was not strangers visiting these places who were at greatest risk, but the 'regulars' and residents.

The dynamics of most offences appear to have remained the same over a long period of time. Thefts largely involved small articles taken without much planning; assaults, too, have a distressingly common set of attributes across the decades. Seen from this perspective, the institutional changes in the apparatus of law and order appear as a mass of largely ineffectual innovations that have tried to deal with persistent problems mainly afflicting the poor. All that said, one hypothesis in this book proposes that the reduction of a great variety of risks has been a principle achievement of the modern organs of law and order. Policing not only maintains the web of power that continues to mediate some social relations in the city, but it has also maintained important agencies of public safety and a bureaucracy that supplements the insurance industry. Accident victims, the suddenly stricken, missing persons, the abandoned family, the homeless, the thousands of youngsters whose bikes have been stolen, the careless merchant who left his shop unlocked – these and other members of the community have been dealt with by the police for decades. While the police participated in traditional 'negotiated transactions' in dealing with many offences, there can be no doubt that they comprised something new, an agency that worked to assemble a coherent system of rules and that used routines to increase public security.

The institutions of law and order have been intrinsic to the net of security as well as the web of power. Perhaps one can find a subtle design in this combination: have the police legitimized their coercive authority by community service? If so, that idea must stand alongside other factors. The roots of policing in Ontario are complicated. Economical public service, demanded by tight-fisted city councils, should not be underestimated in explaining the bundle of chores heaped upon a reluctant police. Moreover, the coercive authority of the police works for many citizens and not just the few. In the city, statutes, by-laws, policing, and courts have greatly affected common life. Arguably, the modern city could not function without the imposition of order, order that we scarcely recognize as such because of its legitimacy and its necessity. Apart from benign critical grumbling, usually softened with humour, citizens in Hamilton have overwhelmingly and essentially uncritically supported the institutions of law and order.

In the first section of this book, chapters 1 to 4, the aim is to describe epochs and institutions and to underscore the replacement of the rule of the sovereign by the rule of law . Chapter 1 describes the old regime as it functioned in the early nineteenth century. Remarkable changes in form and practice characterized the next several decades and these are considered in chapters 2 and 3, which focus in particular on the foundation and early development of policing as well as on major modifications to criminal trials. The expansion of professionalization in the courts and the history of policing through the auto revolution – the growth of functions, technological aids, and training – is discussed in chapter four.

The second and shorter section of the book examines trends in crime and in matters of social and civic order. Chapter 5 studies the long-term trends in law and order data, while chapter 6 presents an account of violence and theft in selected periods of the nineteenth and twentieth centuries. A conclusion summarizes the findings and basic arguments.

1 Criminal Justice and the Waning of the Old Regime

In the afternoon of a pleasant September day in 1828, a ten year-old lad perched on the shoulders of an adult gazed across the heads of the men, women, and children; he could see through the cordon of cavalry drawn up in a semi-circle before Hamilton's frame courthouse. His eyes fixed on a platform that extended out from a wall of hewed logs. The hanging he was about to witness would be the first and last public execution to take place on the original court square. Eight men convicted of high treason at the Ancaster 'Bloody Assize' during the War of 1812 had been hanged nearby in 1814.

The courthouse had been built in 1818 because of Hamilton's selection, two years previously, as judicial capital of the five counties comprising the Gore District in the colony of Upper Canada. Though it was only a decade old, the plain structure – which had also provided the town with a place for religious services – was no longer the most substantial building in Hamilton. Within a year, a stone replacement was under construction on the neighbouring square.

Spectators often gathered in front of the courthouse to watch 'shaming' punishments in the pillory and the stocks, and occasionally the public whippings of male offenders. But the crowd that assembled there on 8 September 1828 was much larger than any seen before; in fact, it easily exceeded the population of the town. Drawn by morbid curiosity, town and country folk started arriving at ten in the morning; the carpenters had the gallows ready around 1:00 pm. Since hangings were the responsibility of the sheriff, he had arranged for the construction of the gallows and the hiring of the hangman. Vendors sold spruce beer and pies.

The condemned man was Michael Vincent, who, to the end, protested his innocence. He had been sentenced to death three days earlier, on 5 September. The judicial system provided no court of appeal and expressed no interest in supporting a petition to the crown for mercy. But Judge Christopher Hagerman had assured Vincent of an early opportunity for appeal to the heavenly judge. And he had provided just enough time for news to spread through neighbouring townships.

During the interval since the trial, several clergymen had spoken with Vincent but all attempts to extract a confession from him failed. While awaiting execution, he had been fed bread and water. District taxes would not be wasted on a dead man. On the morning of 8 September, Vincent met with his aged mother, brothers and sisters, and his two infant children. He talked of inconsequential matters, of debts, and the location of some tools. He was then brought up from his cell in the log basement. For his short walk, his legs were freed of chains.

After the cavalry had formed its line, the magistrates, the grand jury, and leading gentlemen approached the courthouse in a column by pairs. Once they were all assembled, Michael Vincent stopped out of a window and onto the gallows platform. He was asked if he had any final words. The boy, his parents, and all others heard him proclaim: 'I die innocent before God and man.' The executioner – a black man – loosened Vincent's shirt at the neck and placed a thick rope noose over his head. Vincent went stiff with terror. No hood covered his face; some spectators could see the expression of horror. The boy's parents could not abide watching a man who had proclaimed his innocence die before their eyes. They turned and walked away. Someone who had an obstructed view hoisted the boy up on his shoulders. In the lad's words, he 'bade me to tell what I saw.' What he saw, he remembered for the rest of his life. [1]

The drop failed to break Vincent's neck. The knot had slipped around to the front below the chin; it pulled the man's head backward. He was strangling. Writhing in pain, he swung his feet in desperation, attempting to reach the log ledge where the upper and lower floors of the courthouse met. To finish his botched job, the executioner grabbed the legs and jerked them down sharply. Vincent continued to struggle. Hugging the swinging figure, the executioner added his own weight to that of the dying Vincent. Curses from the crowd denouncing the executioner declared that this execution had forfeited the dramatic effect desired by all authorities who staged such proceedings. The condemned man had not performed the role expected of him; he had protested his innocence and this had unsettled some people. Then came the miserable job of the hanging, which transformed Vincent from a convicted wife-murderer into the victim of a dreadfully violent death.

Vincent's relatives tried to get possession of his body, but in keeping with English and Canadian practice the authorities turned the corpse over to surgeons of the district for dissection. Felons convicted of a capital offence were truly at the disposal of the crown. Through the crown's agents, mercy might be granted; if not, the body belonged to the crown, not to the family. The symbolism was plain: the soul belonged to God, but mortal remains belonged wholly to the ruler. Public executions in the old regime reminded all assembled – and all who might read newspapers or hear them read – that they lived under a monarch and were part of a hierarchical social order. The murder had broken the king's peace and now the king had claimed what was due him.

The old regime of law and order, a regime that dealt with more than just felons and executions, had provided the instruments that investigated the death of Vincent's wife and then tried and punished him. The essentials of the system had been fashioned by the Norman conquerors of Anglo-Saxon England in the period from the twelfth to the fourteenth centuries. Yet it was a system that was about to be modified substantially, in the Old World and the New, in the name of efficiency: the goal was not to punish less but to punish better. Hamilton's new stone courthouse would open in the last years of the old regime and close a half century later, by which time the criminal justice system had passed through a series of major reforms.

THE INSTITUTIONS AND INSTRUMENTS OF LAW AND ORDER

The manner of apprehending and trying Vincent exemplified the operation of the old regime's criminal justice system when dealing with serious felonies. It embodied the English approach – rooted in seven hundred years of history – to reconciling local and central authority. While the process culminated in a display of the power of the executive arm of government, prior steps involved local initiatives, district officials, and then, in the setting of the trial itself, a combination of the community and the authority of the crown.

The Norman conquerors and their heirs had established control of their kingdom through a singular blending of local responsibility and central supervision. The latter provided the essential meaning for the common law; uniform or common law was to apply to the entire kingdom. On the continent, numerous regional law codes fragmented kingdoms and the central authorities sought to maintain control by the occasional use of force to suppress uprisings. Only in the mid-sixteenth century did royal justice in France, for example, start to edge its way into regions and towns. England had a much longer acquaintance with royal justice – and it was this brand of justice that Michael Vincent was to experience in all its vigour.

Michael Vincent had farmed in the nethermost reaches of the Gore District in Waterloo Township since 1823. The government had carved this district out of portions of the Home and Niagara districts, responding to increasing settlement at the head of the lake and its hinterland. The first district assize or sitting of a court to deal with serious crimes for the new district was held somewhere in Ancaster Township on 28 August 1817, and the first case concerned an accusation that a certain James Markle had stolen a cow. The first assize held in Hamilton opened on 20 August 1818. In the first case the accused, found guilty of stealing items worth 10 shillings, was sentenced to eight days imprisonment and a public whipping in front of the courthouse.[2] A fall assize would be held in Hamilton – usually in late August or in September – from 1818 to the present. There would be just one assize per year in the Gore District until 1838.

When first established, the Gore District Assize dealt with a mere handful of criminal cases. Thereafter, the criminal calendar grew as the local population increased in the prosperous late 1820s and early 1830s. From 1820 to 1828, the court disposed of an average of six trials per assize and sat for three to seven days at each. The assize that included the trial of Michael Vincent had just four other cases – two assaults, larceny, and grand larceny – and was over in two days. But that was the last of the short calendars and remarkably speedy sittings in the Gore District. From 1829 to 1834, an average of twelve trials were spread over nine to fourteen days; from 1835 to 1837 – a period of extraordinary immigration into the area – the average was twenty trials over nine to twenty-five days. Beginning with the busy 1829 sitting, the dates shifted erratically from early August to mid-October. It is possible that the increase in cases throughout the colony created scheduling difficulties on the circuits. Recognizing the mounting volume of work for each assize, the government in 1837 authorized two assizes per year – one in the fall and another in the spring. On 31 May 1838, the Gore District opened its first spring assize. During the next ten years, assizes meeting in Hamilton had an average of ten trials over as many days, a distribution suggesting slightly more deliberation at trials than in the beginning. Nevertheless, by the time juries had been selected and other court business arranged, it was rare that a trial took an entire day.[3]

From where Vincent had settled, the journey to the courthouse at Newark (Niagara-on-the-Lake) would have been about eighty miles and the trip to the one at York would have been almost as far. Creation of the new district in 1816 halved the distance to a courthouse, although it was still a two-day trip from Waterloo Township to Hamilton. The sudden death of Mrs Vincent meant that a handful of settlers had to journey through the forests and clearings of a new society until they reached the spectacular setting of the village at the foot of the Niagara escarpment.

Vincent's family lived in poverty, dwelling in a dark windowless hovel. Relations between Vincent and his wife were poor; he drank heavily and beat her. Sadly, in these bare facts, there forms a picture of domestic life that was not all that uncommon then or in the following century and a half. The exceptional circumstance was that an assault in late January ended in the death of Mrs Vincent. Or so the prosecution maintained. Her burial occurred on 27 January, the day of her death. Knowing something about the character of Vincent and the good health of his wife, neighbours quickly expressed suspicions about Vincent's story that his wife had died during a seizure. Two days after the burial, a coroner's jury examined the disinterred body.

The coroner in these times had no medical training. Like sheriffs and justices of the peace, they were appointed by the crown and the only professional qualification expected of them was the capacity to draft documents. (In fact, by Upper Canadian statute, justices of the peace – the linchpin figures in the criminal justice system – could not be attorneys, though they had to be 'the most sufficient persons.'[4]) Coroners had existed in England since the ninth century. The term itself derived from *corouner*, an officer of the crown. Initially, the *corouner* acted as a local administrative officer who assisted with the keeping of the peace. The Norman conquest changed the office by making coroners responsible for inquiring into deaths in their regions. In the midst of a hostile Anglo-Saxon population, the Normans paid particular attention to the sudden death of one of their own people. The coroner could fine an entire community where a Norman had died from an act of violence. From this measure, imposed by conquering rulers, there developed the concept of homicide as a crown plea.[5]

Though the medieval coroner retained other administrative duties, his basic task in a criminal justice system that rested on untrained amateurs was to investigate suspicious deaths and to convene a jury to assist him. Like the justices of the peace, he possessed the power to direct the arrest of individuals suspected of homicide and to 'bind over' witnesses to appear in court. The composition of the coroner's jury that examined the corpse of Mrs Vincent is not completely known; how-

ever, one member was a carpenter who, in the course of making cof-
fins, had seen a number of corpses. In his opinion, the body 'had no
appearance of natural death.'[6] Professional expertise was extremely
limited. Under the coroner's orders, a constable arrested Vincent and
brought him to the Gore District jail.

Constables were appointed by the justices of the peace (the terms
magistrate, justice of the peace, and JP may be used interchangeably)
when they met in the court of quarter sessions at the April meeting of
that judicial and government body. Constables could not refuse the
duty without a penalty, but after one year of service they were exempt
for three. Each and every township or place was to have a constable;
even an unincorporated crossroads settlement or mill site with a few
nearby houses might merit one. The indefinite description of the locales that ought to have a constable derived from the medieval assignment of constables to a wapentake, that is, to a small community. They
had to reside in the place; they could not be barristers or officers of the
court.

In addition to serving warrants, constables had the power to arrest by
intervening in an affray or by suppressing disorderly conduct. These
chores involved risks. Therefore, while the justices of the peace looked
for reasonably respectable members of the community to act as constables, they also sought rugged individuals. Unlike the paid constables of
the municipal police forces that emerged in Canadian cities in the
1850s, the constables of the old regime received irregular compensation; the justices of the peace awarded the constables their costs and
such other emoluments as they deemed proper.[7]

The jail that held Vincent came under the jurisdiction of the sheriff,
whose office had the oldest lineage of all the posts in the law and order
system of the old regime as it stood in the early nineteenth century.
The origins of the office are 'shrouded in the mists of the pre-conquest
era.'[8] Once a very important office – J.A. Sharpe has described it as having vice-regal status in the high middle ages – the post had lost ground
to the justice of the peace and the court of quarter sessions. The sheriff
and his under-officers, the bailiffs, possessed a number of duties in the
area of civil law, and, in terms of criminal justice, they had charge of
the jail and courthouse and had to provide jurors for the assizes. Daily
management of the jail rested with the jailer. The jail had once been
a place where the justices of the peace detained suspects for trial; it was
not primarily a place for punishment. In early-nineteenth-century
Upper Canada, however, jails were used for both. Because of the infrequent sittings of the courts, accused persons who could not afford bail
commonly spent long periods in jail. Today's successor to the county
jail – the regional detention centre – is likewise a multi-purpose facility,
but it provides for the separation of prisoners by classification.

Today, most Canadian provinces have two levels of criminal courts; Nova Scotia, Ontario, and British Columbia have three.[9] The Ontario structure was built upon the three judicial levels prevailing in England in the late eighteenth century, although governments subsequently altered the practices, jurisdictions, and titles of the component courts (Figure 1.1). To clarify matters, it is accurate enough to think in terms of superior courts, intermediate courts, and courts with the lowest jurisdiction. In the old regime, the latter courts were known as the petty sessions. Until 1834 in Upper Canada, two or more justices of the peace sitting at times between the quarter sessions comprised a court of petty sessions. An act of that year made it possible for a single justice of the peace to hear and determine – that is, to try – cases of common assault.[10] By the same act, a justice of the peace could free an offender if the latter agreed to compensate the party aggrieved.[11] This arrangement represented a blurring of the line between criminal and civil law since it held out the prospect of damages in a criminal action.

Justices of the Peace – those officials who were so essential to the criminal justice system of the old regime – held an office that originated in the thirteenth century and that acquired additional powers thereafter. Basically, JPs had two main categories of duties associated with keeping the peace: so-called 'ministerial' duties and judicial ones.[12] The former encompassed appointing constables, hearing complaints or accusations, taking depositions, issuing arrest warrants or court summons, bailing suspects, and much else besides. By their judicial powers they constituted courts of petty sessions and courts of quarter sessions. In these courts they tried the cases that had been brought to them in their ministerial capacity. The petty session sittings dealt mainly with misdemeanours, certain felonies, and infractions against local measures, such as those governing market-places. In the larger centres, the petty sessions met frequently.

Sometimes, cases over which the justice of the peace had jurisdiction involved such complicated issues that they preferred to hold them over to the quarter sessions of the peace, the quarterly meetings of the district or – after districts were split into the smaller county units – the county justices of the peace.[13] Typically, the justices of the peace handled all misdemeanours in petty sessions and referred some cases of suspected felonies to the quarter sessions. However, the jurisdiction of the petty sessions with respect to felonies was expanding throughout the 1830s.

A major consolidation act of 1833 specified that, in order to send a case to trial at quarter sessions or an assize, two justices of the peace had to hear the complainant, take down written testimony, show the same to the accused, and permit the accused to cross-examine the complainant or witness. The justices of the peace would then determine if

Figure 1.1
The Evolution of Criminal Courts in the Hamilton Area[1]

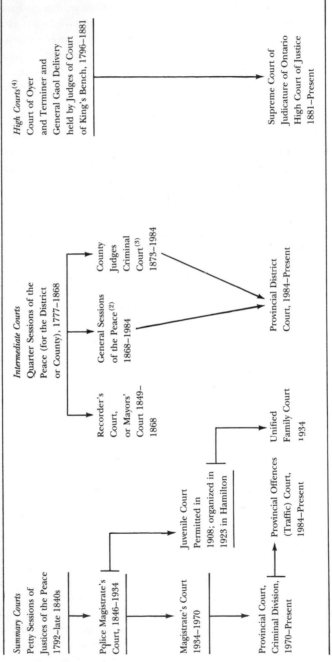

1 Prior to the organization of the Gore District, the area was in the Niagara District.
2 Grand Jury and Petit jury.
3 No juries.
4 The term 'Assize' was commonly used.

bail should be granted. In cases where there was 'positive and credible evidence' of a felony having been committed by the suspect, a single justice of the peace could have that party placed in jail; however, two were still necessary for determining bail. Matters were rendered even more intricate by the fact that the definition of a felony was subject to change with legislation.[14] Furthermore, in cases of larceny, the court of quarter sessions could send the case to the assize.[15] On account of the lack of uniformity on procedure for handling a number of different crimes, two acts were passed in 1853 which attempted to rationalize the duties of the justice of the peace.[16] Yet not even these measures could eliminate the JP's discretionary authority to issue either an arrest or merely a summons to appear in court.[17] Like the modern police constable, the justice of the peace was guided by statute but had to exercise judgment.

Unlike the petty sessions, the court of quarter sessions, which brought a number of justices of the peace together, had a grand jury and trial juries. The quarter sessions – the intermediate court in the old regime – had been constituted in the old province of Quebec by an ordinance in 1777 and were extended into what later became Upper Canada in 1788.[18] Unfortunately, no quarter session records have been discovered for the Gore District, but the records of quarter sessions for several other districts have survived. Those for the Johnston District indicate that only a minority of the justices of the peace for that area bothered to travel to the courthouse town to handle the work of the quarter sessions.[19] Sometimes, justices in quarter sessions heard complaints pertaining to felonies and other serious crimes, and they sent these cases to the next assize – a court with superior jurisdiction. Conventionally, the assize tried 'difficult matters' and those offences that could result in capital punishment. Because of the gravity of these cases, the attorney general, who was the head of the bar and a government official, often attended. The attorneys general of Upper Canada and the Maritime colonies probably had a greater involvement in criminal cases than their model, the attorney general of England and Wales.[20] Attorney General John Beverley Robinson travelled to Hamilton to prosecute Vincent.

Jurisdictional boundaries between the quarter sessions and the assizes had grey areas, but in 1837 the government attempted to clarify one source of ambiguity and at the same time provide for more speedy justice. It erased the distinction between grand and petty larceny, effectively placing all larceny cases under the control of the quarter sessions. The single proviso was that the presiding justice of the peace had to be a barrister.[21] This stipulation was the first of many steps aimed at replacing amateurs on the bench with professionals.

Like the grand jury and the petit jury, the term assize – denoting a specially commissioned royal council – derived from the court French that the Normans brought to England following the conquest of 1066. Essentially, the assizes – even those in Upper Canada – were special assemblies presided over by a judge sent from the capital and empowered with specific commissions for that particular sitting of the court. Using terms once again derived from court French, the assize judge acted under a commission of oyer and terminer and general jail delivery. As the words suggest, the judge's commission authorized him to hear and determine cases and to have delivered before him the occupants of the jail who had been charged with crimes requiring the attention of the assize. The three and later four Upper Canadian judges who received the commissions comprised the Court of King's Bench, which met at the seat of colonial government. The commissions enabled them to travel from the capital on circuit.[22]

In Upper Canada, the lieutenant governor issued the commissions of assize judges, and these commissions were forwarded to the sheriff who arranged the assize. For example, beginning in 1794 the sheriff selected the jurors in the manner and number specified by legislation. He obtained the names of jurors from the district's tax assessment rolls and he had these names called three times in open court.[23] The commissions for an assize – written on parchment and carrying the great seal of Upper Canada – authorized any one of the judges named to hold an assize at the stated place and time. In rare circumstances, a unique commission could be issued for the holding of an assize outside the routine cycle. This occurred in early 1838. A special commission authorized an assize to try a number of men accused of treason for allegedly participating in the failed rebellion the previous December. The proceedings opened on 8 March and finished on 4 April. Judge James Buchanan Macaulay was assigned and he was joined on the bench by four justices of the peace. This level of participation was unusual – normally one or two justices of the peace sat as associates. The larger number in 1838 indicated the importance of the trial as well as the wish of local authorities to become involved in proceedings that affected several of their respected neighbours. The assize, therefore, was a routine but flexible judicial event; it was more of an *instrument* of law and order than an *institution* of law and order. As a postscript, it can be added that the issuing of commissions ceased with the Common Law Procedure Act in 1856 which established the assizes by statute.[24]

The 1828 fall assize that tried Michael Vincent began on 1 September. Judge Christopher Hagerman, elevated to the bench that June, had one local associate, justice of the peace James Wilson. During an assize, the judge from the Court of King's Bench was joined by a local justice of the peace or, as in the 1838 special assize, by several. It is not entirely clear what protocols determined which of the JPs joined the judge, but it seems likely that a justice from the community where an offence had taken place was expected to attend. Regardless of local participation, the judge took the lead, reviewing the law, questioning witnesses, and charging the jury. The trials took a standard form. At the assize, as at the quarter sessions, a crier punctuated the proceedings with proclamations announcing the stages of the proceedings: the opening of the court, the call for the sheriff to return the writs, the calling of the grand jury, the charge to the jury, and the pronouncement of sentence. 'God save the King [or Queen]' concluded many of the courtroom proclamations.[25] Trials presented plenty of opportunities to assert royal sovereignty.

At the assize, prosecuting attorneys and defence attorneys attended capital cases, such as Vincent's and the treason trials of 1838. It is not clear how often they attended other felony cases. At an assize trial the witnesses against the accused were heard first, followed by the witnesses for the accused. The latter might include not only individuals who could address the facts of the case but also character witnesses, for after a conviction the fate of the accused in a capital case frequently depended on issues unrelated to the case and the letter of the law. The circumstances of the crime, the belief that an example was needed, and the character and circumstances of the accused often determined whether or not the sentence would be carried out as specified by law.

Before the trial proper, the grand jury had been sworn in and, if form had been followed, had met in a private room. The stone courthouse that opened in 1829 had such accommodation. Like the assize, the grand jury originated with the Norman conquerors. Initially, it had served to inform the king's judges of crimes committed in the area from which it was drawn. Occasionally, commentators have usefully called it the grand inquest, for it inquired into serious allegations.[26] It also employed the Norman device of enlisting the help of local notables, bringing them before the royal courts and so making them share responsibility for keeping the king's peace. At the Hamilton assize or the Gore District quarter sessions, something like the following proclamation was read when calling the grand jury: 'Oyer, Oyer, Oyer. You good men that are returned to enquire for our Sovereign Lord the King, and the body of this district of Gore, answer your names and save your fine. God save the King.'[27] Centuries after the jury's origin, the proclamation still declared the fusion of local and royal interests. In 1351, the trial jury was separated from the grand jury. Prior to that, when the grand jury indicted someone, the accused had generally faced a trial by ordeal. By the end of the seventeenth century, the grand jury had evolved into a body to eliminate spiteful prosecutions.[28]

Comprising more than twelve men – generally around nineteen in the Gore District – the grand jury, consisting of respectable local citizens and usually many justices of the peace, had to determine whether or not enough evidence existed to try the accused. At the assize where Michael Vincent's case was considered, the grand jury was composed of fifteen men. In this case as in others, the grand jury considered the charge that appeared on the indictment, a formal document that included the name of the case, the place of the trial, and the particulars of the offence. Indictments had to be drafted carefully: an error might result in the release of the accused.[29] Each offence had a particular form that had to be adhered to exactly since the bill of indictment was actually a special plea from the community to the representatives of the crown. A concern about precise form with respect to indictments probably explains the presence of a bound volume of longhand indictments from eighteenth-century England among the papers of judge James B. Macaulay.[30] In the Vincent case, the coroner would have drawn up the indictment.

Throughout most of the nineteenth century, the coroner's jury provided the usual path to court in cases of suspected manslaughter or murder. Yet there was another significant process that generated indictments for felonies. Since 1551 in England, two justices of the peace had the authority to hear a complaint under oath, hear witnesses, and finally determine whether or not sufficient evidence existed to merit a trial at quarter sessions or the assize. If convinced that reasonable grounds for a trial existed, the magistrates would then prepare the bill of indictment. This practice entered Upper Canada and, through a process of reform affecting the office of justice of the peace, evolved into the preliminary hearing through which all serious cases normally would come before superior criminal courts in the twentieth century.

The grand jury, therefore, did not draft indictments; it reviewed them and then either confirmed or rejected them. The originator of the indictment sent it and any depositions or other documents to the clerk of the peace. When presented with the indictment by the clerk, the grand jury did not try the case, for it only had to consider the evidence appearing on the indictment and not the evidence produced by the defence. The accused could not appear to challenge the indictment. To confirm that enough evidence existed for a trial, twelve members of the grand jury had to be in agreement. If they agreed, the jury inscribed the words 'true bill' on the document; if they believed there was no case, they wrote *ignoramus*. In the case of a true bill, the reading of the indictment to the prisoner represented the formal accusation. This procedure contrasted with the continental European system, which put the initiation of indictment proceedings wholly in the hands of a public official.

Though the assize had become a routine criminal and civil court, it retained the forms of a royal council, a meeting between county notables – in Upper Canada, the district notables – and a representative from a central authority, the Court of King's Bench. On such occasions, the judge addressed the grand jury about a number of issues. Besides a general outline of the cases that the assize had before it, the address might include remarks about the political state of the colony and lectures on the social order as ordained by God. One student of the Upper Canadian legal system, Patrick Brode, having located a few charges to the grand jury in Upper Canadian newspapers, concludes that 'the loyalist judges presented a narrow view of society in which the subject owed a duty of obedience to a benevolent government.'[31]

James B. Macaulay's address to the Gore District grand jury in September 1832 seems typical. Long, orotund, and filled with metaphors, the address began with a statement of regret that a 'dreadful scourge' – a cholera epidemic – had delayed the assize. Macaulay then advised the grand jury on how it should seek the truth. 'If we view the facts as they are disclosed with a steady eye and examine the whole at last in a just light ... we shall generally perceive our way clearly to a satisfactory result.' If someone was acquitted who was guilty, that person would escape only 'from temporal punishment' and would be judged ultimately by 'He who seeth in secret.' From general thoughts embodying the orderly universe of an old regime jurist, Macaulay descended to the calendar of 'high offences,' noting that among the latter larceny was conspicuous – 'Cases of Simple & Compound – Clergable [sic] and Capital are embraced.' He elaborated on the meaning of robbery, which he defined as stealing either by force or by terrifying the victim. Finally, in the process of rebuking the magistrates for having granted bail to a prisoner when they lacked authority to do so, Macaulay reviewed some finer points of the common law. Since grand juries were packed with the justices of the peace, the address to the jury provided an occasion for educating them.[32]

The petit jury (also known as the petty or trial jury) of twelve that determined the facts of a case perhaps had the most complicated and controversial history of all the institutions of the old regime's criminal justice system. The jury had begun as an accusatory instrument, namely the grand jury created at a famous royal council, the Assize of Clarendon in 1166. By this assize – an assize in the full sense – the royal authorities had moved vigorously to assert royal jurisdiction over felo-

nies at the expense both of existing institutions and of a process that
had dealt with felonies privately (through compensation worked out
between victims or their families and the those who had offended or
harmed them). According to the terms of the Assize of Clarendon,
twelve lawful men of each hundred – the designation for the smallest
community – were to be chosen and sworn to bring before royal officials information about suspected felonies. With the later elimination
of the trials by ordeal and the splitting of the jury into two bodies, the
trial by jury came one step closer to its modern form.

From the beginning, the jury had a powerful role: it was concerned
with the determination of fact. While a famous 1670 court ruling effectively protected the jury against intimidation by a judge, the relations
of the trial judge to the jury lacked firm definition. When the juries appeared to go beyond the determination of fact and brought in verdicts
that defied the evidence but reflected community values, they were
chastised for exceeding their historical role. Judge William Campbell,
seething about the jury at an assize held at Hamilton in the fall of 1825,
submitted a report to the lieutenant governor in which he claimed that
the large number of acquittals had three explanations: just verdicts,
mistakes, and 'less justifiable causes not infrequent in small communities.'[33] By the same token, judges who sternly addressed or harangued
juries and made clear their reading of the facts were sometimes criticized as behaving unconstitutionally. This was true in Upper Canada in
1828, when tract writers and journalists remarked on the alleged transgressions of either the jury or the judge.[34] The trial of Michael Vincent
extended an opportunity for such editorial comment. However, there
was another subject of controversy about the jury in Upper Canada. As
noted earlier, the preparation of rolls from which jurors were selected
was in the hands of the sheriff.[35] Reformers suspected that, in some
politically important trials, this government-appointed official packed
the rolls with partisans. In 1850 the reform government of Robert
Baldwin placed the duty for filling the rolls in the hands of elected
township officials.[36]

The selection of jurors as well as the appointment, remuneration,
and conduct of the judiciary in Upper Canada exploded as political
matters in the 1820s. Reform politicians and newspaper editors scrutinized the bench, looking for misdeeds. In some instances, they had little difficulty in scoring a fair point – but not in the case of Michael
Vincent. In his charge to the jury, Christopher Hagerman, denigrated
by reformers as a member of the inner circle of the colony's ruling of-
ficialdom, stated that he believed the deceased had been murdered by
the prisoner and that he would share the responsibility with the jury for
making this determination. Francis Collins, editor of the *Canadian*

Freeman and an implacable opponent of the government, took the position that Hagerman violated proper form by turning himself into a prosecutor when he should have protected the accused. The claim was ill-founded, although it expressed the persistent belief of English radicals that the jury had too little freedom and power.

There was nothing unusual about Hagerman's charge: judges' bench books for the period indicate that judges either chose to leave the question of guilt entirely to the jury or directed the jury to find the accused guilty. Moreover, the jury in the Vincent case had good cause to arrive at a guilty verdict and there is no evidence to indicate that the jurors felt that the judge had coerced them or influenced them unduly. Apart from Vincent's past conduct toward his wife, marks on her body suggested that she had been beaten. Except for the condemned man's denial, the case seemed an uncomplicated one. All in all, then, subsequent remarks about the conduct of Hagerman in the Vincent case have to be seen as a minor episode in the ongoing skirmishes between the representatives of the people and official authority.

THE INSTRUMENTS OF COMMON JUSTICE

Judges delivered their sentences on the last day of the assize. The one passed on Michael Vincent went as follows: 'Michael Vincent convicted of murder sentenced to be conveyed from here to the place from whence he came and from thence to the place of Execution there to be hanged by the neck till he be dead.'[37]

Not often had such awful sentences been recorded in the assize register for Upper Canada; indeed, after Vincent, no other men would be hanged in the Hamilton area until 1840. The bulk of the criminal justice business transacted, business overwhelmingly conducted at the petty sessions and quarter sessions until the early 1840s, dealt with petty larceny and common assault; thereafter, moral order offences assumed prominence for reasons that will be considered shortly. Most criminal justice cases, therefore, were handled by the justices of the peace in petty sessions and quarter sessions. Direct attention to law and order remained primarily a local matter managed by men of property and standing.[38] Many of these unrepresentative officials knew that the duties of a JP were a burden, but they realized that the appointment conferred status.[39] still, the prestige was purchased at a cost in the colonial towns.

From the beginning, towns – with their concentration of population, their taverns and entertainments – kept the magistrates busy. The colonial government recognized this and, prior to the incorporation of towns that proceeded rapidly in the 1830s and 1840s, appointed a good many magistrates from urban centres. As for the other JPs, the colony lacked the landed aristocracy and gentry that supplied magistrates in England; rural merchants and millers who would probably not have received commissions of the peace in the old country secured appointment here. Around the time of Vincent's trial, the qualification for office was an income of 100 pounds per annum.[40] For those untrained community notables who accepted the responsibilities of a commission as JP, English handbooks may have been used. The clerk of the peace – the appointee who helped organize the courts and the documents used to prepare a prosecution – may have had copies of statutes and enough legal training to advise the justices of the peace. In 1835 William Conway Keele, an enterprising English barrister who had come to the colony in 1820 and had worked as the managing clerk in the attorney general's office, published an Upper Canadian manual for justices of the peace.[41] By 1858 the thick and dense volume packed with common law and statutes had gone through four editions.

Unlike rural England, with its established families of the gentry and aristocracy, the new society of Upper Canada had a small and scattered population base, no families of long residence, and few men of considerable wealth. The colonial magistracy, therefore, had more in common with the magistracy of metropolitan London, for both consisted of men of lower social status than the country magistrates of England.[42] The scarcity of men of rank and standing in the new district added to the difficulties of finding and retaining magistrates. Richard Hatt, one of the more enterprising millers and merchants near Burlington Bay, at first refused a commission in 1816 because his business required his 'attendance in Lower Canada once or twice every year and would interfere with the Sittings of the Court.'[43] Hatt's neighbour and fellow miller, Matthew Crooks, wanted to resign in 1822 so that he could tend to his own business. As well, he felt that he had had to carry more than his weight because of 'the other gentlemen in the neighbourhood, either refusing or neglecting to [carry] their [proper] shares of the Public duty. [This] makes the situation of Magistrates an extremely irksome [business].'[44] A Mr Ferrier from Mount Forest, a two-day journey from the judicial centre of Hamilton in the 1820s and 1830s, recalled the disgust he felt when, as a JP, he heard that he 'would have to act as a magistrate, and on a very ugly case, too.' He disliked the idea so much that he 'went off to chop in the woods.'[45]

The nettles of responsibility carried by the stock of prestige were not eagerly grasped by all ambitious men. To make the position slightly more agreeable, the government of Upper Canada in 1834 protected JPs against 'frivolous and vexatious actions for mere error in form' so long as they discharged their duties conscientiously.[46] But there were other problems. Initially, owing to distance and the poor state of roads, the notables in one township did not know those in another and the government sometimes lacked a clear idea of local needs, the quality of potential magistrates, or even whether a magistrate still lived in the area. The creation of the Gore District exposed the difficulties of fleshing out a system of law and order in a new society of considerable expanse and light settlement.

Sheriff Titus Simons reported to the government in February 1820 that one of the JPs could not attend the quarter session because he had left the district four years earlier. In the same letter, Simons reported that another justice of the peace actually lived outside the Gore District.[47] In several instances, settlements at the fringes of the district complained about the government's failure to appoint local magistrates. Villagers in Mount Pleasant petitioned for their own magistrate upon the creation of the district, alleging that otherwise they had to travel thirty miles to Ancaster. 'Besides, the want of Authority in this place, we consider as a source, in a manner, of many irregularities amongst us, particularly on the Sabbath Days.'[48] Residents of Trafalgar Township and of Waterloo Township registered the same complaint and selected candidates for the magistracy during public meetings, an unauthorized innovation that surely displeased the administrators of the colony.

As the Gore District grew and the maturing colony developed political factions, enmity affected the magistracy. During the April 1828 quarter sessions, an old and violent political and social confrontation came to a head in a clash between the magistrates on one side and the clerk of the peace and the grand jury on the other. Though the clerk of the peace was an important district official, no English or Canadian statutes authorized the position and its functions would be assumed by the county crown attorney after that office was created in 1857. In the early nineteenth century, however, the clerk was an intrinsic feature of the quarter sessions and operated much like the county crown attorney of later years. George Rolph, appointed clerk in 1816, studied some law after the appointment; unlike England, where legal training by this era was expected, in Upper Canada clerks were not always well prepared.[49] On this occasion, that was not an issue.

Rolph was a reformer. He also lived with a Mrs Evans while he was still married to someone else. The combination of affronts that Rolph represented to the establishment inspired a band of local tories to gag and then tar and feather him on the night of 2–3 June 1826.[50] His assailants also 'threatened to maim and cut' Rolph 'in a way to [sic] horrible to describe.'[51] A grand jury of the court of quarter sessions in

April 1828 sympathized with Rolph and insisted that the case was serious enough to be held over for the assize. However, the magistrates, who sided against Rolph, wished to try the case. They repeatedly threw out the recommendation to transfer jurisdiction over the matter to the assize, saying 'many most unpleasant and irritating' things about the grand jury. Occasionally, it was reported, they qualified their criticisms with 'an assurance that the said Court meant to give the Jury no offense.'[52]

Rolph, as clerk, witnessed the whole proceeding. He retaliated by holding up court business, claiming that 'there were perjured Magistrates' on the bench.[53] The stalemate continued from Saturday, 12 April, until late in the afternoon of the following Monday. Eventually, the case went to the Court of King's Bench for a determination of jurisdiction and there Rolph's petition failed.[54] In turn, a number of magistrates petitioned for the removal of Rolph as clerk. The conflict bubbled up again at the assize of September 1828, when a grand jury once more presented a true bill on the case, and later at the quarter sessions in April 1829.[55] In the end, Rolph dropped his charges and the magistrates succeeded in removing him.

The functions of the justices of the peace in quarter sessions are reasonably well known. Gore District magistrates began their quarter sessions on the second Tuesday in January, April, July, and October. In addition to criminal justice cases of a moderately serious nature that had been referred to them by their fellow justices meeting in petty sessions, the magistrates conducted the local government business of the district. Their activities outside the quarter sessions, either in trying cases at petty sessions or in taking information and subsequently making out warrants, is poorly documented. The letterbook of occurrences brought to the attention of JP Robert Ferrie, brother of Hamilton's first mayor, Colin Ferrie, lists cases that occurred in Wilmot Township – just beyond the region under study – from 1850 to 1857. During these years, the complaints included a theft, a forgery, two instances of wilful damage to property, six assaults, four threats, and two tavern brawls. After information had been presented under oath, Ferrie issued a warrant to the constable. The one he gave to constable John Ginerick in August 1850 was quite open-ended. A watch had been stolen and Ginerick was 'to search persons of a man, woman or child whose names are unknown, also their baggage.'[56]

In contrast to the situation in a far-away township, plaintiffs in Hamilton and other towns showered magistrates with requests for action. The district's jail records provide a means of measuring the volume of work handled by the urban magistrates. Table 1.1 reveals the number of people committed to jail by several active JPs, a figure that

Table 1.1
Examples of the More Active Justices of the Peace in the Gore District, 1833–51

Name	Occupation	Activity as JP	Total Jail Committals	% Thefts	% Assaults	% Moral Order	% Other*
Richard Beasley	Hamilton merchant	1833–41	95	64	17	12	7
Colin Ferrie	Hamilton merchant	1833–42	19	74	21	5	0
Alex Roxborough	Hamilton merchant	1836–45	162	26	33	14	27
Nathan Gage	Brantford merchant	1843–9	100	57	19	17	7
Thomas Racey	Dundas merchant	1838–52	49	30	31	18	21

* Offences against the court: violation of recognizance, contempt, breaking bond.

is not to be confused with the number of informations laid and warrants issued.

The great majority of committals derived from petty sessions. In 1834, as noted already, an overhaul of the Upper Canadian criminal code enabled a single justice of the peace to try common battery and trespass cases; and three years later, further legislation enabled some cases of larceny to be tried at the court of quarter sessions instead of at the assize.[57] In general, more minor criminal cases were to be handled summarily or by the court of quarter sessions. Over time, the unpleasantness of the duties, the complaints by reformers that JPs were lazy, incompetent, and friends of the government, the increase in the types of cases that could be tried in petty and quarter sessions, and the rise of moral reform movements put pressure on the amateur system and helped to effect a change in the magistracy.

The government of the United Canadas took an initial step toward professionalism in law and order when, through a section of the act that chartered the city of Hamilton in 1846, it enabled the governor general to appoint a police magistrate there.[58] For many decades after this measure, the public had the benefit of a paid official whose sole business was to listen to complaints. Presiding over what became known as a police court, the police magistrate heard complaints from people of all classes. The accessibility and simplicity of the police court not only encouraged prosecutions of the poor by the rich, but of the poor by the poor. Until the public became used to carrying their complaints to police constables – a practice that seems to have developed gradually in the late nineteenth century – the police magistrate and his court provided the main recourse to prompt and fairly inexpensive justice for an astonishing range of complaints.

Like the part-time amateur justices, Hamilton's first police magistrate, George Armstrong, had no legal training. However, he had the vital prerequisite for official service in the old regime; he was unswervingly and demonstrably loyal to the crown. A colourful patriot and a practised pleader for official favour, Armstrong was the type of individual who often appeared as a petitioner for office in the early decades of the Upper Canada's development. Holding a commission as captain in the Royal Navy, he had seen action at Trafalgar during the Napoleonic Wars and, while serving in Upper Canada during the War of 1812, at the Battle of Crysler's Farm. Though he was cast adrift after peace returned in 1815, he later resumed military service, fighting in China in the 1820s. The following decade he was back in Upper Canada; in the wake of the rebellions of 1837–8, Armstrong claimed to have set fire to the explosives that destroyed the *Caroline* on the Niagara River, thereby disrupting the supply line of the rebels who had their camp on Navy Island.[59] In short, Armstrong had – in his own words – 'served in all climes.'[60]

Returning to Canada around 1840 from an adventure in the East Indies, Armstrong made a disastrous investment in American securities. Afterwards, furnished with letters of introduction, he sought an appointment with Governor General Sir Charles Bagot. Bagot, dying of cancer, could not see him,[61] but Armstrong persisted. Describing himself as a friend of the government – and one with eight small children – Armstrong had a specific post in mind. In late 1843, he had been made aware of a bill in the legislature that would provide towns and cities with police magistrates. The resignation of the Baldwin-Lafontaine reform government delayed the implementation of this measure, but Armstrong received a commission as a JP.

Armstrong's eagerness for service must have been appreciated, for his brother justices unanimously appointed him acting magistrate for Hamilton in the autumn of 1845. At last, when the reformers returned to office, the city charter establishing a police magistrate was passed in 1846. Armstrong's bid for the new position had the backing of the chairman of the quarter sessions, the city council, Sir Allan MacNab, and other justices of the peace.[62] If the reformers of the colony had hoped to substitute professionals for placemen, they had failed in Hamilton – at least in the short term. When reform leader Robert Baldwin introduced a municipal bill in 1849, it stipulated that the police magistrates had to have three years standing as a barrister. Hamilton council took exception, alleging that 'the duties of a Magistrate do not require the possession of much legal knowledge, and may be discharged equally as well by a person of experience and ability as by a professional man.'[63] As the first and last paid magistrate without legal training to dispense justice in Hamilton, Armstrong, the quintessential patriot and office-seeker, held the post until his death in 1862. His successor, as required by the 1849 act, was a barrister.

PETTY CRIMES AND A DISTRICT IN TURMOIL

The appointment of police magistrates for cities was partly a result of the reform party's many attacks on the magistracy. It also was a reaction to social disorder in the colony, disorder that originated in the United Kingdom and then spread throughout North America. As the revolution in agriculture and the rise of industrial capitalism undermined the patriarchal family unit in England, Ireland, and Scotland, transient wage labourers roamed the employment frontiers of the New World, bringing brothels and taverns to formerly quiet villages. Few regions were affected as sharply as the Gore District of Upper Canada. Situated at the west end of Lake Ontario, it included the present counties of Halton, Wentworth, Brant, Wellington, and Waterloo. The scene of canal construction and railway building, the district also served as a reception point for large numbers of famine Irish immigrants.

Records of incarcerations at the Gore District jail provide clues to the timing of the disturbances. Taken together with changes in colonial statutes, municipal by-laws, and the strengthening of policing and the magistracy, the rates of incarceration for some offences – particularly those against moral order – denote shifts in the attitudes of the authorities. Put another way, the jail incarceration rates capture both sides of a complex process: social disorganization and responses to that disorganization.

Jail committals fluctuated slightly from season to season. Summers facilitated navigation and the movement of immigrants and transient labourers who transformed Oakville, Dundas, Hamilton, Brantford, Paris, and Guelph into lively centres packed with people seeking work and recreation. Assaults, horse thefts, and petty larceny rose slightly above the average during July, August, and September. Yet the seasonal fluctuations were modest, and annual trends showed considerable variation (Figures 1.2 and 1.3). A few years exhibited particular troubles. The mid-1830s, years of heavy immigration and rising local costs, introduced higher rates of committals for property crimes (Figure 1.2). The rate sagged in the depressed late 1830s and then climbed again to peak in the mid-1840s. At that point, the ascent stopped – a fact noted with relief by the grand jury in April 1847: 'It is gratifying to find that the

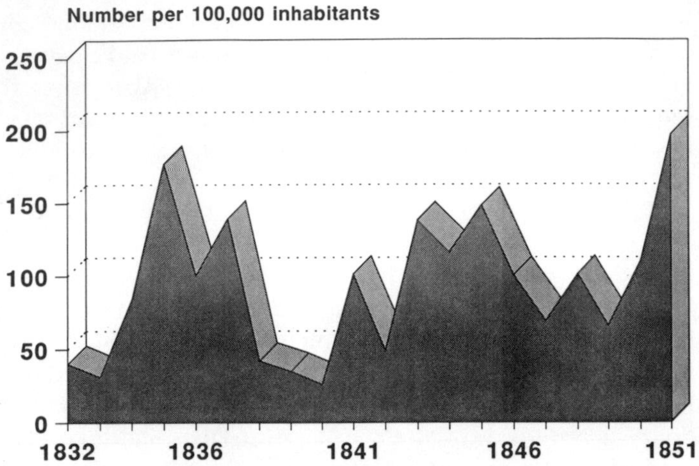

Number per 100,000 inhabitants

Figure 1.2
Gore District Incarcerations: Crimes against Person, 1832–51
Source: Archives of Ontario (AO), RG 20, F–15, vol. 10, Hamilton Jail Registers,
1832–51; John C. Weaver, *Hamilton: An Illustrated History* (Toronto: James
Lorimer 1982), 196.

number of persons of this description [felons] is much smaller than
usual in the District, and the offenses which the unfortunate people
stand charged with, generally of a less aggravated and serious nature.'[64] But the respite was short-lived: the rate rose again in the early
1850s.

In the United Kingdom, the 1840s were also troubled economic
times. Historian David Philips has linked the economic hardship of this
period with trials for larceny in England's industrial 'black country.'
During a period of rising costs, the underemployed and poorly paid
stole articles of modest value to supplement their income. Immigration
and public works in the Gore District made for a different economy
and society than that of the 'black country' but the motives for theft in
the Old and the New World may not have been all that different.

At the head of Lake Ontario, the peak years for crimes against property were times conventionally considered prosperous. Surges in new
arrivals from Ireland and England, an overstocked labour market,
harsh working conditions, and rising prices for food and shelter may
have had an impact on the property crime rates. If the theft of food and
clothing are considered, the hypothesis is supported. In 1846 the district experienced its greatest number of committals (thirty) for stolen
food and clothing; the previous high had been thirteen cases in 1835.
Both were years of considerable immigration and prosperity for district
millers, merchants, and land agents. Yet, for prospective settlers and

Committals per 100,000 inhabitants

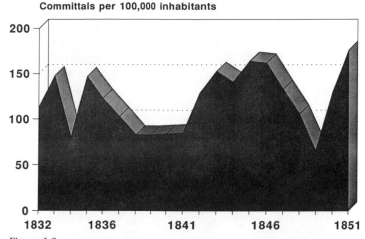

Figure 1.3
Gore District Incarcerations: Crimes against Property, 1832–51
Source: AO, RG 20, F–15, vol. 10, Hamilton Jail Registers, 1832–51; Weaver, *Hamilton*, 196.

the transient labourers who often travelled with their families, conditions frequently boarded on the desperate.[65]

Committals for crimes against persons essentially moved in concert with those against property (Figures 1.2 and 1.3). A jump in committals for violent and threatening acts accompanied the hectic immigration boom and urban growth around Burlington Bay in 1835. In the wake of the rebellions of 1837–8, the region 'settled down.' Of course, the jail was so filled with treason suspects in 1838 that it could not have held many who stood accused of lesser felonies. However, the committal rates for violent acts remained low through 1839 and 1840. Growth had faltered; an international depression and the news of political disturbances along the St Lawrence navigation route stopped or diverted the course of immigration from the Hamilton area. Possibly, too, the suppression of the rebellion served to chasten, terrify, and exhaust the Gore District.

A new round of spending on public works projects – the Welland Canal that lay just outside the district and the Grand River navigation system within the district boundaries – revived the flow of transients, including thousands of navvies. With the arrival of a large casual workforce in 1842–3, violence once again picked up. The committal rate dropped again in 1847, likely because of the completion of the Welland Canal two years previously and the winding down of work on the Grand River. In the early 1850s, however, a new wave of navvies came through the district. The construction of the Great Western Railway – largely a Hamilton venture – caused hopeful labourers to migrate through Hamilton and Dundas on their way to a labour camp near Copetown. Navvies building the long cut along the Niagara escarpment split into two brawling factions of Irishmen, 'Fardowners' (from Cork) and 'Connaughtonians.' An oversupplied labour market, tension over employment prospects and working conditions, the male labour camps, sectional disputes from the old country, and an abundance of whiskey traders helped propel the 1851 committal rate for violent acts to a level double what it had been in 1848.

Fluctuations of committal rates for thefts and crimes against property form a distinct path, one different from the pattern of incarcerations for moral or public order offences. These latter offences – vagrancy, drunk and disorderly conduct, streetwalking, gambling, violation of the Sabbath, and so on – were endured and accepted as of minor consequence until the early 1840s (Figure 1.4). Before 1843, they constituted only 12 per cent of all committals; from 1843 to 1851, they amounted to 35 per cent. Something quite important had happened. It is unlikely that 'sinning' had increased remarkably on a per capita basis, although it may have increased to some degree for reasons that will be outlined shortly. The low rate in the 1830s should not be confused with a near absence of vice.

There was nothing puritanical about Upper Canadian society prior to the late 1830s, although certain Protestant evangelicals were dead set against drink, cards, theatre, dancing, and other dangerous frivolities. Generally speaking, this new society had a firm attachment to drink. 'Taking the horn' – an evocative expression of the time – was a custom that enlivened marriages, christenings, funerals, harvests, and daily labour.[66] A trial report from 1843 described a wedding celebration that ended in insults and a homicide. 'Friends and relations of the parties had been making the rounds nary for three days in succession at different inns in the town.'[67] When the Dumfries Mills were being constructed, the workmen demanded and received the 'usual' ration of rum. At public entertainments such as fairs and circuses, drink brought on the 'rude and boisterous roar of riot.'[68] Drinking and other vices were even evident at religious camp meetings, outdoor assemblies that attracted large crowds in the 1820s and 1830s. Reminiscing about those times, Charles Durand, a former town clerk of Hamilton and a strict Methodist, recalled how 'wicked people on the outside often attended meetings; carried on all kinds of games; even horse racing, wrestling, fighting.'

In the 1830s and early 1840s, the secular Sabbath was a recreational

Committals per 100,000 inhabitants

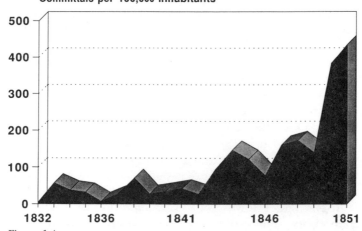

Figure 1.4
Gore District Incarcerations: Moral Order Offences, 1832–51
Sources: A O, R G 20, F–15, vol. 10, Hamilton Jail Registers, 1832–51; Weaver, *Hamilton*, 196.

institution. Sunday revels began on Saturday night and lingered into Monday morning, delivering heavy traffic on town streets. The irate magistrates of Hamilton met on 27 July 1837, during the 'dog days of summer' that they felt brought out the worst in people; they grieved about the desecration of the Sabbath. Sunday had become the 'day on which offences against the Peace occurred: rioting, fighting in the streets, drinking, using foul and abusive language, and driving furiously in the streets.'[69] It was also the only day of full release from toil in an age when the six-day work week prevailed.

Along the waterfront, drinking, gambling, and whoring went on in taverns, licensed shops, and disorderly houses. Hamilton, a town of three thousand in 1840, probably supported some twenty drinking establishments. The public works attracted crude refreshment stalls,[70] and there were many houses that sold alcohol and maintained or attracted prostitutes. Five such places ran into trouble with the Hamilton magistrates in the early 1840s: Marianne Ravelle's 'bad house,' Daniel Tolliver's 'notorious house,' Mr and Mrs Luckey's 'disorderly house,' Joe Case's grocery and beer shop which kept 'common women of the town,' and Mary Lavill and May Lily's 'house of ill fame.'[71] These many outlets for crude entertainment flourished as strangers moved through the city. Their trade increased when, in the spring and summer, circuses paraded into town or the militia mustered. In the summer months, the longer daylight hours, open windows and doors, and the ease of movement along the streets brought disorderly behaviour audibly and visibly to the attention of town dwellers.

Until the early 1840s, the small number of appointed constables and the merchant magistrates were mainly concerned with complaints about thefts and assaults. (They kept a watch on loyalty too. An old-timer reminiscing in 1884 about Hamilton as it had been in 1819 recalled that one man had spent two days in jail for saying 'damn the King.'[72]) Perhaps because of some intimidation of local officials by plebian rowdies, the old regime largely tolerated rough recreation. There were exceptions. In the village of Waterdown, an overly zealous magistrate, Ebinezer Griffin, endeavoured to rid the town of turkey raffles and drinking in 1841. He was ousted by community pressure.[73]

In the larger towns, however, toleration of coarse entertainment soon ended. The groundwork for a campaign against vice was laid locally in 1829 with the formation of a temperance society in Ancaster. The founding of an American presbyterian church in Hamilton also had an influence, for this church was devoted to temperance and it set about distributing the moral tracts produced by the influential American Tract Society in New York. For the first – though certainly not for the last time – the institutions of law and order were exposed to a moral order crusade.[74]

On their own, moral reformers probably could not have greatly affected committal rates; in later years, appeals to the authorities to clamp down on vice would produce only modest results. The moral order offensive of the 1840s and 1850s, however, coincided with widespread fears about social stability. The moral tales of the tract society – tales that warned of rootless strangers as well as the temptations and threats present in the anonymous society of cities – resonated with local events in the 1830s and 1840s. These events occurred shortly after the British parliament had granted local constabularies sweeping powers under the Vagrancy Act of 1824 and this measure appears to have inspired the framing of similar colonial measures.

Immigration was an obvious worry in Hamilton where, in the words of Sheriff Cartwright-Thomas, writing in 1840, 'the immigrant tide breaks.'[75] The population of the Gore District tripled between 1830 and 1842, largely because of an influx of about eighteen thousand immigrants. As the gateway to other districts and as the regional centre, Hamilton witnessed the passage of many transients and attracted purveyors of vice. But other towns were also affected. At Brantford, for example, order temporarily collapsed when navvies' grievances against the navigation company and disputes between the Irish Catholics and the local establishment sparked a flagrant defiance of authority. Bench warrants issued for service by the local constabulary at the spring assize in 1843 were not acted upon,[76] and in July of that year, a mob drove several magistrates out of town.[77] At the very least, the crisis of the early 1840s demonstrated how burdensome the tasks of constables and magistrates could become. At most, the incidents confirmed for some citizens the association of anarchy with vice and strangers.

The government's response to social disorder was not long in coming. Interestingly, its initiatives for re-establishing order largely took the form of measures supporting local action, whereas quite similar concerns in England had resulted in acts of parliament providing for an aggressive response on the part of the central government. Through town and city charters and municipal enabling acts, the parliament of Canada permitted towns and cities to suppress vice and to deal with vagrancy. What Carolyn Steedman has found regarding the English vagrancy legislation seems to apply to Upper Canada as well. It 'provided a daily context for police work in the nineteenth century.'[78] The attention paid to defining and punishing vagrancy seems to have been commonplace in the transatlantic world during the first half of the nineteenth century.[79] Until the mid-twentieth century, local officials in the Hamilton area frequently used charges of vagrancy against transient labourers, strikers, and people suspected of committing serious crimes. Vagrancy served nicely for a century as a vague charge with which to harry strangers and the poor.

Under its old town charter, Hamilton had passed by-laws in the 1830s and the early 1840s that restricted bowling as an indolent recreation, prohibited roulette, established penalties for prostitutes and found-ins, and codified a sweeping measure against drunkards, vagrants, and rowdies. In 1843 council passed another by-law: 'Ordered that all vagrants, vagabonds, or other persons of ill fame, or persons who are drunk or so conducting themselves to be a nuisance and found wandering in the Town at night shall be liable to be arrested and upon conviction thereof shall be liable to a fine of 30 shillings for each offense or in non-payment, 30 days in the district Gaol.' [80]

The 1843 by-law – certainly the spirit it embodied – had an astonishing impact. It led to as many as 50 per cent (516 of 1105) of Hamilton's share of jail committals from 1843 to 1851. The 1846 city charter sustained the mood, for it affirmed the power of the corporation to arrest rogues and vagrants, to appoint a police magistrate, to establish and regulate a police force, and to continue to use the district jail as the town jail. Acts of incorporation for Dundas and Brantford, in the following year, empowered those towns to suppress tippling, charivaris, and gambling as well as to control common showmen, circus riders, mountebanks, and jugglers. Provincially, the government of the Canadas in 1845 passed an act to prevent profanation of the Lord's day; it forbade Sunday tippling, skittles ball, football, racket or any other noisy game, and gambling or races. Moral order had achieved considerable legislative recognition. Indeed, more than this occurred – the new civic charters especially affected the evolution of law and order institutions. The age of policing was about to begin.

THE ORIGINS OF POLICING

Long before the 1850s, Hamilton had institutions that performed police functions. Not only were there a number of appointed constables and a separate night watch, but, as the judicial capital of a district, Hamilton also had a bailiff and deputy bailiffs attached to the court. There were the justices of the peace as well. A paid police force would eventually rationalize the system by combining the constabulary and night watch duties. For a long time, however, budgetary concerns surrounded the city's attempts to rationalize the agencies of order and security. Hamilton was not unique in this respect. Confusion and experimentation was commonplace throughout England and the United States as well.

The terms police and policing complicate an understanding of the situation. Throughout the English-speaking world in the early nineteenth century, the word 'police' had not taken on its modern connotations. Noah Webster's 1828 dictionary for the United States described police as the government of a town or city, as in the police of London, of New York, or of Boston. The government of all incorporated towns of New England was called the police.[81] The usage in England meant all of that, but, very late in the eighteenth century, the term police also referred to a civil force, such as a private group to protect Thames River shipping.[82] The creation of the Metropolitan London Police in 1829 strengthened this new meaning. Thus, while a civic police department was something new, it was not a radical departure. The term had a context; the services performed were not entirely without precedent; the course to innovation in Hamilton was not barred by a fear of a uniformed presence on the streets, but by a fear of expense.

On its incorporation as a town in 1832, Hamilton had obtained a board of police. Among its inaugural deeds, the board appointed a high bailiff who resembled the high constable of the old regime in England. However, in addition to bringing people before the board for the types of crimes that also were dealt with by the justices of the peace, this temporary appointee had to report to a member of the board of police anyone who breached its regulations. When making an arrest, the high bailiff had the authority to command other inhabitants to assist. The offending party had to be brought as soon as possible before any two members of the five-member board. In other words, the members of the board – really town councillors – functioned exactly as justices of the peace except that they had been elected by a small enfranchised electorate. In a study of lower courts in Canadian cities, Greg Marquis has assembled other instances of what he has termed 'civic justice,' justice dispensed by an elected magistracy. There was a brief interlude at mid-century when Saint John, Montreal, Quebec, Toronto, Halifax, Charlottetown, and other centres had courts presided over by elected members of the civic government. The police board and high bailiff system in Hamilton was, therefore, a common and slight nod toward local democracy within the old regime.[83]

The alleged ineptitude of the English local amateur constabulary has been the subject of historical debate.[84] On balance, they seem not to have been as incompetent as once believed. In Hamilton, the bailiffs may not have been bumbling and useless, but there were problems. The public did not always respond to calls for assistance, and two bailiffs were dismissed during the first two years of the system. One of these bailiffs had been accused of the rough handling of a woman and had also had three other unspecified complaints lodged against him. In 1842 the man who had served as bailiff since 1839 was arrested for theft. It is possible that the charges were undeserved, but, even if they were trumped up by disgruntled citizens seeking revenge, they still demonstrate an instability that itself jeopardized public order.

In the summer of 1837, an outbreak of burglaries prompted demands for greater protection, but adverse economic conditions compelled the impoverished town government to reject the idea of a paid police. Instead, ten men volunteered to keep a rotating patrol. The reluctance to resort to a hired force has been regarded by some American historians who have noted the same phenomenon in their cities as evidence of an early republican distrust of standing armies. Cities in the slave states were notable exceptions; Charleston and New Orleans had armed and hired watches. Perhaps knowledge of police forces that supported the institution of slavery caused northern city councils to reject comparable experiments as worthy only of tyrannies. In England, too, adherence to a voluntary system until the County and Borough Police Act of 1856 has been explained as arising from a concern for liberty or as a bid for the retention of local discretion by the gentry. In Hamilton, there were no reported paeans to liberty and no evidence of a gentry or commercial élite wishing to hold exclusively the reins of authority. The delay in establishing a hired force was caused by purely budgetary considerations.

Whenever it felt that it could afford to fortify law and order, the council acted, building a lock-up in 1840, arming constables in 1843 with staves from a local lumber yard, and in 1845 purchasing a hand cart 'to convey vagrants to prison.' The town hired special constables when fairs, quarter sessions, and assizes brought more than the usual flow of strangers. Soon after hiring Armstrong in 1846, the city began to experiment with other hired police officials. In 1847 it employed a chief bailiff, a chief constable, and two subconstables. In 1848 it replaced the two with ten special constables – two to a ward – who received payment only when they turned out to perform an official duty. The city returned to four employees in 1850. Then, in early 1851, there occurred the events that gave the city the critical nudge required for bolder and more costly actions.

Eric Monkkonen has proposed that, in the United States, most cities organized police departments in the 1850s and 1860s in imitation of larger centres such as Boston and New York. In doing so, Monkkonen claims, these cities embraced the prevailing assumption that police departments were signs of modernity and progress. But this view begs the question as to why forces were formed. What were these modern institutions expected to achieve? Moreover, where the origins of policing have been studied in detail, there is a good deal of evidence indicating that riots and demonstrations have played a part. Hamilton provides a Canadian example of what may be a broader pattern.

On 5 February 1851, hundreds of striking labourers on the Great Western line marched through Dundas 'armed with bludgeons and threatening a breach of the peace to the great consternation and alarm of the peaceful inhabitants.' Reports circulated that other labourers, anxious for the opportunity to work, would fight the strikers.[85] A public meeting held in Hamilton sent a petition to the government of the Province of Canada to send in troops to quell the turmoil. The government – as budget conscious as the municipalities – rejected the request and declared that no military force would be sent until municipal authorities had formed a police force and until it had proven inadequate. Hamilton, Dundas, and the railway company immediately agreed to set up a police force of not less than twenty-seven mounted men, and shortly thereafter the governor general sent in two companies of a British regiment. The appearance of a mounted police to deal with labour unrest was not exceptional – a similar response had followed riots on the Welland Canal only a few years before – but now civic authorities were involved. The railway police operated for several years.[86] When disbanded sometime in 1853, several men joined the Hamilton force, which the city now placed on a fairly secure basis as a multi-purpose agency to meet the social consequences of an economic and demographic boom.[87]

THE JAIL POPULATION AND
BIASES IN THE COURT

Did the people arrested in the district differ significantly from the rest of the community? And, if so, why? In attempting to answer these very simple and important questions, it is necessary to enter into a discussion on sources, methods, and theories. The jailer recorded a considerable amount of personal information on each prisoner: national origin, age, and sex were reported for every year from 1832 to 1851. Information also was taken on occupations (1843–7), literacy (1848–51), and moral habits (1848–51). Among other things, these last three variables demonstrate the penetration into a colonial society of a concern with the classification of criminals. This concern had become a part of penology throughout the North Atlantic world in the first half of the nineteenth century.

The national-origins data depict the prominence of the Irish. Although Americans were well represented in the Gore District jail before the rebellion of 1837 – and many of them may have thought it prudent to call themselves Upper Canadians after that event – the number of Irish prisoners was out of proportion to their population in the district. There is an interesting pattern to the charges against the Irish: they were singled out for the moral order charges to a far greater extent than any other nationality. Judging by the committals for crimes against persons or property, they were no more criminal than Upper Canadians, Americans, Englishmen, or Scots. Neither were the labourers who were just over half of the male prisoners from June 1843 to December 1847. Nearly half of the labourers, in fact, claimed Ireland as their birthplace. The offences typically committed by labourers, both Irish and non-Irish, were moral order violations, petty larceny, and assaults. Though there had been dramatic episodes of riot associated with labourers, these were not quantitatively significant.

Regrettably, the jail records do not indicate who stole from whom or beat whom. Undoubtedly, the canal and railway navvies tore up fences and destroyed woodlots for firewood; unquestionably, they threatened authorities. In sum, they represented a problem to some people of property and station. Likely, though, the larceny and violence that labourers committed were often at the expense of other labourers.

This is certainly the impression conveyed in newspaper accounts of the police magistrate's court just beyond this period. It is probable, then, that very few settled people in the district and its towns experienced crime as victims. Their perceptions – which affected the development of law and order institutions – depended to a considerable degree on what they were told or what they read about threats to order. They knew about the flood of newcomers, suspected the Irish of being desperate and violent, and had before them the hard evidence of a few labour riots.

Another aspect of the relatively innocuous nature of the bulk of the jail population concerns gender. The rise in committals for moral order offences was accompanied by a relative increase in the number of women being locked up. About 60 per cent of the women arrested from 1832 to 1851 were Irish, as opposed to 40 per cent of males. Three-quarters of the women taken in for drunk and disorderly conduct – an offence that brought a dramatic increase in arrests after the arrival of the famine Irish – were Irish. In the case of vagrancy, the proportion of Irish women among all women was four-fifths. The moral order onslaught of the 1840s and early 1850s had a marked impact on women, especially Irish women. Women were to be happy at home, tasteful, and tender; they were to be angels of mercy and paragons of virtue. The transient and sometimes abandoned women of the immigration trek contravened social conventions. A relatively young group of women – half of the women arrested for moral older violations were between sixteen and twenty-five – possibly cast up by the dislocations of immigration gravitated to the towns and cities. There, in the 1850s, were found the navvies, the newly arrived mechanics, and tradesmen who had flocked in, drawn by the prospects of employment in a railway boom, and the purveyors of a good time. The combination proved propitious for vice. In dealing with vice, the constables probably found the women easier to apprehend, subdue, and convey to jail.

Much of the over-representation of young Irish Roman Catholic women in the jail data arises from the presence of repeat offenders. Women of all origins accounted for 18 per cent of all committals but 28 per cent of repeat committals. Female repeaters had arrest records that far exceeded those of male counterparts. Young and poor, these women lacked subtlety in their relationship with community values. Jane Ellis, an English immigrant, was twenty-one when first arrested for being a public nuisance in June 1843. Over the next two years, this prostitute was arrested twelve more times on related charges. On one fine Saturday evening in July 1844, she walked arm in arm with Henry Masiah, who was 'playing with her breasts as they walked.' Whether or not such women had succumbed to alcoholism and prostitution on the immigrant trek, they could expect little sympathy from a community that had embarked on a moral order crusade.[88]

Did the repeat offenders represent a criminal class? Did the women and the men who transgressed community norms often become more dangerous in their wayward ways? There is not much evidence to support either proposition. In the case of the women, they amassed records consisting of the same offences; nothing suggests that they descended from petty crime to serious crime. Women were arrested for a cluster of crimes without victims: vagrancy, drunk and disorderly conduct, and prostitution.

Men, however, committed a broader set of crimes that did include violence. Jesse Hickman, a black barber from the United States, had four convictions for assault and battery between November 1834 and May 1835 and two more convictions for threatening in 1843. It is possible to imagine the racial insults that may have led to his problems with the law, but neither in his case nor in most others can the gender of the victim be determined. Wife beating, a crime that figures prominently in later decades through to the present, was evident. James Hall, a nasty drunkard and wife beater who occasionally turned to theft, compiled a local record from 1837 to 1849 that ranks him as one of the more vicious characters encountered by authorities. He was neither an immigrant nor of Irish background.

The repeat offenders among the men truly formed a varied lot. Old Daniel Gorman, a poor, fifty-year-old Irish labourer when first arrested for stealing clothing, spent time in Kingston penitentiary in 1837. He was arrested four more times for theft, but he seems more a pathetic mendicant than a menacing criminal. A conceivably more professional criminal was Caleb Swayze. First arrested and charged with robbery and forgery in 1832 when he was in his early twenties, Swayze was arrested twice in 1837 for theft and returned to jail in 1841 for stealing. Altogether, there were 250 repeat offenders accounting for just 8 per cent of people committed. Of course, a regional study misses the possibility of mobile criminals with long and varied records. Professional counterfeiters, burglars, horse thieves, and pickpockets operated in the province; their activities surface only in rare impressionistic accounts.

There were few homicides in the immediate Hamilton area during the old regime. Indeed, there have been relatively few committed throughout the century and a half considered in this book, probably no more than 150. Michael Vincent's crime – committed some distance from the town – represented a common form of homicide. Domestic violence accounted for a quarter to a third of the community's murders (see chapter 5). Another leading source of violent death – the insult and brawl – had its preview in the nearby village of Dundas on St Patrick's Day, 1834.

As usual, James Owen had come into James Reed's grocery shop and tavern for a glass of beer. A rowdy father and son – Protestants who had consumed a great deal already and 'seemed troublesome very troublesome' – turned their attention on Owen, a Roman Catholic. The younger man grabbed Owen's waistcoat and insisted that he drink with him. Owen rejected the offer. 'Damn your friendship I want no such as that.' The young man tore Owen's shirt and said something about Owen's wife having left him and gone to live in Guelph. 'The reflections on his wife increased his anger.' Rising to the bait, Owen challenged the father and son to a fight. They thrashed him. Breaking free, he returned in twenty or thirty minutes with friends. 'Stones began to fly.' One of Owen's friends, John Rooney, struck the elder man with a whippletree – a piece of carriage harness. An iron hook 'indented the skull' and killed him. Judge James Buchanan Macaulay tried the two men at the Gore assize in early August. His charge to the jury took into account the provocation but also the interval between it and the final brawl. That lapse of time minimized any claim about acting in the heat of passion. Rooney stood especially condemned. He had not suffered the original insult. Macaulay concluded that malice also existed when Owen went for help. He wrote in his bench book: 'It would justify a verdict of Murder but I was not prepared to say it would not justify a verdict of manslaughter.'[89] The jury found the pair guilty of murder; Macaulay sentenced the two to be hanged on 6 September. In the end, as a result of petitioning by the condemned men's supporters, the sentence was commuted to banishment. Curiously, however, Owen died in his cell shortly before his scheduled release; he may have been murdered by the friends of his victim.

What is notable in the witnesses' depiction of this crime is the context, which included a tavern, heavy drinking by at least one party, a boisterous young male, jostling, an insult to manhood, sectarian differences, and a challenge. Many of these significant features leading to the fatal incident surfaced over the years in other male brawls that ended in death. Roughly a fifth of subsequent homicides followed a similar script.

The incidents of violence suggest that no threatening criminal subculture festered in the district. Criminals, whether male or female, did not progress from minor offences to serious felonies or capital offences. Of the eighteen people convicted of capital crimes from 1832 to 1851, only the convicted murderer Henry Van Patten had earlier committals to the Gore District jail – twice for theft. The real story of crime in this corner of Upper Canada was its modesty, something the Gore District shared with the rest of the colony. As John Beattie discovered when reviewing several of the criminal calendars at the assizes and the data on the number of prisoners delivered to Kingston penitentiary, 'Upper Canada was not seriously threatened by crime.'[90] No crime wave posed a threat to society; no criminal class – nursed on petty crime and vice and graduating to felonies – rocked the social order. Plaintiffs and defendants often came from the same labouring classes. It was the confusion of crime with labour protest and fear of the Irish immigrants, along with the upsurge of moral reform, that effected monumental changes to the institutions of law and order in the 1840s and 1850s.

Not all of the men and women whom the constables had committed to the jail were guilty of crimes; many sat for weeks in the damp and awaited trial. If the magistrates could not dispense summary justice, then the prisoners had to wait until the quarter sessions or assize met, unless he or she could produce bail. Two magistrates could admit a prisoner to bail, or the prisoner could petition a judge on the Court of King's (or Queen's) Bench to direct a magistrate to set bail. Thus, the length of time spent in a cell varied with an individual's understanding of the legal system, community standing, and wealth. Understandably, then, Upper Canadians had much more success in securing release by bail than did the Irish newcomers.

Common labourers seldom met bail unless they had assistance from a bondsman or a helpful countryman. John Fennessy, leader of Irish Catholics in Brantford in the early 1840s, appears to have aided friends. In Ancaster, Bucklin Alderman – condemned as 'a troublesome officious fellow' – acted as a bondman in the 1830s. Magistrate John Haycock complained: '[Alderman] sets bond for every scoundrel that requires it, and the more infamous the offender, the more fit for the interference of Mr. Alderman and who on occasions arrays himself against the constituted authorities of the country, when he can do safely to himself and give to the lower orders of people (over whom he exerts considerable influence) an improper bias on every occasion that presents itself.' Yet a few 'troublesome' fellows did not alter the trend of outsiders failing to be released on bail in the same numbers as their Upper Canadian counterparts.

There is no direct testimony about the roles of prejudice or familiarity in influencing the deliberations of juries. However, Irish men and women were definitely under-represented among those prisoners released either for want of a bill of indictment or from acquittals by trial juries. The Irish shared the fate of outsiders throughout the history of criminal justice; they lacked substantial community roots and thus influential patrons. Worse, as outsiders, they were simply suspect. The disadvantages of the Irish continued after the presentation of verdicts. In cases of summary justice, where sentences typically included a choice of paying a fine (usually thirty shillings) or going to jail (usually for thirty days), the Irish more often had to select the former than did the Upper Canadians. The group that most consistently paid the fine was Upper Canadian farmers; Irish women were the least likely to do so.[91]

THE REFORMATION OF PUNISHMENT

In the 1820s the district jail served primarily as a place for prisoners awaiting trial or punishment, which just might include time in the stocks or lashes. The jail was itself a place of punishment, but only in the 1830s did it become the exclusive form of punishment, except in instances when fines applied and when judges saw fit to prescribe a whipping. Before the 1830s, incarceration did not accord well with the prevailing theory of public punishment, which stressed the need to put a prisoner on display as a warning to adults or lesson for children. Indeed, the fact that culprits had long been removed from public view was felt by the grand jury in April 1863 to have been a mistake. The jury believed that prisoners should be put to work on the streets where 'the shame attending such exposure would have a most salutary effect.'[92] The best that could be managed in the late nineteenth century was the marching of people convicted at the police court to the city and later the county jail.[93]

Public punishments had been essential features of criminal punishment under the old regime. The stocks confined the arms and legs of a seated prisoner; the pillory fastened the neck and wrists of a standing prisoner. By an act of 1800 for 'the more effectual punishment of certain offenses,' whipping remained a punishment, though women were to be whipped only in the presence of female witnesses.[94] Besides shaming someone, public punishments notified people about who in their midst could not be trusted. One perjurer in the late 1820s stood with his neck in the yoke on the courthouse square for two days with 'everyone gazing at him.' One traditional form of indicating for public benefit who had committed a felony was abolished early in the history of the colony. In 1800 Upper Canada eliminated the practice of branding a felon's hand because it 'may fix a lasting mark of disgrace and infamy on offenders, who might otherwise become good subjects.'[95]

In 1841 the pillory was abolished in Upper Canada. Another form of punishment, whipping, died out gradually. The last whippings in the district for many years appear to have been administered to two convicted thieves in January 1834. From then on, magistrates and judges normally measured out punishments in shillings and in days spent in jail rather than in lashes with the cat-o'-nine-tails. But there were exceptions. Whipping remained a sanctioned punishment well into the twentieth century,[96] and from time to time police magistrates of Hamilton ordered that prisoners be whipped. One such whipping occurred in 1885, the victim being a convicted child-molester; decades later, in 1910, a wife-beater received one week in jail and ten lashes. These and the whippings carried out occasionally in the penitentiaries were hidden from public view.[97]

Perhaps the elimination of shaming and the gradual decline of whipping expressed humanitarian sentiments. Yet a stay in the jail was still dreadful – even when not exacerbated by lashes. The four cells and six debtor-rooms in the basement of the stone courthouse were several feet below ground level and heated by a hall stove. In 1832 the prisoners received a pound of bread a day, two blankets, and two sets of clothing. In later years, the meals were slightly improved as meat and potatoes – lots of potatoes – were added. There was an exercise yard and prisoners could speak to visitors through the grating in the cell doors. For most offences, the stay was brief. Of those who were convicted of larceny, nine out of ten received sentences of ninety days or less, and three-quarters got sixty days or less. Still, the diet and stagnation 'below the ground where there is no fire, and where the light of the sun seldom shines' affected the prisoners' health. And there was overcrowding. During a 'crime wave' in the spring of 1834, for example, the four cells held eighteen prisoners.

Traditional accounts of the reformation of punishment emphasized the good intentions of humanitarians who hoped to see prisoners not just punished but reformed. Revisionists later proposed that punishment by incarceration, especially in a model penitentiary, represented aspects of the new industrial social order that had come to cherish discipline and routines. Both interpretations agree that the penitentiary represented rationalization, the replacement of discretion and caprice by certainty and design. A district jail was not a model penitentiary, but even here there was evidence of the schemes of the reformers and of a further assault on the old regime.

Under the old regime, jails had been miserable places, carelessly run. Prison reformers believed that, if punishment was to have the effect of reforming behaviour, outside contact had to be controlled: no alcohol could be brought to the prisoners, prisoners had to be classified and separated, jail life had to be governed by rules, and there had to be religious instruction. Most of these measures were in place at the Gore District jail by the late 1840s. There were even plans for a new jail that would include separate quarters for prostitutes, debtors, and felons. The district jail in the old regime had held a mixed assortment of people and some were placed in common cells: debtors, parties accused of felonies and awaiting trial, people serving short sentences for misdemeanours, the young and the old, men and women. Reform plans for the local jail came to naught, but a jail built in 1885 did provide for separate halls of cells for men and women. The real reform of punishment by incarceration, however, involved the building of a penitentiary at Kingston.

Upper Canada lacked the resources of England and the wealthier American states. All the same, by the early 1830s the colonial government had given serious thought to the building of a penitentiary, eventually settling on one of the two main systems then popular in the United States. It is not surprising that the colony looked to the United States for models, because reformers in many lands turned to the republic as a storehouse of improvements. Often in later years, Upper Canada's agents of law and order would examine American practices and inventions. The British colony could not deny geography.

Investigators for the government of Upper Canada found two general systems of penitentiary reform in the United States. The Pennsylvania system kept prisoners apart at all times; the New York system imposed silence on the prisoners but did not provide the paraphernalia to keep them wholly separate. The object in both cases was to force inward reflection on the prisoners. The New York arrangements were cheaper and that appealed to the Upper Canadians. The colonial legislators expressed the hope that, by well-regulated labour and religious instruction, the penitentiary would reform individuals and bend them to the habits of industry. At the new Kingston penitentiary, which opened in 1835, the utilitarian mood that had now worked its way into punishment would even extend to the disposal of bodies: unless the relatives of a deceased prisoner took away the body it went to the local medical society.[98]

The provincial penitentiary had a practical consequence for the exercise of law and order in the Gore District. It permitted judges to eliminate some of the complications that accompanied the sentencing of felons, especially where capital punishment was required by law. In England, the transportation of convicts first to America and then to Australia provided a safety valve of sorts. It was not necessary to execute in every instances; the crown could show leniency. In Upper Canada, the government abolished transportation and replaced it with banishment in 1800. Transportation was reinstated in 1833 but it was seldom used; the rebels of 1837 who were transported to Van Diemen's Land were the exception rather than the rule. While banishment remained on the books,[99] it was never a satisfactory form of punishment.

A typical sentence of banishment was delivered in Hamilton on 2 September 1828 against George Young. Prosecuted by the attorney general of the colony and convicted of grand larceny, he was 'sentenced to leave his Majesty's Dominions for the term of seven years and to depart there from within four Days.'[100] The period allowed to make preparations to leave as well as the period of exile varied according to the severity of the crime. Convicted merely of larceny at the assize of 1827, another prisoner's sentence was recorded as '5 yrs Banishment and to leave the Prov in 8 days.'[101] The expedient of banishment fit the circumstances of a raw colony, for it involved neither expense nor organization. From 1832 to 1851, seventeen individuals resident in the Gore District were banished from the colony: five for horse theft, nine for other thefts, and one each for shooting, rape, and treason.

All of these cases could have gone either way and pitted the word of the defendant against that of the accused or left some doubt in the mind of the judge. Was the horse stolen or did the accused man believe that he had the owner's permission? Was the thief goaded by bad company and less culpable than his mates? Was the convicted rapist John Standish seen clearly by the women picking strawberries? In a few cases, the full weight of the law was harsh and it seemed appropriate to let the community decide what it thought of the individual. There were cases where the banished person returned or never left; the community had spoken, or rather had not spoken. In September 1831, a Gore District grand jury condemned the practice of banishment, claiming that the crown did not prosecute those who returned. Some people were terrified that a returned felon would do them harm; for example, John Standish's victim and her husband petitioned against his banishment, alleging that he would return and seek revenge. The building of the Kingston penitentiary neatly resolved fears and passions fostered by banishments.

The ultimate punishment – death by hanging – did not escape the attention of prison reformers. England had slowly begun to reduce the number of its capital crimes by the early nineteenth century. Similarly, after the American revolution, Pennsylvania eliminated capital punishment for many of the crimes that the English code had forced upon it and other colonies. In the 1840s, campaigns in several states bordering on Canada were waged to abolish capital punishment altogether. Michigan abolished it in 1847; Maine, Wisconsin, Minnesota, and North Dakota eventually followed the same course.[102] Over the decades, Canadian authorities paid a lot of attention to innovations in law and order south of the border, but not with respect to progressive actions against capital punishment. In 1828, judge John Walpole Willis, familiar with reforms in the United Kingdom, criticized Upper Canadian legislators for neglecting to trim capital offences. His blast had no effect. Until 1833 the criminal code of Upper Canada was basically that of England as it stood in 1792. Consequently, shooting at a person as well as horse and cattle theft called for the judge to impose the death sentence. The reality was less draconian. After 1826, in cases where the court believed that the prisoner was a fit candidate for royal mercy, judges no longer donned the dreaded black cap and read the death sentence in open court – they merely recorded it.[103] More significant was the fact that, at the Gore assizes from 1822 to 1832, judges entered nine capital sentences but in the end only Michael Vincent was hanged. Convictions for riot, shooting, livestock theft, and rape all concluded with the crown extending mercy.[104]

The pursuit of mercy brought a ritualized contact between the community and the representative of the crown. The petitions that expressed this contact often included the names of magistrates. When parents initiated a petition, they first established evidence of loyalty to the crown; military service or a loyalist family connection did nicely. They might then proceed to explain their dependence on the convicted party for support; the shame that had already descended upon the family, it was often said, had levied enough suffering. When friend and neighbours drafted a petition, they attested to the character of the prisoner and spelled out any extenuating circumstances that had occasioned a lapse in an otherwise blameless life. Alcohol and unfortunate luck in selecting companions explained horse thefts; insults or threats had provoked attacks or the threatening use of firearms. To function effectively, petitions had to work through the channels of deference; they had to circulate to include important people. But who could vouch for whom in turbulent periods of migration and immigration? Many newcomers lacked patrons who understood the system.

After the opening of Kingston penitentiary, petitioning continued but lost some of its life-and-death quality – convicted felons could now be incarcerated for extended periods. Eventually, moreover, there were other avenues of appeal. A court of appeals was established in 1849, but it could only hear cases that dealt with errors in law. In 1857, legislation extended the right of appeal to errors of fact as well as well as errors in law.[105] The gradual demise of petitioning was part of a larger trend in the early Victorian era. A system of law and order that had focused on the individual in the community was being replaced with one attempting to treat the concerns of law and order as professional matters. Many developments in law and order during the rest of the century – especially from the late 1840s to the early 1870s – involved further retractions of both amateurism in enforcement and discretion in judicial processes and punishment.

Because criminal justice – regardless of era – so often intersects with human relations and the concrete circumstances of life, professional agencies and actors have never really been able to eliminate community-based attitudes. The professional police would encounter many of the same problems that plagued the amateur constabulary of the old regime. Professionalism became firmly implanted during the 1850s; however, the criminal justice system still had to face the old temptations, risks, and evils. Wife beater Michael Vincent, the drunken prostitute Jane Ellis, and the over-forceful bailiff remained stock characters.

2 Expeditious Courts and Muscular Mercenaries

'Poor McConnell, poor McConnell. He deserved better.' So lamented Michael McConnell on the morning of 14 March 1876. Indeed, his predicament could not have been worse. Flanked by constables, a black-hooded hangman following close behind, the convicted murderer walked out of the county jail, into a sunlit yard, and towards the gallows. With hats doffed, the press and prison officials walked solemnly at the rear of a small procession. The stairs to the noose had been painted black. Executions in full public view had ceased in Canada, but a number of people had been issued passes and many more clamoured for a glimpse of the macabre ritual. At 7:00 a.m. a large crowd milled around outside the jail. It dispersed a half hour later when it became obvious that this would not be a public execution. Just before McConnell and his party stepped out into the sunshine, spectators with passes were ushered from the jail's public rooms into the yard.

Remarkably, McConnell had slept for six hours, waking just before sunrise. He had no appetite for breakfast. On the walk to the gallows, he rarely lost his composure. He shook hands with the jailer, praising the humane treatment he had received. When he first perceived the masked executioner, it gave him a dreadful fright. 'My God, my God,' he sobbed. Then, immediately recovering himself, he was reported as saying 'I forgive you, poor fellow' to the silent figure in black.

In a matter of seconds, the sombre procession had crossed the yard. McConnell, the sheriff, the executioner, and a minister mounted the steps. On the gallows platform, the sheriff stepped forward and read the warrant of execution. Leaving nothing to chance, he had consulted doctors about the hanging; McConnell had been weighed and, since he was quite lean and only a few inches over five feet, a ten-foot drop had been prepared. Most sheriffs no longer secured local amateurs as hangmen; hangings had become a matter of state violence conducted by a few itinerant professionals who applied a rudimentary understanding of physics and physiology. McConnell's weight and the distance of the drop assured an appropriate rate of acceleration; the noose would halt the movement of the head while the body remained inert; the opposing forces would dislocate the neck. The execution, like many other matters associated with the case of Michael McConnell, was conducted with professional deliberation.

McConnell, like Michael Vincent in 1829, expressed no remorse. In his final address, he claimed that his victim had wronged him. The executioner then tied his legs and placed a black hood over his head. He sobbed in a choking voice, 'Oh Lord be with me; Oh Jesus stay with me.' After the hangman lowered 'the county kerchief' over his head, McConnell uttered his last words: 'Pull it a little tighter.' When the minister reached 'deliver us from evil' in the Lord's prayer, the trap-door opened in a flash and the butcher from Scotland was – in the parlance of the Victorian press – launched into eternity. A few minutes later, McConnell was certified as dead. At three in the afternoon, a coroner's jury held a formal hearing. There was a post-mortem; details about McConnell's brain and heart made the front page of the *Hamilton Spectator*. The newspaper also carried some of the comments of the doctors attending the *post-mortem.*

Like Michael Vincent's execution, McConnell's initiated a controversy about the law; in his case, the controversy was about whether or not he had been insane. Yet the executions of the two men differed in an important respect: Vincent's was open to the public, McConnell's was not. Prior to McConnell, the last public hanging in Canada had been that of the assassin of D'Arcy McGee in 1869. Throughout the western world, many states had moved executions behind jail walls, ostensibly as a humanitarian reform.[1] Only a select number of spectators who applied for tickets were admitted to Canadian hangings. The newspaper accounts conveyed enough of the terror to satisfy those who trusted in deterrence by an awful example.

McConnell had attacked and stabbed his landlord, Nelson Mills, on 5 January 1876 in broad daylight on a major street. Mills had just instructed the sheriff to have McConnell evicted. Mills did not die until three days following the attack, but it was clear shortly after the stabbing that he had suffered a fatal wound. Someone notified the police, whereupon a detective proceeded by buggy to McConnell's house and arrested him. (Not only had the day of the amateur constable passed, but the Hamilton force in the mid-1870s boasted two full-time detectives.) The police magistrate, with McConnell in tow, went to Mills's house to get a deposition from the dying man. Following the standard practice for justices of the peace and police magistrates when they had a statement from an accuser or witness, McConnell was asked if he had anything to add. He did not. After Mills's death, earnest professionalism surfaced in the coroner's inquest. The coroner was Dr Thomas White. For the post-mortem, he called in a Dr Campbell from Toronto, an examiner in physiology and microscope anatomy for the Council of the College of Physicians and Surgeons of Ontario. A third doctor assisted Campbell. With the deposition taken by the magistrate and the findings of the coroner, the coroner's jury had sufficient evidence to indict McConnell.

Indictment by either a grand jury or a coroner's jury was required before there could be a trial at an assize; however, those felonies normally tried at the intermediate level of courts no longer always required a grand jury indictment. Three years before McConnell's trial, the province of Ontario had created the County Court Judge's Criminal Court, which tried cases without a grand jury or trial jury if the defendant agreed. Meant to expedite criminal justice, this major reform did not affect the procedures for McConnell's trial. By common law custom, the rare crime of homicide required a trial at the assize.

More than the style of execution had changed in capital cases since the trial of Michael Vincent. The arrest of the suspect by a detective and the involvement of doctors at a coroner's inquest were fairly recent innovations. The trial disclosed more of them. Its length – two days – indicated that both prosecution and defence exercised greater care than their counterparts had done at the 1828 trial of Vincent.

There was nothing typical about a murder or a murder trial; they focused public attention on the criminal justice system to a degree unmatched by any other events. At McConnell's trial, which attracted both public and professional interest, detailed reporting indirectly revealed much about police, judicial institutions, procedures, and defence tactics. On the opening day, a posse of police constables struggled to restrain the crowd that had gathered at the old stone courthouse. A large number of lawyers and magistrates attended to watch noted Toronto lawyer B.B. Osler – assisted by the Wentworth County crown attorney – face the local defence counsel, John Crerar. Though the attorney general or solicitor general had frequently prosecuted cases at the assize during the early years of Upper Canada – attorney-general John Beverley Robinson had prosecuted Vincent – it had been customary since about a half century before McConnell's trial for the law officers of the crown to delegate the prosecution of criminal cases at the assize. The creation of country crown attorneys in 1857 had provided the delegated prosecutor with a local assistant. Thus, at McConnell's trial, two attorneys acted for the prosecution.

John Crerar had been practising at the bar for only five years, but he was clever and had presence. The previous year he had helped found Hamilton's Garrick Club, a society dedicated to presenting plays of 'high character.'[2] Crerar initially attempted to postpone the trial, alleging that newspaper coverage of the murder had prejudiced the prisoner. Press coverage certainly had not arisen as a concern a half century earlier at the trial of Michael Vincent. On the grounds that the defence had not proven its point, the judge denied the motion.[3] Crerar then began presenting an insanity defence. He tried to establish that a head injury two years earlier had left McConnell prone to fits and severe headaches. It also had precipitated odd conduct. McConnell dug holes in his yard and filled them; he built a sod fence and then tore it down. The star witness for the defence was Dr Joseph Workman, the former medical superintendent of the Toronto Asylum for Lunatics.[4] Workman had held the post at the asylum for twenty-one years and had criticized the judiciary in other cases of alleged insanity. At McConnell's trial Workman insisted on the defendant's insanity, noting that the accused had not acted rationally in choosing the time and place of his attack. Moreover, McConnell expressed no regret for his crime and this cool indifference, claimed his attorney, marked him as insane.

Until the report of a royal commission on insanity in 1957, Canadian courts adhered to rules on the plea of insanity that the House of Lords had formulated in 1843. Law and medicine never fully agreed about the so-called 'McNaghten rules,' which insisted that to be considered insane the accused had to have acted without knowing the quality of his act or that the act was wrong. Some medical people argued that a few insane people, while appreciating the quality of a criminal act and knowing that it was wrong, still committed it because they were deprived of the reason to resist.[5] Workman's subtle point was that McConnell was insane even though he knew right from wrong.

Judge Patterson's charge to the jury described McConnell as eccentric, cited precedents from three instances of the insanity plea, and concluded that the defence had not made a case for McConnell's inability to distinguish between right and wrong. The jury – taking longer than expected – returned after fifty-five minutes. Seeing its solemn demeanour, Crerar buried his face in his hands. Patterson allowed McConnell to make a statement and then, forgetting to put on the traditional black cap, he pronounced the death sentence.[6]

In a post-trial open letter, Workman insisted that his professional expertise was infinitely superior to that of barristers and judges in these technical matters. The subject of insanity remained a 'sealed book' to all but a few authorities – such as himself. Just because a man had a motive, insisted Workman, did not mean that he was necessarily sane. Insanity was a medical issue.[7]

The trial and execution of Michael McConnell marked a new phase in criminal justice, one marked by the introduction of medical science, the reduction of some of the overt symbolism of punishment, and a more prominent role for defence counsel. The discussions about McConnell's sanity marked a significant change, too, for Workman's open letter implied that only men of science – not the jury nor the judge – could reach a just decision in a matter of life and death. All that said, continuity with the past also was conspicuous at this 1876 trial. The assize retained its solemnity; the juries – grand and petty – remained in place.

CRIMINAL JUSTICE AND THE VICTORIAN POLICE COURT

At mid-century, legislators worked to make the criminal justice system more utilitarian and professional. The assize escaped significant reforms. Instead, changes were directed at the two lower levels of criminal justice proceedings: the petty sessions of the justices of the peace and the quarter sessions.

Murders – indeed all serious felonies such as aggravated assault, assault with a weapon, burglary, rape, and so on – seldom happened or seldom were reported in nineteenth-century Hamilton. With respect to common assaults, petty larceny, drunk and disorderly conduct, and vagrancy, it was an entirely different matter. As stressed in chapter 1, the socio-economic changes in the Hamilton region had at times both helped attract a distressed population and aroused the fears of the élite. The government of the United Canadas, which in the mid-nineteenth century had played a significant role in restructuring the economy by building navigation projects and assisting in the construction of railways, found it necessary to embark on a restructuring of the state to deal with the social consequences of the industrial and urban growth that it had helped launch. This restructuring often involved the institutions of law and order.

Because of their considerable volume of business, the petty sessions invited reform. In Hamilton, modification began when the government of the Canadas enabled the petty session to be taken over by a police magistrate, an innovation initially authorized by the civic charter of 1846. At first, the Hamilton police magistrate had no special powers; the powers he did exercise were also held by the justices of the peace, the mayor, and the councillors. What distinguished the police magistrate from the justices of the peace or the elected officials was that the municipality appointed and paid the incumbent.[8] As noted earlier, a municipal act in 1849 enabled all towns and cities of Upper Canada to have a police magistrate if they so wished.[9] Police magistrates still had to sit with another justice of the peace – the mayor or councillor in the city – in order to try certain felonies. Two years later, an act to facilitate the performance of duties of justices of the peace granted new powers to the police magistrates, powers separate from those of the justices of the peace. Henceforth, the police magistrates could do alone what two justices of the peace acting together had the authority to do. Thus, for example, when sitting alone they could order bail, prepare bills of indictment, and could try certain felonies as described by statute.[10] Justices of the peace were not abolished in the wake of the creation of the police magistrates or the expansion of their powers; they remained significant in the county jurisdiction and they retained useful specialized functions in cities.[11] But in the cities the existence of police magistrates had consigned justices of the peace to relative obscurity.

An overlooked but fundamental element in the composition of criminal justice machinery, the police magistrate had a part in processing virtually all criminal offences in the second half of the nineteenth century in Hamilton. On the same day that he took McConnell to witness the deposition of Nelson Mills, he likely listened to complaints about theft, common assault, and drunk and disorderly conduct. Except for the fatal attack on Mills, it would have been a typical day.

Early in the history of the office of police magistrate, professional qualifications entered the picture. The city's first police magistrate, George Armstrong, had no legal training; however, his successor, James Cahill, had studied law in a Hamilton law office from 1835 to 1839 and was admitted to the bar in 1840. Cahill became magistrate in 1863 and died in office thirty years later. Upon Cahill's death, the post went to George Jelfs who surpassed Cahill's record of service by presiding until 1928, though from 1923 onward he dealt exclusively with juveniles while another police magistrate took over the sittings of the police magistrate's court. Jelfs too was a lawyer but he gave up his practice after his appointment. In fact, by the early twentieth century most police magistrates in Ontario towns were lawyers, though many were not. A few police magistrates continued to practise even as they tried cases. The post was treated as a patronage plum; Jelfs had served on the executive of the Hamilton Reform Association, a Liberal Party club.[12]

Regrettably, Cahill left no interviews or extensive statements about his work, but because Jelfs did it is possible to elaborate on the actions and thoughts of a late-Victorian police magistrate. The hours he spent in court comprised the least onerous part of the job. By statute, he or the mayor, who might relieve him, had to be available six days a week; no attendance at his office was required on Christmas Day, Good Friday, or any day declared a public holiday by proclamation. Jelfs actually maintained three offices: one at city hall, another in a room attached to the police court, and a small one at home. The public came to each. 'Hundreds of unfortunates of one sort or another ... call on him', the *Hamilton Spectator* noted.[13] He was 'bombarded by persons desiring of "having the law" on somebody else.'[14] This feature of the system of law and order is important.

By Jelfs's time, the magistrate and the police handled complaints, but it remained the task of the police magistrate to order arrests or to issue summonses to court on the basis of a plaintiff's initiative. That is why Jelfs maintained three offices; that is why people even roused him from bed. Around 8:00 a.m., Jelfs arrived at the city hall office and was beset by persons who poured forth their troubles in his ear: he listened to complaints about 'a wicked husband, an eloping wife, an employer who won't pay wages.' On market days, constables or patrons sometimes brought in complaints about the vendors at the nearby civic market which opened at 7:00 a.m.

As he left to walk the short distance to the police court where he was expected to preside at 9:30, people acting on behalf of those in jail or appearing before his court attempted to put a word in his ear. George Denison in Toronto recalled the same hubbub of petitioners outside his door in 1877; he immediately abolished the practice of permitting persons to bring letters from aldermen 'telling the magistrate what to do in their cases.'[15] Whether in Toronto or Hamilton, the police magistrate was an accessible, harried, and well-known public figure. From the 1850s to the 1890s, the Hamilton papers frequently printed the police court column on either the editorial or the front page. Newspapers sketched and photographed Jelfs. People in difficulty knew where to go and it was not always to a police constable.

During the second half of the nineteenth century, the police department – among other duties that grew without cease – continued to carry out duties that the amateur constables had executed for the justices of the peace in the old regime. When a constable served a summons or made an arrest under the instructions of the police magistrate, he performed a service intrinsic to the operation of law and order throughout the Victorian era. The summons linked plaintiffs' complaints and the police court. Victims of thefts and assaults, as well as of many other offences, made use of the police magistrate, the police, and the police court. Complainants came to one of the police magistrate's offices and laid 'an information' against someone they believed had wronged them. The magistrate issued a summons and had a constable deliver it to the party named. Ordinarily, constables walked to deliver the summonses. There was no urgency.

On occasion, the complainant convinced the magistrate to do more than issue a summons to appear before the police court. The magistrate could order an immediate arrest, though Jelfs may have been less willing than his predecessors to do this in cases of domestic dispute and feuds among neighbours. When a magistrate ordered an arrest, a constable acted immediately under the magistrate's orders. In Jelfs's day, the police dashed in the police wagon to make the arrest. During the first several decades of policing in Hamilton, constables or detectives rarely inquired into complaints; they simply undertook to deliver a summons or make an arrest. Towards the end of the century, however, the police dealt with more complaints directly. If the complaint sounded reasonable and the complainant wished to prosecute, the police would direct the complainant to the police magistrate's office. A summons or an arrest warrant would be issued. Whether or not the police interceded directly or simply carried out the bidding of the police magistrate, suspects summoned or arrested normally had to appear in court the next day to face an accuser.

In the last decades of the nineteenth century, the Hamilton police court cleared about three thousand cases a year at the rate of five to ten cases a day. Held six mornings a week, sittings lasted an hour or two. This meant that on average the magistrate moved a case through in roughly ten minutes. The city's police court was, as Gene Homel has said of its counterpart in Toronto, a court of 'intuition and speed.'[16] An estimate prepared in 1921 suggested that a city police magistrate in Ontario could dispose of as many as ten times the cases handled by a high court judge. On occasion, to give the police magistrate some relief for a vacation, the mayor or a member of city council sat on the bench. The province divested the mayor and councillors of all magisterial authority in 1948, finally disposing of the elected amateur jurists a century after the creation of the professional police magistrate.[17] In fact, the amateur substitutes were not without some professional assistance, for they appear to have been guided by the crown attorney and on one rare occasion by the police chief. In August 1912, when Jelfs had taken leave for a fishing trip and the crown attorney was touring Europe, 'the chief had his hands full deciding different points of law, and coaching the acting magistrates as to their duties and privileges in pronouncing sentence.'[18] Though rare, such practices clearly transgressed the independence of the bench. They intimate that at this time lower court proceedings ground on daily without much attention to legal niceties or care for the rights of the accused.

After court, Jelfs waited in his second office to hear appeals on fines, to write letters on behalf of some of the people he had sent up to the provincial penitentiary, and to listen to 'more people in trouble.' After lunch, he returned to the city hall office where he heard more complaints, offered advice – on the critical matters of whether or not and how to prosecute – made out warrants for arrests, and issued summonses to court.[19]

Except for the expansion of its jurisdiction, the police magistracy of Hamilton did not change fundamentally from the mid-nineteenth century to the First World War. As the city grew, the commission hired more constables; however, the city retained only one police magistrate until 1923. Not surprisingly, therefore, the number of court cases handled per year did not increase proportionately with the growth of the city's population; the lack of more than a single magistrate was a bottleneck that restricted the flow of complaints.

The police court at the turn-of-the-century functioned as an unpretentious and open forum of justice. Unlike the assize, the court projected simplicity. Paul Craven puts it bluntly. The physical surroundings of the police magistrate's court 'were better calculated to inspire nausea than awe.'[20] Hamilton's police court occupied spartan quarters in the central police station. A balcony that connected the court with a lock-up behind the station bore the nickname 'the bridge of sighs.'[21] According to a colourful and sarcastic newspaper description, the accused sat on the right, spectators on the left; splatters of tobacco juice stained both sides of the floor. A row of 'bright looking and evidently brainy men' sat at a table in front of the judge's desk and swivel chair. They were the lawyers.

Police magistrates donned no judicial robes. A journalist in 1881 described the brisk ceremony that opened the court. Sergeant major Kavanagh of the police force 'trumpeted forth "hats off" which is the signal for the commencement of the Olympian games.'[22] Later in the century, a police clerk opened proceedings with 'oyer, oyer' and declared that the court was ready for business. Unlike the assizes, where the judges recorded details from the trials in bench books, a police clerk merely noted basic information about the accused, the complainant, and the offence. There were thin reminders that the judicial system originated historically with the monarchy. Portraits of the monarch or a coat of arms hung on the wall behind the bench.[23] On the day of King Edward's funeral in 1910, the court was closed and the 'drunks' were discharged from the jail at sunrise.[24] The symbolism of monarchy persisted as one of the rare distinctions between a Canadian and an American court.

A provincial commission investigating the office of police magistrate in 1921 discerned no uniformity of practice from community to community. The forty-one barristers who then ran police courts presumably knew something about the law, but they comprised fewer than half of the province's magistrates. Even knowledge of the law was no guarantee that what went on followed the law. Perhaps he was puffing up his ego, but the colourful late-Victorian magistrate for Toronto, Colonel George T. Denison, boasted that he never followed precedents unless they agreed with his own views.[25] Jelfs made a slightly more cautious declaration in 1901. 'I may have erred in my conception of the law, but at no time have I ever departed from what I considered an honest interpretation of it.'[26] Though some of Jelfs's practices appear odd and unjust in retrospect, workingmen and women in late-Victorian Hamilton were relatively fortunate. At least they had magistrates with legal training and no direct ties to major employers.

The 1921 Ontario inquiry found that the magistrates in several communities were minions of the largest employers in town. The magistrate for Kapuskasing was a manager with the Bruce Falls Lumber Company; Port Dover's magistrate managed a local fish-canning factory; the manager of the labour department of International Nickel ran the police court for Port Colbourne. In farm towns, merchants and millers as well as insurance and real-estate agents held the office.[27] It is common to assume that the Canadian practice of appointing judges has produced a higher calibre of judge than has been realized by democratic processes in the United States; however, the historical situation in one of Canada's richest and presumably most sophisticated provinces challenges facile assumptions of superiority. Stuart Ryan and F.B. Sussman offer this assessment of Canadian magistrates today: 'The consequences of imposing so great a responsibility on so large a class of judicial officers, so diverse in background, education, experience, and outlook as the Canadian magistracy, have not been fully worked out.'[28] Much the same can be said about the magistracy in late-nineteenth- and early-twentieth-century Ontario.

Though Jelfs believed that he interpreted the law 'honestly,' much of what he and other magistrates had to consider was not the law but conflicting accounts of incidents. In assessing the truth of a tale, Jelfs applied tests derived from the prejudices of his class and gender. In dealing with the drunks that constables brought before him, he set free first-time offenders; in fact, he did not bring them before the court at all. In this he made one exception, however: single males from out of town. He fined them 'for the support of the police department.' If this had been a common practice, it would help explain the relatively severe treatment of strangers noted by Michael Katz, Michael Doucet, and Mark Stern in their analysis of Hamilton police court records over the years from 1879 to 1881. They conclude that 'the more lenient sentences received by residents clearly underscored the relationship of transiency to inequality.'[29]

In evaluating the many cases of wife beating, Jelfs preferred not to arrest the husbands on their wives' complaints, but only to have them summoned before the court. It seems that he did this because he often felt that wives had ulterior motives and he did not wish to punish husbands unduly. He seemed relieved that wives often dropped charges. When the parties insisted on a court appearance, he had a rule of thumb for apportioning guilt. 'If the woman demands harsh treatment, I conclude the husband is perhaps, more blameless than the wife. I have found this a pretty good test.'[30] However, Jelfs and the city press agreed that proven wife beaters deserved punishment in kind, namely whippings added to their jail terms. Perhaps because most reports of wife beating arose from the city's poor, the press accorded it considerable attention. Overtones of a wish to discipline the rabble blended with the chivalrous idea that men who beat women were cowards.[31] Wife beating and non-support cases came before police magistrates' court on a relatively infrequent basis, (Table 2.1) and that fact suggests that Jelfs's vivid recollection of them was probably based on complaints he heard in his office and deflected from court.

Jelfs's methods are not the only features of court practice that seem peculiar by today's standards. Armstrong, Cahill, and Jelfs discussed prisoners' records and used them against the accused. In November 1887 George Davis appeared in the court on a charge of shoplifting. The police chief – who could 'spot a jailbird when he sees one' – requested that magistrate Cahill remand Davis, so as to give him time to find Davis's previous record. The Toronto police furnished it and the private prosecutor used it to convict Davis. This case also shows the complexities of prosecution. A victim brought the action; the police chief helped to secure 'evidence'; and the judge bound the prisoner over until his record could be found. Although he doubtless was in court, the county crown attorney, whose origins and functions are considered later on, said nothing. What Friedman and Percival have written about the California police courts applies equally here. 'They never lost completely the flavor of informality and folk justice.'[32]

By all accounts, the Hamilton police courtroom was filled on rainy and cold days. Spectators, defendants, and witnesses – all described in the press as the unwashed – produced odours that defied the description of journalists, who nevertheless tried to recreate the atmosphere

Table 2.1
Sex of Complainants before Police Magistrate's Court according to Selected Crimes and Groups of Crimes, 1859–1918

Crimes	Complainants	
	Males	Females
All Crimes against Persons (n=1312)	89.3 %	10.7 %
Common assault (n=88)	91.9	8.1
Wife beating (n=19)	0.0	100.1
Non-support (n=13)	7.3	92.3
Sex offenders (n=38)	50.0	50.0

Source: HPL, RG 10, Series K, Hamilton Police Court Proceedings. A sampling of every tenth case was created for 1859, 1878, 1898, 1908, and 1918.

for the entertainment of readers. Amidst those who sought justice from the tribunal for the poor, there were merchants who prosecuted shoplifters, middle-class women who decided it was not beneath their dignity to appear to prosecute a servant for theft, tavernkeepers there to answer a summons for selling drinks on Sunday, and gentlemen who had failed to clear the snow from their sidewalks. Despite occasional appearances by the city's more affluent, the court dealt largely with poorer folk.

Lawyers entered the lowly police magistrate's court to defend clients. They appeared in the Toronto court in the 1850s, but perhaps only in rare cases.[33] The limitation on the recourse to barristers by defendants was a practical one: could they afford the services of a lawyer? There was no legal aid and the extent of *pro bono* work is unknown. Certainly, the more affluent defendants used defence counsels. In Hamilton, tavernkeepers by the 1870s retained them to combat the whiskey detectives and paid informers who assisted with the enforcement of the province's liquor laws.[34] The frequency of recourse to lawyers by common folk cannot be determined precisely, but it appears to have been unremarkable before the 1880s and to have increased thereafter. A black servant, James Mallet, retained a lawyer in 1881 when he stood accused of stealing two silk handkerchiefs from the house where he worked.[35] A court reporter in 1893 made a point of writing that Ada Johnston, a burglar, could not afford her usual attorney.[36] According to George T. Denison, who became police magistrate in Toronto in 1877, his family-law practice had never done police court work, but during his first day in court a crowd of defendants and litigants besieged his brother's law office.[37] The episode implies that, in the larger cities of late-

Victorian Canada, plaintiffs and defendants employed counsel fairly regularly.

It is indicative of the established position of defence counsel by the First World War that Jelfs was probably forced to retire to juvenile court because of his snide comments about lawyers who defended 'criminals'. The veteran magistrate had remarked in 1924 that he disapproved of lawyers defending parties when the crown attorney had a clear case.[38] For their part, the crown attorney and the city's lawyers soon made sure that the lowest court was not a one-man show. In 1903 the Hamilton police court retained Budimir 'Bud' Pritich as its first translator. This appointment was testimony to the ethnic aspect of an industrial boom in the city,[39] and it also marked a break from the past – translators had never been employed by the petty sessions of the old regime. In short order, the translators acquired an influential position in the city's lowest court, for they not only translated but explained cultural differences to the court and to complainants and defendants. All the same, the modest innovations of the late nineteenth and early twentieth century took place, as Gene Homel aptly writes, 'within the shell of traditional methods.'[40] The police magistrates retained considerable power.

The power of the police magistrates extended outside their offices and courtrooms, for they also sat on the police commissions. Conflicts of interest inevitably resulted. As an official who dealt with criminal justice matters without benefit of juries, the magistrate was a judge holding great authority; as a supervisor of the police force, the magistrate had a close working relationship with the police. In many instances where the police served summonses or warrants issued by the magistrate in response to a complaint, this dual role may not have been a problem. Yet, once police functions included the serious investigation of criminal cases and the collection of statements, the magistrate's position as judge of criminal cases and supervisor of a body aiding the prosecution violated the tradition of fairness that was supposedly central to the common law. Time and again, the Hamilton magistrates publicly praised the force. 'I repeat again,' said Jelfs in 1913, 'that Hamilton's police force is the best in America, bar none.'[41] His successor made a comparable boast.[42] If these declarations had any spark of sincerity, one may conclude that magistrates were not predisposed to distrust police statements. At the very least, the association of magistrates with the police could have psychologically coloured their weighing of police evidence.

The most serious offences that Jelfs saw with any regularity were assaults that inflicted real injury and a few burglaries. A sample of the cases from 1859 to 1918 summarizes the business of the police magistrate's court. The abundance of moral order charges, particularly ones dealing with drunk and disorderly conduct, continued a trend that had begun in the 1840s when the town and the colony attacked immorality by statute (Figure 2.1). The annual reports of the police chief for the late nineteenth and early twentieth centuries suggest that roughly one out of ten cases that came before a police magistrate was a felony. The magistrate sent about one out of ten of these to a higher court. Rarely did a sentence given by a police magistrate extend beyond a year. Denison's boast that he had tried assorted felonies did not stretch the truth, but it played down the forlorn and petty character of the bulk of minor transgressions. By a federal act in 1869, the police magistrate could try larceny, embezzlement, assaults with or without a weapon, and assaults on females and women not amounting to rape.[43]

The disposition of cases tried in the police magistrate's court adds meaning to the term summary justice. Put simply, justice was unceremoniously fast. Magistrates discharged a minority of defendants. As in the decades of the old regime, the prevailing sentences prescribed the choice of a fine or a few days in the county jail (Table 2.2). Mostly, the plaintiffs and the defendants came from the working class and the poor. Several samples drawn from the late-Victorian police court journals – lists of those convicted that included personal information – establish the prevalence of unskilled labouring men. Over half of late-Victorian offenders came from this body.[44] It seems unlikely that they retained counsel. They certainly posed no grave threat to the property or persons of the affluent, let alone to the social order. However, they could, and often did, do harm to one another, as will be spelled out in chapter 6.

According to Michael Katz, the police court data for 1879–81 suggests that the magistrate's court treated crimes against property and morality more harshly than crimes against persons. 'In their protection of property and propriety the courts revealed the preoccupations of the respectable classes, the primacy of commodities within the acquisitive age and the investment in an ideal femininity that justified the elimination of women from the marketplace and their confinement within the family.'[45] This statement is misleading. There was more to the dynamics of cases in the lower court than class inequality and female dependency. Complaints were the foundation of the process and, since many complainants came from the same class as the accused, the depiction of criminal justice as a process biased by élite values is too simple. Furthermore, Katz's study is wrong in assuming that the bringing of essentially private disputes to the court 'had probably not been envisioned by the architects of the legal system.'[46] First of all, the system never had 'architects.' It was not planned by anyone; it developed over the centuries without benefit of design. Secondly, the system had evolved as a process wherein notions of private disputes and public law

Court appearances per 100,000 inhabitants

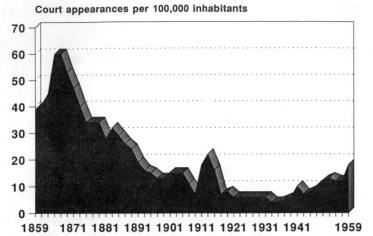

Figure 2.1
Vagrancy, Vice, and Moral Order Charges, Hamilton, 1859–1959
Sources: *Hamilton Spectator*, 21 January 1865, 11 January 1866, 11 January 1867, 17
January 1870, 4 January 1872, 6 January 1875, 6 January 1876, 22 January 1878,
9 January 1879, 26 January 1880, 11 January 1881, 30 January 1883, 7 February 1884,
28 February 1887, 30 January 1890, 16 February 1892, 26 January 1898, 27
January 1899, 31 January 1901, 5 February 1902, 22 January 1903, 3 February 1904,
23 February 1905, 30 January 1907, 20 January 1909, 3 February 1910, 27
February 1915, HPL Special Collections, Records of the City of Hamilton, RG 10,
Series A, Police Department, *Annual Reports*, 1906–70, missing 1906–8, 1910,
1911, 1914, 1916, 1918–19, 1930, 1933; RG 10, Series K, Police Court Proceedings,
Ledgers, 1859–1949.

were often conjoined. Individuals brought complaints about crimes
that could sometimes be seen as private disputes. The volume of borderline private disputes that came before the court was becoming an
issue in the late nineteenth century.

The police and the police court provided help to the working people
and the poor of Hamilton, and this help went beyond handling their
complaints about assaults and thefts. When employers refused to pay
wages, the employees could sue in the police court. From mid-1860s to
the late 1880s, fifty to one hundred cases for wages came before the police magistrate each year. They included labourers and domestic servants suing for non-payment, and wives suing husbands for support. If
Jelfs is typical, police magistrates dealt firmly with guilty husbands. Jelfs
despised husbands who 'hang around hotels, with their wives and little
children perhaps starving. They ought to get a whipping every day.'[47]
In 1921 Jelfs opposed the idea that the names of the accused in maintenance cases should be kept out of the newspapers. The court, he said,
should work to embarrass irresponsible husbands.[48] With his condem-
nation of defence attorneys, his many supportive references to whip-

Table 2.2
Disposition of Cases before Police Magistate's Court, Hamilton, 1859–1918[1]

Year	Discharged	Choice of Fine or Jail	Fined	Sent to Prison (Felonies)[2]	Referred to Higher Court[3]	Held Over on Remand[4]
			Percentages			
1858 (n=367)	38.8	42.2	17.7	4.1	3.4	1.7
1878 (n=289)	32	47.4	7.3	5.5	0.0	3.1
1898 (n=161)	46.6	8.1	23.0	7.5	2.5	11.8
1908 (n=253)	23.3	31.6	21.7	4.3	4.0	14.6
1918 (n=480)	19,0	46.5	12.9	2.1	4.8	7.7
All Years	28.1	34.9	17.7	4.1	3.4	8.0

(1) Every tenth case was selected.
(2) This percentage may approximate the percentage of felonies tried, though some were discharged and hidden in the discharged column.
(3) In 1858 the process involved the referral of a case to the Recorder's Court. After 1878, the police magistrate conducted a preliminary hearing before a felony was tried at the general sessions (County Court) or at the assizes.
(4) The increasing practice of remanding an accused may imply the intervention of the crown attorney; more and more crown attorneys postponed proceedings until they had finished preparing their cases. This practice in turn reflects the professionalization of the criminal justice process.
Source: HPL, RG 10, Series K, Hamilton Police Court Proceedings

pings, and his appreciation for the embarrassing glare of publicity, the Liberal Jelfs was no milktoast liberal. Neither was the police court just an instrument for emergent capitalism.

EFFICIENCY AND PROFESSIONALISM IN THE INTERMEDIATE COURTS

From the early 1840s to the late 1870s, Ontario governments extended their reforming zeal to the intermediate courts, as they had done with the lowest courts when they expanded the lists of crimes to be tried in petty sessions and when they provided for the appointment of police magistrates. The United Canadas and then the province of Ontario –

which had the responsibility for organizing courts under the terms of the British North America Act – passed a fair amount of legislation aimed at raising professional standards and improving the efficiency of the intermediate level of courts. Not all innovations lasted, a fact that complicates any narrative review of the subject. Two trends, however, were visible in all the experiments: trained barristers gained control of the courts, and juries were marginalized. Both developments resulted in the displacement of amateurs, supposedly in the interests of efficiency, sound legal judgments, and impartiality.

The first jabs against the old regime's courts struck at the justices of the peace meeting in quarter sessions. JPs had always been controversial figures in Upper Canada, and so it proved a simple matter initially to undermine their authority on the grounds that they lacked the training to handle criminal law. By an act of 1845, the justices meeting in quarter sessions to deal with criminal matters could no longer elect one of their own number as chairman of the session. Instead, the government appointed a judge to preside over the judicial business of the quarter sessions. Such appointees had to be barristers. Titled the district and later the county judge, this official's duties grew with subsequent reforms.[49] In 1873 the Ontario government went the final step and provided that the county judge could sit alone; the justices of the peace were no longer required at what had been the court of quarter sessions.[50]

Even before the demise of the quarter sessions in the 1870s, legislators had experimented with intermediate courts in the cities. Tucked into the comprehensive act that overhauled Upper Canadian local government in 1849, the government of the United Canadas created the new judicial post of city recorder for Toronto, Hamilton, Ottawa, Kingston, and London. The name recorder derived from the English concept of a court of record, or a court whose records were permanently maintained. Akin to the police magistrates, the city recorders were to be assisted by one or more aldermen,[51] and they had to have been members of the bar in the colony for five years. They could be police magistrates, and that is what they were in Hamilton, where a recorder's court functioned from 1849 to 1868.[52] The police magistrate referred his more serious or difficult cases to the recorder's court, which, like the quarter sessions, met quarterly and operated with grand and petty juries. In essence, the government had created something like a court of quarter sessions specifically for the cities.[53]

In 1868 a provincial law reform act abolished the recorder's court and for judicial purposes the cities were reunited with the counties. The 1868 act also abolished quarter sessions and replaced them with a semi-annual general session of the peace presided over by the county

judge. By these rationalizations of the court system, the province reduced the number of occasions when juries had to be assembled but
also substantially lengthened the waiting time for anyone facing trial.[54]
Meanwhile, the government of the new Dominion of Canada tried to
introduce the practice of trials without jury into the counties by a
'speedy trial' act of 1869.[55] Much of the rhetoric supporting the reform alleged that innocent parties stood to gain, for they could be tried
before wise and well-trained men and – if innocent – could secure early
release without having to post bond.[56] The federal measure invaded
provincial jurisdiction and soon had to be replaced by comparable provincial acts. Ontario authorized the practice with its own statute in
1873.[57] Beginning in 1874, accused parties sent by the police magistrate to be tried at an intermediate court could elect either to be heard
before a judge alone in a new court – the County Judge's Criminal
Court – or to wait for a trial by jury at the general session of the peace.
The County Judge's Criminal Court handled from its inception the
great majority of criminal cases destined for an intermediate level
court.

The creation of a new criminal court increased the efficiency of the
provincial court system, expediting cases and eliminating the costs of
assembling jurors. But did those who elected for trial before a judge
alone receive gentler treatment? Not if conviction rates are any indication. Those defendants who opted for a prompt trial without jury had
a conviction rate in the years immediately after the reform three times
that of those who elected for a jury trial.[58] A broken set of statistics collected by the province from 1909 to 1919 likewise depicts a higher conviction rate for those defendants who elected for trial without jury,
though the difference was not as dramatical as that suggested in the
earlier report.[59] It is hard to say what these trends mean. It could be
that they challenge assertions that innocent parties would overwhelmingly choose a trial before a judge alone; innocent people may well
have calculated that they would receive justice from a jury while the
guilty opted for a prompt resolution. The one sure fact is that the new
court processed far more cases than the other intermediate court, the
general sessions.

To summarize, by the time that McConnell stood trial in 1876, complainants in serious cases who lived in the city would bring information
to the police magistrate. If the matter was serious enough, he would
order the arrest of the individual rather than issue a mere summons.
The accused would appear in police court, probably the day after the
arrest. Occasionally, the police magistrate would remand the accused
until the crown attorney had assembled his case (Table 2.2). The magistrate would hear the basic evidence and determine whether or not to

send the case to the general sessions of the peace or even to the assize. If the former, then the accused could elect to be tried without jury at the County Judge's Criminal Court or to wait and have a trial with a jury when the general sessions held its semi-annual sitting. By lengthening the waiting period for a trial, the reduction of the number of sessions from four to two increased the desirability of selecting a trial by judge alone. Of course, if the case went to the assize, then there was no speedy trial, no trial without both grand and trial jury.

The last notable innovation in the conduct of trials applied to prosecutions. When Michael Vincent had been tried in 1828, the prosecution of felons at the assize – especially in capital cases – had engaged the law officers of the crown: the attorney general and the solicitor general. Yet, as observed in chapter 1, these law officers increasingly delegated to crown counsels their right to prosecute. Apart from the criticism that the appointment of crown counsels was rife with political patronage, the system for prosecution was flawed because neither the attorney general and solicitor general nor the designated crown counsels took part in prosecutions at quarter or petty sessions. The clerk of the peace helped to prepare the documents necessary for prosecutions at the former and complainants could secure private counsel to conduct a prosecution at the quarter and petty sessions. If complainants did not secure such counsel, it was alleged that they might not know what evidence was required to secure conviction.[60] Critics declared that this state of affairs allowed many culprits to escape punishment at the quarter sessions owing to poorly prepared cases.[61] The government of the United Canadas recognized that there were problems with the system of prosecution. In 1850 a committee of the legislative assembly investigating public expenditures heard from the reform leader and then attorney general Robert Baldwin. Baldwin maintained that, because of the accumulation of work at the capital, the law officers of the crown could not personally direct the business at the assizes. He thought that the criminal calendar 'would have to be done by some other gentleman of the Profession specially retained for the purpose.'[62] The government contemplated following the lead of states in the republic and establishing the office of local prosecutor, an office that did not exist in England.[63] Yet no action was taken until the legislature passed the County Attorneys Act in 1857. This measure established the office of county crown attorney.[64]

Under the County Attorneys Act, justices of the peace, police magistrates – who were pivotal to this process in the cities – and coroners were instructed to turn over to the new functionaries all depositions, recognizances, inquisitions, and papers connected with criminal cases.

The crown attorney, as the office became known, had to examine these documents and, where necessary, order further investigations to collect more evidence. By placing someone with legal experience in charge of the preparation of the prosecution, the government hoped to eliminate the possibility that malefactors would escape on technicalities. Beyond preparation, the crown attorney helped to prosecute at the quarter sessions (after 1873, its two successors, the general sessions and the County Judge's Criminal Court). The crown attorney also had the authority to appear at police court and offer advice to the police magistrate. Evidently, the chores of the police magistrate had become so complicated by legislation that it was believed they would need legal counsel from time to time and they should not have to pay for it out of their own pockets.[65] The responsibilities for prosecuting cases did not fully extend to the assize, where the provincial government still appointed crown counsels; however, the county crown attorney could prosecute at the assize in the absence of a crown counsel.[66]

By fashioning the office of crown attorney, the government of the United Canadas maintained a symbolic distinction between its courts and those of the United States. In the republic, the public prosecutor or district attorney presented the case for 'The People versus John Doe,' whereas in Canada the crown attorney or an appointed crown counsel argued the case for 'The Crown versus John Doe.'[67] A further distinction between Canadian crown attorneys and American district attorneys was that the latter were elected while the crown attorneys were appointed by the governor and later the lieutenant governor. (It would long be argued, though not very convincingly, that vice-regal appointment kept the crown attorneys out of the clutches of politicians.) The 1857 act also marked a departure from the legal system of England, which avoided establishing local prosecutorial offices. In the judgment of Paul Romney, 'the office of county attorney was a distinctive Upper Canadian creation, and like other distinctive Canadian institutions it was a blend of American and British ideas.'[68]

The government intended that the crown attorneys would fill a gap in the machinery of criminal trials at the intermediate courts. In this, it appears to have succeeded. By the end of the century, private prosecution both at the general sessions of the peace and at the County Judge's Criminal Court had become rare. In 1895 it was reported that 'no county judge will try a person accused unless the prosecution is conducted by a crown officer; neither will a judge of the assize.'[69]

Crown attorneys also attended the police magistrates' courts. Though procedures in these courts had become complicated by the last decades of the century, they remained extremely flexible and informal.

Private individuals could still prosecute a case, and, even when a private prosecutor brought a case before the police magistrate, the crown attorney might intervene and provide the prosecutor with a helpful precedent.[70] At the same time, the attendance of lawyers and the crown attorney at the lowest court during the second half of the century altered the nature of trials even for minor crimes. Confrontations between the accuser and the accused now were often replaced with actions pitting crown attorneys against barristers acting for the accused. In Hamilton's lowest court, the crown attorney appears to have been an active participant who spoke out – not only against defence counsel but also against the magistrate himself. Jelfs declared, in a case involving a juvenile, that the boy's parents ought to whip him. The crown attorney demurred and recommended a bit of parental love.[71]

The crown attorney did not intervene in all cases, leaving prosecution in most common assault and larceny occurrences to the complainant. In fact, the provincial government expected the crown attorney to watch just such cases as these for questionable private prosecutions. As the *Upper Canada Law Journal* put it, 'the grand defect [of allowing unbridled private prosecutions] lay in requiring or allowing public prosecutions to be conducted by private individuals – permitting them to shape a charge of a public nature as their private feelings urged.'[72] One 1888 case intimates how the crown attorney checked a prosecution. Catherine Deardon had hired John Townsend to clean her chimney. After he left her house, she noted that three dollars had vanished. 'That was the only evidence against Townsend, and as Crown-Attorney Crerar didn't think it was strong enough to convict, he was discharged.'[73] This crown attorney was the same barrister who had defended McConnell; his obvious talent recognized, he had been appointed crown attorney for Wentworth County in 1881.

The crown attorney's statutory authority to advise the magistrate made him a prosecutor in some cases and nearly a second member of the bench in others. Innovation and specialization to achieve greater professionalism had, in this instance, established an office that jeopardized the independence of the judiciary and meddled with the court's impartiality. How could someone who was basically a prosecutor remain impartial when making recommendations to the magistrate? A century later, an Ontario law reform commission looked into this enduring function of the crown attorney. The commission concluded that 'it is not consistent with our concept of the independence of the judiciary ... that they [crown attorneys] should advise the justices of the peace in specific cases.'[74] Another implication flowed from the crown attorney's ambiguous role. Along with the rise of police intervention in criminal justice matters, the advice of the crown attorney to the police magistrate and to complainants may have effected a major transition in how the public used the courts by reducing the frequency of applications for a summons or warrant. As we have seen, the crown attorney had to watch over private prosecutions in the court of quarter sessions 'where justice towards the accused seems to demand his interposition.'[75]

Public officials in the late nineteenth century had started to deflect access to the lowest courts, and the crown attorneys were a part of this broader process. Police magistrates also could deal with 'nuisance' prosecutions at their discretion by ordering a 'prosecutor or complainant' to pay the costs of a failed action. It is difficult to determine when the overburdened police magistrate seriously began to work to deflect complaints away from the court. But it did happen. In June 1893 Jelfs issued a caution in court that signalled a reversal of an earlier practice which had permitted all manner of 'private' disputes to come before the court.[76] During the late-Victorian era, formal and informal changes to the lowest court began to discourage public use of the criminal courts and, thereby, to shunt more of the frontline burden of dealing with complaints onto the police, a relatively new institution which was maturing precisely at the moment when legislators and magistrates introduced monumental changes to practices in the lowest courts.

THE TRIUMPH OF CIVIC POLICING

The evolution of Upper Canadian policing was closely tied to dramatic changes in the colony's social landscape. In the mid-nineteenth century, Upper Canada's élite feared that the arrival of thousands of impoverished wage labourers from the United Kingdom posed a serious threat to property. This fear was not groundless, for, as we have seen, Upper Canada experienced its share of collective violence in the mid-1840s and early 1850s. As far as the Hamilton area was concerned, the *Spectator* in 1856 editorialized that the region around the city had become 'the highway between the western part of the American Union and the seaboard'. Geography and the railways had ordained that Hamilton would experience problems because of 'the large floating population.'[77]

Against this background, one of the notable shifts in law and order at mid-century involved the mechanism used for dealing with crowds and the potential for collective protest and violence. In the past, the government had used troops to quell disturbances and had encouraged companies and municipalities to assume responsibility for the maintenance of order. Gradually, however, the idea of a Canadian gendarmerie began to attract support. In the aftermath of the rebellions of 1837–8, a mounted police patrolled areas of rural Lower Canada and the Niagara frontier.[78] Later, in the wake of religious riots in Montreal and Quebec City in 1853, an inquiry had recommended a provincial constabulary for the Canadas,[79] but nothing was done until 1856. In that year, the government introduced a bill to reorganize policing in the province. By then, the persistence of labour and religious violence had underlined the need for such a measure. The case for police reform was also strengthened by the decision of the English parliament to take up the same issue.

Supporters of the 1856 Canadian scheme argued that, like Ireland and England, Upper Canada needed better protection than that supplied by scattered municipal police forces, justices of the peace, and county constables. The government recommended scrapping nascent municipal forces; they would be replaced by a provincial force stationed in barracks at Quebec, Trois Rivières, Sherbrooke, Montreal, Ottawa, Kingston, Toronto, Hamilton, and London. In the event of an emergency, the government could order units of this mobile mounted force into any part of the colony.

Attorney General John A. Macdonald claimed during the parliamentary debate on the police bill that the protection of order 'should no longer be entrusted to men living among the citizens, sharing the prejudice and the excited feelings of the populace against whom they might be called to act. It was only by separating these men from the populace that their efficiency could be secured.'[80] Essentially, Macdonald was calling for the creation of a national police force that represented national interests and could suppress public protests without qualms. His comment suggests how far some politicians had moved from accepting the practices of the old regime; a system that placed the onus for law and order on local worthies was to be replaced by one that stressed the benefits of a mobile force in the name of efficiency. The liberal opposition pounced on the bill, particularly its blatant assault on local government.[81] Of the nine cities designated to receive barracks, six petitioned against the bill. Typically, the cities approached the question of policing from the perspective of costs and benefits. They would be expected to pay two-thirds of the expenses and would lose the benefit of a force that undertook a set of municipal functions. In the end, possibly as part of a bid to sustain a coalition of moderates, the government dropped the measure.

The parliamentary, municipal, and newspaper debates about the advantages and risks of a provincial police force represented one of the

more significant discussions in central Canada on the issue of policing.[82] Municipal policing had nearly bent and broken before the arguments of the rationalizers and centralizers, the admirers of the Irish
constabulary and the European gendarmeries. Instead, however, something different resulted. Owing to the failure to create a provincial gendarmerie in 1856, policing retained local touches that proved important in themselves and that provided Canadian police forces with several facets of what would become a complex public image. Because
the old system survived, policemen continued to be appointed by local
officials and to retain a civic identity; they were compelled to carry out
civic duties and allowed to live in neighbourhoods and not in barracks.
From a liberal perspective, the consequences must not be taken lightly;
the police in Ontario municipalities were not conceived of as an external force imposed to discipline unruly local folk. However, this does
not mean that in the area of policing, Upper Canada/Canada West followed a remarkably distinctive course of development. While Upper
Canadian policing did differ from its counterpart in England – the
Home Office exercised a centralizing influence over county and borough forces[83] – it essentially represented a variation on a theme. In
terms of long-term trends such as professionalization and the cooperation and integration of police forces to achieve uniformity in police
conduct, the civic police of Canada West/Ontario developed along the
same lines as police elsewhere.[84]

The controversy over policing in 1856 also had more tangible results. It is likely that the establishment of the North-West Mounted
Police by John A. Macdonald in 1872 owed something to the earlier episode. More immediately, an important innovation issued from the debates. Colonial politicians were now interested in doing something to
reform local constabularies. In the process of revising the Municipal
Act in 1858, therefore, the government placed municipal police under
the direction of boards of local commissioners. These consisted of the
mayor, the police magistrate, and the recorder. Upon the abolition of
the last office, the county court judge became a member of the civic police commission.[85] New York state had attempted to implement comparable schemes for the city of New York in 1853 and for metropolitan
New York in 1857,[86] and the state of Missouri passed a law in 1861
to put the St Louis police in the hands of a commission during the political crisis of the civil war.[87] Yet these experiments did not last;
Ontario's police commissions did. In Canada West, police hiring and
management were forever removed from city councils and ostensibly
from the intensely partisan civic politics that affected policing in
American cities.[88] The commissions provided Ontario policing with an
element of distinctiveness.

PROFESSIONALISM AND MILITARISM

Like leaders of other groups in the late nineteenth century, police officials pursued a professional standing.[89] The process was complicated, diffuse, incomplete, and more diverse than the label 'professionalism' would seem to imply.[90] In Hamilton, at no single point did senior police officials determine to make policing a profession, but there were a number of steps from the meeting of the first police commission to the organization of detective and traffic branches that indicate incipient professionalism.

Professionalism as an occupational goal meant the detachment of the police from civic politics and the establishment of a force of individuals who could serve as experts in relations with assorted groups within the city. This goal possessed inherent risks because – as the opponents to the 1856 police bill recognized – there is a fine line between a body of detached experts and an agency of the state's coercive power. Moreover, for a variety of reasons, the ideal of detachment was not only risky for civil society but also psychologically difficult for constables. The origins of the constables, turnovers in their ranks, and the nature of their work at times checked the drive for detached professionalism.

The campaign for professionalism in United States police forces has been described as 'an attempt to bring functional order and dignity into a disorganized, low-status occupation.'[91] The reference to disorganization and low status oversimplifies. The work was extremely difficult, sometimes hazardous, occasionally unpopular; there are grounds, then, for thinking of policing as low-status employment. But policing also held many attractions, such as steady employment and eventually retirement benefits. Those who shaped policing wanted it to approximate a profession, but the work itself – with its numerous challenges – made that objective elusive.

It is impossible to construct a detailed social profile of the Hamilton force in the late-Victorian era – the records simply do not exist. Yet, by drawing on newspaper reports, one can sketch the broad outlines of a picture. Press stories about troubles on the force and the deeds of particular constables contain incidental items about the men. No less valuable from our point of view are newspaper accounts about how the police commission selected recruits. During the 1870s and 1880s, the commission minute books faithfully reported the hiring of constables while revealing nothing about the process: the constables were taken onto the force 'after due examination.'[92] Newspaper reports, however, fill in the gaps. The press made sport of the selection process on at least four occasions: January 1878, March 1881, October 1881, and March 1887.

In 1878 ninety applicants assembled at the police station and marched by twos to the city hall where the commissioners interviewed them. Height and age were important.[93] During the October 1881 interview, the three commissioners considered twelve men. Candidates formed a line in the council chamber at city hall and pinned the numbers of their applications to their coats. The commissioners checked their height, which had to be at least five feet nine inches. All were asked if they had military experience.[94] The previous March, the commissioners had inspected and interviewed eleven applicants. Formerly, such applicants had to be younger than forty-eight years of age, but a new policy required that they should be younger than thirty. Also, applicants no longer had to be residents of Hamilton.[95] This change appears to have been a deliberate move to enlarge the pool of available men at a time when it seemed to critics that the chief was converting policing from a fairly congenial stroll among neighbours into a demanding job with regimentation. In any event, it was alleged that out-of-town men would not play favourites and that by widening the search more men who were familiar with policing would apply.[96]

For the March 1881 interview, applicants lined up and Judge Sinclair asked them to take off their coats. This being done, Sinclair felt 'their thighs and sinews,' poking them with a finger 'in the manner practiced by the gentry from the rural districts when examining a prize bull.' Next the men had to walk about, turning left and right while the commissioners commented on the good and bad points about their backs and shoulders. To measure stamina, five were singled out and asked to jog around the council chambers. At the conclusion, Thomas Johnson of Sarnia – tipping the scales at 175 pounds – and Alexander Campbell of Brantford – weight 185 pounds – were declared fit candidates.[97] Literacy was not mentioned, but an account of interviews in 1883 specified that the men had to read, write legibly, and have certificates of good character from previous employers. The commissioners preferred married men, claiming that they were 'steadier.'[98] Married men were also less likely than single men to leave town in search of better work, for policing had become a more difficult occupation than in the past.

Although the Hamilton force went through a reorganization in the early 1880s, the process for selecting the men remained the same. Value was still placed on size and physical fitness. In March 1887, fourteen men – 'as fine looking, stalwart fellows as you would want to see'[99] – applied for a single position. The applicants followed the commissioners into the council chamber, formed a semi-circle, and took off their coats. The judge 'examined their points', after which they marched around the room so that the commissioners might judge their paces. Cheeky reporters wagered on the outcome. Nine of the men were mechanics and they gave a desire for 'a steadier job' as the reason for applying. The appointee stood six feet and weighed 200 pounds.[100]

Along with the rigors of the probationary period, when green constables pounded the beat at night, the selection process was – to appropriate the apt words of a Toronto commissioner – 'a survival of the fittest.'[101] To direct fit young recruits, the commission hired experienced constables and sergeants who often had served with another force or a military unit.[102] Not until 1913 did the commissioners speak of securing 'bright young men', but by the 1920s they employed a psychologist to test the candidates' intelligence quotas.[103]

From their beginnings and across all cultures, police constables have found themselves in unpredictable situations.[104] Until fairly recent times, however, police forces did not train constables in the methods for handling different kinds of problems. All forces adopted one basic approach – 'taking charge.'[105] This strategy depended on authority, the ability of the police to restore calm through their physical bearing. Failing this, there was sheer brute force. In the city and era under review, drawing the handgun had not become a stratagem in 'taking charge'. Rowdies set upon Constables Smith and Robinson and beat them terribly while they were on night patrol in August 1874. Smith fought back with the butt of his revolver, 'but forbore to shoot.'[106] The main criteria for selection to the force – bulky manliness – must be evaluated in the context of what commonly brought dangerous situations under control. A constable's size, not his handgun, did that.

It is impossible to estimate the frequency with which the police found their safety jeopardized. Yet, anecdotal evidence substantiates the claims of the constables that their work entailed extraordinary risks. Heads were bashed, teeth knocked out, ribs kicked, faces slashed, and beards and hair pulled. The rowdies who assaulted Constables Smith and Robinson in August 1874 robbed them of their batons, caps, coats, and whistles.[107] Several years later, during an attack on three constables, Constable Spence suffered a clubbing about the head and chest, was kicked, and had his whiskers pulled.[108] On both occasions, the police magistrate treated the attacks as serious enough to send the perpetrators to the Central Prison in Toronto. Just a few months after Constable Spence's assailants were jailed, someone took a shot at the constable during a night patrol.[109] This was especially reprehensible for it came as 'a cowardly act.'[110]

Constables understood the routine hazards of the job. The danger of physical assault came as part of the accepted burden of the policeman's lot, for hefty constables normally could confront these risks in a manly fashion, trusting in their strength and nightsticks. Firearms in the hands of criminals threatened the lives of policemen and also undermined the face-to-face encounters upon which the tactic of 'taking charge' depended. A veneration of brute force explains the mystique attached to the hickory baton brandished by the oldest man on the force in 1888, Peter Ferris, who wore badge number I. Polished with goose grease, the baton bore 'evidence of having been repeatedly brought in contact with some pretty hard craniums – at a time, too, when No.I's arm was more lusty that it is at present.'[111]

There was nothing simple and easy about street confrontations; 'taking charge' demanded restraint as well as strength. In September 1905 a pair of constables tried to make an arrest at a tavern and thirty 'lads' chased them down the street shouting, 'Lynch the bull. Take the boys away. Don't let them get your names.'[112] Needless to say, no arrest was made. On other occasions, taking charge led to complicated encounters that placed the police in real jeopardy in spite of their brawn and cherished nightsticks. In September 1887 two constables tried to arrest Bob Brown for drunk and disorderly conduct. Brown broke free and one constable pursued him; the other constable – the ancient Ferris – puffed along behind. Constable Hallisey caught Brown, who proceeded to beat the officer savagely. A crowd gathered, and, though it remained neutral, it egged on Brown. Ferris arrived and soon other constables came to the scene[113]; Hallisey recuperated in bed for more than a week.[114] The most interesting aspect of this episode concerned Hallisey's decision not to wield the nightstick; instead he clung to Brown until help arrived. 'He was afraid the roughs who were around encouraging Brown would pile on him also' if he used his 'club.'[115] Strength, size, and speed were assets when the police were arresting men who had friends in the crowd; constables believed that crowds would stay neutral as long as they refrained from swinging their clubs.

In the early 1880s, constables experienced a different kind of attack, one that rattled the self-respect of many experienced men. That attack took the form of efforts on the part of police administrators to enforce discipline and rationalize police work. In effect, the drive toward professionalism immediately disturbed the status of policing and, in the eyes of some constables, diminished their work. In the muscular realm of policing where the authority of the constable was his main instrument, independence in the workplace – freedom to use discretion on the beat – was felt to be intrinsic to masculine identity and thus to authority. If, according to the assumptions of the age, marriage and a domestic life or a very few occupations such as teaching defined femininity, then policing provided a masculine ideal. Consequently, efforts to alter the conduct of police work collided with fiercely held values about work and identity. The crisis came in the early 1880s.

During the 1870s, the city's economy recovered somewhat from a catastrophic depression that had lingered into the mid-1860s, but it did so unevenly. Civic leaders remembered the dreadful economic collapse of the last decade and nothing in the 1870s restored their confidence. Concurrently, the city grew and so did the demands on the police force. The public demanded better service and the chief begged for more men. City council – which had lost control of many aspects of policing with the establishment of the police commission – retained authority over funding; city politicians held fast to austerity. In these circumstances, a reorganization of police work was a natural remedy. The extraction of more service from a fixed labour pool is a practice common to all employers, particularly in periods of retrenchment or when labour is scarce.

Another cause of police reorganization was a growing climate of legalism. Not for decades would this effloresce into notions such as conflict of interest or civil rights; for the moment it was legalism from the top down. Railway employees beginning in the 1850s were bound by strict codes of conduct; local government became more bureaucratically structured; reformers on both sides of the Atlantic proposed civil service examinations; the German model of administration interested a number of American observers. Throughout the English-speaking world, the concept of codification challenged the old regime's vision of justice dispensed by wise and influential men aware of local conditions and conscious of precedent.

Hamilton's police commissioners started to restructure the force in the fall of 1879. Judge Sinclair, the county judge and by statute a member of the police commission, made a trip to neighbouring Buffalo, reputed to have 'the model department on the American side of the line.' There 'much valuable information was obtained,' and the commissioners subsequently resolved to remodel the force and thereby make it 'more effective.'[116] One prior reform had divided the city into three patrol areas and put patrols under the direction of patrol sergeants. The words chosen to describe the measure in the annual report for 1878 could not have been more meaningful: 'a very beneficial management.' Professionalism certainly had entered the picture, though it came as an attempt to effect savings rather than to enhance the status of the work involved. Violations of department rules and regulations were now strictly enforced and fines levied against lax constables. These were preludes to a sweeping revision of policing.[117]

The only models of professionalism available to police reformers in the 1880s were those provided by other police departments and the military. Throughout North America in the late nineteenth century, police forces adopted new uniforms – that of the English 'Bobby' was especially popular – and undertook drills that resembled military exercises. Hamilton was typical. In the early 1880s, the Hamilton force was led by Chief Alexander D. Stewart. A powerfully built former bank clerk, Stewart was a fuss-and-feathers militia enthusiast. Within a few months after taking charge, he outfitted constables in new uniforms with white helmets 'similar to those worn by the colonial forces.'[118] In addition, while civic policing was still the entrenched model in Ontario, the trappings of a European gendarmerie or a colonial mounted police came in through the backdoor in the name of efficiency. Once a week, under chief Stewart's regime, the force was drilled. The average day's work of the sergeants and the constables was eight hours, not as long a day as that of the average mechanic but the constables trudged around outdoors the whole time and Stewart put the men on rigorously managed work schedules. Until Stewart took charge, constables set out on their beats from their houses. Extending back a few decades to the night-watch, this practice allowed the men some independence but also led to charges of neglect of duty: Constable Davison, for example, excused his oversleeping on the night of 20 June 1875 by blaming his wife for failing to call him.[119] A three-shift system introduced by Stewart made it possible for two-thirds of the entire force to be on duty during the night. The city was portioned off into numbered beats, each with a defined route.

Beginning in December 1880, constables going on duty assembled for parade and it was then that reports, special instructions, warrants, and so on were read, so that the men began their patrols with a knowledge of what they should look for and do. While the adoption of an army parade and inspection could not be complete because of the lack of officially condoned firearms, military form was closely followed none the less. At parade the constables had to present their full equipment of memorandum book, handcuffs, whistles, batons, and badges. Not only did this review and briefing hint at the conduct of a gendarmerie, but it marked the beginning of a formal shift in the relations between the police, the public, and the police court. Citizen complaints had been the basis of most police court actions in criminal matters; the police now began to inquire and investigate.

Constables marched out from the station house in single file under the direction of a sergeant and proceeded to the head of their respective beats where they relieved men on duty. The retiring constables paraded back to the station and were discharged. While constables patrolled the beat, sergeants came around at irregular intervals to check on them. Besides this routine of the beat, every constable was liable to be assigned extra work, as emergencies dictated. They were on call twenty-four hours a day and forbidden to 'moonlight.' If absent because of illness, they forfeited one-third of their pay for the period. Every man received tens days of holiday annually in the 1880s.[120]

Stewart's martial system furnished the force with many essential routines. It also provoked rancorous controversy within a year of implementation. At first, the press reported enthusiastically about the new direction in the force which – in the hyperbole that often accompanied reports on the successes of policing – allegedly made it 'as capable and as efficient as anyone could wish.' Soon enough, however, the city saw another side of police reform. To critics – including many of the constables – the chief used the force to ennoble himself, holding parades in front of crowds of 'ladies and gentlemen,' the police commissioners, and the officers of the local militia unit.[121] Contests for the best-dressed constable and the chief's speeches – 'which for pomposity of phrase might have suited Napolean [sic] for an address to the grand army of the Rhine' – were lampooned as ceremonial flummery.[122] Other criticisms went to the heart of the nature of police work and revealed how the constables viewed themselves.

The introduction of spit and polish, of regulations and drill, stirred resentment. Stewart had attempted nothing less than to overhaul the conduct of police work in a way that anticipated the introduction of time-and-motion studies to factories and offices several decades later. He also attached some superficial characteristics of gendarmerie policing to civic policing. Constables had been used to some flexibility and to exercising individual judgement; in the words of a newspaper editorial, 'a police force resembles a factory, not a barrack.'[123] Under Stewart, all this changed. The constables scoffed at the drill system and believed that the military model turned sergeants into martinets. They also felt that the new regulations blocked discretion. If a constable saw a sack of flour on the street or boxes piled on the sidewalk in front of a shop, the regulations demanded that he order its removal. In their capacity as guardians of the city's thoroughfares, constables always had to work to assure the circulation of traffic, but formerly they had been allowed to use common sense. From their perspective, they had acted as responsible individuals. Now, under the new regime, they felt ashamed of some of the petty regulations that they had to enforce. They protested against a loss of dignity.

They also resented the added work associated with the Stewart system and voiced plausible arguments against it. A bitter constable gave this account of why the chief's system would not reduce crime. 'I have to meet the visiting sergeant at a certain point and time. Suppose I see some suspicious characters on my beat and get the idea they are up to some dark job, I daren't linger ... because if I'm late for the sergeant ... all I can assign as an excuse is the fact that I was shadowing some suspects.'[124] Similarly, the use of sergeants to check up on the men irritated constables. It also prompted questions about the waste of scarce manpower.

The initial shock of a revolution in the conduct of policing precipitated the resignation of several proud, experienced constables. John Campbell, a six-year veteran, resigned in October 1881 and went public with his reasons. Campbell avowed that Stewart demanded unswerving loyalty to himself. Men who wanted promotion had to toady and cringe to the chief in everything. The man who replaced Campbell – not a resident of Hamilton – lasted one night. He discovered he was 'not cut out for a policeman.'[125] The model force had its problems.

Undoubtedly, the Stewart reforms represented a critically important shift in policing. There would be no going back. Previously the multifarious duties of the police had expanded as provincial statutes and municipal by-laws mounted, but Stewart launched a sweeping offensive on how that work would be arranged and how diligently it would be executed. The explanation for this disruptive and controversial set of innovations is complicated. The local force was participating in an international movement to 'modernize' policing, with Stewart playing a central role in gathering and spreading information among Canadian chiefs. A few weeks after becoming head of the Hamilton force, he sent forms to other chiefs in the country and expressed the hope that these would allow him to compare various police systems.[126] At a chiefs of police conference in 1881, Stewart presented a paper on 'the internal economy of our police forces'.[127] The conference formed the Chief Constables' Association of Canada.[128]

In Hamilton, the new order not only affected the constables on the beat; it also translated into pressure to professionalize the character of detective work. Detectives did not fit comfortably into the hierarchical structure of the force. Since the 1860s, the role of the detectives in dealing with theft had been to contact thieves or fences and to recover property. In Boston in the same era, Roger Lane has written that for this job 'the quality needed was familiarity with criminals.'[129] The same was true in New York where, according to Wilbur Miller, the detectives formed an 'empire within the force.'[130] Cash bonuses encouraged the practice of seeking out criminals, for victims and insurance companies supplemented the detectives' wages with rewards for recovered property. Detective work could be profitable. As late as 1875, the Hamilton police commission hired a special detective to snoop about for violations of the liquor licence act. He was to receive a reward of five dollars per conviction and to have the occasional advance.[131]

Scandals about the handling of stolen property had rocked the force in 1860 and twenty years later suspicions about the detectives making private deals rather than enforcing the law surfaced occasionally. Putting the matter bluntly, a *Hamilton Spectator* reporter questioned the honesty of detectives in 1881. 'Is it friendship or a mere mercenary motive that permits the offender always to escape?'[132] There were questions too about the efficiency of a system that encouraged detectives to be tight-lipped about crimes in order to horde reward money. In the early 1880s, the city's two detectives could not work together because of distrust and apparently neither the chief nor the constables knew about the cases being investigated by the detectives. Additionally, the detectives were suspected of extorting protection money from houses of ill repute.[133]

Stewart tackled the independence of the detectives and promulgated new orders for their management. He put them on a shift system which included night duty. They had to report at 8:30 in the morning and write up reports and be ready for assignment.[134] Not long after this, the commission dismissed a detective for withholding information.[135] In a later move, Stewart created a separate detective branch, because he noted that the detectives felt themselves superior to the sergeants and would not follow instructions. By 1905 the detectives worked out of police headquarters in city hall, where the chief and police magistrate maintained their offices.[136] They constituted a special branch, set apart from the main station, and under close supervision.

The effort to curb the free-wheeling activities of the detectives was an important development in the evolution of policing. It made this branch of the police more clearly responsible for upholding the law as opposed to looking after the property of individual or corporate interests. The latter approach to detective duties may well have fostered more crime, since the settlement of cases by police mediation between owners and thieves opened up the possibilities both for corruption and for thefts designed to generate rewards. In the development of the idea that the police had to enforce all laws and leave discretionary action to the courts, the 1880s were crucial years. The establishment of this idea of a uniform enforcement of the law helped to fix the public's belief in the basic honesty of the force, something that did not take root in all societies which were also forming police forces. Nevertheless, the Hamilton force could never entirely shake allegations of corruption. Nor could it purge every rotten apple before some damage had been done.

Repercussions from the creation of a detective branch eventually rippled outward to touch court rulings about evidence. Once the police, through the new branch, began to investigate serious crimes in earnest, the courts started to formulate rules governing the conduct of interrogations of witnesses and the accused. To protect citizens and to assure that police evidence was sound, assize judges and appeal court decisions put detectives on notice that their techniques were under close and critical scrutiny. In the higher courts of Ontario, street wisdom from the station house sometimes clashed with common law scruples about the coercive implications of the state vigorously pursuing a prosecution. Police detectives unquestionably introduced a complication for, and even a challenge to, the common law tradition.

TRAINING, DEMERITS, AND RESIGNATIONS

Professionalism extended only so far. It applied to the command structure of the organization, to the regimented beat, to an insistence that men enforce the letter of the law, and to weaning detectives from the indecent pursuit of reward money. As yet, however, there were no bold claims about crime fighting and the science of detection. The checkered nature of police professionalism actually surfaced in some of Stewart's pronounced eccentricities. His penchant for things military and his determination to go by the book stirred up ressentment on the force, but these and other features of his regime undoubtedly appealed to some men. The smart uniforms, the parades before the city fathers, and the rising physical standards smoothed over a transition that ruffled many constables and several detectives. Masculinity, jeopardized on one front by the diminished independence of policemen ('We are not children and toadies but men'), was bolstered by another. Policing remained a job for 'real men.' Perhaps by chance, Stewart stumbled upon a way to affirm masculinity. He cloaked professionalism in the natty garb of male pride. More particularly, this most influential chief in the early history of the Hamilton force applied his theatrical flair to associating policing with the manly adventures of empire building. Seen from this perspective, the choice of uniforms was ingenious. Whether or not Stewart recognized what he was doing, acted intuitively, or was just a ham is not as important as the fact that somehow he made the person of the chief – and thereby the force – appear rugged and heroic just at the moment when well-publicized exploits of empire-building caught the public imagination.

Stewart even paraded in the national limelight. At the conclusion of the rebellion of 1885, the Canadian government wanted a single citizen to lay the formal complaint against Louis Riel. Hamilton's chief was selected. In Regina on 6 July 1886, in the time-honoured fashion, he laid an information before the stipendiary magistrate.[137] In itself, this represented a public-relations coup for Stewart. But he pushed it farther. After a sojourn of four months, during which he allegedly collected evidence for the prosecution of other rebels, he returned to

Hamilton's streets sporting a Buffalo Bill hat and hunting attire.[138] He soon clashed with the mayor and resigned.[139] Afterwards, Stewart briefly worked in the United States as a Pinkerton detective, returned to Hamilton, failed in business, and served three terms as mayor. Like many adventurers, he undertook the odyssey to the Klondike in 1899. He died of scurvy on the trail from Edmonton.

In choosing a successor, the Hamilton police commission tried to find someone who could likewise function as a reformer and appear as a dashing figurehead. It settled on Hugh McKinnon, the former chief of the Belleville force. McKinnon had some of the right stuff, for he claimed to have been the general and heavyweight hammer- and stone-putting champion of America for four years. He posed with twenty-one gold and silver hurling medals arranged across a great chest. Some ladies swooned, as we shall see. With its hiring of McKinnon, the commission declared that the Hamilton force remained a bastion of muscular maleness. Lacking the initiative of his predecessor, the new chief was a humdrum administrator whose reports are interesting for what they disclose about conventional police thinking in late-Victorian Canada. Policemen of the era believed in the value of apprenticeship as fervently as any skilled craftsmen. Wisdom came with experience and the main device for keeping the streets tranquil and safe was keen observation.

In his report for 1886, McKinnon listed the ideal qualities for a detective. The first talent was described as follows: 'a useful detective must be a good physiognomist.'[140] Flexing his vocabulary to its limit, the chief meant that a detective had to practise the 'art' of determining character from the features of the face and body. At this time, physiognamy was assuming the status of a science. Access to the wisdom of this science was believed to come with years of constant practice; there was no formal training. Faith in experience also argued in favour of a detective branch comprised soley of permanent appointees and not constables transferred on a temporary basis. The chief opposed the assumption that a 'policeman in plain clothes is a detective.'[141] 'Old detectives,' asserted the former hurler, 'add continually to their connection and establish additional confidences of the highest consequences to them in following a criminal trail.'[142]

To see the modern detective branch as the heir of that which developed over a century ago misses significantly different practices and a distant context. Matters of internal discipline and a trust in accumulated experience all led to administrative innovations that established a detective branch as a distinct entity under close scrutiny. Later, the expectations of the public would be raised by the next stage in professionalization, namely the notion that a high percentage of crimes could be solved by the application of science and social science. But this idea was foreign to the late-nineteenth century. What was then deemed a well-planned police action strikes us today as very ordinary. One example can illustrate the point. William Tucker had abused his wife; she moved out to live with her father. Tucker shot at her through a window, wounding her in the arm. Off hurried the father to make a complaint at the police station. The magistrate authorized Tucker's arrest. Constables searched the assailant's boarding-house and favourite taverns; a detective was placed at the railway station. He nabbed Tucker as the fugitive attempted to board a train. Except for the gun, the episode had much in common with countless other cases. Wife beating was involved; a citizen made a complaint; the police magistrate issued a warrant; the police made some inquiries and 'staked out' a station. Yet, in its time, the apprehension of Tucker was considered a 'clever performance.'[143]

McKinnon introduced a few innovations. He insisted on constables receiving instruction in the proper treatment of injuries and 'in the means of telling a case of drunk [sic] from a case of sickness.'[144] In general, however, the talents of a boxer were more valuable than those of a doctor in the rough world of street work. The system that Stewart had shaped and McKinnon now administered continued to stress masculinity. Constables received no training worthy of the word. The commission hired men who could survive on the streets and alleys; it expected the men to learn from these classrooms of life. In the early 1880s, the new constable went through a month-long probationary period. At first, he worked alongside the station duty-man, in order to assimilate the varied features of police work. Next, he went on the street with an older constable for several weeks. Whenever possible, he would accompany constables executing warrants to become conversant with this extremely important part of police duties. At the end of the trial period, the chief tested him on rules and regulations.[145] If he passed, he became a second-class constable, eligible for advancement by good conduct.

The department published a training manual in 1889. Despite its promising title, it provided very little detailed information on the work of policing. Instead it spelled out the rules of proper conduct and reinforced a faith in the wisdom of the street. These two principle features of the manual contradicted each other. For example, the rules prohibited constables from stopping to talk to people on the beat, but they still were expected to get to know all the 'regulars'. The street really defined the constable's work. He was expressly instructed to 'learn thoroughly each street, building, alley, etc.' Although having to walk at a pace of two and a half miles per hour, he had to inspect the beat rigorously; report street lights that were out; inspect all low windows for signs of illegal entry, and check doors in commercial areas to make certain that they were locked at night. Many directives steered the constable to places that constituted the dark corners of the city and of Victorian anxieties: gaming houses, second-hand shops, pawn shops, houses of ill fame, and cab stands.[146]

The instructions for detectives mirrored those for constables and made it clear that detectives now operated on a short leash, having to report daily to the chief.[147] As for the chief, his responsibilities classified him as a budding bureaucrat, although the colourful Stewart successfully defied such a bland description, a fact that might explain why he soon had to resign. McKinnon, too, fell short of a bureaucratic ideal. Much of the chief's work pertained to record keeping. He had to record all personnel changes; inspect stations and their books; prepare, when necessary, written charges against constables; inspect applications to the force; keep records on the property of suspects and on the property returned to victims. The chief also had to supervise the general functioning of the force, with one important exception: he could not issue guns to the men unless the commission so ordered.[148]

It is not surprising that professional conduct and institutional order were introduced into the city's principal agency of order. Neither is it remarkable that the culture of the station house and the beat appeared rough and crude to bourgeois contemporaries, or that racial slurs were occasionally uttered in the police magistrate's court. The Hamilton police force in the late nineteenth century was no company of large choir boys. If any constable had been an innocent when he joined, the work soon changed his character. In any case, many constables – besides being young – came from a cultural background that accepted some of the very pleasures that they now had to suppress. Moreover, their instructions, which called for the surveillance of gaming houses, taverns, and persons and places of ill fame, put the temptations of gambling, drink, and prostitution regularly before them. The contradictions of the cultural position of the constables surface in newspapers stories, demerit books, and police commission hearings. On the basis of hearings before the commission from 1872 to 1896, it is possible to describe the frequency and character of the infractions committed by policemen.

Roughly 120 men served with the force during these years. Some were either lucky or truly morally upright: 22 per cent of the men retired with no reported reprimand. Another 15 per cent left soon after joining, many departing with the notation 'unfit'. The remainder all had marks against their names: 28 per cent with one, 17 per cent with two, 8 per cent with 3, and 10 per cent with more than 3. Another way of expressing the data is that 80 per cent of the men who served for several years – that is, those who had not been promptly dismissed as unfit – had earned one or more demerit. What mitigates the impression of a force rife with problems is the distribution of the demerits over time. Not only do the five to ten reprimands a year suggest that the men did not often slip into moral turpitude, but it underlines the strictness with which regulations were enforced in the early 1880s. Most transgressions were minor.

Several service records make surprising revelations about the ineptitude and foibles of a few members of the force. Drinking and sleeping on duty were the most frequent offences and were often combined in the career of a constable. Constable Beatty joined in November 1880 and within five months had been absent from the beat, found asleep, and twice caught drunk on duty. The commission promptly sacked him. Constable Sutherland, hired in 1878, demonstrated soon and often that he lacked proper moral fibre for police work. Within months of joining, the commission fined him for a visit to a house of ill fame; two years later, he appeared drunk on duty on the queen's birthday. A year after that incident, he tendered his resignation after a charge of insubordinate and insolent conduct. The commissioners declined the resignation. They dismissed him instead.

In contrast to these dismissals, the force tolerated the drinking problem of Constable Cable for seven years. The chief fined him twice in 1892 for being drunk on duty and in 1893 for being under the influence when off duty – the infraction of indiscretion. Caught drunk on duty again in 1898, he promised to take the pledge, but the next year he had to resign after being found unfit for duty 'due to liquor'. Another constable, hired in 1875, had to leave the force in 1879 after two episodes of dereliction of duty. On the first occasion, he allowed a prisoner to escape and, on the second, he stood accused of cowardice.

Some positively odd careers – moral reversals with rewards – dot the police annals. Constable Coulter began inauspiciously. Hired in March 1878, he was fined ten days pay that November for being found in a house of ill fame. After being released from beat duty at midnight, constables Coulter, Sutherland, and Moore paid a visit to Jennie Kennedy's whorehouse and dallied for an hour. A little over a year later, Coulter fell asleep on duty. In 1882 he paid a fine for disobedience. But he must have had ability and straightened up, for the commission awarded him a good conduct badge in 1891, appointed him detective in 1895, and in 1911 made him inspector of the detective division. Like Coulter, Constable Fenton got off to a very bad start in 1872: he was dismissed as unfit. But a sudden retirement created a second chance in the same year and he endured the beat for thirty years. He also survived a reprimand for being drunk on duty and after twenty-one years earned a good conduct badge.

The commission dismissed some men because of to their attitude, not the bottle. Constable Harris signed on in 1878 and endured police work until 1909. Except for a fine levied after entering a house of ill fame in 1880, all other demerits pertained to his independent attitude. In 1883 he refused to doff his cap in the presence of a superior; in 1887 the commission fined him for insubordination; in 1905 he left the city without permission; in 1909 he was reported as disobedient, insolent, and neglecting his duty. He never received a good conduct badge! Constable Littlehales, a proper joker and free spirit, seemed totally misplaced during his six years on the beat from March 1875 to April 1881. He let a prisoner go without proper authority in 1879 and a few months later lost a week's pay for refusing to get his hair cut and for talking back. He yielded to the commission and had his hair cut but in a few months earned another suspension without pay for insubordination. He followed this up almost immediately with a comedy sketch at the station house. The sight of the aptly named Sergeant Pinch bent over to scrub the floor inspired Littlehales. He mimicked the patrol sergeant 'in an insolent manner.' Two weeks without pay! When he failed to get fitted for one of the new helmets introduced by Stewart in 1881, Littlehales demonstrated his lack of serious attention to the job – or at least to the new order. He was asked to resign.

Although the chief and the commission punished infractions, they accepted that even police constables could err. When long-service constables who had moved up the ranks got into trouble, they were demoted, watched, and then sometimes restored to their former rank. Constable McKenzie became a patrol and drill sergeant in 1878, after eighteen months on the force. He must have demonstrated exceptional ability, for he was moved up to sergeant in 1880 and became a detective in 1881. He had a splendid record until 1892–4, when a series of drinking offences resulted in the commission demoting him to constable. But in 1895 he was elevated to patrol sergeant.

A major arrest could turn a career around. Constable Bainbridge joined in 1881 and made some small slips in the 1890s; however, his arrest of a murderer in 1900 earned him a commendation. Long service rather than a perfect record or brilliant career seems to have been the key factor in promotions. Bainbridge finally became a sergeant in 1910, long after his great deed. Careers with less remarkable incidents plodded along the same path that Bainbridge trod. The commission hired Alex Campbell in 1881 and he too had blemishes on his record – falling asleep on duty and refusing to obey an order. Never commended for anything, he also became a sergeant in 1910 when the force was expanding. Constable Gigg, hired in 1889, received his good conduct badge ten years later, was reprimanded for insubordination in 1901, and made patrol sergeant in 1911. Even for policemen who behaved flawlessly, advancement was often slow. Donald Campbell became a constable in 1875, earned a good conduct badge in 1891, and was transferred to the detective department in 1905. After thirty-five years with the force, he was finally promoted to inspector of detectives. In summary, the dismissal, promotion, and reduction in rank of men was not, generally speaking, a capricious business. The commission apparently weighed performance, experience, and good behaviour. Temptation and boredom caused a number of men to slip; some were caught and fined or otherwise punished.

For his troubles, the constable, the hired citizen, received a modest wage; the daily rate certainly was below that of skilled labourers. In addition to his salary, during the 1880s he got two pairs of trousers and one summer tunic every year, a winter tunic, fur cap, and gloves every two years, and an overcoat and helmet every three years. It was not much, but then not many workers had any clothes supplied. The rules forbade constables from accepting gratuities and rewards as well as from influence peddling.[149] Detectives had long been exempted from the rule which instructed policemen to decline rewards and some constables may have hoped for promotion to detective or to sergeant. The city paid sergeants about half again as much as the constables received, and the sergeant-major had free use of a house and fuel.

Perhaps the greatest benefit that accompanied employment on the police force in the late-Victorian era was job security. Police commissioners relentlessly countered the pay petitions of the constables with the argument that they benefitted from guaranteed employment during the entire year. In 1883 and 1884, the men and the chief made comparisons with the wages of other Canadian cities in order to strengthen their case for salary increases. Ignoring this argument, the commissioners retorted that the constables were well paid by the standards of the Hamilton labour force. The mayor alleged that the policeman 'was as well off as the mechanic whose work and income are uncertain. He had mechanics apply to him for a position on the force on the plea that the steady job was better than the unsteady one.' Judge Sinclair agreed. 'A bricklayer could get $3 a day but he couldn't get steady work all the year round.'[150] Moreover, except for the interlude in the late 1850s when the force was young and the city bankrupt, the force experienced no mass reduction in its complement.

What awaited the faithful civic servant toward the end of a career? For the very few constables who stayed with the force long enough to approach retirement, their duties were changed somewhat in recognition of a diminished capacity to pound beats and crack skulls. Removed from the rigours of the beat, they put in long hours at tedious chores. The reports of constables falling asleep in alleys, on doorsteps, or at the station guarding the lockup testify to the tedium of police duty which seemed to overcome most constables at some point in their careers.

'The kindly old man' who wore badge number 1, Peter Ferris, was the oldest constable on the force in 1885. Indeed, the scrawny veteran who looked like 'Uncle Sam' had been with the force almost from its beginning and in 1879 was thought to be 'the oldest wielder of a baton in Ontario.'[151] A Scottish immigrant, he had joined the mounted force sponsored by the Great Western Railway and in May 1851, along with another veteran – Sergeant-Major Kavanagh – he had helped to suppress strikes by the navvies and to break up riots in the Copetown construction camp. Ferris kept as a souvenir the club that he had used in the labour camps of the railway. He joined the Hamilton force in 1857 and became a sergeant in 1860, but he lost his rank though not his job when the city cut back the force in the autumn of 1860.[152] His record was fairly typical, for he had been admonished twice in the 1870s for insubordination and once for being drunk on duty. But there were no black marks against his name in the 1880s and 1890s.

In 1883, when a number of constables had threatened to strike over a pay dispute, the mayor summoned Ferris. On parade and in front of the other men, the mayor asked him whether he intended to strike the next day. Old Peter 'rugged, stern, and weather-beaten, looked up uncompromisingly, smiled, and answered firmly: 'Oi do not, sur.'[153] All of the men then chimed in with the same answer. The old employee of the railway police was the perfect minion, for he truly believed in never shirking his duties. He did 'his duty like a man.'[154]

We know something about the tasks assigned to this elder and obedient servant with 'the characteristic scotch face' because of his memorandum book for 1885. During that year – only seven days are unaccounted for in the book – he worked every day of the week. He was granted two days off duty to recuperate from injuries received while arresting one William Rowe, ten days leave in May, and a day and a half sick leave. In sum, he definitely reported for duty on 345 days. Most of the time he worked a split shift. He had no time off for Christmas or New Year's Eve. Typically, he went to the city market at 8:00 a.m. and enforced market regulations. He often doubled as the police court constable, guarding prisoners, collecting fines, and accompanying some prisoners to jail. Around 1:00 p.m., he went home and had 'dinner'. At 7:00, he returned to work. Usually, he kept order at the opera house, returning home after the play at 10:45. Many times in the evenings in 1885, he went to the Salvation Army barracks and stood guard at meetings or watched to maintain order among the people whom the army was helping. Invariably, his Sunday chores involved further guard duties at the 'sal. barr.' From time to time, Salvation Army meetings had been broken up by rowdies and Ferris was the token of law and order. Sometimes in the evening, he also delivered summonses and collected fines.

For forty weeks in 1885, Ferris plodded through this routine, experiencing unmitigated tedium. For five weeks, his lot was the graveyard shift (8:00 p.m. to 7:00 a.m.), during which he protected the city's water works from vandals. As he noted in his diary, it was 'quite' [*sic*] work. It also was uncomfortable, for in 1887 Ferris blamed a cold and sick leave on the lack of heat in the water works office.[155] During two weeks in February, when civic taxes were collected, he guarded the tax office. On a score of other days, he had assorted tasks, such as tending to the horse patrol wagon, guard duty for a procession, some unspecified work at a fire hall, and taking children to St Mary's orphans' home.

Occasionally, Ferris was challenged by situations more commonly dealt with by younger constables. His arrest of William Rowe after opera duty on the night of 26 January resulted in injury. He made no further arrests until 11 July, when he caught a boy stealing. On 14 September, he achieved a moment of glory when he took charge of a runaway horse and wagon. Yet such incidents were exceptional. Ferris's work life consisted overwhelmingly of unrelenting routine. As a consolation, he had attained some recognition as a congenial fellow, the familiar, decent and helpful officer who conveyed the notion that the police were in and of the community. It was symbolically important that Ferris wore badge number 1 and that its bearer – a man bound to duty – appeared often in public places. If people trusted old Peter, perhaps they would trust other constables too.

The numbering system had been introduced in 1875 so that the public could identify constables, but within the force there was an element of prestige in holding a low number.[156] A low number, however, eventually translated into an unhappy retirement. Financially the retired policeman had bleak prospects. Ferris should have retired in 1895 but he was allowed to continue for another year.[157] When he did retire, the commissioners voted to give him $500 in consideration of his forty-five years of service. Upon reconsideration at another meeting, the commissioners lowered the bonus to $350.[158] Other retired policemen literally threw themselves on the tender mercies of the police commissioners. In 1883 ex-sergeant-major Kavanagh pleaded for a bonus on account of long service. Like Ferris, Kavanagh had been with the railway police and had a solid reputation confirmed by promotions. His petition was not entertained.[159] Old Fenton, a constable deemed unfit when he first joined and who had a checkered career thereafter, retired in 1902 after thirty years of service. Forty-five patrolmen petitioned for the commission to pay him $15 a month for life. The commissioners, perhaps with benefit of actuarial tables, may have sized up the sixty-year old constable as a durable survivor; they granted him a lump sum of $425.

It was Chief Stewart who initiated thinking about a significant measure that promised to reward men who had long service with a force. He suggested the formation of a national policeman's benevolent fund 'to keep the wolf from the door and keep the dear ones from suffering and want.'[160] According to his scheme, all policemen would pay a dollar a year and another dollar upon the death of a member. This scheme was not implemented, but on 8 December 1890 the Hamilton commissioners created a local benevolent fund. Constables paid into it 3 per cent of their pay. As well, all rewards and money from the sale of lost articles went into the fund, a practice followed in the Toronto benevolent fund.[161] The commissioners invested the money in mortgages and municipal bonds.

PROFESSIONALISM AND TECHNOLOGY

Citizen participation in the formal maintenance of law and order shrank greatly over the nineteenth century, especially in urban centres. Barristers replaced local amateur worthies on the bench of the lowest and the intermediate courts; a police force with military features patrolled the streets. The juries remained, but they had never been part of petty sessions and police court proceedings. As for their standing in the intermediate courts, that had been whittled down by the creation of the County Judge's Criminal Court. Moreover, by the 1870s and 1880s, grand juries persisted, in the opinion of some, largely as costly ornaments. They still received the assize judge's address, courteously replied, and toured the jail. Their indictments frequently seemed *pro forma*, and presentments – cases that grand juries knew about and put before the court – were unheard of. Editorials called for the elimination of grand juries, denouncing them as frills that the counties could ill afford. Law and order was becoming less and less a matter of community involvement, and more and more a concern of specific professions and economy drives.

In the same period in which all these developments were taking place, police administrators began their ceaseless quest for technological aids, a quest that took them beyond the city and province. This fascination with technology owed something to the dilemma that police administrators faced when dealing with their political masters. Though the police commission managed many aspects of policing, city council established the budget. As explained, the political challenge of reconciling economy and better service affected the organization of policing, and the resulting innovations did not stop with Stewart. His successors, pushed by the commission, carried on the work. The next phase involved the application of technology.

Every year, the chiefs of police appealed for more men to protect the taxpayers, balancing lists of accomplishments with interjections that more men would increase the city's security. In 1887 the mayor replied to the chief's call for more men with a counter-proposal. 'The fact of the matter is that the introduction of the patrol wagon and the telephone has revolutionized the police.'[162] The mayor insisted on a system of alarms similar to fire-alarm call boxes; citizens would be able to use these to summon a patrol wagon at any time to a vicinity.[163] The city adopted a call-box system for police use and the commissioners continued to explore other innovations that would improve police service. In doing so, they invariably looked to United States cities, travelling to Detroit in the winter of 1888 to inspect innovations in that city's system of policing.[164] In policing, as in much else in urban Canada, the agenda was set by economic imperatives, the public's demands for improved services, and examples from the big cities of the republic.

The fascination with technology persisted, broadening the character of police work and fostering minimum levels of education for admission. However, street wisdom endured. In recent times, the police force has embraced an extreme dualism in its institutional values. The records and communications officers pull up information from computers while the constables on the street still rely on memory and instinct.

3 Human Agents of Civic Order

The Toronto newspapers could scarcely contain their glee, for they had stumbled onto a story certain to wound the pride of boosters in the neighbouring 'ambitious city'. In early January 1895, 'a man known well in athletic circles' checked into the Grand Union Hotel on Simcoe Street in Toronto and requested a suite. The room he obtained opened onto a parlour. So did the adjacent one occupied by two ladies 'of most attractive appearance' who had accompanied him. The party of three were registered as H.B. Collins, Miss Maude Collins, and Miss Ella Collins, all from New Haven, Connecticut. For three nights, they had a dandy time. H.B. Collins consumed a good volume of spirituous liquors at the hotel bar and in his room. The ladies always appeared in splendid humour.[1]

When presented with the bill, Mr Collins signed the cheque as Hugh McKinnon. McKinnon, a chap well-known in sporting circles, ordinarily took pride in announcing his lofty standing as Hamilton's chief constable. Not on this occasion. His conduct in 'Toronto the Good' 'shocked the moral sense of the community.'[2] Another story soon surfaced. One of the women at the Grand Union Hotel, whose real name was Mrs Tommy Gould had accompanied McKinnon to Milton during the previous summer when the chief – a champion hurler – had judged events at the Scottish Games. Tommy Gould announced that he would initiate divorce proceedings and name the chief as co-respondent.[3] While the police commission waited until McKinnon recovered from what his doctor described as a severe cold, police magistrate Jelfs went to Toronto to investigate. Later, Jelfs led the interrogation of the chief before the police commission. The burly chief could not deny the facts, but he tried to wriggle out of charges of impropriety, denying that he had been caught on an tipsy stroll down the primrose path. He even worked to turn the tables completely by alleging chivalrous conduct. From time to time, he boasted, he had aided women in distress, pursuing men who had trifled with ladies and had put them in a delicate way. In the chief's rendition, some cad had misused Mrs Gould's sister and the trio had charged off to Toronto to deal with the bounder and put things right. The chief admitted to no misconduct, except that he had imbibed heavily. He then submitted his resignation.[4]

Chief McKinnon's escapade was clearly at odds with the image of Hamilton's reorganized force. During the history of civic policing previous to 1895, police forces in North America had evolved from haphazardly founded civic departments into bureaucratically administered agencies with codes of conduct. Even if the path of change was strewn with sensational episodes of irregularity, professionalization continued none the less. As discussed in the previous chapter, police in the larger Ontario centres had been placed under the authority of appointed commissions in 1858 in an attempt to keep partisan politics and corruption out of the management of this important new civic service.[5] In Hamilton, the Stewart regime in the early 1880s had altered the conduct of policing as work by strengthening its military attributes and insisting on strict law enforcement rather than discretionary conduct. Some specific innovations, such as drills and the marching of the men to the head of their beats, would fade and return only to fade again, but the military model persisted as an ideal of police conduct promoted by chiefs and sergeants.

On the surface, many developments in the Hamilton force at the turn-of-the-century accord with Eric Monkkonen's model of changes in American police departments. After 1890, according to him, civic police were evolving from agencies of class control into crime-fighting bodies attuned to technological advances.[6] However, this depiction of a transformation in policing has been challenged by Helen Boritch and John Hagan. Their study of crime and policing in Toronto stresses the persistence of class control and moral order campaigns even while the force did try to improve its crime-control activities.[7] In their estimation, it is not clear that 'reforms also resulted in a major reorientation of police enforcement policies.'[8] While Hamilton's experience appears similar to that of Toronto, there are variations. In Hamilton, the force and its constables did not make a smooth and immediate transition to progressive policing. That much accords with Boritch and Hagan's study,

but in contrast to the persistent attention of Toronto's finest to policing working-class entertainments, the Hamilton force seems to have
been a far more reluctant agent of moral order.

The image of policing cultivated in Hamilton certainly resembled
that of contemporary departments across the continent. By 1900 the
'telephone signal boxes' enforcing specified beats,[9] the many publicly
stated missions for the police, and the statistics selected for annual reports contributed to an impression of the force as an exemplar and en-
forcer of civic order and an up-to-date crime-fighting organization.[10]
The élite expected this from the police and, in the half-century after
the founding of the Hamilton force, the force itself had been moved
toward at least outward compliance with standards of military and
moral conduct. Increasingly since the 1880s, constables were not just
to be civic servants who protected persons and property; they were by
their very conduct to express the ideal moral standards of the community. The resignation of McKinnon in 1895 was one symbolic turning-
point. His protestation that his plight was 'owing to wine and not
women' elicited no expressions of sympathy.[11]

A parallel set of developments saw the force embrace technological
aids and detection systems. The first of these innovations was the telephone installed in the chief's office in April 1878.[12] Within several
years, the telephone became commonplace in the stations and new
constables in the early 1880s were instructed in its use. When in 1898
the force embraced the international Bertillon system for identifying
criminals – a system whose nerve-centre was at the Bertillon headquarters in Chicago – it obtained the latest fad for institutions aligned
against crime and disorderly living. Based on the idea that no two individuals were alike, the Bertillon system involved the measurement of
eight standard body features. The Hamilton force adopted fingerprinting in 1912, but some wanted posters forwarded to Hamilton continued to cite Bertillon measurements into the 1920s.[13]

Alert to gadgets and international innovations in the young field of
criminal detection, Hamilton's constabulary resembled hundreds of
others across North America. But had policing become an effective instrument of social control or, at the level of the constables' beats, an
urban profession?

AN INDIFFERENT AGENCY OF MORAL ORDER

That the police had been missionaries for middle-class values was a
compelling revisionist thesis proposed by historians writing in the
1970s. These historians dealt with the policing of British working-class
communities in the mid-nineteenth century.[14] When labour historians

of the transatlantic world subsequently dealt with the police, they too focused on its function as protector of property, particularly corporate property during labour actions. In the United States, however, historians of the police, meanwhile, have tended to stress the disorder in urban policing caused by political tampering. They allege that the class mission evident in British policing had been diluted in the United States by ethnic participation and by an assortment of social service tasks assigned to the police when city councils cast about for cheap ways of providing new urban services.[15] Other historians of policing have been struck by how policemen, through their work, recreation, and even family connections, have formed a society or caste apart from other citizens. The Hamilton experience illustrates all of the above.

Policemen in Hamilton were directed to exemplify and to impose standards of conduct derived from the values of the governing class of a newly prosperous and largely Protestant colonial society. However, the evidence also demonstrates that, while pressure for regimentation and separation from the rest of society came from the police commission, the response of the workingmen in uniform to such demands was mixed. Though Hamilton was not unique in this respect, the historical literature on policing long ignored the issue of internal friction within police forces as well as such mundane matters as hiring, training, daily work routines, and wages.[16] Yet this is beginning to change. Policing is now written about as a job and from the perspective of the constables. When considered in this light, notions of social control and professionalism are found to be incomplete descriptions for policing in the early 1900s. Significant tension between order and disorder existed within the police force itself and the police were not entirely outside urban working-class society.[17]

At the turn of the century, what the established grand bourgeoisie of Hamilton wished for was a disciplined corps of morally upright and energetic guardians of public order. They wanted their commercial property and industries inspected at night, their payrolls guarded, their homes watched over during their holidays,[18] and their streets free from begging and unlicensed activity.[19] These things the police did do, but how effectively? Certainly, special requests for extra attention to the protection of private property proved problematic. Constables felt that inspection of private residences should have generated extra revenue for their benevolent (retirement) fund.[20] It did not, and, for this reason among others, many policemen appear to have been at times lackadaisical defenders of property. There also were limits on how far the police commission would go in having private interests protected by a public agency. An attempt by the Hamilton Iron and Steel Company to have its watchman appointed a special constable was rejected by the commission as incompatible with its authority.[21] What all this suggests is that an analysis of policing must take into account facts that point to conflicts other than those involving class: conflicts between constables and the administrators, and between administrators and special interests.

If the arrangements for protection of private property were problematic, those for the defence of moral order were even more so. Across North America at the turn-of-the-century, many pressure groups pushed for state, provincial, or local laws restricting gambling, drinking, prostitution and other morally dubious activities. Enforcement of such laws, however, was generally lax. In Hamilton, for example, the years from the 1880s to the First World War were the heyday of crusades against alcohol, gambling, prostitution, and violation of the Sabbath. During this period, the police commission heard sporadically from moral crusaders, but, when it did, it tended to deflect their entreaties or heeded them only in the short term. The American literature on police forces stresses how the often deep involvement of the police in local political machines became a factor where the enforcement of unpopular laws was concerned. The Hamilton force was less overtly political and corruption was modest. Like forces in other Canadian cities, however, the Hamilton constabulary failed to enforce moral order laws rigorously.

Hamilton reformers participated in the same temperance movement and Sabbath campaigns that earned Toronto its sobriquet – 'the good.' Yet the city's leaders lacked the evangelical zeal of their Toronto counterparts. In Toronto, William Howland, elected as mayor in 1884, steered the city toward righteousness, and the Toronto police force established a morality department in 1886.[22] The Hamilton Temperance League in 1884 tried to goad the Hamilton force with charges of failing to enforce the liquor licence act; the chief and commission politely requested the league to provide specific information.[23] In other words, the police in Hamilton were not going to devote more energy and resources to the matter but instead placed the onus on the temperance group. Similarly, a petition in 1885 to enforce strictly the Lord's Day Act with respect to barbers and hairdressers elicited no special action 'as the Police have instructions to see to it that all laws are strictly enforced.'[24] It is possible that the eyes and ears of the temperance and Sabbatarian advocates may have assisted the police. The number of cases of police action for breaches of the liquor licence act and for violations of the Lord's day rose slightly. However, the tepid response differed significantly from what was happening in Toronto.

Nothing more was heard from moral reformers until the mid-1890s, when the 'Christian Endeavor Societies' complained about the sale of cigars and candy on Sundays and a deputation from the Ministerial Association alleged that the force allowed gambling dens.[25] Following this outburst, the moral reformers fell silent until 1903. Then, led by two prominent Presbyterian women – Mrs John Gibson, wife of a provincial cabinet minister and corporate lawyer – and Mrs Samuel Lyle, wife of the minister at Central Presbyterian Church – the church favoured by the civic élite – the Local Council of Women requested censorship of naughty theatre posters.[26] Alas, reported the commission, the city had no applicable by-law. The question resurfaced in 1910 when a portrait of a passionate embrace – which shamed even the devil in the background – advertised 'The Soul Kiss.'[27]

Sermons and petitions on issues of moral order increased from 1907 to 1914. In 1907 a Hamilton clergyman revived the spectre of sin on the stage. 'I view with anxiety,' he exclaimed, 'the increasing thirst for entertainment in this city.'[28] He and others reiterated earlier calls for a morality department within the police force.[29] The Citizens League petitioned the commission in late 1908 and early 1909 to assign members of the force to a detachment devoted to enforcing the laws on liquor licensing, gambling, and prostitution.[30] In fact, the league – inspired by the international crusade against the 'white slavery' of prostitution – insisted that Hamilton form a morality department like the one in Toronto.[31] The commission promised to give the matter full consideration, but prevaricated. Indeed, the police magistrate had resisted imposing morality after prior encounters with the armies of virtue.[32] He wondered if the league could distinguish an immoral act from an illegal one. He explained that, in Hamilton, the police commission allowed houses of prostitution as long as they 'were decently conducted.' The county judge supported the practice. 'The police could not take the place of fathers and mothers,' he concluded.[33] With attitudes like these, it is little wonder that the trend in moral order cases tried before the police magistrate's court dipped from the 1860s to the early 1900s (Figure 2.1 and Figure 3.1).

The Citizens League's persistence was rewarded with temporary results. During 1909 and 1910, the police staged more than the usual number of raids on gambling establishments and houses of ill fame, and the police magistrate handed out more severe fines than in previous years. The vice crusade of 1910 seems to have been reluctantly initiated and required direct orders from the provincial attorney general.[34] In any event, it was short-lived; raids declined in subsequent years.

Prosecutions per constable

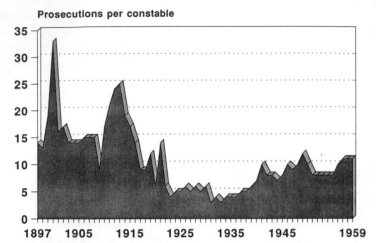

Figure 3.1
Moral Order Prosecutions per Constable, Hamilton, 1897–1959
Sources: Hamilton Spectator, 21 January 1865, 11 January 1866, 11 January 1867, 17 January 1870, 4 January 1872, 6 January 1875, 6 January 1876, 22 January 1878, 9 January 1879, 26 January 1880, 11 January 1881, 30 January 1883, 7 February 1884, 28 February 1887, 30 January 1890, 16 February 1892, 26 January 1898, 27 January 1899, 31 January 1901, 5 February 1902, 22 January 1903, 3 February 1904, 23 February 1905, 30 January 1907, 20 January 1909, 3 February 1910, 27 February 1915, HPL, Records of the City of Hamilton, RG 10, Series A, Police Department, *Annual Reports,* 1906–70, missing 1906–1908, 1910, 1911, 1914, 1916, 1918–19, 1930, 1933; RG 10, Series K, Police Court Proceedings, Ledgers, 1859–1949.

What accounts for the lack of police enthusiasm for moral order campaigns? Corruption springs to mind, but it seems less probable than other considerations. The police department had likely not eliminated entirely the exercise of discretion by constables, and so the latter may have been inclined to caution and to refraining from action if there was doubt or risk. As well, constables may have been indifferent or even hostile to measures that forced them to look for trouble among folk of their own class background. One 1912 incident shows what could happen in spite of orders to enforce the laws strictly. Constables Aitkin and Creen discharged a prisoner under arrest for drunk and disorderly conduct because they knew it was his first offence. The commission ordered them and the deputy chief, who knew of their action, to adhere strictly to regulations.[35] But how many more discretionary actions went unnoticed? In the nineteenth century, American police, according to Joseph Tropea, adopted avoidance and discretion as two major options in moderating the dilemma of how to represent a new system of rational legal administration while being responsive to neighbourhood situations.[36] It seems that the police in Hamilton pursued the same awkward strategies, and their critics noticed.

Yet crusaders for moral purity lost neither heart nor energy. The YWCA and the Salvation Army alleged in 1912 that Hamilton figured at the centre of the white slave trade in Canada,[37] and other reformers claimed that promises of theatrical work lured innocent young women to the city and prostitution.[38] Perhaps. Such charges, however, suggest another explanation for the want of reforming zeal among Hamilton authorities: police officials drew the conclusion that some crusaders were fools. The notion that promises of theatre work undermined virtuous women struck Jelfs as complete nonsense and he said so, questioning whether women were lured into prostitution out of stupidity.[39] None the less, the reform crusade made the police commissioners squirm and they made a concession in 1910 by hiring as deputy chief a man who eagerly took up the task of Sisyphus. 'I am going to make this city morally clean,' boasted William Whatley in 1914.[40] A sharp upturn in morals prosecutions per constable that commenced when the commission hired Whatley as deputy chief proves this zealot meant business (Figure 3.1).

The police force's conduct undercuts the idea that it functioned as a consistent – let alone a forceful – agency for social control. When it did choose to listen to the moral-order interest groups, it seemed to act from contrary impulses – the cultural biases of its middle-class directors and the working-class culture of its men. Unfairness resulted. In reluctantly enforcing moral order laws, the police chose routes of least resistance and hauled in members of visible but marginal groups. Constables arrested the clients of prostitutes less frequently than the prostitutes themselves. A local branch of an anti-white slavery association criticized this approach in 1912. In reply, the police commission insisted that constables could do nothing else because the criminal code made it illegal for males to frequent a house of ill fame and it was difficult to prove that men had been 'frequenters.'[41] Along with prostitutes – many of whom were Afro-Americans – the police arrested an extraordinary number of Chinese for gambling and clamped down on 'foreign' boarding-houses for the illegal sale of alcohol.[42] Chief Smith, pressing a charge of street-walking in 1912, barked a racial slur in the magistrate's court. 'There's a colony of these coloured women in town, and all they do is walk the streets.'[43]

There was nothing unusual about the police force's tendency to focus on marginal groups, especially those who were also visible minorities: its forerunners had been doing the same thing in Hamilton as early as the 1840s.[44] Indeed, the pattern was so entrenched that only one conclusion can be drawn: racial prejudice was rampant among

Hamilton police.[45] Of course, the police were not unusual in this respect. Newspaper reports of that era spewed out disgusting racial slurs; the constables on the beat were no worse than the journalists who reported on them. And journalists, who aimed at catching the public's interest, likely mirrored public opinion. After a 1909 raid on a 'craps' game which netted twenty-seven black males – an interesting episode in itself – the *Spectator* reporter remarked on the cheerful singing in the no. 3 station house: 'It was the strangest combination of crap shooters, coon shouters, and dark town revivalists that the police have met in many a day.'[46] Similarly, racist comments invariably littered reports on the arrests of Chinese gamblers.

Sharing popular assumptions of the day, the Hamilton police believed that certain racial groups were inclined to criminal behaviour. This 'differential treatment' was based on the assumption that some minorities possessed a 'weakness' or a toleration for 'immorality' that offended the majority. Conceivably, Chinese immigrants gambled in an open way that annoyed the majority, although some of the attention paid to them evidently stemmed from a pervasive popular outlook that equated Chinese laundries and restaurants with even worse offences. Moral reformers implicated both locales in opium trafficking and white slavery. Even Chinese Canadian names attracted suspicion; the Hamilton police actually proposed that the Chinese should adopt 'reasonable' names, since that might help in identifying them.[47] In 1915 Chinese restaurants roused civic wrath because they stayed open into the early hours of the morning. 'They are becoming the resorts of objectionable characters at night,' asserted Chief Smith, 'and the police have no power to order these people out of the restaurants.'[48] The discovery of a drugged woman in a Chinese café in 1917 kept the issue alive for several years.[49] Nationally, the belief that the Chinese had introduced narcotics into Canadian society peaked in the early 1920s with the publication of Emily Murphy's *The Black Candle*, an exposé of drug traffic.[50]

Many recent European immigrants were conspicuous in activities that interested moral order reformers and the police. In the booming Hamilton of the early 1900s, single immigrant males flocked to bootleggers, the entrepreneurs who catered to the illicit liquor traffic. The bootleggers posed a threat to social order, for occasionally they clashed violently over territory. All the same, the frequent raids on immigrant establishments seem suspiciously nativist; rarely did the police nab middle-class citizens at their 'resorts.' On one occasion, however, they did precipitate a major civic scandal by going after prominent citizens for immoral conduct. In March 1914 the police subpoenaed fifty young girls in a case against two prominent businessmen who stood charged with luring the girls to a house for immoral purposes. One of the men committed suicide and the other escaped conviction on a technicality and moved to his ranch in Alberta.[51]

On balance, the police shared conventional contemporary stereotypes; however, constables were unique in having the power to disrupt peoples' lives. Sometimes they did so on the basis of appearances, acting on beliefs that accorded with the popular attitudes of the majority and the behaviour of a few within a minority group; sometimes they were simply behaving dishonourably. On the night of 6 January 1912, the liquor licence inspector and Constable Bleakley raided an Italian house looking for liquor. They forced the women in the house to get out of bed. Bleakley allegedly tickled a woman under the chin and made improper advances. A delegation of Italians complained formally to the commission, which heard witnesses on both sides before deciding in favour of the constable. Nevertheless, Bleakley left the force in June, convicted of neglecting his beat.[52] Misunderstandings and improper conduct might have been minimized if the Hamilton police force had hired minorities; the commission began to recruit constables from European ethnic minorities only in the late 1940s.

Like accurate crime rates, police misconduct and prejudice have always been elusive subjects, partly because information about transgressions have depended on victim complaints. Lacking the material for a precise rendering of accounts, there is no better summary for the behaviour of the police at the turn-of-the-century than Friedman and Percival's description of the force in Oakland, California. 'They were prejudiced against the Chinese, they despised "tramps," they tolerated gambling. They twisted formal law, sometimes unconsciously, in accordance with everyday values, and sentiments. The police were not legalistic.'[53]

Some features of moral order enforcement invited more scorn than others and the judicial system recognized this fact. It seemed foolish to many contemporaries that Sunday ice-cream vendors should be issued the 'blue invitation' – the summons – to stop by and see the police magistrate. The police also served summonses on Greek peanut vendors. The law demanded these actions, but the police magistrate convicted very few of those arrested and then levied light fines. Another example of how the criminal justice system exercised discretion surfaced after the interlude of moral order raids. So-called respectable first-time offenders – 'the lambs' – coaxed favours from the fellows at the station; relatives, friends, and even bankers were informed so that bail could be met. Early in 1912, consistent with a recent history of an alternation between softhearted favouritism and blind justice, the commission ordered the force to stop this messenger service.[54]

Putting the moral order crusades in perspective adds even more complexity to discussions on social control. Not all pressure-group activity falls readily into the category of moral order or social control. At the turn-of-the-century, the Civic Improvement Association complained several times about the failure of many citizens to remove snow from their sidewalks and it got results.[55] A number of surprised residents found themselves in police court facing fines for lack of attention to civic responsibilities. In fact, throughout the late nineteenth century the police force hauled into court individuals who had failed to clear the snow from their sidewalks.[56] On the one hand, therefore, selective use of historical evidence easily can cast the police as more oppressive and harmful than they were. On the other hand, the omission of activities can strip the police of a record of useful if mundane service. And always there was the fluctuation between leniency and rigidity, a fluctuation that expressed shifts in policy or personality at the top. These shifts were mediated by the men on the beat.

THE POLICE AND ORGANIZED LABOUR

The conduct of the police during major labour actions offers further opportunities to consider their situation within the context of urban social relations. The Hamilton police were called upon to protect property and persons during strikes. The most publicized occasion was the November 1906 street railway strike. After strike-breakers were bought in to operate the cars, the union's sympathizers responded with force: they attacked Hamilton Street Railway cars and also buildings where the company housed the strike-breakers. The police found that they could not readily separate antagonistic crowds from the strike-breakers. On 5 November, the first night of violence, several police were injured. Ordered by the commission to be more forceful in dealing with crowds in future, the police chief expressed his reluctance. The crowds included women and children and the force lacked the numbers to deal with a riot.[57]

The inadequacy of the force came to the fore on 23 November when a crowd near city hall jostled and jeered the police. That same night, in an attempt to protect strike-breakers from a mob, a few police fired over the heads of the assailants and then lost a number of their recently acquired Colt revolvers in a mêlée. The following day militia units from out of town arrived and enforced the Riot Act. Backed up by militia, the police charged a crowd which had not dispersed and people now were beaten by constables. The force defended these actions on the grounds that people had been given a chance to disperse quietly after the reading of the Riot Act.[58] But the beatings were denounced by several aldermen and the Trades and Labour Council later called for an investigation of the actions of the police.[59]

After the strike, the company paid each member of the force a ten-dollar gratuity for protecting its property.[60] Certainly, the force had compromised itself, but the events also revealed it as a hesitant and ineffectual auxiliary of corporate capitalism's union-crushing tactics. Small and comprised of city residents, the civic force was not capable of large-scale and sustained duty on behalf of an unpopular enterprise. The company had used private detective agencies to obtain 'intelligence' about the union and to secure tough strike-breakers, and in the end it was the militia that actually restored the order necessary for the running of the streetcars. In many comparable instances across Canada, local police were supplemented by outside forces.[61]

One later incident deserves mention. In mid-July 1914 Deputy Chief Whatley ordered constables to break up a 'socialistic mass meeting.' He defended his action on the grounds that language used at the meeting defamed Great Britain, the United States, and the institutions of law and order and that people were being incited to riot. Public and press opinion ran against the decision and the officer was left on his own to defend it. He later spoke with socialist leaders and promised to allow future assemblies if they were 'of a quiet nature and not calculated to create ill feeling or disorderly conduct.'[62]

Local governments had not maintained civic police departments principally to intervene in labour disputes; rather, tight-fisted councils kept forces busy performing a multitude of services to earn their civic salaries.[63] If the roles of municipal police forces as defenders of persons and property integrated them into corporate union-breaking tactics, this situation derived from the provocative and aggressive actions of companies and not directly from the civic police. When a reactionary officer went beyond what public opinion would accept – as Whatley did – public protests checked the threat to liberty.

Moral order campaigns and strikes have secured prominent places in the writing of social history in Canada. Dwelling on them as features of urban policing, however, is no less misleading than maintaining that policing concentrated soley on the apprehension of criminals. To critics, police forces oppressed the workingman and 'foreigners'; to supporters, it prevented crime and caught malefactors. The forces did all these things, but they did them almost incidently and largely ineffectually. Through no real fault of their own, policemen could not solve many crimes; moreover, they often had only an auxiliary role in some crimes that were solved.

In Hamilton, much to the dismay of some powerful citizens, the police force was far from being a well-oiled, crime-fighting machine.

In 1901 lawyer and politician S. C. Mewburn demanded that the commission 'investigate the methods of the Police Department in the attempt to capture parties breaking into his premises' on the night of 9 July. The commission concluded that there had been 'negligence and mismanagement' on the part of the sergeant-major and the chief.[64] In late 1908 Constable Duncan lost a day's pay for failing to report a robbery which had occurred on his beat.[65] The capture of burglars was so noteworthy a demonstration of 'bravery and courage' that, when it occurred early in 1908, the commission advanced the policeman involved one year towards becoming a first-class constable.[66]

Policemen could not have been expected to prevent or solve the majority of crimes. Most thefts left few clues and often no suspects; the police had little with which to work. Moreover, given the volume of incidents requiring police attention, many crimes simply had to be written off. As if the volume of criminal incidents with real victims was not enough of a burden, the city council and the police commission added to police work by continually passing regulatory by-laws that required police enforcement. The chief and constables might protest but they were bound to act and to leave discretionary judgment to judicial authorities.

Forces were financed by local governments which, though interested in order, were headed by civic boosters who measured progress in serviced lots and rising assessments, not more uniformed guardians. The chiefs' annual entreaties for additional men and new stations were met, but typically the increases lagged behind the expansion of the city and followed a series of petitions from citizens in lightly patrolled areas. Not only did local governments expect more and more from the police, but by the turn-of-the-century the province and the federal government initiated extensive regulatory measures on professions and trades, food preparation, and many more areas of economic activity – to say nothing of restrictions on the manufacture and sale of alcohol. In the absence of a provincial gendarmerie, the civic police had to enforce the measures of senior governments. The police constable's lot still retained the physical challenges of previous decades, and increasingly it was becoming more complicated. Yet, despite the growing workload, the new century brought no remarkable shifts in the qualifications for constables or much innovation in their training.

BEEFY LADS WHO TOOK CHARGE

Poking fun at the terribly serious antics of the commission reviewing applicants for the police force in late 1888, a reporter referred to 'the usual goose-stepping.'[67] The same comment could have been made in later years, for military ideals continued to permeate the structure, conduct, and rules of the force. Regimentation, regulations, incentives for advancement, and patrol routines worked to discourage intimacy with the community. This fascination with and imitation of military conduct contradicts the belief that policing in the English-speaking world avoided the militarism of continental European forces. Civic forces lacked the weaponry and the detachment from the local community that characterized a national gendarmerie, but they tried hard to pose as companies of soldiers. Police culture quickly took on paramilitary dimensions.

Group photographs of Hamilton constables expressed eloquently the uniformity achieved by enlistment requirements and dress. The men stood shoulder to shoulder for the good reason that physically they were alike. From 1900 to 1945, most stood between 5'11" and 6'1" and weighed between 170 and 190 pounds, with chest measurements of 37 to 40 inches. The *Hamilton Times* – when covering the hiring of new men – listed their vital statistics as if the recruits had paraded as prize livestock. Unsuccessful applicants were slightly smaller on average than the probationary constables. This observation and the very fact that measurements appeared on the application forms and in a newspaper attest to the importance ascribed to size.

In seeking descriptive adjectives and labels for the force, journalists fastened onto 'stalwart,' 'good specimens,' 'every inch men,' and 'the local squad of huskies.'[68] Hiring remained an examination of brawn, much like what it had been in the 1880s. The commission quite literally 'sized up the men.' In February 1892 'a very fine squad of men' – seventeen applicants – stood with their backs to the wall while Charlie Smith, the city messenger, tugged at the blinds to let more light into the council chamber. On this occasion, the commissioners grilled candidates for an hour. Regrettably, they had to reject Gideon Perry – 'a fine specimen of manhood' – because he had not lived a year in Hamilton (that residency requirement applied then to constables, but not to senior men).[69] By 1910 a doctor also examined the men, but only after the commissioners had sized them up first.[70] The importance of size, reminisced Chief Smith in 1914, drove desperate applicants to pad their shoes with felt to raise their height or to place lead on their person to increase their weight.[71]

Although the nature of their work would change substantially, particularly in the 1920s as the automobile overwhelmed policing, the commission still wanted constables to establish a commanding presence and be able to subdue malefactors. Once on the force, the men were expected to keep in shape. Yet the commission's aspiration to maintain a physical standard ran into the independent views and conduct of the men. In the late 1890s and early 1900s, instructors conducted foot drills for all men at the armouries about every two months. In 1900 the commission heard complaints about these assemblies and entertained a recommendation from the men that Indian club drills and dumb bells be employed instead.[72] Constables insisted that walking the beat kept them fit enough. In an effort to keep the men trim, the department in 1912 took out a group membership at that quintessential expression of muscular Christianity, the YMCA.[73] Athleticism, however, proved no more popular than drill; in 1913 the commission dropped group membership at the YMCA 'on account of so few members of the force taking advantage of the gymnasium.'[74] None the less, physical uniformity was achieved and maintained. The turnover in constables and the hiring of new young men as well as the obligatory trudging over a beat achieved more in this regard than drills.

The desired physical attributes also extended to outward appearances of full natural sight, speech, and hearing.[75] Constable Springer was reported as unfit for duty in June 1907 because of 'an impediment in his speech.' With notice that 'his articulation had improved,' the matter was dropped.[76] At least as late as 1914, constables were permitted to wear glasses only temporarily and with special permission.[77] Constable Meyers, suspected in 1913 of deafness as a consequence of having been struck in the head by tackle in the police stable, had to have his hearing monitored for a year.[78] The commissioners had slight compassion for physically 'sub-standard' men. If a man was unfit, he was unfit.

As in earlier years, accounts of the force in the press stressed the connection between physical presence and the tactic of 'taking charge.' Following a parade of the force in 1907, a reporter remarked on the gratifying spectacle of 'big strapping fellows, who looked as if they could put up a strong argument in making an arrest and were a typical terror to evil-doers.'[79] Several commonplace routines of policing unquestionably demanded brute strength; for example, a crowd that assembled to watch a road race on 30 October 1907 attacked a pair of constables who had attempted to arrest a drunk.[80]

The force's emphasis on physical strength left little room for firearms. Guns were carried and fired by policemen on duty before being prohibited in the late 1870s.[81] After constable John Lowery had to apply great force and risk his life in subduing a burglar in 1884, the commission yielded to demands from the constables and permitted them officially to carry arms on night patrols.[82] Later the practice seems to have been prohibited again, though a few constables on night duty still carried concealed guns. There was a considerable amount of soul-searching and vacillation until the fatal shooting of a constable in 1904 resolved the issue once and for all.[83] Essentially, for the first half century of its existence, the Hamilton force relied upon truncheons and muscle which could inflict awful damage, though nothing like that of firearms. Furthermore, at least since 1889, the commission ruled the use of clubs or night sticks acceptable only for self-defence.

Not surprisingly, chief A.D. Stewart proposed that constables carry pistols on night duty.[84] Stewart, the militia enthusiast, was also something of a martial-arts fanatic who opened a city club for fencing and boxing. It was not just an American fad to equip the police with revolvers, it was a proposition based on an international martial outlook. The English bobby may not have carried a sidearm, but his Irish and colonial counterparts were certainly less restrained.[85] None the less, guns were reserved for very exceptional circumstances. Day-to-day police work required brawn, not bullets.

There was more to the physical requirement than an equation between brawn and performance of duties. Police officials believed that this requirement helped build an élan that added to the satisfaction of the job; policing was not open to just anyone, but to a special muscular breed. In an age of bloody empire-building, bare-knuckles boxing, and flourishing amateur athletics, physical prowess and size merged with popular notions about manliness. This physical and martial atmosphere, however, was not associated with frequent brutality on the part of the police, although the actual level of unnecessary violence may never be known.[86] Given the thousands of arrests for street fighting and drunk and disorderly conduct which could have involved violent encounters, the complaints against the police for acts of violence were surprisingly rare. Yet it is also plausible to think of the complaints against the police as a fraction of the total sum of incidents where police violence occurred. Indeed, the low number of complaints may be an indictment of the complaint procedures. Today within the force, rumours persist that constables have roughed up people in custody, particularly those who have assaulted officers. Rarely do these parties lodge a complaint, because they may have had enough experience on the street to know that the force possesses a long memory.

In any case, the records show that, from 1900 to 1914, the police commission dealt with only five complaints against constables for use of excessive force. One episode involved Constable Duncan, who roughed up a young boy when moving the lad's wagon off a sidewalk. Duncan had to pay for a broken crock and a witness's time and was 'directed to use more judgment in handling these small offenses.'[87] Duncan had other black marks against his name. In less than a year on the force, he had failed to respond to a robbery, committed an act of insubordination, and released a prisoner without authority. The commission dismissed him.

The remaining four actions concerned Constable Campaign, who qualified as the force 'bully.' He had applied and been rejected twice before being taken onto the force in 1883. The commission denied him a good service badge after a decade on the force; he had neglected duties on two occasions. A hint of more serious troubles ahead appeared in July 1898 when a Major O'Reilly complained that Campaign had ordered him – 'in a very offensive manner' – to move along as he talked to a friend on King Street.[88] 'Move along' orders were one of the great sources of friction between policemen and citizens in American cities and apparently in Canadian ones too. Also, it has been alleged that American policemen in the late nineteenth century developed, through training on the street and station-house lore, a practice of swift pre-emptive action against perceived danger; they responded to verbal abuse as if it was going to lead to physical assault.[89] Campaign appears to have adopted this strike-first-and-ask-questions-later approach.

In 1902 Campaign was caught drinking on duty and fined. His slide from obvious unhappiness into dangerous behaviour, however, took a few more years. Dennis Bennett complained that Campaign had struck him over the head with his baton on the night of 5 November 1906, the first night of rioting during the streetcar strike.[90] Of course, the commission, which took a hard line on the mobs assembled against the company, concluded that the constable had done nothing other than circumstances required. But a pattern of dubious conduct now unfolded. Campaign broke Andrew Wilson's jaw while arresting him on 12 January 1911, assaulted Charles Layton on 24 May 1912, and 'acted in an ungentlemanly manner' toward J.M. Farewell on 24 December 1913.[91] In every instance, a mitigating side to the story could be found and Campaign was officially exonerated, although encouraged to resign.[92] He alone of the sixty to seventy men on the force between 1900 and 1914 had a record of rough conduct.

The force embraced many types of individuals. The taxing work, the modest pay, the sparse rewards, and the very limited prospects for improvement made few constables contented employees. When constables got seriously out of line, they were removed. Perhaps 'the problem constables' – especially if they had years of service – were not dealt with as early and as firmly as they could have been. All the same, most constables rarely used excessive force and their superiors seem to have listened to and recorded public complaints. The exceptional case of Constable Piper shows both the potential for serious harm by a constable and the clear recognition by the commission that unstable constables like him had to be dismissed. Piper – who had just finished his probationary term – arrived drunk at the station house in early December 1912. Worse, he waved his gun about. At that point, the men quickly overpowered him and the commission sent him packing a few days later.[93]

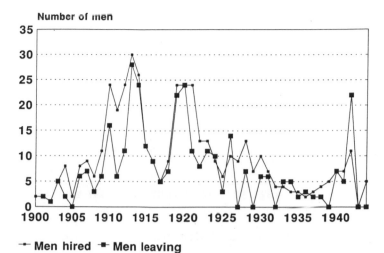

Number of men

-•- Men hired -■- Men leaving

Figure 3.2
Turnover in the Hamilton Police Force, Men Leaving and Hired, 1900–45
Source: HPL, RG 10, Series A, *Annual Reports*; Series E, Personnel Files, 1883–1942.

Besides the job security and the authority that went with the position, some of the attraction of the force may have come from its outward qualities of being apart from the broader community. Male vanity and esteem were served by the uniform and identification with a cadre of mighty physical specimens. After all, the men who joined the force were young. They themselves remarked upon their appearance and uniform, claiming that these made them irresistible to women. Three-quarters of those taken onto the roster from 1900 to 1914 were between twenty-one and twenty-five; twenty-one was the most common age for successful applicants. There was a simple explanation for the age profile. Regulations governing eligibility had lowered the maximum age from forty-eight to thirty sometime around 1880, and in April 1900 the commissioners set a rule fixing the age of applicants at twenty-one to twenty-five.[94] In 1910 they raised it to thirty.[95] Youth was a factor in the high turnover rate in the Hamilton force in the years just before the First World War (Figure 3.2), when the discipline and low pay for probationary constables drove a number of recruits out of the force. Wages rose very gradually except for the substantial increases in the inflationary period just before the war; the salary received by the chief sharply separated him from his men (Figure 3.3).

Whatever the managers of the force sought to create through recruitment standards, codes of conduct, and drills, they had actually assembled a mixed body of material with which to work. The body of personnel was never so uniform and so fully 'apart' from the public as

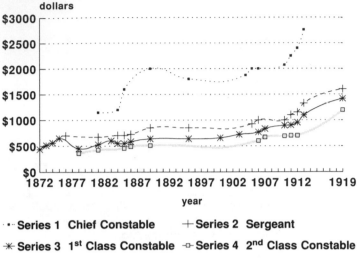

Figure 3.3
Annual Wages for Selected Ranks, 1872–1919
Source: HPL, RG 10, Hamilton Police Commission Minutebooks.

to jeopardize its image as an agency that could serve most citizens. Moreover, the personalities, backgrounds, and expectations of the men who joined was varied; the labour market in the city was often in such a vigorous state that the force found that it could not readily secure and retain good men. Only in the economically troubled 1930s would the department really have an exceptional number of applications in relation to posts (Figure 3.4).

Labour relations or working conditions might have contributed to the departure of many men. What Greg Marquis has observed for the Toronto force in the same period holds true for Hamilton. Many young recruits became dissatisfied with their prospects, rejected the discipline and authoritarianism, or simply could not endure the monotony of the beat.[96] Petitions from Hamilton constables to the board mostly dealt with wages and the benevolent fund.[97] There is evidence of well-organized and vigorous negotiation on the part of the constables in the years between 1905 and 1918. A brief for a wage increase in January 1912 included 'a tabulated account of the scale of wages paid in other cities, including Ottawa, London, and Montreal.'[98] In 1913 there were rumours of 'a threatened desertion from the ranks by the men' over the refusal of the commissioners to raise salaries.[99] The chief later denied that men were 'quitting wholesale.' In the end, no great exodus occurred; only three men resigned.[100]

Resentment flared up on several occasions over the fact that the men

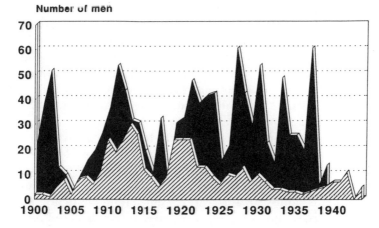

Figure 3.4
Growth of the Hamilton Police Force, 1900–45
Sources: HPL, RG 10, Series E, Personnel Files, 1883–1942; unlisted Series, Application Forms.

paid a greater percentage of their wages into the benevolent fund than did the chief and sergeant-major and that official fees earned for attending coroner's inquests went into the same fund.[101] Attending constables wanted the rewards of extra duty. The work itself led to organized complaints and silent protests. In June 1896 thirty-nine constables – virtually the entire force – protested against the reorganization of beats. They complained about insufficient time 'to thoroughly examine doors, windows, and gratings.'[102] Constable Myers, found guilty of neglect of duty, had absented himself from his beat on the night of 20 August 1905. He stated that 'the reason he did not go over the beat was that he had too many doors to try.'[103] Using 'the closet' – the toilet – provided a common alibi for being absent from the beat.[104]

In December 1909 the members of the force raised a petition for an additional day off duty per month; they had been granted one day off a month at the chief's discretion beginning in 1905. The request was granted three years after its first presentation.[105] Policemen who kept their noses clean were spared layoffs and unemployment; they or their widows received retirement benefits from the benevolent fund. A 1913 inquiry into their living conditions concluded that they had done well by their work, for over half appeared on the assessment rolls as home-owners.[106] However, the work was as physically demanding, as tedious, and as vulnerable to 'speed-up' measures as industrial employment.

In the early twentieth century, Canadian cities swelled with new arrivals. To cope with the mounting demands on existing services, local governments built and hired at great speed. In Hamilton, as branch plants and working-class suburbs mushroomed across the east end, the city simultaneously tried both to modernize and to expand urban services. Unglamourous but essential work extended sewers and strengthened health services. As for the police, hiring became frantic after 1900. Yet much also remained the same.

The force continued to be relatively homogeneous. In terms of its religious cast, it was still overwhelmingly Protestant. Many successful applicants between 1900 and 1914 failed to cite religious denomination, but of those who did 85 per cent claimed to be Protestant. In subsequent eras, almost all applications stated religious denomination. From 1915 to 1918, 90 per cent of the new members were Protestant; from 1919 to 1929, 94 per cent; as late as 1940 to 1945, it was 88 per cent. Of all the Protestant denominations, only Baptists, possibly manifesting their historic distrust of the state, shunned police work.[107]

The religious cast of the department did not go unnoticed at the time. Reviewing the annual report for 1914, the *Spectator* saw evidence of bias. Of the three men hired that year, two had previous experience and the third came 'from the north of Ireland. It was alleged that this was sufficient recommendation for the chief.'[108] Whatever the circumstances in this instance, evidence for bias in hiring is indirect and supported only by a few newspaper innuendoes. The *Times* reporter covering the hiring routine in February 1892 thought it curious that the commission spent so much time sizing up and questioning the men – 'as if they did not know beforehand who was likely to get the job.'[109] Discrimination is difficult to prove, but something was happening, because Roman Catholics accounted for approximately 25 per cent of the city's population during the late nineteenth and early twentieth centuries and they were but 10 per cent or less of the force.[110] A possible explanation may lie in how employment opportunities on the force were made known to the public. The commission advertised for constables in the city's newspapers from the late 1870s on, but a friendly suggestion accompanied by tips about the application procedure was more likely to draw men to the force than an employment notice. Notwithstanding the newspaper advertisements, word that the force would be hiring likely circulated initially through networks of friends and lodge brothers.

In Toronto, the police force had a reputation for being connected with both the Orange and the Masonic lodges.[112] Police magistrate George T. Denison of Toronto remarked that he 'had never been connected with any secret organization of any sort. I was never a free

Mason or Orangeman and consequently have had a free hand in working only for the real benefit of the police administration.'[113] His declaration was true, but it did not apply to many others associated with
the force. In Hamilton, the Masonic connection was important. Chief
Alexander McMenemy, who died in 1880, was a mason.[114] Chief
Smith, whose twenty years as head of the force was certainly long
enough to affect its composition, was not only a prominent Mason but
a Presbyterian from northern Ireland. As a past master of the Acacia
Lodge AF & AM, past principal sojourner of the Knights Templar, and
a member of the Scottish Rite, Smith figured prominently in the city's
network of fraternal connections.[115] Even in the early 1950s, senior
men told recruits that to 'get ahead' they should join the lodge. And
they did.

Yet one should not make too much of the Protestant character of the
force. The 1889 training manual made it clear that members of the
force were not to express offensive political or religious beliefs.[116]
Moreover, the force had much in common with the populace. The city
itself was not only predominantly Protestant but very British. Recent
immigrants to Hamilton had come from England and Scotland by and
large and the police force had a very substantial English and Scottish
contingent from 1900 to 1914. Roughly four out of every ten men
hired in the period were from either England or Scotland. The proportion would fall to three in ten from 1915 to 1930 and tumble thereafter
to about one in ten. At all times, Canadians formed a majority, but the
British minority remained significant.

In the early 1900s, the city took in thousands of Canadians as well as
immigrants; the police force roster followed the undulations of the mi-
grant flow. Fewer than 10 per cent of the new men recruited in the first
fourteen years of the century were born in Hamilton, a proportion that
would rise to 24 per cent in the period from 1919 to 1929 and to 44
per cent during the Great Depression. Yet, in the early 1900s, seven out
of ten recruits resided in the city at the time of their application.
Significantly, one-third of newly hired constables in all time periods
from 1900 to 1945 came from at least thirty miles away from the city.
During these years, the component born overseas would decline, but
because of the large number of constables from elsewhere in Ontario,
there always would be a fair number of men who were not 'homers'. In
some of its cultural and demographic traits, then, the force was ambig-
uously located. It did not perfectly reflect the city; it was not wholly of
the city. Neither could it be said that it intruded as an alien presence.
All things considered, police hiring captured the flavour if not the
exact proportions of Hamilton's labour force.

The trade background and social standing of members of the force actually mirrors the youthfulness of applicants. Young men, twenty-five and under, had little opportunity to have formed a strong attachment to a trade. Consequently, in the dynamic first years of this century, the force may not have embodied the aspirations and values of the city's skilled labour force. The police department, an organization that occasionally was instructed to intercede on behalf of employers, was not predisposed to strong fraternal identification with striking labourers. Here again, however, ambiguities enter the discussion, for policemen appear to have been eager to unionize themselves. In 1918 police unions were formed in London, Ontario, and Saint John, New Brunswick, and the Hamilton Trades and Labour Council enthusiastically welcomed an effort to organize that city's force. During the summer, two-thirds of the men signed and paid dues.[117] Chief Whatley (elevated in 1915), backed by the commission – especially magistrate Jelfs, who maintained that the police provided an essential service – decreed that 'no member of the police force will be allowed to remain on the department if he becomes a member of the Dominion or American Federation of Labor or its branches.'[118] The commission later met demands for higher pay and for a day off each week, and in 1920 it permitted members of the force to form a police association. Over the next several decades, the Hamilton Police Association became less of a labour relations body and more of a social club and community-relations organization that organized dances, picnics, concerts, and Christmas parties. During another 'red scare,' after the Second World War Ontario legislated a ban on police associations affiliating with labour unions.[119]

The extensive hiring completed just before the First World War had implications for the character of the force for many years, because only after the Second World War was there a greater period of expansion. The average of twenty-five new constables hired annually from 1911 to 1914 was double the number taken on during the best year from 1921 to 1945 (Figures 3.2 and 3.4). Since the booming industrial labour market readily absorbed skilled labourers and clerks, the force had to draw heavily upon farm lads and the common labour pool. Over 40 per cent of the new constables (fifty-four men) from 1900 to 1914 came off the farm or considered themselves common labourers (Figure 3.5). Unable to pick and choose as readily as they could at later times, the commissioners accepted about a half of the sons of the soil and a third of the common labourers who submitted applications. The proportion of skilled labourers who joined was at its twentieth-century nadir. When a few clerks applied, they achieved a high success rate. Even at this early stage in bureaucratic growth in policing, the chief and commission sought clerical skills. The first typewriter had been purchased in 1895 and in that same year the commission ordered the chief to maintain a

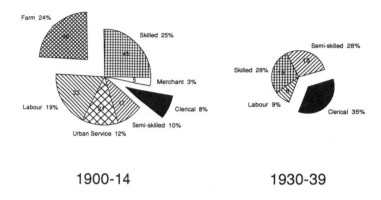

1900-14   1930-39

Pies are in proportion to number hired

Figure 3.5
Background of New Constables, Former Occupations, 1900–45
Sources: HPL, RG 10, Series E, Personnel Files, 1883–1942; unlisted Series, Application Forms.

book for recording reports of incidents by 'telephone or otherwise.'[120] By 1912 the commission had hired a clerk-inspector to manage financial and clerical duties which had grown too large for the police court clerk to handle.[121] Modernization coexisted with inertia, overwork, and backwardness.

More than just large rustic youths donned the blue. More than at any other time, the local force in the early 1900s attracted men with prior police experience. Out of 495 applicants from 1900 to 1914, seventy-five or 15 per cent came with prior police experience and their 40 per cent success rate exceeded that of all other groups of applicants. By far the largest body of former officers applying came from the United Kingdom (fifty) and they surpassed the success rate of any other set of men in getting onto the force. To be more specific, twenty-two former policemen joined the Hamilton department from the turn-of-the-century until the beginning of the war. Two of these men had served with the Royal Irish Constabulary and another with a South African constabulary.

CIVIC ORDER AND SOCIAL SERVICES

A court appearance for theft or assault during the late nineteenth century usually stemmed from a victim's complaint or – to use the proper terminology – an information; moral order offences, in contrast, originated primarily with the police (Table 3.1).

The annual rate of charges laid for moral order offences charts re-

Table 3.1
Source of Complaints to Police Magistrate's Court according to Selected Crimes
and Groups of Crimes, 1859–1918

Crimes	Individuals	Source Police	Company	Other*
All crimes against Persons (n=118)	85.7	14.3 %	0.0 %	0.0 %
All Larceny and Theft (n=155)	72.9	10.3	16.8	0.0
Petty Larceny (n=84)	73.8	10.7	15.5	0.0
All Moral Order (n=593)	19.6	78.0	2.4	0.0
Drunk and Disorderly (n=275)	5.1	94.9	0.0	0.0
Gambling (n=52)	3.8	96.2	0.0	0.0
Violations of Motor Vehicle Act	1.1	98.9	0.0	0.0
All Cases (n=1312)	33.1	60.7	3.2	3.0

* *Truant officers and Dominion Police.*
Source: HPL, RG 10, Series K, Hamilton Police Court Proceedings. A sample of every tenth case
was taken for 1859, 1878, 1898, 1908, and 1918.

lations between the police and an assortment of people: vagrants, drunks, street-walkers, inmates of bawdy houses, found-ins, and gamblers. Many of the accused came from the working poor; however, in the course of the second half of the nineteenth century, fewer and fewer of these people came before the police court. The quality of the city's moral conduct is unlikely to have improved over this period and the police were not necessarily less vigilant. While never abandoning the practice of arresting vagrants and drunks, the local authorities added a more subtle approach to the maintenance of social order.

From the 1840s to the 1860s, the city's judicial records were crammed with citations against vagrants, but the rate of arrests for moral order offences started to fall by the 1870s (Figure 3.1). Some unknown portion of the decline in court appearances for drunk and disorderly conduct and especially for vagrancy and begging came about because the police force undertook to aid the transient homeless and a number of unfortunate alcoholics. This practice originated in the late 1850s or early 1860s; the earliest known reference to police sheltering describes the force helping about 300 persons in 1864. At times, the police shelter and arrests for vagrancy were connected. In hard times, for example, the police discouraged individuals from staying in the police shelter for longer than was thought proper and sent them to jail as vagrants.[122] In some cases, the police sized up the petitioner and packed him off as a vagrant to the police court the next day[123]; in others, eviction from the shelter prompted a request for a stay in the jail.[124] Despite connections with the criminal justice system, the police dormitory was separate from the jail and entry was by request. The Hamilton force continued to furnish lodgings on a temporary basis in the jail cells of the central station and in other stations occasionally, but it also maintained an official shelter.

Police shelters were common throughout North America. In Hamilton, the provision of temporary shelter by the police may simply have been another instance of local government heaping tasks upon a fairly new civic department. Still, the police shelter continued an old municipal practice: the city had maintained crude sheds at the waterfront during the 1830s for ailing immigrants and the local government accepted some responsibility for destitute people. The shelter occupied the upper floor of station number 2, a stone station built in 1856 adjacent to the railway yards.[125] Civic authorities had located this outpost near both the wharves and the railway station in order to monitor the new arrivals. In all of Hamilton's early relief activities, authorities attempted to strike a balance between showing compassion and deterring outsiders from overwhelming the city's relief budget. The practice of having the police department open the doors of station number 2 to the unemployed, transient job seekers, and the needy fit this dual concern. It also placed some transients under supervision.

The shelter's role in keeping an eye on transients was appreciated by many Hamiltonians. Throughout the late nineteenth century and into the twentieth, panics about the supposedly lawless activities of transient young men swept through the city. Anxiety like that which accompanied the canal and railway navvies of the 1840s and 1850s stirred mightily again in 1872–3 and to a lesser degree and for a specific reason during 1909. Fear arose once again during the First World War and the Great Depression.

As an industrial city experiencing bursts of growth and sharp economic downturns, Hamilton often had many single men seeking employment. Early in 1872, however, employers' resistance to the nine-hour day intensified social tension in the city. Concurrent with workers' demonstrations and employers' lockouts, the mayor announced that the authorities would take firm steps to put down rowdyism. By the summer of 1872, labour actions of major dimensions had failed, but bitterness lingered among some of the city's machinists and moulders who were not rehired. For months, alleged ruffians gathered at several places, harassing passersby.[126] The *Spectator* denounced the protesting workers as rowdies, ruffians, disreputable men, worthless vagabonds, and blackguards,[127] and it joined other newspapers in calling on the police and magistrate to deal firmly with men gathering on the streets.

The next burst of hysteria concerning transient men occurred in 1909, when the mysterious murder of Ethel Kinrade – an unidentified tramp was blamed – and the shooting of two policemen investigating a burglary sparked a crusade to round up 'the vags.'[128] The campaign continued into 1910 with plain clothesmen circulating through the city to capture 'professional hoboes.'[129] In the 1920s the 'canned heaters' – men who dissolved their troubles with a swig of Sterno – replaced tramps as the evil of the day and during the 1930s and 1940s the police kept a sharp eye on gypsies. The police chief in 1925 expressed neatly the police perspective on strangers, especially those who were both young and male. 'The permanent residents of Hamilton, generally, are all law abiding, and serious crimes were invariably done by outsiders.'[130] He did not elaborate and he probably had erred. But this exaggeration demonstrated the perceptions that underlay the police's conduct.

Until 1930, the free bed at the police hostel allowed supervision of 'the vags.' Moreover, the ability of the police to determine who might stay an extra night, who was to be ejected, and who would be sent on to the police court insinuated an element of social control into this charitable practice – such as it was. The charity extended by the Hamilton force was modest, rough, and sometimes touching.

At the threshold of the Hamilton hostel, the desk sergeant personified the exercise of social control and worked to prevent 'abuses' of hospitality. On account of the sermons he delivered to his guests, his desk was nicknamed 'the pulpit.'[131] The hostel itself – a loft 12 feet by 16 feet – had a distinctive odour, the origin of which can all too readily be imagined. For many years in the late nineteenth century, the sleeping area – 'the Dormitory' or 'lofty retreat' – consisted of an unsanitary attic with planks for beds.[132] The filthy state of the lodgings annoyed the constables assigned to station work, but it accorded well enough with the civic policy of discouraging 'unproductive people' from lingering in the city at taxpayers' expense. While American historian Eric Monkkonen deserves much credit for unearthing the widespread existence of police shelters, a closer consideration of them may reveal unpleasant abodes with multiple purposes.[133]

The sheltering of large numbers of people was firmly established by the early 1870s. A reporter alleged in late 1874 that the King William Street police station had assumed 'its condition of last fall and winter,' noting, 'a large number of irresponsible, shiftless vagrants, who either have no work to do nor try to obtain it, come night after night to the station for lodging.' Those who came repeatedly in the winter of 1874

– a year that set a local record for numbers sheltered – were threatened with a stay at the central prison.[134]

Over the decades, the numbers sheltered were considerable. In one week in February 1876, 163 nights of lodging were provided to seventy-three applicants, an average of over twenty persons per night.[135] That may have been a record, for even during a cold snap in January 1874 – the busiest year for which there are reports – when the hostel provided lodgings for 476 persons, the average was fourteen per night.[136] From 1 January to 6 April 1878, the number lodged was 1396, or again about fourteen per night.[137]

By the 1880s the occupants had declined to just over one thousand each year. Names were kept in what the police nicknamed 'The Doomsday Book' or 'A History of Wasted Lives.' These records have vanished, but accounts of the occupations of those who sought shelter in the police station have survived. For that record week in February 1876, the *Hamilton Spectator* cited the professions of seventy-three applicants: forty-eight labourers, five iron moulders, three clerks, and the remainder representing assorted trades.[138] A reporter saw the dormitory registers in 1910 and listed occupations for those who had sought shelter between 1892 and 1910: '... phrenologist, embalmer, actor, musician, doctor, steamship captain, papermaker, shoemaker, boiler-makers, blacksmith, servant, vagrant, machinist, tailor, farmer, miner, carpenter, baker, coachman, carriagemaker, carriage-trimmer, cabinet maker, housekeeper, peddlar, painter, plumber, locomotive engineer, locomotive fireman, metal finisher, riveter, shipbuilder, bootblack, newsboy and urchin, soldier.'[139] The same reporter counted up the names from 1 January 1892 to November 1910, arriving at the sum of 24,026 or a mean of more than 1200 per year. Distress, as Judith Fingard has established in a classic study of colonial poverty, soared in the brutal Canadian winter.[140] And so it was that the Hamilton hostel invariably had its busiest months from November to April.

The provision of shelter was distinct from the police magistrate's practice of despatching some of the city's homeless alcoholics to jail for a number of days on vagrancy or drunk and disorderly charges. The magistrate sent a few of these poor people to the jail cells after they appeared in the police court; however, the police sheltered people who came directly to the station and requested aid. In a few cases, the police magistrate also sent people to the lodgings and not to jail cells. Thus, in March 1872, Charles Mason, who could not work due to an injured hand, was sent by the magistrate to the police station 'to be taken care of for 20 days.'[141]

Were the people whom the police aided 'unproductive' unfortunates dependent on by minimal and miserable municipal assistance?

Some were. Dr Alfred Case qualified for this description and was the most frequent lodger. 'Who has not seen the haggard little doctor wandering about the streets with unsteady stride, his old bent cane, worn satchel, and high silk hat?'[142] The fluctuations in the numbers of men and women (about ten men for each woman) who were sheltered appears to have varied with circumstances in the labour market and with seasonal temperatures. The onset of cold weather in November 1877 pushed up the number who applied for lodgings and the reporter covering the story noted that 'many were healthy looking specimens, but declare that they cannot obtain employment. When they are admitted they are hungry, and they ask the policeman on duty for bread.'[143] Sometimes employment opportunities drew transients to the city and to the door of the police station. In early 1876, the dormitory and the cells housed an exceptionally large number of men; they had come to Hamilton looking for jobs on the construction of the waterworks or on the Hamilton and North Western Railway.[144] Other times, a sudden layoff precipitated the arrival of a handful of men from the same trade or locale. On 1 December 1878 thirty men entered the police station. Most hailed from around Collingwood, Ontario, and had laboured as railway navvies on the Hamilton and North Western Railway extension. They suddenly found themselves out of employment. The number of lodgers rose early in boom periods and early in depression years; it declined as depressions wore on, as in the 1890s.

The numbers of people sheltered increased again when the city's industries underwent remarkable expansion in the early 1900s. The police shelter then functioned as a common place of resort for men on the tramp who were drawn to reports of jobs or to those people who were 'down on their luck.' In some cases, that luck had been negligible. A report about the lodgings in 1920 included the pathetic sketch of a recent resident. A seventy-year-old man asked for help. He had lost his job and his savings had been wiped out by the funeral costs for his wife who had died just a week after his layoff. He had been living in farmers' fields and begging food until the cold weather arrived. His daughter in Toronto could not help: 'she had enough to do to look after herself.' As well as sheltering him, the constables brought a sandwich and tea and took up a collection.[145]

On a few occasions, the lodgings provided a refuge for children and whole families in distress. As winter threatened in October 1874, Dora Martin, a half-clad girl was brought to the station by her mother who asked for lodgings overnight. 'A home in the jail has been allotted to her for twenty days.'[146] Ten years later a newspaper reported briefly on the plight of Elizabeth Halliday who with her three children – aged four, six, and nine – spent Saturday night and Sunday at number 3 station. They had no means of support and subsequently were given an order by the mayor for support.[147] Somewhat later in the century, a family of nine German immigrants arrived at the railway station in the midst of a blinding snow storm. They had nowhere to go, no food, and no money. A police constable took them to number 2 station where they were quartered.[148]

The reporter who published the sample of occupations in 1910 also remarked on the character of police treatment of the men and women sheltered: 'If those of the public who are inclined to talk unkindly of the police could see behind the scenes, watching the bluecoats gently assisting the doctor to the lodgers' quarters, doling out the lodgers' free lunch, bread and sometimes giving him money at the break of day when he starts on the tramp.'[149] In sum, many of the men, women, and children who came to the police station do not appear to have been exploiting the city's 'hospitality' or to have been 'unproductive' residents. They were people in need and the police constables may well have had more compassion for them than did the city fathers who scrutinized the annual accounts of the force and constantly deferred improvements to the lodgings. A number of other residents, however, were sized up as suspicious vagrants.

The history of the shelter complicates interpretations of policing. Constables were compassionate and prejudiced, helpful and hectoring. The masters of the force, however, directed shifts in policy, and they surely used the hostel to try to help control male transients and other undesirables. Another important point that needs to be made is that the intervention of the police commission and of city council into the running of the shelter renders its statistics useless as a measure of community distress. When the employment situation in Hamilton deteriorated in the mid-1870s and the shelter was overwhelmed, the city announced that access to the dormitory might be cut back because of its use by 'unsavory people'.[150] Similarly, during the First World War, the police magistrate curtailed lodgings. Men arrested for vagrancy or brought before his court as habitual residents of the attic were given the choice of joining the army or taking 'the winter course at the castle' – hard labour on the rock pile at the county jail.[151] Not surprisingly, in 1918 the police lodged only eighty-four people.

The police engaged in at least one other relief effort. Interestingly, it was specifically directed toward families; in many activities, the police magistrate and the department favoured families and family men over single males. The institutions of law and order presumed that able-bodied but unemployed single men from out of town were shiftless.

During the very hard winter of 1914, when unemployment soared in the city, the police detachment in the east end organized a charitable drive for families. The police relief fund of the Sherman Avenue station raised nearly $600, enough to supply 321 families with some Christmas cheer. Each got five pounds of roast beef, a basket of potatoes, a pound of beans, butter, sugar, and presents and oranges for the children. Baskets and stockings were stuffed in the station poolroom, which the men gave up for charity. The selection of gifts for the boys and girls under eight years tells us something about the obviously conventional cultural values of the force. The boys got books and the girls got dolls.

But the spirit of charity ought not to be too severely assessed; 1604 persons benefitted, 642 adults and 962 children.[152] Moreover, Chief Smith issued instructions in January 1914 that station-duty men were to furnish lodgings to all who sought it. Even after spare cots were filled, the men were to provide shelter. The chief countered criticism that a station would become a 'hangout for hoboes' by claiming that most who pleaded need were deserving.[153] Chief Smith was not predisposed to think harshly of people.

The special shelter service at number 2 station ended in the Great Depression by a combination of accident and design. Canadian National Railways built a new railway station on the site and none of the other police stations had a refuge for transients other than the cells.[154] An order from the deputy police chief in 1932 tried to put an end to the practice of letting some people sleep even behind bars: 'the salvation army will be able to house all transients in future.'[155] In great metropolitan centres in the United States, the police departments had divested themselves of the lodging function much earlier than in Hamilton.[156] Interestingly, the demise of the shelter nearly coincided with the beginning of an upturn in the rate of moral order offences, a rate that had been declining since the mid-nineteenth century.

Aid to the poor – meagre though it was – was not the only social service provided by the Hamilton police: the force also operated an ambulance. During the 1880s the expansion of the city created a problem: suburban residents appealed for police protection and yet lived in areas with population densities that did not justify a patrol. The commission debated in 1884 whether to have a few mounted constables who could dash to the suburbs or whether to employ a wagon. Not surprisingly, the arguments centred on efficiency and cited American examples. Judge Sinclair advocated mounted men and recommended that Chief Stewart write 'to say New York, Chicago, Boston, and Buffalo.' The chief successfully argued that a wagon – used in Chicago – provided a swift response and saved wear on the horses. He may have been correct, for 'Barney,' one of several police horses, put in twenty-five years of service before being replaced by an automobile in 1913.[157]

Yet an even more compelling argument favouring the wagon was that, according to Stewart, the wagon could deal with suburban crime 'and more too.' The chief 'dwelt at length upon the varied uses that a wagon could be put to,'[158] noting, for example, that it could double as an ambulance. This struck a responsive chord among economy-minded city councillors, and the patrol wagon-cum-ambulance began operation.[159] In 1909 alone the wagon made 6684 trips.[160] Chiefs from Winnipeg and London observed the Hamilton system in the fall of 1884, thereby illustrating the diffusion of ideas among the North American urban governments.[161] Not all of them selected identical resolutions to common problems, but they certainly evaluated practices with little regard to the border. In 1943, the force eliminated its ambulance service.

UNDER THE BATON OF A MARTINET

Normally, the Hamilton police responded without enthusiasm to the outcries of moral reformers and seldom orchestrated crusades on their own. However, when the commissioners went outside the force and the city to hire William Whatley as deputy chief in October 1910, a new era dawned. More and more, the police would now lead the offensive against crime and moral disorder.

In any police force, the hiring of a senior officer from outside heralds a campaign for greater discipline.[162] The chief in 1910, prominent mason Alexander Smith, had held that office for fifteen years and had been on the roster for thirty-eight years. Described as a good man in his own way, the chief had little drive, had not lived up to the expectations of the moral reformers, and had allowed discipline to falter. There is also a possibility that Smith's fraternal-order connections had encouraged the spread of a dry rot of favouritism and leniency. 'I think,' said the mayor to his fellow commissioners, 'it is wise to get a man for that position [deputy chief] who has no personal feelings in connection with the force.'[163]

In settling on Whatley as the new deputy chief, the city and police commission choose the ideal person to shake up the force. Physically, Whatley met the era's requirements for police leadership: square-jaw, moustache, and a six-foot three-inch frame. Some enthusiastic estimates added three more inches. That Whatley looked every inch – however many that was – a policeman was confirmed by police magistrate Jelfs in a 1924 tribute: Whatley was 'a man in every sense of the word.'[164] Born in Somersetshire, England, this Lord Kitchener look-alike had served in the Boer War, stayed on with the Cape Mounted Police, and eventually accumulated seven years experience with South

African constabularies.[165] His boast that someone from his clan had been in military service since 1727 may explain his public deportment. He enjoyed parading solo about the city, brandishing an ebony cane with silver handle.[166] Whatley was to the force in the 1910s what Stewart had been to it in the 1880s: a military dandy as well as a tough and active leader who stuck his neck out and made enemies quickly.[167] But he lacked Stewart's panache and generosity of spirit. Whatley's public displays of moral zeal bordered on the ludicrous.

The hiring of Whatley put a bit of starch into Smith who now decided – with about as much resolve as the affable veteran could muster – that 'it is almost time the force was cleared of tipplers.'[168] Demerits rose accordingly. But it is what Whatley did in the city – not to the men at the station houses and on beats – that showed how an outsider could upset relations between the force and the community. One misadventure occurred only weeks after joining the force. Whatley introduced a rigorously enforced 'move along' campaign that called for constables to disperse clusters of people on major streets. Citizens were dumbfounded. When he had cards printed so that he and his men did not have to repeat themselves to astonished citizens, people initially thought that the police were distributing advertisements.[169] The strain on the police, mused a reporter from the *Times* who may well have been tipped off by an outraged constable, was dreadful: "The stony stare, the indignant look, the muttered words of rebellion, and the sarcastic shrug of the shoulders must be aggravating. That job would make anybody a drivelling idiot inside of a week.'[170] The campaign died. In the meantime, Whatley managed to grab more favourable headlines.

Raids on gambling joints and houses of ill fame, with Whatley at the head of a specially selected squad, earned praise and front-page photos. After descending upon the Central Athletic Club where he rounded up thirty-seven men for playing craps, this militant newcomer had his men take down the names of flashily attired winking maids who walked 'the pike' – as King and James streets were called. Constables also kept a watch out for country girls stepping off the radial street cars and corrupting city lads.[171] Whatley ordered constables to disturb men and women sitting intimately on park benches and – in some instances – constables escorted the women home. This did not sit well with all parents, for some accepted or even encouraged the idea of courting in parks, given the lack of privacy at home.[172]

Among his controversial pronouncements, the aggressive deputy insisted on enforcement of an anti-spitting bylaw and the proper licensing of dance halls.[173] He had the audacity to suggest that merchants who left doors unlocked would be fined.[174] An overbearing man who revelled in the power of his office and the boom of his voice, Whatley could not resist ordering civilians. At a public event in 1913, he could be heard shouting from his seat: 'Sit down'; 'Stand back.' When a crush occurred at the exit, the deputy chief sounded off: 'you will reach that gate without scrambling in a few minutes. You women are only making yourselves and others hot and uncomfortable and are doing no good.'[175] Ever the martinet, Whatley both introduced revolver practice in 1912 and, as noted earlier, ordered the breaking up of socialist meeting in 1914.[176] Elevated to chief after Smith's death in 1915, Whatley continued to pursue a strict regime and busied himself with the details of moral order. (Figure 3.1) Reviving police interest in the city's population of Chinese origin, in November 1920 he instructed all members of the department to report to him forthwith if they knew of any 'white girl being employed in a Laundry, or Restaurant etc. owned or controlled by a Chinaman.'[177] Constables exacted a measure of vengeance against their chief after he had commanded them to get tough with by-law violations. When citizens groused, some constables told them to call the chief if they had a complaint. They did. Whatley was not amused.[178]

With Smith and Whatley, extremes in administrative styles of law and order stand out clearly and, because of this perfect contrast, it is possible to reflect upon the role of police leadership and upon alternate concepts about policing. Smith, the aging lodge brother, adopted the view that a chief should cultivate ties of personal loyalty with his men, tolerating their imperfections and coaxing them through their tedious chores. He himself was only too familiar with these chores, having worked his way up through the ranks. As well, as a chief constable, Smith appreciated the social and political composition of the city and felt that firm action to meet the demands of interest groups for the suppression of this or that vice would horrify a good many other citizens. In short, Smith apparently assumed that a chief could do little to reform a society but a lot to disturb it. His instructions to the men during Hamilton's centennial celebrations in 1913 summarize his philosophy. 'Let them [people celebrating] have a good time so long as they do not injure any person or destroy property. Do not arrest any person unless it is absolutely necessary to do so. We have done well so far.'[179]

Whatley, in contrast, assumed that a chief had to act assertively and that his men had a mission to impose order on the city. The law was the law. Its instrument – the police – had to enforce its very letter and then some. An apologist for his conduct might see in him the police officer as the detached crime fighter. If that is what he was, then he exemplifies the flaw in this strategy of policing: he jeopardized local respect by acting like a coercive agent of an outside power. Perhaps Whatley was misled by his experience in South Africa, for his approach to policing seemed influenced by an alien sense of the city. He failed to appreciate that he was not occupying it for King and Country, not holding it for the rule of law against rebellion. Because the 1856 police bill had been defeated, he was merely a municipal servant.

Neither Smith nor Whatley would have understood today's concerns about minority rights, although Smith at least had the sense to realize what his city would accept as appropriate police behaviour. Smith may have developed this sensitivity by muddling together lodge, force, and city. Whatley, for his part, confused an imperial mission with policing, the force with the city, and he sought to discipline both the men under his command and the community they served.

SINNERS ON THE BEAT

The force itself had no single identity; Whatley certainly did not epitomize it. Some constables were detached from the city and may have felt comfortable imposing the rule of the law; others, from the tarnished character of their records, had a more flexible attitude. The blend of experienced men and raw recruits must have made for interesting banter. Of course, we know next to nothing about the conversations that would have enlivened the tedium of the beat or night-desk duty. Yet some of these conversations were surely not pleasant, for insubordination was a common internal charge. In this regard, Greg Marquis is right to call attention to 'the rough culture of the station house.'[180] In November 1912, for example, the commission suspended Constable Coombs thirty days for assaulting Constable Wallace on duty.[181]

It must have been difficult to maintain a sense of order and discipline when the physically similar men in the uniforms were not the same from year to year. The hiring of youths on the margins of a strong labour market led to the employment of many who soon left. The turnover rate among new constables from 1900 to 1913 was over 40 per cent (66 out of 146). The average length of service for those who left during these years was twenty months; if four long-term constables are removed from the group, the mean length of service for those leaving falls to seventeen months. A similar volatility affected the Toronto force during the same years.[182] Nearly half of those who departed (twenty-nine out of sixty-six) from the Hamilton force did so in official disgrace. They were let go because they failed to set an example, not because they had done any injury to the public.

From the 1880s onwards – that is, beginning with Chief Stewart – the department maintained two default books. One of these ledgers, the departmental default book, recorded offences of a more serious nature: insubordination and drinking on duty were prominent. The divisional ledger listed minor charges such as sleeping on duty and gossiping. The commission had to hear and confirm a complaint before the black mark was entered into either ledger. A default could result in a fine, the loss of merit points, and dismissal. Defaults expressed human frailty, but also the boredom of tedious work and the desire of men to fraternize at work. The default books and actions against constables reported in the police commission minute-books confirm important observations made by Greg Marquis. 'It was the very working-class origins of the police and the roughness of their culture that disturbed, and continues to disturb, liberal critics and police reformers.'[183] Further, while entries in the default books and minute-books add little to the picture of police misconduct assembled from the newspapers in the 1870s or 1880s, they do underline the frequency of that misconduct. Above all, however, some of the incidents are worth recounting simply because they vividly affirm the roughness of the culture and the way the men tried to shape their work in spite of regulations.

The men listed in the default books had been found guilty of loitering, appearing drunk on duty, entering saloons or houses of ill fame in uniform,[184] habitual gossiping on the beat, and insubordination. Constable Sharp found a way of relieving the boredom of walking the beat on the night of 28 October 1909. Patrolling the city 'accompanied by a girl,' however, was not believed to be in the public interest.[185] The chief in 1913 vowed to put a stop 'to the flirtations which some of the constables carry on.'[186] Constable Springer dealt with the ennui of Sunday duty by playing cards in a boathouse.[187] Exhausted and unlucky, Constable Merritt was heard 'snoring in a privy' away from his beat. He was dismissed.[188]

Often the chief and the commission dealt with seasoned constables who committed transgressions by imposing fines and issuing warnings. In November 1900 Constable John Clark confessed to the board 'that he was while on duty slightly under the influence of liquor.' His good record saved him.[189] When Sergeant Vanotter brought charges of insubordination against constables Gibbs and Tuck, the board found them guilty. However, 'in consideration of the circumstances under which the offence occurred and the good character of the men,' they were let go with a reprimand.[190]

Popular constables sometimes garnered public support. Newcomers were less likely to have had patrons; the chief and the commission seem to have culled out promptly what they might have referred to as 'the bad apples' from the barrel of novices. The commission also upheld the dismissal of several new men for poor health, including one young man committed to the 'insane asylum.'[191] Another 40 per cent of those leaving (twenty-six out of sixty-six) resigned, although the personnel records suggest that many had been invited to do so. The rest of those who left had deserted.

DRUDGERY ON THE BEAT

Despite changes in leadership, the basic core of police routines remained the same under Whatley as under Smith. The pedestrian beat endured – as it had to – as the centrepiece of policing. On the eve of the Second World War, the men were concentrated on night patrols. Of the four squads, three worked after dark. One squad took the daytime shift from 7:00 a.m. to 2:30 p.m., the second took over at 2:30 and remained out until 10:45 p.m. It was joined by the third squad at 6:50 p.m. and that party of constables patrolled until 4:00 a.m. The fourth came on at 10:50 p.m. and was relieved by the first squad at 7:00. Half the force worked through the night and everyone was on call. The fortunate first squad, though relieved of night duty, had to take drill under Whatley on Friday afternoons. The men were rotated through the squads once a month.[192] Probationers drew night duty for the first six months.[193] Little wonder that a few were caught catnapping! Until they protested in 1910, they received only one day off every two months and sometimes were denied that; by 1913 they had succeeded in forcing the commission to grant one day off every other week.[194]

The extraordinary expansion of the factory district and of the working-class blocks in the city's east end forced the department in 1910 to send out several men to walk around these areas.[195] Strapped for constables, the chief tried the expedient of night patrols by bicycles in new suburbs.[196] The old beats that radiated out from the city centre no longer served the entire city. The opening in late 1911 of an east-end station on Sherman Avenue in the heart of the immigrant district technically solved the problems posed by annexation, but no non-Anglo-Celtics were on the force. The two senior men in charge of the station had little understanding of the culture of eastern and southern European immigrants. Sergeant Bainbridge had joined the Hamilton force in 1881 and had experience with the County Durham Constabulary in England. The head of the detachment was none other than Inspector of Detectives Coulter, who had visited a house of ill fame just a few months after coming onto the force in 1878. Coulter proved to be a humane officer who worked at achieving good relations with the community.

Work on the beat itself had not changed substantially between the 1880s and 1914. A Toronto reporter looking at the Hamilton force in

1913, in order to support its appeals for higher pay and challenge the claims of the commissioners that a constable was better off than a labourer, stressed the rigours of the beat. The constable patrols 'his beat, walking over the same territory like a veritable machine, stopping only to ring in at the signal box at stated periods, speaking to no one except to give information.' Of course, the constables were expected to suppress 'all natural inclinations.' Night work was nerve-racking and constables sometimes saw things 'which are most repugnant to the senses and which would turn the ordinary man sick.'[197] The description gave a highly favourable impression of the special qualities needed for police work. It also ignored what routinely happened to the men on duty. The constables, felt one reporter, 'held many titles.' 'Besides being a city directory, he is a timekeeper, and a timetable; and a general information bureau. He is also a weatherman, and a butt of long cracked nuts that wouldn't make a hyena laugh; a lady's escort, and a horse catcher, incidently being a policeman.'[198]

But some changes had occurred in the way policing was conducted. There was greater attention paid now to paperwork; the constables had to make out monthly reports on arrests and summonses. As well, all probationary constables had to take a first-aid course. The introduction of firearms compelled the force to conduct instruction in firearms and about 'the way to handle a man with a gun or rifle.'[199] Technology also affected work. The call box and telephone became more prominent instruments of policing. The former was being used both to report in and to call for 'the hoodler' – the local moniker for the paddy wagon. A late-nineteenth-century signal system combined the telephone and call box. A light on the box told the constable to call in; otherwise he merely pulled a lever which sent an electronic impulse back to the main station where his progress around the beat was recorded on a paper tape. The system did not always function properly. In the summer of 1911, call boxes jolted nearly all the constables with electricity; one of them, Constable Wallace, arrested a drunk, went to the call box, inserted the key, and was thrown against a nearby tree suffering burns to his hands.[200] The availability of technological aids – and underlying these the demands for efficiency – had 'industrialized' police work.

As far as the police were concerned, the most important technological innovation was the automobile. It eventually took many constables off the beat and distanced them from the neighbourhoods they patrolled; it also vastly increased their workload. Starting in May 1910, the chief recognized the dangers posed to citizens by the 'street burners.' Interestingly, the three owners singled out as serious offenders who deserved substantial fines for speeding were members of the city élite: tobacco manufacturer George C. Tuckett, Dr Leeming Carr, and

Joseph Levy.[201] As the authors of a previously cited study on Alameda County, California, remark, traffic violations were the one aspect of 'law enforcement that fell more heavily on the wealthier classes' because only the well-to-do owned cars.[202] That trend changed as the ownership of cars became more widespread. By the end of the Second World War, motor vehicle violations approached one thousand per year. What is more, the powers conferred on the police to deal with traffic represented the greatest increase in their power to lay charges since the creation of the force.

Data on the sources of complaints heard at the police magistrate's court, besides reaffirming the persistence of the old-regime's common law practices as citizens laid formal complaints for traditional offences, register the impact of moral order crusades and motor vehicle regulations in advancing the authority of the police (Table 3.1). By the fall of 1912, the commission had discussed the need to purchase motorcycles and automobiles to pursue speeding drivers.[203] Meanwhile, the sheer increase in the volume of traffic of all kinds compelled the chief to separate traffic direction from beat work; a new squad dealing purely with traffic was formed.[204] Policing was poised to embark on a struggle for order and safety, one that grew naturally out of its historical civic functions but that concurrently minimized the beat, thus weakening the vital link between city and police.

In the twentieth century, the police had to retain the ability to take charge of a situation while keeping abreast of by-laws, statutes, and court procedures. Their range of tasks and rules grew, and failure to adhere to the latter eventually led to reprimands from the bench. From the 1880s through to the 1920s, considerable effort had been put into professionalising the police force. But what Wilbur Miller has concluded about the New York cop in the mid-nineteenth century applies also to the Hamilton constable. 'The policeman was more a man than an institution.'[205]

4 Forced Liberalization and Technological Enthusiasms

On 7 March 1947 a substantial crowd braved late-winter winds and collected around the courthouse, a Second Empire structure completed in 1879 – the third incarnation for a Wentworth County courthouse. The curious had come to hear the verdict in a new trial ordered by the Ontario Court of Appeal. The trials of Evelyn Dick – the original, the appeal hearing, and the new trial – comprised a three-act drama and the most sensational criminal case ever witnessed in Hamilton. Arguably, it was the most sensational Canadian trial of the mid-century. Reporters arrived from across Canada and the United States.

The contrast between Dick's trials and those of Michael Vincent and Michael McConnell are plentiful. Most obviously, the trials of Evelyn Dick were time-consuming: the first trial alone took nine days; it included sixty hours of testimony or half a million words and 100 exhibits.[1] The Dick trials also had a long-term importance that both the Vincent and McConnell trials lacked. Unfortunately, sensationalistic coverage of the case deflected attention from rulings that affected the conduct of Canadian police investigations and emphatically confirmed important rights of suspects. Grisly details, the expressions and dress of witnesses and especially the accused, and even the courtroom ritual were reported at length in newspapers across the continent.

Everything about the Dick case was outrageous, and unpredictable, but it is possible to penetrate the fantastic story and discover general points about the criminal justice system and more common crimes. One obvious feature of the courtroom spectacles that centred on Mrs Dick was that they exuded tradition, something that the superior court judges and county officials believed important. In this respect, the Dick trials were typical rather than exceptional.

At the Dick trial as at all assizes in twentieth-century Hamilton, the sheriff appeared in a cocked hat and, bearing his drawn sword, escorted the judge to the carved walnut dias surmounted by a royal coat of arms.[2] The judge sat on one of the two chairs; the other – slightly behind him and empty – was reserved for the king or his representative. The procession and the dias affirmed that an assize concerned matters of life and death, and that its authority flowed from the sanction of local government, the criminal law-giving monopoly of a central state, the sovereignty of the crown, and historical practice.

Nowhere else in the modern Hamilton had tradition persisted as it did at the courthouse. The court crier still declared 'oyez, oyez, oyez! All persons having anything to do before my lord, the King's justice, draw near.'[3] On those rare occasions when either the assize or the county general sessions of the peace had no criminal cases, the sheriff presented the judge with white gloves to signify a clean calendar.[4] In addition to tradition, decorum prevailed and women had their heads covered with a hat or scarf.[5] A judge at the fall assize in 1926 had to remind the women present to cover their heads, 'the same rule prevailing in courts as had for centuries prevailed in church.'[6] While much about the conduct of criminal justice in the lower two levels of courts had succumbed to significant change in the mid-nineteenth century, the assize retained trappings from the old regime. Judges assumed postures that reminded spectators of the chasm separating the assize from the police magistrate's court. The latter processed a parade of the petty and profane; the former remained the theatre of far more serious matters.

After five hours, the crowd assembled on 7 March 1947 got its reward. The jury found Evelyn Dick not guilty of murdering her husband. Had she been found guilty, the crime would have been extraordinary. Domestic homicides almost invariably involved males killing females. Had she been sentenced to hang, the punishment would have stirred up a controversy about hanging women. In the orderly fashion of a Canadian courtroom at mid-century, reactions to the verdict were respectful and muted, devoid of emotional outbursts. 'Well, that's that. The jury has spoken,' sighed the special crown prosecutor who had assisted the local crown attorney.[7]

At the words 'not guilty,' the accused cupped her hand over her mouth to suppress a smile, but a few minutes later, free of the courtroom, she leapt up and hugged one of the guards in the prisoner's room. As she left the courthouse, flash bulbs popped everywhere. A taxi whisked her back to the county jail; she faced an additional charge. Officers searching her house for clues to John's disappearance discovered the body of an infant – John and Evelyn's son – packed in cement and stuffed into a satchel. Charged with manslaughter, the stylishly attired courtesan who claimed to have slept with 150 men, including the police magistrate's son and several lawyers, would eventually be sentenced to life imprisonment for this crime.

The trail of events that had brought Evelyn Dick to court began a year earlier, 6 March to be exact, when John Dick vanished. At 10:00 on Saturday morning, 16 March, five children hiking along the slope of Hamilton mountain discovered his torso. The oldest boy ran up to a road and hailed a passing car. Within a few hours, the authorities had initiated an investigation. The coroner ordered a post-mortem and the police checked the missing persons files. On the following Monday, the county crown attorney contacted the Ontario Provincial Police and requested that an inspector with the criminal investigation branch take charge of the inquiry; the municipal character of policing had its limits in an era when criminal detection seemed to demand special skills.

The crown attorney's central role in initiating a thorough investigation captures well his stature in the local, criminal justice machinery. From its beginnings in the mid-nineteenth century, the crown attorney's role in criminal justice proceedings remained peculiar and powerful. Among the courthouse establishment, it was improper to profess that the crown attorney laboured in the mills of justice as a mere prosecutor. Judges, crown attorneys, and the attorney general of the province all maintained that the crown attorney did not seek to convict people but only to assemble facts and place them before the courts, especially before the jury. In his charge to the jury, the trial judge in the Dick case had said 'the purpose of the Crown is not to seek the conviction of any person, or to seek an acquittal. The purpose of the Crown is to function as fairly as possible and as impartially as possible so that you may form a conclusion based on the facts.'[8] Months later, the attorney general of Ontario, still smarting under the defeat in the Dick case, stated with reference to that setback that the crown never wins or loses cases.[9] Yet, in fact, the crown – truly the state – had tried very hard to win. The new trial had provoked the attorney general to send two attorneys to join a prosecution team that included the county crown attorney.[10] Although not a factor in the Dick case, the crown's tactics remain a matter of concern to this day. The crown sometimes has felt, for example, that it has no obligation to disclose all evidence to the defence. Surprise witnesses and evidence that could help the defence have occasionally been kept back. This issue of 'discovery' adds to arguments that the crown functions as a prosecutorial authority, as was the government's intent when it created the office of crown attorney in 1857.

Declaration at the time of the Dick trials concerning the neutrality of the crown glossed over the adversarial process in a criminal trial and painted the crown's prosecutorial role as neutral and benign. More than that, the mythology concerning the office of crown attorney betrayed a feeling of superiority on the part of the state. The crown attorney's office by its very name invoked the historic concept of the just ruler, of the bond between the people and the crown. In most Canadian provinces at mid-century, loyalty to the crown was widespread and, in some circles, passionate. In Ontario, where historical mythology had insisted for decades on the idea of loyalist origins and a rejection of republicanism, the crown was thoroughly integrated into the symbolism of the political and judicial systems. This was emphatically true in Hamilton. Wentworth County crown attorney S.F. Washington, active early in this century, adopted a crown that radiated shafts of light as a device on his stationery.[11] An Ontario crown attorney had the best of all judicial worlds: the legitimacy of a powerful label appropriated from the old regime, the investigative backing of the modern state, and the myth that the crown could not lose a case because it merely presented facts.

Prior to the Dick case, the notion of crown superiority had not been seriously challenged in Hamilton. The police department, the crown attorney, and the police magistrate, in frequent contact, shared assumptions so perfectly that they could convey them without even benefit of a wink or nudge. For example, the police first held Evelyn Dick on a spurious vagrancy charge, an all-too-common practice in Hamilton that was malicious in law.[12] When she came before the police magistrate on this charge, he denied bail, averring dryly that 'there may be a lot behind this vagrancy count.'[13]

Time and again, the Hamilton authorities had used the nominal vagrancy charge to hold someone until a more serious charge could be laid.[14] In later years, they would employ – more tentatively to be sure – a convenience charge of drunk and disorderly conduct.[15] On the occasion of taking Evelyn Dick to the station, the police and the crown attorney happily used the delay afforded by the vagrancy dodge to pry statements out of the none-too-bright accused before the crown attorney actually charged her with murder. Four days after the initial appearance before the magistrate, the crown attorney and Evelyn Dick returned to the magistrate's court and the crown introduced the murder charge. The police magistrate, helping the crown attorney along, reminded him that the vagrancy charge was no longer necessary. 'Do you wish to *nolle prosse* the charge?' The crown attorney replied in the affirmative.

In the Dick case, the crown attorney walked a fine line between collecting the facts and finessing the process to achieve a successful prosecution. Yet the police strayed perilously and improperly over another line, that separating the authority of the law and the rights of an accused person. Indeed, behind the spectacle of the trial and the gruesome findings that had precipitated it, the Dick case disclosed a tale of arrogance and error in the criminal justice system. But when the case had concluded, it showed how this same system which could be abused could also be redeemed. Concurrent with the strengthening of the repressive potential of the modern state, the judiciary and the bar had started to work out principles of conduct to restrain state agents in the future.

CRIMINAL INTERROGATION, INDICTMENT, AND PROTECTION OF THE ACCUSED

Despite the summoning of an OPP inspector and the occasional use of forensic laboratories in Toronto, the investigation turned up no physical evidence to connect Evelyn Dick directly with the act of murder. The entire case rested on statements that she had given to the police.

Throughout the world at this time, statements remained an essential part of police investigations. It could not be otherwise. 'Despite modern advances in the technology of crime detection,' wrote Felix Frankfurter, 'offenses frequently occur about which things cannot be made to speak.'[16] Discerning the truth of statements has perplexed judicial officials from the middle ages to the present. Whereas medieval criminal justice systems had recourse to oath-taking and trials by ordeal, and early modern systems in Europe used threats of torture, torture, and examinations of witnesses by skilled judges, the twentieth-century approach in common law societies involves inquiry and debate led by lawyers with either a judge alone or a judge and jury determining the truth.

In her statements, Evelyn Dick concocted fantasies about gangs cruising the city in autos, seeking to kill her husband. She related yarns about angry husbands whose wives had allegedly been seduced by the late Mr Dick, who, contrary to these tall tales, seemed to have been a decent fellow. Statements by the accused caught her in contradictions and also helped to assure that the jury would try her for wickedness rather than on the charge of murder.[17] Hamiltonians clucked their tongues about shameful Evelyn but voiced little disapproval about the grey-haired gents who had decked her out in elegant clothes and fur coats. Reputation persisted as a factor in criminal justice proceedings in all three layers of courts during the nineteenth century and most of the twentieth. However, in the instances of serious crimes, the trend of the twentieth century inclined toward a more strict trial of the charge, a more complete application of judicial principles. There had been progress. But Evelyn's reputation clouded the trial.

Not only did Evelyn Dick make bizarre and contradictory statements, but the city police obtained them in cunning ways that jeopardized their admissibility.[18] As one authority wrote some years later, it is in the hours when the police have a suspect to themselves that 'their role subtly alters from agent of the law to that of embryo judge. Without using physical force they can cajole, insinuate, bluff, threaten, exhaust and perhaps most effectively of all, suddenly turn friendly.'[19] He may well have had the Dick case in mind. The Hamilton police manipulated Dick with a show of friendship. A police sergeant who knew Evelyn and whom she trusted took her for a ride to places she had mentioned in an earlier statement, her fourth. He failed to mention that anything she might say on the drive could be used against her. In fairness to police administrators, it must be said that in 1932 the chief had ordered that prisoners were to be informed that they did not have to say anything.[20] How well the force subscribed to the rule is another question.

The taking of statements by the Hamilton police had already occasioned remonstrances from the bench. In 1935 Justice Nicholas Jeffrey warned the police that, if statements by an accused were to be submitted in court, they had to be verbatim. The best way to achieve authenticity, he pointedly advised, was to use a shorthand reporter and take down every word.[21] Yet, while the courts had made it quite clear that the police had to proceed very carefully when taking statements, not all judges agreed on what precisely constituted a valid statement.

Over a decade after Jeffrey's sharp judicial warning, Evelyn Dick's friend on the police force noted her comments in the course of their drive. She said a great deal but, at the end of the outing, refused to sign a statement based on her comments. Thus, she believed that her remarks in the car could not be used against her. In a *voir dire* – a hearing conducted by the judge without the jury to determine the admissibility of evidence – the trial judge made a dubious decision to allow the statements from the officer who had taken her on the ride. There was a further police transgression. When Mrs Dick sat down to make corrections to her initial statement, the same friendly sergeant who had taken her for a ride saw her lawyer entering the station. 'I stalled him off until she had signed it,' he testified at the first trial.[22] In fact, the officer lied to the attorney and told him that Evelyn was talking to her mother on the telephone.[23]

Justice in the English tradition had evolved differently from that in continental Europe. Historically, English courts had viewed confessions by suspects with suspicion, believing they were unreliable. On the continent, however, confessions had once been considered the only true proof, a stance that for centuries encouraged the use of threats of torture or even torture itself to extract admissions of guilt.[24] In the Dick case, the Hamilton police had not obtained statements by 'third degree' methods. No, they had been friendly to a fault. Yet, having used trust to secure amendments to a statement, an officer denied Dick's lawyer immediate access. It proved a costly error in judgment, and, of course, was a blatant violation of the suspect's rights. Understandably, then, the Dick case was long cited as an example of outrageous police conduct.[25] Evelyn Dick had been arrested without a warrant and taken to the police station with no charge against her. Later, having been charged with vagrancy, she made statements while her lawyer was kept from her. In fact, one of the investigating detectives lied to her lawyer,[26] stating that Evelyn could not speak to him at the moment as she was talking to her mother by telephone. In fact, the police were attempting to get her to sign a statement.

A recent study has offered this critique of police interrogation practices: 'Historically, Canadian interrogation law has suffered from a number of key weaknesses. By failing to require police to inform suspects of their right to refuse to speak to them, allowing the use of tricks, lies and psychologically coercive interrogation techniques ... the law failed to protect adequately the fundamental right of an individual to remain silent.'[27] It is difficult to prove or disprove the validity of this strong assertion. The Dick case definitely supports it, but a number of surviving statements indicate police caution and adherence to rules in serious cases. As early as 1920, for instance, murder suspect Giovanni Maranga concluded his statement to the police by declaring 'I make this statement after being warned in the usual way by Mr Taylor [the police translator].'[28]

A more complete and proper phrasing appeared in some later statements. A Polish immigrant who shot one of his tenants in 1924 gave a statement through an interpreter with a stenographer recording the interview. The deputy police chief began: 'Tell him he may be charged with murder. Tell him he is not obliged to say anything but whatever he does say will be taken down and used against him at his trial. Ask him if he understands what we are saying?' The suspect signed a declaration – which soon became a stock feature of statements by accused persons – that he had made his statement 'without fear or favor or promise of any kind and after being duly warned in the presence of the interpreter and of my own free will and accord.'[29] This evidence, combined with Jeffrey's 1932 order, reinforce the notion that the Hamilton police knew about and often honoured the strict requirements for a statement. From time to time, however, detectives thought that they could escape scrutiny.

The case against Evelyn Dick was first presented in a very lengthy preliminary hearing before a magistrate, who then prepared the indictment against her. Magistrates had become the essential agents in preparing indictments. Increasingly through the nineteenth century, governments had concentrated the indictment process in the hands of the police magistrate; reforms marginalized justices of the peace and the coroner without eliminating them.[30] The next step was taken with the Canadian Criminal Code of 1892, which eliminated indictment by a coroner's jury – the proceeding that had begun Michael Vincent's walk to the gallows in 1828. Henceforth, at the end of an inquest, after the coroner had summarized the evidence, the coroner's jury might still assign culpability. However, if the decision of that jury indicated homicide, the coroner would deliver the suspect to a preliminary hearing before the police magistrate. No one could be tried upon the results of a coroner's inquest without a preliminary hearing. In practice, by the mid-twentieth century, the coroner acted in consultation with the crown attorney and the police. The crown attorney, working with the police, would either direct the coroner to hold an inquest or actually determine that an inquest would be redundant because there would be an arrest and a trial.

A 1939 case illustrates how far the coroner's inquest had fallen as a central and autonomous institution in the criminal justice system. A boy had been killed by a stone thrown by another youngster. The crown attorney ordered an inquest, which ended soon after it began. 'In view of the fact that the boy who threw the stone was later placed under arrest, the Coroner's Investigation was terminated forthwith.'[31] Step by step, the crown attorney had replaced the amateur officials who made the crucial decisions about indictment in the old regime. Barristers and the law had edged aside the community. Relegated to an ancillary position, the coroner's jury still performed useful service to the community. In the auto age, this jury brought to the attention of civic and provincial authorities measures that could save lives. During the 1930s, 1940s, and 1950s – peak years for auto carnage – coroner's juries proposed reductions to speed limits along certain roads, street lights at intersections, and a ban on parking near schools.[32] As in the nineteenth century, they made recommendations for industrial safety.[33]

As for the office of police magistrate, it also experienced significant changes in the twentieth century. Because of some public confusion that associated the office with the police department – in truth a tellingly accurate mistake – the province shortened its title to just magistrate in 1934. The responsibilities of the office also changed; indeed, in terms of the preparation of indictments, magistrates had more authority than ever before. Nevertheless, the lowest court was still the poor stepchild of the justice system when a 1959 editorial in the *Criminal Law Quarterly* complained about miserable facilities across the province.[34] A significant boost to its status occurred in 1968–70, when Ontario's magistrates' courts became provincial courts presided over by provincial court judges.[35]

After Hamilton's magistrate prepared an indictment against Evelyn Dick, the case proceeded to trial at the assize. At the assize – and also for the general sessions of the peace – the sheriff drew grand jurors and a pool of trial jurors by lot. The grand jury quickly found a true bill in the case of the crown versus Evelyn Dick. The crown and the defence attorney reviewed potential jurors until twelve men had been selected. Evelyn's mother testified for the crown; a charge laid earlier against her had been dropped. Newspaper stories about the case were circulated to crown witnesses to refresh their memories, and, at the trial's close, the judge gave a very damning charge to the jury. The jurors returned a guilty verdict on 17 October; the judge sentenced her that day to be hanged on 7 January. No woman had ever been hanged in Hamilton and the city had not had a hanging since 1930.

'I want my case appealed,' said Mrs Dick immediately and without emotion. Toronto lawyer John J. Robinette petitioned the Ontario Court of Appeal for a new trial, citing twenty-five causes. In reviewing the petition, the court expressed dismay at the conduct of the Hamilton authorities. In reference to the vagrancy charge, one of the five judges declared that 'if that can be done in Canada, it is time we found out about it.'[36] The court also ruled that the police's use of a friend of the accused to extract information from her, as well as its action in denying Dick legal protection at a critical moment, constituted a breach of law. The court's order of a new trial jolted the provincial government.

Unexpectedly, the appeal court's ruling raised a crucial question for all Ontario – possibly all Canadian – jurisdictions. 'When is a statement admissible,' queried a dismayed attorney general, no doubt voicing the concerns of police departments across the province.[37] Certainly Evelyn Dick made her statements voluntarily and that fact accorded with basic principles of the justice system. One reason for insisting on voluntary statements was to promote trustworthiness; another was to protect citizens against the power of state. Yet what constituted a voluntary statement? In a classic formula from an English decision in 1914, it was maintained that an accused's statement must not 'be obtained ... either by fear of prejudice or hope of advantage exercised or held out by a person in authority.'[38] Judges still had to interpret advantage. In the Dick case, the appeal court took into account the ignorance of the defendant, her predicament, and fact that the police had at one point deviously denied her access to a lawyer.

The attorney general appealed the decision and lost. The province next appealed to the Supreme Court of Canada, which declined to hear the case.[39] That exhausted attempts to block a new trial for Evelyn Dick. To the attorney general, the failure to overturn the appeal court's decision reinforced other rulings that threatened to hobble the police. The police had to caution witnesses that their statements might be used against them. They also had to proceed carefully when questioning so as to avoid a leading examination. An area of criminal justice that had not existed until around the 1890s, the law of police interrogation and statements by suspects, was growing into an area of precedent and rules. It is sometimes said that lawyers have rendered the law unnecessarily complex and, by conjuring loopholes, they have made it possible for criminals to wriggle through them to undeserved liberty. That allegation provides an incomplete account. The formation of police departments and developments drawing the state into prosecutions have necessitated the elaboration of the common law and the erudite counter-thrusts of defence attorneys.

As already recounted, the jury acquitted Evelyn Dick at a new trial. She may have been an accessory after the fact to a murder, but on the murder charge her lawyer John J. Robinette made sense. 'One would not hang a dog on the evidence you have heard.' She was not a good person, but that was not the point. She should not be hanged on the basis of flimsy evidence. After her acquittal on the murder charge, another jury found Dick guilty of killing her infant son. She then spent eleven years in prison before being granted a ticket-of-leave from the parole board in 1958.

The importance of the Dick case is not to be found in the private life of the accused, though her sexual conduct certainly fascinated Hamiltonians. Its importance rather rests on the fact that Dick's acquittal on the murder charge not only helped solidify rights for the accused but also launched the career of Robinette, the so-called dean of Canadian lawyers. For good luck, whenever he addressed juries in subsequent cases, Robinette carried his notes for the address to the jury at the second Dick trial.[40] The case advertised the role of the high-profile and astute defender who put the crown and the police on their guard.[41]

Other aspects of the Evelyn Dick case demonstrate the increased standing of lawyers in the criminal justice process and the demise of community-controlled processes. Had it been left to the community, 'that filthy woman' likely would have followed Vincent and McConnell to the gallows. Yet it was not just the defence that had come of age and become professional. Trial practices more generally had come to reflect professionalism, transforming centuries-old English institutions so that they better reflected the modern world. Consider, for example, what happened when Evelyn Dick had appeared before a police magistrate for a preliminary hearing prior to her first trial. The magistrate found enough evidence to draw up an indictment against her. In essence, he heard the evidence against her and determined that the crown had assembled enough to merit a trial. Grand juries were still empowered in Ontario to hear the evidence in such cases and to decide whether or not to proceed to trial, but this ancient and once important institution – which had barely survived the nineteenth century – was now a judicial ghost that many wished to exorcise.

Once police magistrates sitting alone could hear the evidence for a case and prepare an indictment, critics of the grand jury could claim that it shared its power of screening prosecutions.[42] Strictly speaking, this was not accurate. The preliminary hearing by a single magistrate had merely pared down the indictment-preparation role of the justices of the peace by authorizing a visible and full-time professional to perform the same duty. Reform had struck at the justices of the peace, not yet directly at the grand jury. While the magistrate prepared an indictment, it was the unique task of the grand jury to screen it. Effectively, however, the standing of the grand jury had been damaged. The preliminary hearing had the benefit of simplicity and promised a professional review, scrutiny of the evidence by someone with legal training rather than by a certain number of inconvenienced laymen who wanted to be elsewhere.

Another measure truly undermined the grand jury. The previously mentioned act of 1873, which permitted defendants facing certain criminal charges to elect to be tried before a judge without jury in the intermediate level of courts, deprived the grand jury of a considerable portion of its workload. As was shown in chapter 2, cases handled in this fashion received a preliminary hearing and then a trial. Neither grand nor petit juries heard these cases. Late-nineteenth-century estimates proposed that between 75 and 90 per cent of criminal cases were tried without a jury.[43] The denigration of grand juries proceeded farther. In 1879 Ontario passed legislation reducing the size of the grand jury from twenty-four to fifteen, but the act was not proclaimed.[44] In 1892 the province legislated a reduction in the grand jury to thirteen

and in 1955 to seven. Federal jurisdiction over criminal justice procedure complicated the actual reductions.[45]

The first grand jury of seven persons in Ontario sat at Hamilton in
January 1961.[46] Long before them, however, the grand jury – indeed
both the grand and the petit jury – experienced one monumental reform. Mary Ryan taught school, but in early January 1953 she had to
miss classes and appear at the courthouse. Another woman was to have
joined her, but she failed to appear when the sheriff performed his traditional role and called their names. Thus, Mary Ryan had the distinction of being the first woman in Hamilton to serve on any jury; she
drew duty on the grand jury of the assize.[47] Men alone had questioned,
charged, tried, defended, and judged Evelyn Dick. In fact, one of the
most striking general features of the criminal justice system from enforcers to judges was its domination by men. In this respect, the fraternal aspects of the police department stand out because the men
incorporated masculinity into their *esprit de corps.* They were not alone
in treating the criminal justice system as a male club, for as Constance
Backhouse has documented, women seldom embarked on careers as
lawyers until the 1970s.[48]

A provincial measure that enabled women to serve on juries created
a new topic for lawyers, one that stimulated crude psychological speculation. In 1959 Arthur Maloney, a prominent lawyer lecturing to
other lawyers, recommended that in cases involving sex offences the
defence should argue against the inclusion of women on juries. In
other instances, however, he believed that women could be helpful to
the defence because 'the maternal instinct of the woman juror is very,
very, strong.' He also alleged that women might be attracted to a hand-
some defendant.[49] The introduction of women to the judicial system
clearly did not dispel gender stereotyping. Members of the bar had
toiled long in an all too exclusive and all too exclusively male club.

The jury on which Mary Ryan served was an institution that had come
under frequent attack over the years. The first bill for its abolition came
before the Ontario legislature in 1876. In line with its unreflective enthusiasm for efficiency in the courts, the *Canadian Law Journal* welcomed the idea of at least abolishing the grand jury in the cities, because there the existence of police magistrates guaranteed that compe-
tent officials would be at hand to manage the duty of committals.[50] But
the bill failed. The last attempt to eliminate the grand jury in the nineteenth century began in 1889 when Senator James R. Gowan launched
a crusade in the red chamber. Gowan had no use for the essentially
moribund institution. As a judge, he had first denounced it at Simcoe
in 1880 when – appropriately enough and according to the very cus-

tom he disparaged – he addressed a grand jury.[51] It had long been the practice of judges to lecture grand juries on the law and their responsibilities. Gowan's charge to the Simcoe grand jury may have caught his audience off guard, but it could not have upset the jurors who had found the sheriff's summons an inconvenience. Gowan's campaign ended unsuccessfully in 1891.

Owing to Gowan's initiative, the parliament of Canada canvassed the country's judges. Their replies indicated that the process of criminal prosecution had passed through an important transition which some favoured and others distrusted. Those who supported abolition of grand juries stressed that the public had nothing to fear; magistrates and crown attorneys would protect the public against vexatious prosecutions. Behind this claim lay the assumption that malicious or dangerous prosecutions most likely originated with individual complainants.[52] It is significant that a number of jurists still viewed prosecutions as actions brought by individuals. To their way of thinking, the community, through the grand jury, had once checked prosecutions brought out of spite, but now the court itself and a new officer, the county crown attorney, would ensure that accusers did not manipulate the criminal courts to exact private vengeance. To the advocates of modernity, this interposition represented an improvement, because learned professionals now could protect the public. Therefore the expense, inconvenience, and unnecessary pomp that accompanied the grand juries could safely be eliminated. With a lean, efficient, and professional system in place, the public required no archaic institution comprised of amateur and reluctant champions paid for by councils that resented compensating jurors.

Not every judge believed that the greatest threat to the people came from malicious or improper prosecutions by individuals. Those who supported grand juries harboured suspicions about the state. They distrusted the dual functions of the crown attorney and wondered if the new system skewed the criminal justice apparatus against the accused when the crown attorney advised the magistrate, assembled the documents for a prosecution, and then also looked out for malicious prosecutions.[53] Did the gathering of duties into the hands of the crown attorney jeopardize or protect the rights of the suspects? In the context of what was happening in all other departments of criminal justice – such as the advent of the police and the increased powers of the magistrate – the critics of abolition had a point. The centre of prosecutorial authority had begun to shift from the public to the state and now it was being proposed that the check on prosecutions of serious crimes also shift from the public to the state, or at least to the bench and the crown attorney. Holders of these offices might proclaim that they stood in a neutral realm outside the state, but the daily conduct of justice argued otherwise.

Another participant in the debate was the Hamilton Law Association, a body whose very existence further illustrates the trend toward professionalization in the local criminal justice system. Incorporated in 1879 under an act respecting libraries and mechanics institutes, the association not only promoted social occasions but also founded a fine law library, addressed contemporary legal issues, and produced recommended fee schedules. 'The increasing influence of the legal profession and the power of making their views felt through the means of law associations,' it recorded in its annual report for 1885, 'should be taken advantage of to give expression to any suggestions for the better administration of justice.'[54] Within the tortured prose of that declaration resided an assumption regarding the authority of the profession. Earlier in the century, the crown, the parliament, the bench, and the justices of the peace considered improvements to the administration of justice. Now, a new agency, a professional interest group, edged its way into the process. Legislators helped by requiring that assorted judicial officials have experience as barristers. In 1889 the legal profession in Ontario modernized its educational standards by creating Osgoode Hall Law School, which remained the society's law academy until 1957. Courses were mandatory for all law students, though a vestige of the apprenticeship system endured – articling remained a part of training. Ontario legal education followed the continent-wide trend toward the creation of law schools, but uniquely the provincial law society retained control over the program.[55]

On the issue of grand juries, the Hamilton Law Association opposed abolition on the grounds that this venerable institution countered the power of the state. In a memorial to parliament, the association warned against placing too much authority in the hands of one person – a public prosecutor – and described the grand jury as an institution of the people. Critics met this argument for retention by claiming that events had already gone so far that to oppose one more utilitarian change would merely leave behind a useless vestige. To them, the grand jury was a relic that duplicated or rubber stamped the findings of a preliminary hearing. On these grounds, a county judge from Hamilton supported abolition. With nearly all the committals to trial by jury in cities being made by the police magistrates, most of whom were lawyers, the grand jury, in this jurist's estimation, had outlived its usefulness.

Canada's first Criminal Code, in 1892, declared which provinces had already requested the abolition of grand juries. Provinces wishing to eliminate them had to petition for an amendment to the federal code.

Ontario retained the grand jury and Wentworth County – ever frugal – worked its grand juries hard to get a decent return for the daily expenses paid each juror. For example, at the winter assize in January 1920, the Wentworth County grand jury listened to a speech from the judge who called upon it to consider how crime might be reduced. In an address reminiscent of those of almost a century earlier, he commented on social strife. Next the jurors inspected the county house of refuge for the indigent, the hospital for the insane, the home for boys, and the jail. In the grand jury room, they considered the bills of indictment and drafted a report on these and their visitations.[56] Such duties were not unusual. In its last decade of existence in Ontario – the 1970s – the grand jury continued to inspect jails, hostels for the homeless, and senior citizens' lodgings; they also continued to reject a few bills of indictment and even changed the charges in indictments.[57]

Though many states in the United States retained the grand jury, Ontario was one of the last jurisdictions in the British Commonwealth to retain it into the 1970s.[58] On behalf of Ontario's attorney general, the master of the Supreme Court of Ontario prepared a report in 1939 that advocated, in the name of efficiency, the reduction of the petit jury from twelve to six and the abolition of the grand jury. Still, the grand jury survived because its defenders praised it as 'a valuable adjunct to democracy.'[59] The final and critical blow came from the Ontario Law Reform Commission, an on-going agency established in 1964 and assigned the task of modernizing Ontario's civil and criminal law. In a 1973 review of the grand jury, the commission compiled new arguments against it. Defence lawyers felt that, since the grand jury only heard the evidence of prosecution witnesses, it gave them experience and confidence denied to defence witnesses. Some believed that a true bill put additional authority behind the prosecution; the designation 'true bill' and the idea that another jury had seen the evidence might psychologically affect petit juries, biasing them toward accepting the truth of the indictment.

For their part, the crown attorneys indicated that the abolition of grand juries would free them for other tasks and lessen the inconvenience experienced by prosecution witnesses. As always in the reform of legal institutions, cost-cutting provided an additional rationale. 'It was on the ground of efficiency and economy,' reported the commission, 'that in England the grand jury was abolished.'[60] England had done so in 1948.[61] In Canada, the commission noted, the campaign against the grand jury had faltered in 1892; however, the establishment of Canada's first Criminal Code in that year had 'introduced an epochal change in the status of the criminal trial jury.' It abolished a common law prohibition against a defendant being retried for an offence of which he or she had been acquitted. 'The Code empowered the Crown to appeal on a point of law and the Provincial Court of Appeal to order a new trial, if it found the appeal valid.'[62] A 1930 revision of the code more radically pruned the role of the jury by giving the Court of Appeal the authority to reverse the jury's verdict and return the defendant to the trial court for sentencing.[63]

The law reform commission inquiry of the early 1970s – indeed the debate about the grand jury in the 1890s – showed how far the legal profession had come since the early nineteenth century. In less than a hundred years, it had gained control of all levels and all aspects of criminal justice, replacing instruments that for centuries had drawn broadly upon the community or – more correctly – community élites. By the late nineteenth century, legal training had become a prerequisite for judges, crown attorneys, and police magistrates. Lawyers had even moved into the police magistrate's court in the last decades of the nineteenth century, while lawyers in the attorney general's office and jurists on the bench of the Court of Appeals could act to overturn the verdict of a jury.

The cry of efficiency and conflicting perceptions from both the defence and the crown finally undermined the grand jury: in 1976 Ontario abolished the grand jury by requesting the federal government to amend the Criminal Code. Perhaps this was not an error, only the way of the world and, in some regards, an improvement. After all, the refinement of the practices of defence lawyers such as Robinette, the evolution of case law on matters such as witnesses' statements, and legal aid had all occurred while the grand jury faded and eventually vanished.

As yet another symbol of the modernization of the justice system, legal aid deserves a few words. As early as 1921, legal aid had been recommended by a commission examining police magistrates' courts in Ontario.[64] This idea was not acted on for three decades. Though assorted social service agencies and the charity-based *pro bono publico* work of the legal profession provided limited aid,[65] demands for legal assistance grew so substantially in Ontario that in 1951 the province subsidized a plan prepared by the Law Society of Upper Canada. Under the terms of the aid scheme, members of the profession supplied some of the funding and local societies such as the Hamilton Law Association put the plan into operation. It worked as follows. When an accused appeared before the court without counsel, the clerk of the court would inquire if he or she needed counsel. If the answer was yes, the magistrate adjourned the case until the trustees of the law association appraised the accused's situation and assigned a lawyer or rejected the request on the grounds that the accused could afford counsel. After

several years, the legal aid plan in Hamilton dealt with hundreds of requests annually.[66] It soon attracted more clients than the local association felt it could support. Mounting demand compelled the province
in 1966 to establish a plan that provided complete government funding but left the law societies in charge of its administration.[67]

THE OLD AND NEW REALMS OF POLICE WORK

A discussion of the Dick case leads naturally to the subject of police interrogations. For, as noted, Evelyn Dick landed in court not because of
evidence uncovered by the police but because of her own confessions.

From the mid-sixteenth century until the formation of police departments, the justices of the peace in cases of felony and manslaughter
were responsible for examining witnesses and for submitting examinations and depositions to the court.[68] In the mid-nineteenth century,
the state began to strip the justices of the peace of many of their historic functions and reassigned them to the police magistrate, the crown
attorney, and the police. Yet the justices of the peace did not vanish
from the scene altogether. They retained the power to issue summonses and warrants, including search warrants. While the general
public in the late nineteenth century appears to have come to the police magistrate and 'laid upon oath information' about assorted offences, the task of hearing complaints and issuing summonses or warrants in the early twentieth century was increasingly shared by justices
of the peace.

The sheer volume of cases in a growing and highly regulated city re-
suscitated the justices. Once again they became useful functionaries.
No longer representing the local élite, the officeholders now performed a bureaucratic service while carrying out traditional legal functions. A period of puritanism in the 1920s increased their work.
Supplied with appropriate forms and rubber stamps, they authorized
search warrants in connection with the enforcement of the Ontario
Temperance Act. Besides authorizing the police to deal with bootleggers and gaming houses, the justices of the peace continued to sign
warrants for other crimes.[69]

As well as issuing warrants, the justices of the peace have continued
to remand suspects. That is to say, they have visited the police lock-ups
and determined whether prisoners should remain in custody to await
further proceedings or be released on recognizances. This power of
the justices of the peace had its roots in the problem created by the establishment of police forces in common law jurisdictions where complainants traditionally had had to prosecute. In certain cases, the police
would detain a suspect before the injured parties could be notified and

bring charges. The processes of remand or release on recognizance bridged the gap, giving legal cover to the holding or binding of a suspect.[70]

By the 1920s, then, a variety of officials – including JPs – could issue summonses and warrants on the basis of information laid by private citizens or by the police department. Nevertheless, the critical role of assembling statements in serious criminal matters had become the task of the police, an establishment that in its first century accented its brawn, operated from station houses with lock-ups, and outfitted most of its members with uniforms. While some justices of the peace in the old regime likely intimidated suspects and witnesses, a profound institutional shift had placed the collection of statements in the hands of a rather more rough, street-wise, and distinctive body of interrogators. As the police assumed the duty of securing statements, the courts eventually recognized the new, often threatening situation and issued countervailing warnings meant to assure the voluntary quality of statements.

On the surface, the modern constables had little in common with the citizen amateurs isolated in a crossroads community in the early 1800s, except that both delivered summonses and made arrests on the authority of warrants. Increasingly staffed by well-trained men and (after 1944) women, the local police headquarters exemplified the professionalism and internationalism typical of regulated life in modern societies. Financed locally, scrutinized by the provincial government, linked with the provincial police and the RCMP, the Hamilton police also monitored police developments in the United States with interest.

From the late nineteenth century onward, a veritable cascade of inventions in communications, transportation, and identification technology tumbled into civic police work throughout the continent. Always the strictures of the city budget influenced innovation, restraining the purchase of new equipment or, occasionally, providing a pretext for a new system of one description or another. It was typical of the association of economy and technology that, when the Hamilton police commission initially introduced one-way call boxes around the city, it did so to enable sergeants to monitor better the progress of constables on the beat. The goal was as much to keep the constables moving as to improve contact between stations and constables on the street. From time to time, chiefs had hoped for a two-way system that would enable the station to notify the patrolmen that they should call in for special directions. Radio communications for patrol cars soon overtook paging by call box.

Economy also had something to do with the introduction of autos and motorcycles. To cope with the expansion of the city between 1905 and 1930, the police force built a new station and hired more men.

Still, the scale of the city and its capacity to grow rapidly at the outer edges challenged the traditional logistics of policing. Foot patrols based at stations could not keep pace with the expansion of the city, and building more stations to reduce the time required to get out to the beats or to answer calls was a costly remedy. From 1911 to 1950, the financially strapped city built no stations in new suburban locales. A station was erected in the far east end in 1950, but not before the frugal city council had obtained the approval of the electorate in a referendum by proposing to include police, fire, and public health services in the same facility.[71] How did the force manage during this period of expansion? The very device that made urban sprawl possible presented the solution. The police commission purchased its first auto in 1912 and its first motorcycles several years later. By 1920 motorcycle officers – not constables on foot – patrolled the outlying areas of the city throughout the night.[72] The same year, the Bank of Hamilton donated an auto to the detective department in the belief that it would help them get to the scene of a crime more quickly than a streetcar.[73] In 1921 the force had its first fatality associated with the new technology when Constable Pryer's motorcycle collided with a streetcar.[74]

The equipping of patrol cars with radios came in 1936 after several annual appeals from the chief, whose clinching argument was that this 'greatest aid to police work ever developed' would permit the force to cut its roster by two.[75] In fact, the size of the force moved in concert with the size of the city; regardless of technology, the ratio of one non-civilian employee of the force for every thousand citizens has been consistent (Figure 4.1). In any event, no sooner had the commission authorized the one-way radios for cars and had the call boxes removed from the streets than the chief appealed for two-way equipment.[76] Five years later, in 1944, Northern Electric installed these radios. During the first full year of operation, the airwaves filled with serious and frivolous conversations. Roughly 3500 calls dealt with fires, prowlers, lost children, fights, domestic violence, and loud parties; more than 16,000 others were categorized as miscellaneous.[77] Bored constables were not quite so lonely anymore.

The Hamilton force rounded out its radio system in 1949 when it established direct radio contact with the Ontario Provincial Police. There was ample precedent for such inter-force cooperation, for, almost from their beginnings, North American police had kept in contact. At first, they used the mail. By 1900 the Hamilton force routinely received wanted posters from across the continent; a surviving group of posters dating from 1909 to 1925 reveal frequent contact with Toronto, Ottawa, Buffalo, and Detroit. In its criminal justice activities as in so much else, Hamilton was a North American city. Departments in

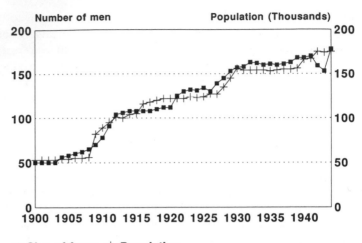

Figure 4.1
Relationship of Size of Police Force to Population of Hamilton, 1900–45
Source: HPL, RG 10, Series A, *Annual Reports*; Weaver, *Hamilton*, 196.

Savannah, Louisville, Selma, and San Francisco sent wanted notices and prisons in Arkansas and Colorado reported escapees. Generally, such communications reproduced photographs. If the suspect had been arrested before, the photographs followed the format of the Bertillon system. Introduced in North America in the 1890s, this system offered the classic 'mug shot' of full face and profile with one of the system's registration numbers fastened to a shirt. It also provided, as noted in chapter three, the measurement of eight different body features.

Alphonse Bertillon, the Parisian founder of the identity system, believed that ears were unique and should be depicted clearly. Often posters gave descriptions loaded with the physical and occupational stereotyping of the era. Suspects had Roman or Jewish noses. Italian fugitives could be found working on construction sites while Chinese suspects might be located labouring in laundries.[78] It is easy and proper to see underlying racist attitudes lurking behind a few of these official communications among police departments. Yet objectionable statements arose from more than raw racism; they reflected the persistent and universal police practice of relying on street wisdom. The associated stereotyping may have laid up a store of serious liabilities and ill will for police departments as they dealt with minorities. But to the police it represented a set of reasonable assumptions.

A ledger recording communications from 1932 to 1936 about wanted persons from outside Hamilton averaged roughly 300 notices annually.[79] Police departments that initiated wanted notices followed up with reports of arrests. About one in five parties wanted were later reported as arrested. Notices came from places as far west as Regina and Denver, as far east as Boston, and as far south as Tennessee. Beyond indicating how immigrants were perceived and implying how North America had grown into a community with considerable freedom of movement and networks of information transcending jurisdictional boundaries, the wanted posters and notices underscored a problem. How could the police make positive identifications? Bertillon measurements of certain features of the head offered an early solution. However, while the FBI cited Bertillon measurements on wanted 'flyers' as late as 1929,[80] the system was imperfect – its measurements were proven not to be always unique. In time, photographs with additional identification features noted improved the situation, and by the First World War the Hamilton department was sending photos of arrested felons to a central bureau in Ottawa.[81] Beginning in 1925, photographers also were routinely sent to the scenes of accidents and crimes.[82]

Fingerprinting provided the ideal technique for establishing identification once an ingenious system of classification for fingerprints had been developed in India by servants of the Raj.[83] The RCMP set up a fingerprint bureau in 1910–11.[84] Afterwards, in 1912, the Hamilton department acquired the necessary equipment from the federal government and began sending fingerprints to the RCMP. Twenty-three sets went from Hamilton to the capital in that first year. It was typical of lingering amateurism and the overlap of duties compelled by frugality that the first fingerprint officer was the crier for the police magistrate's court.[85] In 1917, the force scored its first positive identification by fingerprints, catching a 'clever' English swindler bearing the appropriately inflated and implausible name of Percy DeWilloughby.[86] Significantly, fingerprinting originated as a technique for establishing identity in a world where people were increasingly transient. Only later, by lifting latent prints from the scene of a crime, did fingerprinting become a method of detection.

Initially, specialized fields within policing that possessed professional potential developed almost accidentally, as if they were hobbies. Fingerprinting illustrates the point. Bill Pinch worked as a window-dresser in 1916. Then he happened to read a book about fingerprints. He sent away to Scotland Yard for a manual and in 1920 a relative on the force turned to him for some help on a case. Pinch joined the force four years later. By the time he retired in 1951, the fingerprinting files had forty thousand cards comprised of anyone who had ever been in trouble in Hamilton since the system had been put in place in 1912.[87]

But the age of the self-taught amateur detective had extended for just the length of one career. Leonard Lawrence, appointed acting chief in 1951 and confirmed as chief constable in 1952, introduced a new era. In the condescending words of one newspaper, he was 'no dumb flatfoot.'[88] He had joined as a constable but seemed aloof from rough conduct around the stations. 'There was a lot of roistering, but he was never a part of it.'[89] Lawrence introduced advancement by merit and he accented training. In 1967 the International Association of Chiefs of Police elected him president. This kudo serves to remind us that, though policing enhanced the power of the specific governments that paid its bills, it had achieved an international outlook and formed institutional links.

By the early 1960s, perhaps because of its pivotal location between Toronto and Buffalo, the Hamilton force had taken the lead in co-ordinating the exchange of criminal information among five Ontario Provincial Police districts, the RCMP, four United States law enforcement agencies, and twenty-eight municipal departments.[90] Like other institutions – public and private – police forces recognized the value of collecting and disseminating information. Similar to business corporations, they endeavoured to overcome distance through communications innovations and association. Standardization of information facilitated the organization of networks. In the 1960s the Hamilton force promptly followed corporations in introducing computers, uniform standards for reports, and public-relations divisions.[91] The new policing required a new style of leadership.

Constable Gordon Torrance, a Lawrence protégé who took charge of the fingerprinting operation in 1952, had attended a six-week course at the RCMP training school in Ottawa where he had specialized in fingerprints and photography.[92] His appointment as chief in 1973 confirmed the new route to the top, a path that passed through courses and bypassed seniority. To be chief, it was no longer sufficient to embody one of the earlier management styles, no longer adequate just to understand the city or to make the pavement quake under the tread of a heavy boot. Leaders now required evidence of specialized training. The Police Act of 1949 had empowered the police commissioner for Ontario to establish and operate a central police college.[93] Constables who had attended the Ontario Police College established near Aylmer were said to have received their BA: 'Been to Aylmer.' Training not only honed skills, it established knowledge about the realm of policing outside the community. Through access to facilities, training, and personal contacts, the Hamilton force integrated itself into a network that within Canada included other municipal forces, the OPP, the RCMP, and the services of the provincial attorney general's office, which by the 1950s employed laboratory technicians and criminologists.

Better record keeping, the sharing of information, and scientific approaches to investigations could not replace traditional detective work. This fact surfaced in the Dick case but it was also a feature of all of city's major crimes in the twentieth century. One example – a crime that claimed more lives than any other – illustrates the point. For an inquiry into the catastrophic fire at the Moose Hall in 1944 which killed ten people, a coroner's jury called upon a Toronto professor to conduct tests to determine how the fire had spread through the building. Yet it was not science but the testimony of witnesses that led to the arrest of a pyromaniac whom the police also suspected of having started fires in a church, a school, and a factory.[94]

With the creation of police forces and the formation of detective branches within them, the state – even in common law systems which had always had an ambiguous regard for statements and confessions – turned to a greater use of witnesses' statements and interrogation of suspects to extract evidence. Not long after the Dick trial, an officer with the detective branch stated the obvious in a newspaper interview. 'Co-operation with the public plays an indispensable part in police investigations.'[95] He felt that this cooperation began with the first knowledge of trouble, usually 'via a telephone call from an hysterical citizen.'[96] As noted earlier, police procedures resembled those of the justices of the peace in the old regime in that both relied on the public to report crimes and to supply vital evidence. The critical difference was that the justices of the peace had been amateurs and the police were at first 'mercenaries' and later professionals. They possessed uniforms, lock-ups, nightsticks, and an intimidating appearance. It was one thing for a supposed gentleman-amateur to record statements and quite another for the police to extract statements.

When the justices of the peace had heard from a complainant, they certainly asked questions; when they examined an accused to determine whether they should draw up a bill of indictment, they would have asked questions; during assize trials, the attorney general or crown attorney interrogated witnesses and sometimes the judge did too. In the courts of the lower two layers of the system, the police magistrate or the justices of the peace or the county court judge all asked questions. In sum, interrogation historically had been the task of justices of the peace and judges. Police involvement came later. From what we have seen about police and crime in the nineteenth century, detection, capture, and conviction depended on luck or a witness making a report to the police. If the police questioned prisoners closely in Victorian Hamilton, the process left no traces; this, of course, does not mean that it did not happen.

Voluntary statements and questions asked in open court were quite different from police interrogations conducted in secret. At first, in

England, the idea of police interrogations struck many judges as repugnant. Voluntary statements could be accepted, but questioning by formidable agents of the state could jeopardize the value of statements. In the course of the evolution of nineteenth-century Canadian policing, at some point between 1860 and 1890, detectives started to question persons in custody. This practice first received legal sanction in Ontario in 1890. In 1927 the Supreme Court of Canada likewise endorsed the use of statements obtained by police questioning, but in enunciating the court's decision Chief Justice Anglin inserted an important condition: 'Questioning of the accused if properly conducted and after warning [of the right to remain silent] duly given will not *per se* render his statement inadmissible.'[97] In the annual report of the Hamilton force in 1929, the inspector of detectives observed that 'violent deaths and inquests require a very considerable amount of time in preparing statements, interviewing witnesses for the assistance of the Crown Attorney and Courts.'[98]

Police interrogation seems by the late 1920s – if not earlier – to have been an established practice ostensibly guided by court applied rules. At some point in the subsequent decades, special handbooks were developed to assist the police. They may well have developed in conjunction with police training courses and they dealt with psychological techniques for extracting confessions, statements, or incriminating evidence. Such methods, however, repeatedly collided with the courts' prohibitions of threats and inducements. From the confrontation between police practices and the defence of the rights of the accused, there unfolded an ample body of criminal case law. The Evelyn Dick case came precisely at the moment when the courts had set about to refine this area of the law.

To assist with the significant task of securing useful statements or helpful witnesses who could identify a suspect, the police had recourse to artists and the line-up room. Hamilton had a line-up room early in 1955.[99] However, like the taking of a statement, the staging of a line-up had to withstand the scrutiny of the court. In a 1958 case, Hamilton detectives picked up a suspect in a robbery and put him in the line-up. All the men in the line-up looked different; only the suspect appeared even slightly like the description given by a witness. Understandably, another witness made an identification which the trial judge dismissed, commenting that the Hamilton police had acted like 'a village constabulary.'[100] The police should have secured for the line-up men who had some features like those described by one of the witnesses, for only then would there have been a satisfactory test of identity.

Unquestionably, even in a middle-rank city such as Hamilton, police investigation by the 1920s had become a complex business.

Technology certainly compounded police work. Moreover, the seemingly straightforward practices of dealing with suspects and witnesses required great care owing to the rigours of the rules of evidence shaped by the courts. With respect to the police line-up, for example, authorities on evidence stressed that the arrangements for the identification parade ought to be made by an officer other than the one in charge of the case; the accused should select his own position in the line and be placed among persons who as far as possible were of the same age, height, general appearance, and position in life; witnesses should be called in one at a time and not allowed to communicate with one another. Further, the entire business of line-up identification became ever more complicated as crown attorneys – seekers after the truth – called only witnesses who identified the suspect. In any event, the rules respecting the police parade should have been known to the Hamilton police. By making it humiliatingly clear that procedure meant a great deal, judges helped to effect changes in the recruitment and training of the police.

While science and technology may have helped solve a very few cases, the real story of police work in criminal detection in the twentieth century took place in the courts, not in the labs. It was in the courts where professionals on both sides clashed over statements by the accused, alleged accomplices, and witnesses. Increasingly, as the police and the crown attorney developed methods for assembling statements, the preliminary hearing – in effect the successor to the grand jury hearing – provided defence attorneys with an important field of activity. Here they worked on witnesses to obtain fullest disclosure and discovery, so as to minimize the chances of surprise by the crown. The old community-based check on indictment that the grand jury had provided had been replaced by a setting where professionals worked to lay a foundation for a thorough defence. In Hamilton, this process appears to have been under way by 1900, possibly earlier.[101]

THE MODERN REGULATORY REGIME AND AUTO ANARCHY

Criminal data can reveal a great deal about policing and urban society. However, courts and police forces produced other sets of statistics which also demonstrate the evolution of police and how, at several junctures, services apart from the criminal justice system changed.

Policing has always entailed the regulation of many aspects of urban life. The initial regulatory concerns of early Hamilton had centred on streets and the town market. Assuring honesty and quality at the market and keeping the streets clear of obstructions remained police duties into the twentieth century. These activities did not suddenly vanish, but the city council and the police commission identified new sets of regulatory functions for the police and added them to the older responsibilities. Furthermore, from the 1840s through to the early 1900s, assorted moral order questions and trade regulation matters led to local, provincial, and federal laws that required enforcement by local police in the absence of a national gendarmerie.

The modern regulatory state grew out of public policy concerns about the threats to society at large – and often to specific interest groups – that followed from a modern capitalist economy. There was undoubtedly a link between many of the new regulatory statutes and the old civic watch against forestalling, bad market produce, and the petty cheating by market vendors. However, the twentieth-century regulatory state attempted to impose more universal and exact standards. And it largely called upon the local police to enforce these new standards as well as the prior accretion of regulations.

As Friedman and Percival discovered in their analysis of the police court records in Oakland, California, the police 'do not spend most of their time battling robbers, burglars, and murderers ... Police work was mostly other, more mundane tasks: breaking up fights, handling drunks, enforcing traffic rules, catching runaways.'[102] Yet this view woefully underestimates the range of mundane regulatory tasks undertaken by local forces. The annual police reports for Hamilton from 1905 to 1914 cited offences against more than thirty senior government regulatory measures. A sample of these miscellaneous acts gives some indication of the range of policing duties: Bread Act, Childrens' Protection Act, Contagious Diseases Act, Egg Grading Act, Food and Drug Act, Game and Fisheries Act, Gas Company Act, Gold and Silver Marketing Act, Harbour Commissioners' Bylaws, Hotel Registrations Act, Lottery Act, Moving Pictures Act, Pawnbrokers Act, Power Commission Act, Public Health Act, Rabies Act, School Act, Weights and Measures Act. Of course, the most important of all was the Motor Vehicle Act. In 1910 there were 33 violations reported; by 1914 the number had soared to 311. And this only marked the beginning. For the sake of statistical compression, the data from provincial and federal regulatory acts has been added to that of the city's by-laws (Figure 4.2). The latter were the overwhelming source of actions.

It was difficult enough to enforce the old market rules, street by-laws, and moral order measures. The police now had to enforce new ordinances which effectively turned the force into a watch-dog for several civic departments and other governments. The passage into this new era of regulating civic conduct beyond the markets and streets was rocky at first. Enforcement of the city's newer by-laws had been a sore

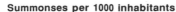

Summonses per 1000 inhabitants

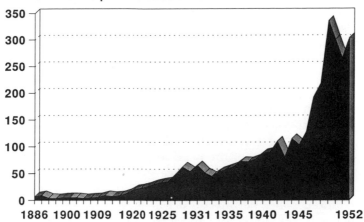

Figure 4.2

By-law Summonses per 1000 inhabitants, 1886–1952

Source: *Hamilton Spectator*, 21 January 1865, 11 January 1866, 11 January 1867, 17 January 1870, 4 January 1872, 6 January 1875, 6 January 1876, 22 January 1878, 9 January 1879, 26 January 1880, 11 January 1881, 30 January 1883, 7 February 1884, 28 February 1887, 30 January 1890, 16 February 1892, 26 January 1898, 27 January 1899, 31 January 1901, 5 February 1902, 22 January 1903, 3 February 1904, 23 February 1905, 30 January 1907, 20 January 1909, 3 February 1910, 27 February 1915, HPL, Records of the City of Hamilton, RG 10, Series A, Police Department, *Annual Reports*, 1906–70, missing 1906–8, 1910, 1911, 1914, 1916, 1918–19, 1930, 1933; RG 10, Series K, Police Court Proceedings, Ledgers, 1859–1949.

point with the force since at least the 1880s. In 1883 the city's health officer had requested assistance from the police to carry out public health measures, and he even appeared at parade to address the men. The chief grumbled that the force was too small to undertake such 'extra duties.'[103] But the police commission emphatically directed the police to enforce all by-laws. If constables did not, they would be considered neglectful in their duties. Their function in the civic scheme of things was not to use discretion, not to select which laws they would or would not enforce, but to summon all suspected offenders to appear before the magistrate who then would exercise discretionary power. This firm directive to accept without hesitation or questioning the measures laid down in police commission and city council by-laws piled more work on the constables precisely at the moment when Chief Stewart was instituting his reforms of police work.

A sense of duty among most of the men carried the force through a critical time when there were rumours of a strike and the defection of several experienced men. Police administrators, dealing with city councils that liked to see value for their money, worked hard to demonstrate the force's efficiency. A consequence of these goals of police commissions and chiefs was that, in the larger scheme of things, the police assisted with the transition from pre-industrial social behaviour to more orderly conduct supportive of urban-industrial routines and class relationships. The police set an example by following the routines of the beat. More important, by grudgingly enforcing the community's regulatory laws, they became intrinsic to an orderly city and its regulated social and economic life.

In retrospect, the police took up some regulatory chores assigned it by the federal government with a speed and pride that would alarm anyone conscious of the need to guard civil liberties. In 1915 Ottawa instructed the Hamilton police to keep a register of enemy aliens. These individuals had to report twice a month to the police station and required police permission before they could leave the city. The local police forces also enforced the rationing of food and fuel and were responsible for press censorship. Similarly, on the day that Italy declared war on the Allies in the Second World War, the Hamilton force moved to arrest within an hour or two 'practically all the dangerous members of Hamilton's considerable Italian population.' In addition to assisting again with the enforcement of rationing, the local police worked with the RCMP in screening applicants for war work.[104]

The local police heartily cooperated with the national state in these matters. On an individual basis, too, patriotism and a martial spirit stepped to the fore during the wars. An unusually large proportion of police officers enlisted in the war effort: in 1944, when the force's strength stood at 150, it saw thirty-five men and thirty-four sons and daughters enlist.[105] The impressive level of wartime patriotism derived partly from a strong *esprit de corps* and partly from the militarism that had always been inherent in the force. The same militarism eased the force's incorporation into national-policing campaigns in times of war.

In the 1950s the police maintained an active war veterans' association, complete with 'marching unit.'[106] Around 45 per cent of the force belonged to the association.[107] These facts and the preference in the nineteenth century for hiring constables with military experience fly in the face of facile claims that the police were civilians who discharged civilian duties and who wore uniforms so that those needing their help would know where to look.[108] Yet the militarism of the police should not be exaggerated. Despite its aggressive image, the civic force could not on its own – in the estimation of political leaders – deal decisively with mass protest or serious disturbances. During an organized protest demonstration of several hundred unemployed people in 1932, the fire department was deputized to aid constables in dispersing the assembly. Similarly, to control violence at the picket lines at Stelco in 1946, the city called upon the OPP.[109] From time to time, the city government might have wished it had had a stronger arm, for even if the police were willing they apparently were not numerous enough or sufficiently trained to handle mass demonstrations.

In the enforcement of non-criminal statutes and by-laws, the police were required to cope with the significant social changes caused by the advent of the automobile. Until around 1914, this omnibus category of activity consisted primarily of assorted offences against city, province, and federal regulations. Afterwards, it came to be dominated by violations involving the auto.

Originally, by-law enforcement meant serving a summons on a party who had violated one of the regulations passed by the city council or by the police commission. The latter authority had the power to issue licences to taxi-cab operators and second-hand shops. Meanwhile, city council passed numerous by-laws that regulated the use of the streets. The automobile caused the numbers of street offences to soar astonishingly. In 1886 the police dealt with about seven by-law infractions per constable per year. By 1921 the number had tripled to twenty-three and by 1928 it had tripled again to sixty-four (Figure 4.2). The crucial legislative factors in this increase were several Hamilton by-laws and amendments passed between 1905 and 1910. Responsible for all matters relating to vehicular traffic, the force found its chores increasing year by year. The province, too, added greatly to the regulation of the automobile; the 1912 revised Motor Vehicle Act ran to nearly five times the length of the original 1903 act.[110]

It has been assumed that 'the growing case-loads in police magistrates' courts' in early-twentieth-century Ontario resulted 'from stringent enforcement of morality laws.'[111] This was not quite the case in Hamilton. By 1920 the auto revolution more than anything else burdened the lowest court in the city. The police magistrate's court passed a threshhold of sorts in 1917 when city by-law offences first surpassed the traditional leading offence, drunk and disorderly conduct. To be sure, special circumstances caused the immediate shift in emphasis. The passage of the Ontario Temperance Act in 1917 drastically curtailed the consumption of alcohol. As one contemporary remarked to explain the fall in drunk and disorderly cases, 'Hamiltonians either carried their loads better through fear of the OTA or else discovered that it was possible to exist without booze.'[112] The OTA may have advanced the year in which auto offences led all others, but by the early 1920s the former class of transgressions would have held the top spot without any artificial reduction in drunk and disorderly charges.[113] Auto offences continued to pile up, growing year after year. To ease the burden on the judicial system, in 1958 the city adopted 'the uniform ticket system' by which violators were served with a summons on the spot, releasing some constables who still performed the historic duty of serving summonses.[114]

With growing popular access to the auto in the 1920s, the efficient circulation of vehicles started to perplex civic authorities. While engineers and planners took up the particular challenges imposed by a new technology, the police dealt not only with traffic flows but also with the loss of life and property damage. Homicide in the steel city was rare, but after the Second World War traffic deaths became disturbingly commonplace. Without stop signs, traffic signals, and public awareness of safe-driving habits, the city was undisciplined in matters of traffic. Drunk or careless motorists had a catastrophic impact.

Besides their traditional task of managing the city's traffic, the police had a further motive for inquiring into auto carnage. The police along with the coroner had the responsibility for attending to the bodies of those who died suddenly on city streets or in any other unusual circumstances. The police not only responded in the first instance to reports of dead or dying individuals, but a sergeant usually assisted the coroner by assembling a coroner's jury if the latter deemed this necessary. In the late nineteenth and early twentieth centuries, the police and the coroner dealt primarily with suicides, industrial accidents, and people dying of natural causes on the city streets; homicide – to repeat – occurred infrequently. The city's first auto fatality likely happened in 1911. By 1921 more sudden deaths investigated by the police involved automobiles than any other cause. For the next half century, the police devoted considerable resources towards ensuring a reduction in auto accidents.

The city responded to the rising number of auto accidents apparent in the early 1920s with the introduction of a by-law in 1924 that compelled drivers to stop at intersections. This by-law, affecting thousands of people daily at hundreds of points in the city, required many prosecutions before stopping at intersections became a habit.[115] Next, the city installed 'beacons' at the major intersections to remind drivers of the requirement to stop; still, intersections remained danger zones. The safety innovations did not exclusively serve public safety. In the name of efficiency, they also sorted out the chaos on the streets and contributed to the efficient running of the city.

The first years of the depression of the 1930s reduced pleasure driving and cut into the number of commuters who dashed off to work in cars. But as the city's economy picked up in 1935, so did the rate of auto fatalities. To the consternation of the police, this rate continued to move upward during the war years despite gasoline rationing, the impossibility of buying new tires legally in the city, and the conversion of auto assembly lines to war production (Figure 4.3). Police officials

Number per 100,000 inhabitants

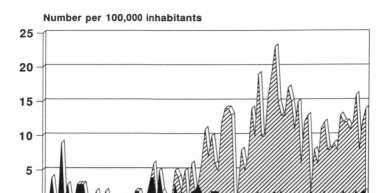

Figure 4.3
Violent Deaths: Homicides and Automobile Accidents, 1870–1970
Source: HPL, RG 10, Series A, *Annual Reports*; coroners' inquest books; assorted
newspaper scrapbooks on Hamilton murders.

worried greatly about the deaths and injuries caused by automobile accidents. Just when it was ceasing to run a hostel and ambulance service,
the department turned to matters of public safety. The new cause of
saving lives and limbs put constables in the schools to teach children
public safety.

Beginning in the late 1920s, the Hamilton police started to analyze
the information that they collected from their reports of accidents.[116]
Automotive accidents easily outpaced industrial mishaps twenty to one.
The most frequent type of auto accident involved two vehicles; the second most frequent, autos and pedestrians; autos and bicycles were a
distant third. Sixty per cent or more of the auto accidents happened at
intersections. Having isolated the problems, the police went to work on
remedies. Late in 1929, the department started to assign school-traffic
officers. In 1936, confessing that 'the traffic problem is one of the most
complex with which the police are confronted,' the Hamilton force established an inspectorship to deal with traffic and to ensure public
safety and the enforcement of laws relating to motor vehicles.[117] To assist them in countering the two great sources of accidents – speeding
and drunk driving – the police turned to technology.

The Hamilton police introduced the breathalyser in September
1957. This instrument allowed constables to make a quick and reasonably accurate judgement about whether or not someone who was driving in a suspicious fashion was legally intoxicated. On New Year's Eve
1960, constables tested 323 drivers with the breathalyser and charged

316 of them. Only 32 of the charges were later dismissed. Altogether, efforts to regulate traffic and the conduct of drivers revolutionized the court system as well as policing. The lowest courts of the province, the courts that historically had dealt with moral order offences, became traffic courts. Just as the recognition of juvenile delinquency as a discrete area of concern came to influence the creation of special sittings of the magistrates court in 1923, so did the automobile compel the setting apart of days for traffic cases.

The automobile had three general effects on policing. The most obvious one was how it came to occupy the time of constables. Parking tickets, speeding citations, accident reports, and traffic violations swiftly became the predominant means through which the police met the public. The second effect lay in the management of traffic; traffic control was well suited for specialization and the development of skills technically quite distinct from all other aspects of police work. The Hamilton force had men on the beat handle the direction of traffic at busy intersection until late 1910 when it established a squad to direct vehicular movement.[118] Finally, the automobile took constables off their feet and put them on their seats. In 1922 the leading American police reformer August Vollmer alleged that migratory criminals in cars caused an endless amount of trouble. By the end of the decade, the idea had surfaced in Hamilton too. 'The police situation to my mind,' said Mayor Burton, 'is that many members of the department have been left walking beats, whereas in the past decade or two every regular crook or law breaker has resorted to high-speed cars.'[119] The assumption – or was it a justification for unsolved crimes? – that high-speeding strangers plundered a city or neighbourhood and then roared off to a new area ripe for the picking was one of many popular notions, however erroneous, that perpetuated the fear of strangers. It also supported an exaggerated faith in crime-fighting technology and promoted an unfounded belief in the idea that crime fighting could be highly successful.

The civic police force constituted an imperfect instrument for the protection of property and social control, which is not to say that police administrators had not hoped for more or that the police force had not stringently enforced social control measures from time to time. The Hamilton police had managed by the First World War to introduce a degree of professional rigour, particularly among the leadership cadre. In their backgrounds and day-to-day activities, however, the constables proved to be a mixed lot displaying varied degrees of dedication to their work. On the whole, David Johnson's appraisal of American policemen seems applicable to their Hamilton brothers. The police had the appearance of an emerging professionalism, but lacked the substance.[120]

Added to the risks of their work, constables have had to deal with uncertain status and after 1950, increasing public scrutiny. In coping
with these challenges, the Hamilton Police Association has fostered an
image of itself as a fraternal body that sponsors social activities and
community functions. Its 1959 report declared that 'several stags were
greatly appreciated by members.'[121] Chiefs naturally reported on the
harmony between the association and the police hierarchy, but, if true,
such statements raise questions about how the inevitable tensions between management and employees in an unusually taxing line of work
were dealt with . It also poses as yet unanswerable questions both about
the depth of police solidarity across all ranks and about the values that
might have enabled policemen to overcome discontent and frustration.

Police work defies tidy summary. When requested to enforce moral
order, they did so inconsistently and with no permanent effect; when
asked to protect property during strikes, they did so without having the
resources to cope with major disturbances. What they did do routinely
on a very large scale was listen to citizens' complaints concerning petty
theft or domestic disputes and assaults, though the last category of offence was declining relative to the growth of the city and the force. At
mid-century, the beat still remained a demanding part of police work.
The *Hamilton News* in 1953 noted that 'the beat cop must ... have good
judgment. He is required to know when to make an arrest, when to
charge a person and have him later summoned to court and when to
merely warn the offender without laying a charge.'[122] Yet while the
beat demanded much of constables, the truth of the matter is that the
proportion of constables who worked a beat fell significantly in the
twentieth century. Moreover, in the 1960s, the city phased out one of
the oldest functions of the local constabulary – the serving of summonses – and cut costs through the use of registered mail.[123]

Police work, therefore, changed even as constables discharged the
traditional duties of a constabulary. Besides their other responsibilities,
constables spent time trying to locate lost children and missing adults;
the Hamilton department ran its hostel on a shoestring until 1929 and
operated an ambulance service until 1943. Increasingly after 1920, it
also had to cope with new burdens occasioned by the automobile.
None of the other emerging city professionals – engineers, planners, or
social workers – had to respond to so varied a set of sensitive urban
tasks; this represented a line of continuity from the days of the village
constable. The streets literally and figuratively provided links with the
past. What might be called the culture of policing continued to draw
upon street wisdom, contact with some of the social elements feared by
the urban élite, and familiarity with the recreational activities and
values of working-class males.

In the 1950s, constables were still advised to know the city well[124] –
a fact that reinforces the argument that policing from the early 1900s
to the middle of the century remained an urban service fashioned
more by street wisdom and coarse experience than professional training. An important and fairly recent question for historical and contemporary inquiry, therefore, is not whether urban police forces have or
have not been agents of social control, but whether they have been and
are adequately trained for their extremely difficult and shifting missions within the changing Canadian city.[125] To a significant degree, the
balance between learning by apprenticeship on the street and professional training tipped toward the later in the 1950s. Yet much of the
overall complexity of policing originated in the persistence of old
habits and values, old chores and pressures, in an age of new demands.
Some attributes of policing retained a nineteenth-century crudeness
and a well-deserved reputation for brutal encounters. In Hamilton, the
old policing with its rough conduct has reputedly endured even into
the 1990s, away from the modern headquarters and in a station located
in the industrial east end. All along, politicians have nudged the force
onto progressive paths that it has not pursued on its own.

'It's sissy stuff now,' jested Russell Buttenham on his retirement from
the force in 1952. He had joined in 1921 during hard times that had
cost him his job as a machinist at Westinghouse.[126] Lighting a pipe and
settling back in his armchair, he recalled the days when men were men
and so were the police. Unquestionably, the force had changed during
the span of his three decades. Technology caused a fair portion of that
alteration in police work. Buttenham himself had ended his career in
the radio room, calling patrol cars on the two-way radio. He remembered the initial one-way system and how he could call the cars but not
be certain they had received the message. By 1960 patrol cars had even
affected the size of policemen. Car designs no longer allowed tall constables to wear their hats while on patrol, and so the height requirement was lowered to five feet nine inches.'[127]

Buttenham's remark about 'sissy stuff' ought to be taken seriously to
this extent: the Hamilton force went through an uneasy transition from
the age of fraternal muscularity to one of professionalism and greater
inclusiveness. It was said of one popular inspector at his funeral in 1924
that he was 'a real mixer ... one of the stalwart pillars of local fraternal-
ism.'[128] At this time, the force retained a reputation for hiring strapping members of the masonic lodge, and a hint of a Scottish accent –
as well as the presence of a relative on the force – certainly did not hurt
one's chances. By the mid-1930s, however, the Hamilton force – when
it could afford to hire new men at all (Figure 3.2 and Figure 3.4) – required them to pass an exam as well as appear intimidating. The rituals

of physical assessment persisted: the annual report for 1936 noted that thirty-six applicants 'were examined, weighed, measured.'[129] Yet, at about the same time, a constable trained at the police school in Toronto began coordinating a four-week course for Hamilton's police.[130] Reputed to be the second police training school in the province, the course included lectures on statutes and court procedures. By the 1940s, every constable had to attend several weeks of classes, studying procedure, evidence, deportment, civility, criminal law, and by-laws.[131]

Chief Len Lawrence stressed in a 1951 interview that 'the public need have no fear that we will ever admit physical weaklings to the force.'[132] The chief's reassurance came after the force had first lowered its height requirement and following a declaration by the mayor that the force had better place more emphasis on intelligence in its recruiting.[133] In fact, for several decades, the backgrounds of constables had altered notably. Men with clerical experience were increasingly likely to be hired (Figure 3.4). By 1951 new requirements insisted on a grade 10 education at the very least. The police checked the applicants' home life, contacted past employers and other police departments, and scanned school records. Next came a written test that examined the candidate's spelling, familiarity with world affairs, and general knowledge. To clear the final hurdle, applicants had to write a convincing composition on why they wanted to join the force.[134] Following hard on the heels of this new policy on hiring, the commission jumped the seniority queue and hired forty-year-old Len Lawrence as chief. Henceforth, education – not seniority – influenced promotions. Lawrence – like Stewart in the 1880s – implemented a number of additional reforms.[135]

The 1950s have a reputation for conservative attitudes, but in terms of policing that decade brought practices which started to remake the composition of the force. Ethnic groups began to have representation on the force and, by 1957, the department took pride in the linguistic talents of those of its men who comprised an unofficial translation pool – a 'United Nations Committee.'[136] Furthermore, the police commission accorded new roles to women on the force.

The several women who worked for the force prior to the 1950s occupied an employment ghetto defined by the commission. The male commissioners and the women of the civic élite had basically agreed for decades about what females might do on the force: they should deal with women prisoners. But the two groups did not always see eye to eye. In 1894 the police commission recognized the need for a police matron to attend to women brought to the lock-up; however, it clashed with the Women's Christian Temperance Union over the hiring of Mrs

Lewis, a black woman. The commission defended her at a meeting with WCTU representatives: 'Mrs Lewis may not be highly cultured, and it is true her complexion is dark; but she is a good, kind women.'[137] The delegation from the WCTU stormed out of the meeting.

From at least the early 1930s on, major businesses employed women in security positions. For example, Hamilton's department stores employed women as floor detectives to catch shoplifters.[138] But the police commission moved incredibly slowly. It took a push from another association of prominent women to expand the hiring of women, even if just marginally. The Hamilton Local Council of Women lobbied in the early 1940s for having women in the Ontario Provincial Police and in civic forces.[139] Hamilton's police chief saw no need for such an innovation, but events soon overtook him; civic politicians were sensitive to the pressure from women's organizations and the popularity of councillor Nora Frances Henderson. She put the fire to the mayor's toes such that the commission hired two women in 1944.[140] These constables, joined by a third in 1947, continued to do what Mrs Lewis had done. They searched and escorted female prisoners, one of whom was Evelyn Dick. By the early 1950s, they also took part in investigations that involved women and children in morals offences, either as victims or offenders.[141]

Later in the 1950s, confessing that Hamilton had fallen behind other cities, the commission announced that it would hire more women and assign them the tasks of interrogating prisoners, interviewing witnesses, and conducting investigations, as well as dispensing parking tickets and participating in public-education programs.[142] This meant that, though the hiring of women increased in subsequent decades, women were directed into particular areas, ones mostly associated with paperwork. While juvenile delinquency was thought of as 'women's work,' criminal investigation and walking the beat were not. A provincial inquiry into policing in 1973 indicated that the Hamilton force of 500 should have had more than eight women. The commission took heed, but many constables seethed aloud, lending sour notes to the official fanfare accompanying the hiring of women. Despite the commission's efforts to make the force more inclusive, gender stratification continues to characterize police work.

THE REFINEMENT AND REFORMATION OF PUNISHMENT

At the local level, the parsimony of county councils retarded the improvements in jails called for by the provincial inspectors who began touring the jails in 1859.[143] Presumably inspectors were expected to provide more independent and professional assessments than the local amateurs on the grand jury. However, judging from the repetition of complaints from year to year, they were not very effective. In the end, it was the problem of a shortage of space rather than adverse reports by inspectors that prodded local authorities to construct a proper jail.

Before the city and the county built the new courthouse in 1879, they had had to deal with the shortage of cells at the jail in the courthouse basement. In 1875 they constructed a grim fortress-like jail that at least housed most prisoners above ground level, although four dark punishment cells were located in the basement. The new structure provided for sixty regular cells, twenty of which were reserved for women. In this place, in the company of a jail matron, Evelyn Dick awaited her trials in 1946. Unlike the old jail which had originally separated only the debtors from other prisoners, the new jail kept aside a corridor for boys under sixteen, another for hapless drunks and vagrants, another for prisoners who had been convicted of a first or second offence, and another for more hardened cases. However, sound carried readily in the jail and undermined a vital goal of the classification or segregation system, namely the isolation of hardened criminals from other inmates.[144] The fact that classification existed in any form at all indicated a trend to imitate the specialization occurring more emphatically in the provincial penitentiary system.

Many of Ontario's county jails offered worse accommodations by far. The county jails held prisoners sentenced for only a few days or at most several months. They also incarcerated prisoners awaiting trial or execution. Under these circumstances, the jails were never thought of as reformatory institutions with disciplinary regimes designed to alter the soul. Still, reform ideas appear to have penetrated 'Ogilvie's Castle' in the late nineteenth century. James Ogilvie, the governor, and his turnkeys prohibited improper language or misconduct in the exercise yard; they sometimes shadowed the prisoners to listen to their language.[145] They also employed the male prisoners in cutting wood, breaking stone, and tending the garden. Asked specifically in 1890 whether he felt the silence system would help reform a prisoner, Ogilvie replied that he felt it was cruel. Besides, he said, it gave 'more facility for self-abuse, which is already practiced largely amongst prisoners, and is causing a great deal of insanity in our prisons; we have found this out by constant watching.'[146]

The reform commission that extracted this information wondered whether the province should take over the local jails,[147] but it was not until 1968 that this step was taken. The colonial and provincial governments inaugurated important reforms to the penal system, establishing a reformatory for boys at Penetanguishene in 1859 and the Andrew

Mercer Reformatory for girls in Toronto in 1880. The provincial hospital at Hamilton also opened in 1880 and received the criminally insane. In 1887 the province founded the Victoria Industrial School for Boys at Mimico and the Alexandra Industrial School for Girls at Scarborough. During the 1890s, however, there began to develop 'a network of voluntary foster-home care societies which gradually supplanted the industrial schools in the province's emerging child welfare system.'[148] In 1904 the 'child-savers,' who aimed at reforming street children by taking them out of institutions as well as off the streets, succeeded in closing the reformatory at Penetanguishene.[149]

A growing concern with juvenile delinquency, coupled with the drive for specialization and professionalization, also affected the organization of the lowest court. A federal act of 1908 enabled municipalities with a police magistrate's court to establish a separate juvenile court. With its typical parsimony in matters of social reform, Hamilton responded only in early 1923, when the police magistrate's court held a special Saturday session to process juvenile offences. Formerly, the police magistrate had tried the cases as part of the daily roster and the press had freely reported on juvenile offenders. Many of the cases heard in the new juvenile court concerned boys who got into mischief, throwing stones at trains, filching fruit, and stealing bicycles. However, the occasional theft of coal suggests that a few juveniles stole with parental consent and out of family need.

Another group of cases originated from the complaints of parents – usually mothers – who came before the court to plead that their sons had become 'incorrigible.' In these circumstances, the magistrate might send the lad to the Mimico industrial farm or assign the case to the Children's Aid Society. Magistrate Jelfs – the aging police magistrate who presided over the first juvenile court – believed in whippings and, with the parents' consent, often ordered such punishment.[150] That Jelfs served as the judge of the juvenile court confirms what his Vancouver counterpart and contemporary thought about juvenile courts generally. Helen MacGill exclaimed that they dealt out sentences like 'a puppy of the Police Court.'[151] Interestingly, the second inspector of the Children's Aid Society in Hamilton was John Pinch, an ex-sergeant of the Hamilton police force.[152] As late as 1929, the apprehending of juvenile offenders was conducted almost exclusively through the police force, which even used the 'Black Maria' to transport juveniles to detention. Thus, contrary to legislation, there was no complete separation of juveniles from the criminal justice system.[153]

In 1934 the juvenile court became part of a larger unified family court division within the police magistrate's court. This new branch of the old court heard cases involving juveniles and assault cases arising from domestic disputes. The unified family court indicated again the city's *ad hoc* and parsimonious approach to the criminal justice system. City council had piled many distinct burdens on the police and now it refused to set up a juvenile court outside the structure of the police magistrate's court.[154] This new court worked closely with the police department's morality division, which had been organized in 1932. After 1960, it also worked with the department's new juvenile branch.[155]

With regard to domestic disputes that involved violence, the police typically dealt with such cases by first establishing order and then directly advising the victim on how to lay charges or recommending that the victim see an officer in the morality department who would suggest courses of action. A justice of the peace assigned to the family court could process the information laid by a complainant. In effect, the basic outlines of processes from the old regime endured beneath the surface changes of specialization. The victim remained the complainant and the justice of the peace retained a function. Chapters 5 and 6 will provide more details about domestic violence and relations among the police, the police magistrate, and victims.

By the late nineteenth century, professionalization had spread to the practice of hanging – the only form of capital punishment authorized in Canada. The sheriff had to administer the carrying out of the sentence of the court and, owing to the traditional contempt for executioners, always contracted the work to a hangman. For most of the nineteenth century, sheriffs secured willing individuals from their vicinity. As time passed, however, train travel and the English example of hiring a professional hangman led to the organization of the trade in Canada roughly into an eastern and western section. The first professional hangman in Canada, John Robert Radclive, had apprenticed with William Marwood, the official hangman of England. Radclive immigrated to Canada in 1890.[156]

As a hangman, Marwood's goal was instantaneous death for the condemned. To that end, he had devised a special noose and worked out a series of tables using the condemned person's weight to calculate the drop necessary to dislocate the neck. Radclive also attempted to improve hanging and invented a gallows that dispensed with the climb up the steps, for he believed that this last walk was 'terribly trying and their [the condemned] knees get terribly weak before they get to the top.'[157] Imperfections in his invention, however, caused him to return to the traditional gallows. Radclive advertised his services by writing to the various sheriffs of Ontario. In the east, he had no rivals. In the west, a hangman operating out of Regina worked the territory from Winnipeg to Victoria, though occasionally the famous Radclive hanged men in that region too. After hanging at least 132 prisoners, Radclive died an alcoholic in 1912. In an interview toward the end of his life, he said that he had 'argued with myself that if I was doing wrong, then the government of the country was wrong.'[158] During the First World War, a small band of MPs argued that the government was indeed wrong, but four private member's bills abolishing capital punishment were defeated handily.[159]

After Radclive's death, a retired English army captain who worked under the professional name of Arthur Ellis served for a dozen years as the country's pre-eminent hangman. His successor also worked as Arthur Ellis, establishing for awhile the nickname of 'Mr Ellis' for all Canadian hangmen.[160] The original Mr Ellis eventually came to believe that hanging was cruel and recommended the electric chair; however, a small number of parliamentarians still hoped to eliminate capital punishment entirely. In 1923 William Irvine, the Alberta Progressive, introduced a private member's bill that failed by a wide margin.[161]

While parliament held intermittent debates on capital punishment, juries, judges, and the federal government exhibited some reluctance in hanging murderers. Of 108 murder cases tried in Hamilton between 1876 and 1970, no more than eight ended in hangings.[162] About half of the cases ended in acquittals and another third resulted in convictions on the reduced charge of manslaughter. Five prisoners received life; five were judged insane. Private members kept the issue of capital punishment before parliament throughout the 1950s and 1960s. Although capital punishment remained on the statute books, the last executions in Canada occurred in 1962. Finally, in 1976, after years of tinkering legislatively with capital punishment, parliament abolished it by a narrow margin on a vote free from party discipline.[163]

By the 1960s and the 1970s, the criminal justice system had lost its direct capacity to inspire awe. This does not mean that the police no longer intimidated suspects or that they failed to establish order by their presence. Nor does it suggest that some minority groups were not afraid of the police, that a stay in a provincial or federal penitentiary was a happy prospect, or that 'socialized justice' helped every deserving prisoner. Rather, it means that criminal justice institutions, buildings, and punishments could not rely on fear alone to achieve their ends. This change was the culmination of a process that had begun in the nineteenth century, when the ending of public executions and the separation of juveniles from adults in jails and courts mitigated the tactic of terror as a strategy in crime prevention. No longer would it be possible for children to see executions from the shoulders of an adult; no longer would children be tried along with adults in the miserable surroundings of a police magistrate's court.

In the 1960s and 1970s, newly constructed jails and police stations resembled modern low-rise business buildings. Moreover, at Hamilton in 1965, the police magistrate's court – officially then called magistrate's court – moved out of the main police station and into a nearby office building, separating entirely the city's lowest court from the police department after more than a century of intimate – and in retrospect some would say improper – association. [164] Serious crimes continued to attract attention from the media, but without a life resting on the outcome of a homicide trial the horrifying intensity once apparent in courtroom reporting vanished. While the criminal justice system in Hamilton has had much in common with those in the United States, it has seldom shown the violent face of the state in post-war decades. That stands in contrast to the majority of American jurisdictions which have retained capital punishment.

Important judicial rulings, liberal reforms, and technology forced more changes to the criminal justice system in the mid-twentieth century than at any other time since the radical innovations that ended the old regime. The creation of detective branches eventually compelled the formulation of a suspect's rights; these rights in turn fostered police training in procedure. Science held out the promise of better techniques of detection and identification. In the wake of the enormous expansion in the number of trials without jury introduced just after Confederation, the province began to tinker with the grand jury, eventually abolishing it. The political leaders of city, province, and country slowly liberalized the criminal justice system. They abolished the death sentence, overhauled jails, created a juvenile and then a family court, and broke down a few barriers to ethnic minorities and women in the police force.

Politicians often forced shifts that ran well ahead of attitudes in that basic institution of contemporary criminal justice, the police department. Able and ambitious police officers swallowed the reforms and thereby advanced their careers, but they found that they could not revise police culture over night. Constables continued to feel misunderstood and overwhelmed, burdened with paperwork, frustrated by regulations, and worn down by the grind of dealing with public complaints. In fact, the topic of public complaints represents another indicator of change in the criminal justice system. The following chapter discusses the matter of complaints in the context of how to interpret crime statistics. This discussion also underscores the fact that, at least since the turn-of-the century and probably as early as the 1870s, the police have come to replace the justice of the peace and the police magistrate as the party to whom the community takes it woes.

5 The Meaning of Trends in Crime Rates

The local news for Christmas weekend 1920 mocked the season's message of peace and goodwill. On the night of 23 December, four young Hamilton men had stolen a Gray Dort automobile in the city and roared along county roads to the crossroads village of Binbrook, planning to rob a general store. Several of them entered the store at around 11:30 p.m. The manager, a veterinary surgeon, Dr T.J. Whitworth, surprised one of the robbers, Wilfred Meharg, and tried to prevent him from grabbing forty dollars out of the cash register. Meharg pulled a revolver and fired twice; Whitworth would die the next day. Although all four felons were Anglo-Saxons, the fatally wounded Whitworth described his assailants as Italians.[1] On Christmas morning, two Italian men did shoot and kill another Italian on a city street. The immediate press response to two unrelated incidents proposed three lessons about local violent crime. First, 'foreigners' had not learned to respect Anglo-Canadian standards of law and order and carried handguns with greater frequency than other residents did; second, the city was in the midst of a crime wave; and third, motorcycles or high-power cars were needed to enable the police to combat crime more effectively.

The three conclusions deserve attention. As it turned out, the first did not apply to the Whitworth murder. However, there were some sensational facts that explained the popular belief in the violence of immigrant males; these facts will be discussed toward the end of the chapter. The third conclusion belongs to a set of beliefs concerning efficient policing and technology. As we have seen, a trust in technological remedies was not unusual. It had surfaced in the 1880s and would arise again and again in the years to follow.

This leaves the second conclusion – that the city was locked in the grip of a crime wave. The *Hamilton Herald* conveyed this view in a panic-charged editorial. 'These two week-end homicides, together with the recent attempted hold-up on South Locke street, and sundry cuttings and stabbings, indicate that the 'crime wave' which has been overrunning the States, has reached us here.'[2] The belief that American 'evils' were corrupting Canada was commonplace in the 1920s; many Canadians assayed the cosmopolitan republic with the jaundiced eye of suspicion. More generally, however, Canadians suspected all cities of fostering immorality and criminals. The *Hamilton Herald* took note that crimes leading to the shooting of Whitworth, a country vet and merchant, had originated in the city. At his trial, Meharg, the city-bred hoodlum, confessed to having robbed farmers on rural roads.[3] In the simple and quickly composed reactions of the press, crime waves appeared to be endemic to communities that seemed restless, mobile, and composed of strangers. All three characteristics were ones that applied to cities.

Since the 1960s, the idea of crime waves and of their alleged urban origins have come under close and critical scrutiny. To deal with the question of crime waves, researchers have worked with assorted criminal justice records to construct crime rates. Of course, there are pitfalls along the trend lines of any *longue durée*, and crime rates in particular invite controversy. American, British, European, and Canadian data on nineteenth- and twentieth-century crime rates have generated considerable speculation about the connections between major social change or economic conditions and crime. Among historians of western industrializing societies, the flourishing enterprise of explaining crime rates has produced a number of divergent explanations. American historians of criminal justice differ from British counterparts even when largely parallel observations are chronicled. This chapter considers some of the parallels and differences and offers an independent line of discussion that questions the results of statistical probes into crime rates by historians and social scientists on both sides of the Atlantic.

The following account takes up leads from Jennifer Davis, whose work on nineteenth-century London has considered how people in that metropolis interacted with the criminal justice system.[4] Amidst her assessments of how and why people complained to authorities about offences against them, she raises the point that data must be understood in relation to the institutional and behavioural contexts within which they were generated. Criminal justice statistics cannot be dismissed as so completely compromised as to be worthless. The challenge is to coax meaning prudently out of imperfect sources. For several reasons, long-term shifts may be less reliable as social indicators than their advocates have believed, but they retain value as indicators of social and institutional changes. Short-term moves in crime rates have been set aside by the proponents of long-term analysis who favour bold conclusions about deep changes in culture, the state, or the economy.

The study of crime and society is not a new research endeavour. Statistically based theories required for launching the social sciences stemmed in part from the collection of data by governments, and much of this data concerned crime. Of special interest to the early social scientists were the statistics pertaining to deviance. From the French through the Darwinian revolutions, European and North American reformers and states blended speculation about human nature with a fascination for the topic of criminal reformation. Almost invariably, their reports included tables. Most focused on the character of criminals and on whether and how individuals could be weaned from deviant habits and restored to society.[5] Some treatises, however, proposed that a high incidence of crimes was associated with urban growth.

Different North-Atlantic communities formed distinctive approaches to statistics. The French excelled in argument grounded in data. Credit for initiating statistically sophisticated discussions about society and deviants belongs to the brilliant and sceptical French lawyer A.M. Guerry, who felt that what we call criminology might – with great effort – approximate an objective science. He never underestimated the challenges of his task and, in his 1833 study of crime and society in France, he undermined several myths to register a warning against simple conclusions. He tried to show that some of the poorest regions of the country had the lowest rate of crimes against property, suggesting that misery did not necessarily breed crime.[6]

Whereas French rationalism made crime and the judicial system subjects for statistically based inquiry and the English at least collected and displayed reams of tables, American evangelicalism sustained the imagery of Sodom and Gomorrah and American romanticism depicted the city as unnatural.[7] While this characterization of national cultures may exaggerate, it is true that anti-urbanism surely has flowed in the mainstream of American life. During much of the nineteenth century and the first decade of the twentieth, visceral anti-urbanism was a prominent trait in American social commentary. In the first half of the nineteenth century, the expanding centres of the United States, increasingly containing concentrations of immigrant population, came to be seen as sinister and menacing, places of turbulence, crime, and riot. Novels, penny dailies, religious tracts, and city-based moral order crusades helped sustain the stereotype of the wicked city. More immigration and labour unrest late in the century added to the menacing picture.[8]

This one-sided and rather grim depiction of the evil city possibly peaked in the early twentieth century. Without any pretence of deducing broad social principles – except that, the greater the city the greater the depravity – popular authors wrung their hands on the topic of the city, exposing poverty and corruption and marshalling statistics on crime. Josiah Strong in *The Challenge of the City* offered this contrast between town and country: 'Philadelphia and Pittsburg are not exceptionally bad cities, but in Philadelphia there are seven and a half times as much crime to a given population, and in Pittsburg and Allegheny City nearly nine times as much, as in the average rural county of Pennsylvania.'[9] In Canada, J.S. Woodsworth praised Strong's book as one that should be in the hands of all readers, warning that 'unless certain tendencies are checked at once, it is appalling to think what will result with the growth of the city.'[10]

Though robust city-bashing did not stop in the twentieth century, more positive outlooks began to compete with flagrant anti-urbanism. Researchers now could state that the concept of the wicked city was seldom supported by any concrete body of data.[11] The urban riots of the 1960s, however, revived a vigorous popular debate about the city. In the years after the riots, historians of criminal justice and crime as well as social scientists aggressively combatted an assumption that an increasing crime rate is invariably the price of urban growth. Through studies that interpreted imperfect data, authors of major works on the history of crime in the United States succeeded in demonstrating that historical realities concerning crime are exceedingly complex, far more so than a simple axiom to the effect that material progress or 'modernization' pulls a society down the slippery slope into criminal anarchy. Yet these challengers of conventional wisdom replaced old assumptions with a few generalizations of their own. It is one aim of this chapter to suggest that the topic of urban crime rates is more complicated than has been maintained by American social historians.

THE TAMING OF THE CITY

While disputing one set of shaky conjectures, historians of crime introduced other sets. With the benefit of hindsight, it seems clear that their conclusions are riddled with unstated assumptions, understated methodological problems, and overstated conclusions. Americans researchers Theodore Ferdinand and Roger Lane, in separate studies in the late 1960s, used historical data derived from police arrests (Ferdinand) and jail records (Lane) to suggest that crime had not increased. As Ferdinand put it after reviewing graphs, 'This downward drift ... stands in stark contrast to the popular belief that crime is growing rampant and more serious every year.'[12] These authors searched for direct and simple explanations. Neither, moreover, showed much curiosity about the auspices of their data. Ferdinand used Boston police-arrest data for

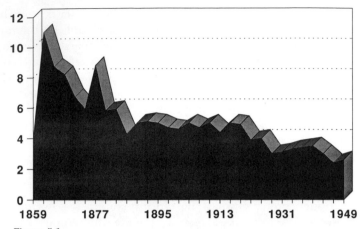

Figure 5.1
Larcenies per 1000 Inhabitants, Boston, 1849–1949
Source: Theodore Ferdinand, 'The Criminal Patterns of Boston since 1849,'
The American Journal of Sociology, vol. 73 (July 1967–68), 95.

the period from 1849 to 1951 (Figures 5.1 and 5.2). He saw in this data a decline in serious crimes when murder, manslaughter, rape, robbery, assault, burglary, and larceny were lumped together.[13]

In retrospect, Lane's early research on crime rates seems unsubstantial, consisting of selected statistics from Massachusetts at three points in time: 1834–6, 1860–2, and 1899–1901.[14] Despite the absence of any interest in understanding the sources of the data he used, Lane asserted that the trend of decline was 'even greater than the statistics indicate.'[15] That is, without discussing biases in the collection of data, he claimed that any errors that might have arisen would run in favour of his argument. Lane was in a hurry to make a bold statement about industrial America. He attributed an alleged drop in crime to industrial development, which 'provided the means of absorbing raw immigrants, of fitting them into a "system" which socialized and accommodated them into more cooperative habits of life.'[16] In Ferdinand's summary to his study, he likewise proposed that the 'adjustment of the descendants of the Irish and Italian immigrants to the urban patterns of Boston' had unquestionably resulted in a reduction in the city's crime rate. A rising standard of living also had contributed to adjustments in life that made for a more civil society.[17] Ten years later and armed with more sophisticated approaches to data, Lane continued to argue that 'criminality was not rising but rather falling beneath all the movement, noise, and smoke of urban growth.' The assertion remained unrevised as recently as 1989, having survived a long run as an unchallenged truth.[18]

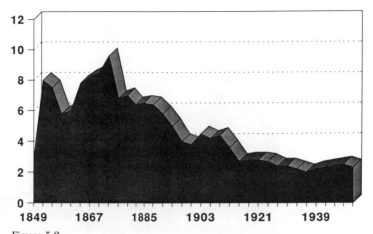

Figure 5.2
Assaults per 1000 Inhabitants, Boston, 1849–1949
Source: Theodore Ferdinand, 'The Criminal Patterns of Boston since 1849,' 96.

The relatively brief discussions by Ferdinand and Lane – laced with the American themes of prosperity, classlessness, and assimilation – were distinct from those of the British social historian V.A.C. Gatrell, who, writing with more sophistication about the very different society of Victorian England, dealt with topics that had intrigued British historians far more than American ones: namely, class and state power. The Ferdinand and Lane studies had inverted conventional thinking about an alleged association between crime and urbanization. Gatrell agreed with this view, at least to the extent that he felt industrial prosperity mitigated the conditions that fostered crime (Figures 5.3 and 5.4). It is worth noting that Gatrell's study, appearing over a decade after the articles by Ferdinand and Lane, had the benefit of some debates about the value of criminal justice statistics that had occurred in the intervening years.

Urban historians, who could not accept the anti-urbanism behind remarks by the likes of Josiah Strong, blithely embraced the arguments of Ferdinand and Lane. Lane himself pressed on impressively with the rehabilitation of the city. Using coroners' reports from Philadelphia, he pursued the theme of the industrial city's civilizing functions in *Violent Death in the City*.[19] More recently he has looked at the 'post industrial surge in violence,' disturbed that 'whatever created the earlier, urban industrial, decline is no longer working.'[20] He has not relinquished his central proposition that serious crime had declined in a period of great urban growth. In the only other notable empirical study of the city and crime written in the aftermath of the urban riots of the 1960s, an examination of court dockets for Columbus, Ohio, from

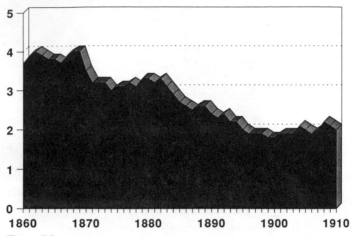

Figure 5.3

Offences against Property without Violence, England, 1860–1910

Source: V.A.C. Gatrell, 'The Decline of Theft and Violence in Victorian and Edwardian England,' in V.A.C. Gatrell, Bruce Lenman and Geoffrey Parker, *Crime and the Law: The Social History of Crime in Western Europe since 1500* (London: Europa Publications 1980), appendix A4.

1859 to 1885, Eric Monkkonen replicated the results and accepted the interpretations of Ferdinand and Lane.[21] Similarly, a study of Toronto policing by Helen Boritch and John Hagan published in 1987 included a graph of the 'arrest rate for crime.' Aggregating all crimes, it too showed a clear downward trend.[22]

From the 1960s onwards, American urban historians, conscious of the dismal recent history of their urban cores, have looked to the past. What had gone right and what had gone wrong? The Philadelphia social history project, directed by Theodore Hershberg, exposed the effects of racism on economic opportunity in the city. Crime was found to have fed on poverty and racism; thus, urbanization and progress were not plausible independent variables explaining crime and violence.[23] While more precise factors than urbanization could explain urban misery and crime, Lane's proposition that the city had actually civilized people received collateral support. In *City People*, Gunther Barth speculated upon how various popular institutions in late-nineteenth-century urban America might have helped rural migrants and immigrants to adapt to city living. Alienation, anonymity, mobility, and the extremes of wealth and poverty were not the sole social realities in and of the city. The cheap press, department stores, vaudeville, and baseball indirectly furnished city people with sets of lessons about con-

Court appearances per 1000 inhabitants

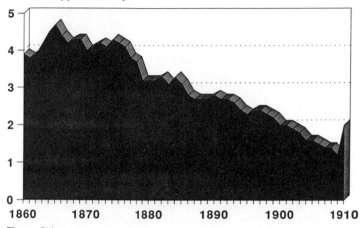

Figure 5.4
Court Appearances for Assault, England, 1860–1910
Source: V.A.C. Gatrell, 'The Decline of Theft and Violence in Victorian and Edwardian England,' appendix A5.

duct and an identification with the community. For Barth, the demise of the inner city – not simply the growth of the city – destroyed important popular institutions that once upon a time had restrained the forces of urban decay. He maintained that 'the shortcomings of urban life are less an intrinsic defect of the city and more a reflection of the fact that people's search for the better life leads as often to greed as to selflessness, which affects country as well as city existence.'[24]

By the 1980s in the United States, intellectuals had reasserted what was – in a broader transatlantic context – the old proposition that environment did not necessarily induce bad conduct. But they seemed compelled to go farther by attempting to prove the point with reference to long-term trends in crime data. As recently as 1988, Monkkonen, in a survey history of the American city, has repeated his earlier conclusions and those of Ferdinand and Lane: 'The evidence assembled by some historians suggests that until approximately World War II, crime and violence in the Western world had been on the decline.'[25] A 1975 article by Howard Zehr on crime in France and Germany ended on a similar upbeat note. 'The decline in violence reflects an acclimatization to city life, a victory for urban values and social organization.'[26] Moreover, one of the most influential promoters of the study of crime trends over time and across cultures, Ted Robert Gurr, drew on secondary literature to produce a graph that charts a drop in homicide rates; it begins in 1200 and stops just short of 2000.[27]

Gurr's downward curve is arresting and it caught the fancy of Lawrence Stone, who leaned on it to carry the weight of a generalization to the effect that the English today are far less prone to casual violence than in the middle ages and early modern period.[28] In a detailed response to the claims of Gurr and Stone, J.S. Cockburn raised a number of questions about the trend line for homicide. Establishing population figures, he pointed out, is never an easy or satisfying exercise; the steps in the fall in homicide need to be considered in association with an account of the history of the treatment of wounds.[29] Homicides are the outcomes of deeds and leave much to be explained about the deeds even on a case by case basis.

Gurr and Lane have steadfastly insisted that, while homicide rates have their problems, they are necessarily the best indicators of violence because it is difficult to hide a body and the accused was likely to have been known to the victim and witnesses.[30] 'For reasons of precision,' states Lane, his work deals with single jurisdictions and 'for reasons of statistical trustworthiness ... with the single crime of homicide.'[31] Yet the issue of the trustworthiness of the data is not settled and, even if it were, there remains the question of what a falling homicide rate says about violence. As Cockburn puts it, 'Our perceptions of violence ... depend on where we look.'[32] To read the newspaper columns on the police magistrate's court in the nineteenth century or a few surviving volumes of the police occurrence books for Hamilton in the 1950s is to descend into a world of domestic violence and tavern brawling. Exposure to that world throws serious doubt on the alleged resurgence of violent crime in the 1960s and 1970s or on the time-worn portrayal of Canada as a peaceable kingdom.

In a lengthy article published in 1980, Gatrell provided a masterful, though partisan, assessment of the value of long-term statistical information and the meaning of Victorian and Edwardian British crime trends. On the surface, Gatrell's detailed account of an alleged decline of theft and violence in Victorian and Edwardian England also sought to undermine the proposition that urban-industrial societies had necessarily fostered crime. But he challenged the idea of an assumed link between material progress and crime by questioning the concept of material progress. How could there have been a correlation between crime rates and progress, he asked, when the latter term does not readily yield to definition or testing?[33] He did not exactly concede that crime rates themselves are slippery items. While many serious questions remain about the way in which criminal justice records – and hence data – have and are being generated by contemporary law enforcement agencies, Gatrell maintained that the rich enterprise of criminal justice history has at least dispelled some crude generalizations about crime and social change.

Nevertheless, Gatrell himself proposed why the findings of historians on trends in crime have failed to shake popular perceptions about the social origins of crime. Capitalism and the city have furthered social tendencies identified with what Gatrell called 'criminogenic pressures': the anonymity of urban life, mobility of the population (especially the poor), the abundance of stealable property, alienation, as well as rising but unfulfilled material expectations that cannot be met. Finally, he alleged that crime rates have been rising enormously in nearly every industrialized society during the twentieth century.[34] Thus, even though he and others demonstrated the case for historical complexity, thereby weakening the historical props for a theory on the inexorable rise of crime, Gatrell did not resoundingly dismiss the existence of a relationship between crime and urbanization.

Gatrell's full-blown argument includes the point that firm state actions against crime – indeed state action in a number of areas of social policy in the nineteenth century – caught criminals unaware; the shock of state power checked crime for awhile. 'A "progressive" State matched itself against an as yet undefended adversary.'[35] On the basis of his article, it could be argued that the state in nineteenth-century England capably managed the symptoms of an increasingly pathogenic society. Yet Gatrell himself does not reach this conclusion. Instead he argues that, if a fall in crime occurred, it resulted not from the actions of the state alone but also from the fact that after the 1840s the poor did not have to contend with rising food prices in periods of unemployment. The arguments fit neatly together; they also rest on a rich body of secondary literature and a set of national data on crimes known to the police.

But what exactly did crimes known to the police mean in the context of the nineteenth century? While criminal justice statistics cannot be ignored, questions concerning their reliability and meaning need to be addressed. Given the methodological challenges and the temptation to reach a startling conclusion, Gatrell's inquisitive style with its tone of a quest for truth does mark his study as perhaps the most significant statistical examination of crime in nineteenth-century England and Wales.[36] It stands in stark contrast to the declaratory tone of American accounts. Nevertheless, one can argue that Gatrell's influential article – indeed every study that has sought out a connection between crime and society for the nineteenth century – moves too quickly over the subject of prosecution. That is, many authors have assumed that ongoing innovations in the criminal justice system necessarily meant greater vigilance by the authorities and hence a statistical bias that – if anything – should have increased the number of crimes known to authorities. The fact that crime rates actually seemed to fall with the refinement of criminal justice innovations apparently bolstered the case for a decline in crime.

This theory, as we will now see, is seriously flawed.

THE CERTAINTY OF IMPERFECT KNOWLEDGE AND WHAT THE POLICE KNEW

The literature cited above indicates how some historical accounts of crime have been related to the city. The city has been correctly excused as the paramount source of crime, for city and industry were never plausible independent variables.

Still, uncritical assumptions about an alleged decline in crime ought to raise a sceptical eyebrow; one can admire the cleverness and openness of Gatrell without necessarily accepting the meaning he gives to the data. Using police court records and police department annual reports for Hamilton, it has been possible to duplicate the now-familiar decline in crime between 1860 and 1900.[37] Yet what we now know about how the entire criminal justice process functioned in this city raises a degree of uncertainty about the generally accepted thesis of a decline in theft and violence.

Ferdinand, Lane, and Gatrell supposed that the local, state, and national data that they employed fundamentally had a consistent definition over time. Of course, they realized that criminal codes changed, that what society defines as criminal is subject to modification. Accordingly, they endeavoured to make what they felt were appropriate adjustments. Furthermore, Gatrell employed data that appeared to be close to events, namely the statistics on crimes known to the police. While that phrase – known to the police – has a firm and reassuring quality, it is in fact burdened with a serious problem: the police, who generated the statistics, did not leave any record of how they were compiled or of the assumptions on which they rested. Placing the data on the grand stage of cultural changes and excited by the detection of what seemed to be significant and unconventional findings, the historians who compiled and analysed pioneer crime rates did not delve into the institutional origins of the statistics.

More is involved here than just the real possibility of sloppy bookkeeping by nineteenth-century clerks or desk sergeants. We must begin, as Jennifer Davis has, by asking some important questions: Why did people report a crime? To whom did they report it? Did the report

necessarily become part of a surviving public record? Were people discouraged from prosecuting? These questions are simple enough to ask,
but difficult to answer empirically. It has been generally assumed that
criminal justice agencies must have intensified the prosecution process
during the nineteenth century, but the evidence from Hamilton on
this point is at best ambiguous. Public reporting of crime has been subject to various cultural considerations and has changed over time, but
it has always occupied a central position in criminal justice. It will be
recalled that a sample of cases heard before the police magistrate from
1859 to 1918 highlighted the role played by individual complainants
in every category of offence except moral order violations (Table 3.1).

A further but related complication arises from a shift in the Anglo-
American institutional apparatus that has dealt with crime. Over time,
victims of crime – in the city of Hamilton at least – redirected their
complaints from the police magistrate's office and courts to the police
officer on the beat who may or may not have forwarded the case into
a bureaucracy that sorted out whether or not to proceed with an investigation, and whether or not to encourage the complainant to prosecute. If this has been the case elsewhere – and the fact that Hamilton
participated in the basic reforms of common law institutions in the
nineteenth century suggests that it was – then data based on court records are certainly compromised. To repeat: Why did people report
crimes? To whom did they report? Did the official charged with hearing the complaint encourage or discourage a prosecution? Did the re-
cipient of the complaint operate under orders and sufficient bureaucratic rigour to record the complaint?

To pursue these questions, it is important to retrace a few steps over
familiar ground and outline what was meant throughout most of the
second half of the nineteenth century when a case came to the attention of the police magistrate. A case of theft or assault normally came
before the court by direct action of the victim or complainant, listed often in the records as a plaintiff. Without evidence, Gatrell proposed
that in the late nineteenth century people were 'increasingly cooperative with the law, and ever readier to report, prosecute, and give evidence against suspected offenders.'[38] This claim assumes a prior
reluctance to use the criminal justice system. Thus, he argued, if errors
in reporting do exist they favour the interpretation that a real decline
took place in the latter decades of the century, for even with a more active public the rates fell. In fact, the Hamilton police court proceedings, paralleling the London ones studied by Davis, suggest that many
citizens in that community were far from reluctant to make formal
complaints in the mid-century. Until the city established a police department and until its functions were more or less mapped out and

known to the public, the magistrate's office handled the public's complaints. From the kinds of cases that made it through to that office and into court where they were reported, it is evident – as we shall see – that the magistrate was not considered distant and unapproachable. Possibly the newspaper coverage of police magistrate's court indirectly publicized his services.

Authorized by a city charter in 1846, the police magistrate provided a full-time adjunct to the city's justices of the peace. The office invited complainants and became in the mid-nineteenth century a clearing-house for all manner of problems that stretched the meaning of crime. For example, children who fought were reported; parents even brought rebellious children before it. The lower courts may not have been places where great deliberations transpired, but they kept required forms and maintained records. When the newspapers and police department reports cited a certain number of assaults, larcenies, or robberies, there is no doubt that they simply had tallied entries in the police-court ledger. These were the crimes known to the police in Hamilton.

On their own, the police routinely prosecuted only transgressions against the by-laws, including the very significant ones dealing with vagrancy and drunk and disorderly behaviour. Very rarely in the nineteenth century did a Hamilton constable or detective introduce into court an action for theft; these appear to have been entered as a special charge – *suspicion* of theft. Constables were empowered by statute to arrest without warrant when they caught someone in the act.[39] The police detected larceny by watching for suspicious conduct, observing former thieves, and keeping tabs on second-hand dealers.

In the middle of the century, action on suspicion occasionally involved an arrest and then a search for a victim. In November 1857 the police arrested a man suspected of heading a gang of thieves. They put him in jail and then went looking for the owner of a dressing case that had another person's initials on it.[40] A week later, two men were reported to the police as skinning cows in suspicious circumstances. The police arrested them on suspicion of theft and then put the cow skins on display in the police office. One skin was recognized and the police had a complainant for a charge of cattle theft.[41] When, in July 1863, Constable West watched in amazement as Archibald Quinn lurched down the street with a calf over his shoulder at 1:00 a.m., he had cause to give pursuit.[42] Quinn, who was overtaken because he refused to let go of the animal, had lifted the calf out of a butcher's wagon. In April 1873, Constable Bennett observed a women walking in a peculiar way and discovered that she had thirty yards of stolen material under her shawl.[43] He had her locked up and then questioned merchants to find a complainant. These latter two cases suggest that street wisdom for the police sometimes meant applying the adage 'if you see a poor person with riches look for a crime.' Of course, they could scarcely act on the reciprocal notion that 'behind every fortune there is a crime.'[44]

Many arrests for theft praised as demonstrating police ingenuity involved a citizen's report, sheer luck, or street smarts. A detective nabbed George Smith after a report that he had sold boots for a third their value to a second-hand dealer.[45] One night in March 1883, a constable stumbled across an odd quarrel. Hiding behind a tree, he heard two men disputing the division of spoils from a burglary. He arrested them.[46]

Very seldom could the constables and detectives claim such successes as these and even their accomplishments occasionally involved what would be regarded today as extremely dubious practices.

In the overwhelming majority of cases, individuals brought their concerns to the police magistrate and the police constables then acted primarily as processors of summonses that channelled cases directly into police court. As for the detective branch, it was, in an era of an alleged decline in crime, secretive about its investigations even within the force; detectives, it will be recalled, sought rewards for returned property. Perhaps policing practices and the public's use of policing in Canada were so distinctive that we should not question Gatrell's trust in data based on crimes known to the police in England. In Hamilton, however, what the police knew and accomplished on their own, from their founding at mid-century to their modernization around 1885, is unimpressive.

Nineteenth-century data for Hamilton and possibly beyond, therefore, was principally derived from complainants' actions, not from the deeds of the police. In some cases, the plaintiff, having shaken up the accused, reached an accommodation, or, having intimidated the other party, never bothered to press on with the case. The court clerk often wrote: 'Plaintiff did not appear Discd'; or, 'Complt did not appear.' Still, the provision of a full-time and readily available magistrate – remember that Jelfs had three offices including one at home – permitted a torrent of complaints and many of these did end up in court. Various motives inspired the complainants. Certainly some complaints originated among feuding neighbours; battered wives used the complaint process to achieve a measure of protection and a modicum of personal power; a few individuals likely used it maliciously. Describing similar phenomena for Alameda County, California, Friedman and Percival believe that the many 'on again, off again cases of quarrels among relatives or neighbors were essentially private matters and court officials felt "used." '[47] It is a moot question whether the quarrels really were 'private matters'; the important point is that officials may have started to treat them as such. A concern about malicious action led to a measure designed to reduce private prosecutions in Canada.

As recounted in chapter 2, the government of Canada in 1857 established the office of the county crown attorney who was charged with several important duties related to the preparation of criminal prosecutions and to advising the police magistrate. However, as Douglas Hay and Francis Snyder have indicated in an account of prosecution in common law jurisdictions, the county crown attorney in Canada was 'justified in part by a reference to the evil of malicious prosecution.'[48] By statute the crown attorney attended to this issue only in the court of quarter sessions and later the court of general sessions of the peace, not at the police magistrate's court, but the fact that malicious prosecution had been mentioned in legislation denotes a serious concern. Until the 1880s, newspaper reports of the police magistrate's court seldom mention the crown attorney. References then begin to appear that show the crown attorney both assisting with some private prosecutions and discouraging others.[49] The dual thrust of the intervention was to see to it that, on the one hand, the more serious cases like aggravated assault were vigorously prosecuted and that, on the other, prosecution for minor offences like common assaults were treated neutrally or discouraged.[50] As was seen in chapter 2, the innovation of the crown attorney was one of many measures in the mid-Victorian era that sought to make more efficient use of the courts.

The ability to assist or discourage a prosecution gave the crown attorney a power that may have been used to the disadvantage of the city's unionized labourers. That was certainly the outcome of an incident in 1892. In that year, a union man brought a complaint against a nonunion labourer for stabbing him. The union man had to hire his own attorney. The defence thought that the prosecution should have been in the hands of the crown attorney; that individual 'stated that he would watch the case on behalf of the crown, but preferred to have Mr. O'Heir (the complainant's attorney) conduct the case.'[51] More generally, the discouragement of prosecution pursued in the late nineteenth century by both the crown attorney and the police magistrate narrowed access to cheap justice and to settlement by criminal process of what sometimes amounted to private disputes.

It is impossible to know what transpired in the police magistrate's office when he heard a complaint and a request for a summons to court or a warrant for an arrest. One hypothesis of this book is that from the 1860s to the early 1900s magistrates shifted from a fairly routine issuing of summonses and warrants to discouraging them in several kinds of cases. Reminiscing in 1914 about a career on the bench that had begun in 1893, George Jelfs thought he might write his memoirs. Surprisingly, he thought that he would not deal with the cases that came up in court, 'but rather the ones that I have been instrumental in settling before they came to court.'[52] Now this is an illuminating confession. Jelfs did more than intimate a pride in reducing private prosecutions, he most certainly discouraged prosecutions in three areas: common assaults of a trifling nature, wife beating, and feuding neighbours.

With respect to the first category, Jelfs dressed down a complainant in court in 1893, dismissing the case and 'telling the young man that when he got older he would consider that prosecution was ill-advised.'[53] Concerning drunken husbands and wife beating, Jelfs said in 1901 that the more insistent that a wife became in wishing to prosecute a husband, the more likely it was that she was primarily at fault.[54] He claimed in 1912 that 'years ago ... his efforts to discourage the custom of carrying ... differences to court were so successful that his docket rarely recorded a dispute of this kind.' He described the process whereby he trimmed the docket, a process that he may have used in other circumstances too. He never declined to take action. Instead, if a party was intent upon having someone brought to court in the manner that would cause the most embarrassment, namely by arrest, then Jelfs would offer only to issue a summons. In Jelfs's words, 'This invariably wet-blanketed the applicant, who wanted immediate action.'[55]

These rare glimpses into the mind of a pivotal figure in Hamilton's criminal justice system suggest that prosecutions were subject to official discouragement by at least the 1890s and probably earlier. In this regard, the attitude of police magistrates toward complainants is doubly important. Not only could they directly dissuade parties from laying charges, but their discouragement had an added edge. They were, after all, the officials who also would try the case if prosecution were insisted upon. Who would want to lay charges knowing beforehand the judge's adverse opinion?

At some point in the late nineteenth century the police became important to complainants, and increasingly so. Perhaps by the 1870s or 1880s, the public came to view the police as accessible, convenient, and useful and so carried complaints to them. For their part, the police eventually helped make decisions about prosecution or intervened in ways that gave complainants some satisfaction. Constables were taking over the work that police magistrates had begun to avoid. Still, for many years, there must have been a mixed system: some victims stepping forward as plaintiffs alone, others coming with the aid of the police and bringing complaints before the police court, and still others calling upon the police force to investigate. The proportions of the mix can never be known. Nevertheless, this complication and the obscurities of police record keeping ought to disturb faith in the idea that nineteenth-century 'crimes known to the police' or 'court appearances' resembled modern conceptions of those phrases.

THE THEFT RATE AND THE REPORTING OF THEFT

With all of the preceding caveats in mind, let us scan the Hamilton theft data for 1859 to 1970 (Figure 5.5). The data came from the annual reports of the police force and represented the total of theft, larceny, robbery, housebreaking, burglary, horse theft, cattle theft, pickpocketing, fraud, and other crimes. Simple theft comprised the overwhelming majority of the offences; consequently, the insertion of robbery with violence into this category rather than that of violent crimes – or vice versa – will not affect the rates. Two obvious and broad trends are that thefts per thousand residents fell from the 1860s to the 1880s and that, from the turn-of-the-century to the early 1950s, the rate fluctuated moderately just below a mean of 4.0 per thousand residents. Stability followed a sharp decline. But does this mean that theft had declined?

Gatrell reported a similarly sharp fall in the larceny rate for England and Wales. He attributed the drop to the deterrent effect of new instruments of social control and the fall in the cost of food. In contrast, Zehr stated that theft rose in France and Germany; therefore, he built his central argument around the notion that one consequence of modernization was to alter the ratio of crimes against person to crimes against property – the latter rose relative to the former. Urbanization raised expectations; the factory system 'taught' labourers to work 'beyond what was required simply to maintain previous standards of living.'[56] Whereas Gatrell implied that the kind of need that might drive some people to steal was an absolute and desperate need, Zehr proposed a relative need.

The contrast between the findings of Gatrell and Zehr indicate some of the problems of explaining theft rates. It is apparent from the accounts of theft in the police magistrate's court of Hamilton that need often played a part in theft, but so did opportunity and other factors. Moreover, the way society – both the victim and the authorities – perceived and responded to theft in this city calls into question the value of thinking about long-term declines in theft.

Until the 1880s in Hamilton, it is more than likely that abundant plaintiff-based court actions originated in minor occurrences. When the police assumed more responsibility for bringing actions near the

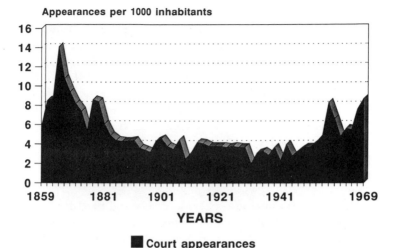

Appearances per 1000 inhabitants

■ **Court appearances**

Figure 5.5
Theft Rates in Hamilton: Court Appearances, 1859–1970
Sources: *Hamilton Spectator*, 21 January 1865, 11 January 1866, 11 January 1867, 17
January 1870, 4 January 1872, 6 January 1875, 6 January 1876, 22 January 1878,
9 January 1879, 26 January 1880, 11 January 1881, 30 January 1883, 7 February 1884,
28 February 1887, 30 January 1890, 16 February 1892, 26 January 1898, 27
January 1899, 31 January 1901, 5 February 1902, 22 January 1903, 3 February 1904,
23 February 1905, 30 January 1907, 20 January 1909, 3 February 1910, 27
February 1915, HPL, Records of the City of Hamilton, RG 10, Series A, Police
Department, *Annual Reports*, 1906–70, missing 1906–8, 1910, 1911, 1914, 1916,
1918–19, 1930, 1933; RG 10, Series K, Police Court Proceedings, Ledgers, 1859–1949.

end of the century, doubtful and minor incidents were kept out of the
courts. In the 1870s, by way of illustration, youths suspected of filching
apples from an orchard were taken to court by the irate proprietor who
would have had the court issue a summons. The police served the summons; propertied men have always had a knack for comprehending the
workings of the law. Forty years later, the proprietor would have complained to the police, who then might have closely questioned and
sternly warned the lads. If a report of this latter episode were made –
and the police commission's directives on the matter suggest carelessness until around the 1890s – it would have been penned into the occurrence books and not have been a part of the police court proceedings. And what did Jelfs mean when he suggested that he took pride
in his handling of cases that never left his office? Was the police magistrate in the late nineteenth century increasingly engaged in the
resolution of disputes out of court?

It is possible that the late nineteenth-century slide in the so-called
theft rate actually captures the phasing in of new intermediary roles for

both the police and the police magistrate, roles that heaped more work on the constables, altered the functions of the magistrate, and reduced the case load in the courts. As working-class households grew used to the police constables, many of whom shared class and cultural origins with the common folk of the city, they took complaints directly to constables who at first were – unlike courts with their system of statutory forms and the increasingly unsympathetic magistrate – casual. The first task of a constable answering a call was to restore order to a situation and, in the course of that exercise, he may well have recovered the property and given a stern rebuke, measures that satisfied the complainant. After all, most occurrences of theft involved items of very little value.

There is no denying cyclical and seasonal hardship as factors affecting the number of thefts. A depression and the onset of winter may help to explain the rash of actions against young people on 19 December 1862. Eliza Myers made a complaint against Catherine Clancey, described as 'a little girl,' whom she alleged had stolen two white aprons; the magistrate committed her to ten days in jail. A boy was convicted of stealing a pair of boots from Dayfoot's emporium, while another 'little boy' was charged by James Sturgeon with stealing a board from his fence. The theft of wood was seasonal.[57] Winter and distress may also have been behind the theft of meat from a stall in the market that sent a twelve- and a fourteen-year-old to jail for twenty days in February 1874. In summer, the necessities stolen by children shifted to garden produce. Charles Taylor, thirteen, had taken potatoes from Thomas Kern's garden; his defence that his parents had done the actual stealing and that he had merely assisted with hauling the spuds away earned him one month in jail.[58] A few young thieves were brought to court by their parents. After George Combs made an information against his son, alleging he had taken two silver spoons and a watch, 'he declined to prosecute.'[59] Late in 1871, sixteen-year-old John Mahon ran off to Buffalo with his father's gold watch and $20 in rent money. He was not greeted as the prodigal son upon his return.[60]

The long run of data may not yield a harvest of insights about crime and the economy or crime and urban alienation once so eagerly sought after by social scientists. Yet the data does highlight or suggest very short-term shifts in social conditions and law-enforcement patterns. The relatively low rate for the late 1850s may have been a consequence of the massive out-migration from the city that was in full swing because of the collapse of the local economy. Transients were not coming into Hamilton. It is possible too that the sudden up-turn in the early 1860s owes something to a depression and also to the unusual circumstances created in Hamilton by the American Civil War. The war gave an economic fillip to the city, promoted 'crimps' who recruited local men for the union army, and precipitated the despatching of British troops to protect the colony during a rough period in Anglo-American relations. The city also became home to a number of 'Yankee skedaddlers.' In the court ledgers, there appear a notable number of theft cases involving 'a soldier of the 47th,' the illegal possession of military boots and 'milt. clothing,' and the light-fingered actions of the visitors from south of the border. Virtually a border city and now one with a garrison, Hamilton experienced some exciting times that spilled over into the courts. Thirty years later, an inquiry into the prison and reformatory system of Ontario reported in passing that 'the great civil war disturbed all the social elements and created a liking for an idle shiftless life.'[61] The social analysis implied in the comment was superficial, but the statement testifies to the memory of an upheaval that touched even neutral communities.

The unusually high theft rate for 1914 and the notable dip for 1946 can be explained by comparable institutional and social considerations. In both periods, economic conditions make a tempting explanation for a change from the norm; however, the circumstances are more complicated. The rise in the theft rate that began in 1913 and continued for several years appears to have been indicative of something. By that year, a number of annexations had been completed by the city; the population base used for this year was, therefore, much higher than that in 1909. Thus, there seems to have been a real increase in crime rates and it likely was related to an economic crash, the high unemployment experienced by the city's labour force, and the fact that these labourers, made up largely of newcomers, had recent and shallow roots in the city. The depression was a necessary condition for the rise in the rate, and the significance of the working-class, boarding-house society of unattached men was surely an important consideration as well.

The actual number of thefts may have increased, for the boarding-houses and taverns that flourish in economic booms were always notorious locales for theft. Concurrently, the civic authorities most likely saw a social crisis brewing; a crisis of unemployment in a city with many immigrants triggered a firm policy of investigating cases and laying charges. This hypothesis – joining many others on crime and society questions – cannot be proven conclusively. Yet, taking into account the internal atmosphere at the police department and the social changes in the city, the analysis is plausible and comes as a refinement over explanations that posit a raw correlation between unemployment and theft. The force had just experienced an internal shake-up under the baton of Whatley, the ambitious deputy chief backed by a police commission that wanted an aggressive force. The department – in common with many residents – was suspicious of immigrant and boarding-house life in the industrial quarters of the city.

The inadequacy of a purely economic explanation is underlined when the crime data for the twentieth century is considered. By the 1930s, the clash between 'foreigners' and a police department under zealous leadership had subsided, and, in contrast to the 1860s, the city had a rudimentary welfare system. Likely for both these reasons, the theft rate during the Great Depression displayed no remarkable fluctuations. As for the following decade, the exceptionally low index number for 1946 adds further support to the belief that the resources and attitude of the police, varying over time, affected the handling of reports, the quality of investigations, and finally the number of charges laid. Lengthy and bitter labour disputes preoccupied the department in that year, leaving little time for an aggressive response to crime.

The next notable variation from the mean occurred in the 1960s, when the rate of theft began to rise. Part of the increase could have been the result of the way in which the data was assembled; that is, the index may have been pushed up artificially by a relatively low divisor, low because it consisted of an underestimated population base. However, even a 25 per cent error would not help to explain the really sharp move upwards in the late 1960s. Assuming that something was happening and it represented a break from the past, what was the underlying reason? Some of the increase could have been the result of improvements in investigation, and it also could have stemmed from the police's increasing propensity to bring charges – the police laid more charges per reported incident in the 1960s than in prior decades. Yet another factor was an astonishing increase in the reporting of thefts by citizens. Most likely, increases in reports were related to insurance claims.

All of the above reflections on a commonly used form of crime rate recommend that, for the modern era at least, indices for theft should be treated warily and, with the possible exception of short-term changes, not even as an indirect measure of real crime. Changes in the institutional paths taken by the public when complaining about theft, the receptivity of the lowest court to hearing complaints, and the availability of police resources have played their part in determining the rate of theft. So has the public's willingness to report crimes. The virtually automatic willingness of individuals to report theft today is indicative of widespread insurance coverage and accumulations of temptingly light and mobile mass-produced articles spread widely across the community.

On the last point, some thoughts on Zehr's hypothesis concerning modernization are in order. Zehr explained acts of theft in the nineteenth century by arguing that urban workers were pinched between rapidly rising expectations and slowly rising standards of living. While Zehr's conjecture about motives centred on the thief, there is just as much reason to focus on the victims and their reporting of theft. After the Second World War, diffusion of prosperity and of credit spread consumer items abundantly across Hamilton and increasingly these articles were protected by insurance as more and more young families purchased houses and secured home-insurance coverage. More recently the interchangabilty of many standardized articles and the democratization of insurance have altered the strategy of recovery and changed the role of the police in that process. A report to the police is no more likely to result in convictions that it did in the past, but at least it leads to the replacement of the lost items. Modernization is likely to have influenced theft reports in several respects. Neither Zehr's theory nor the one suggested here can alone explain trends in theft data.

In the details of the short term, then, reside the facts for a consideration of policing as an adaptable instrument, an authority involved in the web of modern public and private institutions that operate to counter loss and sustain bourgeois comfort and confidence. Illustrative of this point are statistics compiled from police occurrence books. Covering the period from 1896 to the 1960s, these statistics are based on reports to the police (Figure 5.6).

From a detailed study of the occurrence books in the 1930s and 1940s, it is possible to argue that occurrences included an enormous number of low-value articles and that they looked very much like the petty-theft reports that plaintiffs had once brought before the police court. In the past, the police had simply dropped investigations of many occurrences, thus deflating the court statistics that they cited in their annual reports. This practice continued until 1961, when the police started to report routinely and ever more fastidiously on occurrences. Again, the switch from the magistrate to the police as the locus of complaints makes it difficult to reconstruct a reliable time series.

The occurrence data has gaps, but despite these, the trend indicated by the data is clear enough. Above all, the number of 'occurrences/ offences known to the police' per thousand residents – an index of reported thefts – is distinguished by a steady rise from the 1890s to about 1961. Several unaccountable peaks and troughs disturb the incline and cannot be explained. All the same, the trend projects a rise. What is again fascinating about the numbers for the 1930s – the decade of the Great Depression – is the apparent lack of any dramatic increase or decrease in reporting. To the extent that there is any sharp jump in the reporting of theft, it occurs in the late 1930s and the early 1940s when

Appearances per 1000 inhabitants

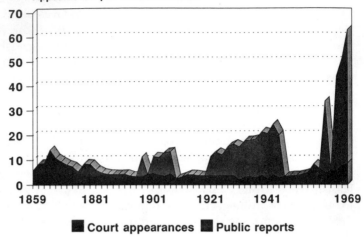

■ **Court appearances** ■ **Public reports**

Figure 5.6
Theft Rates in Hamilton: Public Reports and Court Appearances, 1859–1970

Sources: *Hamilton Spectator*, 21 January 1865, 11 January 1866, 11 January 1867, 17 January 1870, 4 January 1872, 6 January 1875, 6 January 1876, 22 January 1878, 9 January 1879, 26 January 1880, 11 January 1881, 30 January 1883, 7 February 1884, 28 February 1887, 30 January 1890, 16 February 1892, 26 January 1898, 27 January 1899, 31 January 1901, 5 February 1902, 22 January 1903, 3 February 1904, 23 February 1905, 30 January 1907, 20 January 1909, 3 February 1910, 27 February 1915, HPL, Records of the City of Hamilton, RG 10, Series A, Police Department, *Annual Reports*, 1906–70, missing 1906–08, 1910, 1911, 1914, 1916, 1918–19, 1930, 1933; RG 10, Series K, Police Court Proceedings, Ledgers, 1859–1949; Series A, *Annual Reports*.

the index reached the high teens and edged toward twenty. Wartime prosperity in this industrial city provided an abundance of articles worth stealing (including ration coupons and tools), a casual attitude about money, places of entertainment where people relaxed their guard, and strangers.

Because of missing information, the reports per thousand residents for the post-war era can only be interpolated, but it seems likely that the pattern of gradual increase was sustained until the early 1960s. Some of the sharp rise that surfaced after 1961 could have been a result of new practices in the reporting of crime that had been instituted by the Dominion Bureau of Statistics. Obviously, however, the adoption of a different approach to the collecting and classification of data in the early 1960s cannot explain the very notable jump in reporting that occurred from 1968 to 1970. Once again, it is possible that a combination of insurance and new portable consumer articles are mixed up in the events. By the late twentieth century, the police functioned as an orderly public aid to the restoration of private property. In effect, they had added a function to their evolving activities in the city, becoming a white-collar adjunct of the massive state and private-service industry that cushions some of the risks of everyday life.

FROM MEAN STREETS TO CLEAN STREETS?

On first glance, the data on assaults seem to express the familiar proposition that violence declined from the mid-nineteenth to the early twentieth century (Figure 5.7). It should be pointed out that the data summarizes the annual reports by the police department and that assaults included common assault, assault and battery, assault with intent, felonious assault, wife beating, shooting, stabbing, and rioting. Common assault dominated the annual returns.

From the annual totals it is possible to fashion an explanation along the lines of Gatrell's argument that the institutional weight of the state had an initial impact on crime and violence. Certainly, the modernization of the Hamilton police that began in the 1880s (the introduction of disciplined and supervised beats, signal boxes, patrol wagon, bicycle patrols, and a station in the working-class east end) represented a parochial and somewhat later version of what Gatrell proposed. While the idea of police effectiveness is open to question – the ideal of policing, as espoused by contemporary police administrators and the police commission, fell short of realization – one simple inference to be taken from the data is that an agency of the local 'state' made enough of an attack on the casual violence of the streets to promote prudence among citizens.

There is another set of explanations for the apparent decline of violence which does not exclude the possibility that policing itself had something to do with the phenomenon. Culturally and physically, the city changed over the decades from the 1870s to the 1920s. The moral reformers may not have persuaded the police to enforce vigorously their every whim and fancy, but they surely exercised a degree of authority on the population at large as well as some influence on the liquor-licensing laws of the province. Concurrently, the city's housing stock improved and overcrowding declined, particularly beginning in the 1920s; perhaps a greater proportion of city residents than ever before found reasonably spacious accommodations and the opportunity to entertain at home rather than having to pursue recreation in the taverns.

In the first few decades of the twentieth century, radio, automobiles,

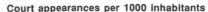

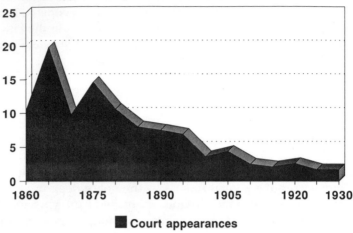

Court appearances

Figure 5.7

Trend of Assaults per 1000 Inhabitants, Hamilton, Five-Year Intervals

Sources: *Hamilton Spectator*, 21 January 1865, 11 January 1866, 11 January 1867, 17 January 1870, 4 January 1872, 6 January 1875, 6 January 1876, 22 January 1878, 9 January 1879, 26 January 1880, 11 January 1881, 30 January 1883, 7 February 1884, 28 February 1887, 30 January 1890, 16 February 1892, 26 January 1898, 27 January 1899, 31 January 1901, 5 February 1902, 22 January 1903, 3 February 1904, 23 February 1905, 30 January 1907, 20 January 1909, 3 February 1910, 27 February 1915, HPL, Records of the City of Hamilton, RG 10, Series A, Police Department, *Annual Reports*, 1906–70, missing 1906–08, 1910, 1911, 1914, 1916, 1918–19, 1930, 1933; RG 10, Series K, Police Court Proceedings, Ledgers, 1859–1949.

and cinema altered entertainment. These gifts of technology to a consumer society – along with bigger houses – also propelled the city toward greater compartmentalized activity and reduced instances of interpersonal contact. A larger proportion of the population than ever before enjoyed a middle-class style of life, one less fraught with assertions of power through physical confrontation and perhaps more obsessed with material display than nineteenth-century working-class life had been. New forms of leisure redirected resources away from boisterous entertainment. In the city by the mid-twentieth century, significant social and technological phenomena of advanced capitalism had trimmed the opportunities for rowdy contact, braggadocio, and rumbumptious conduct.

Plausible though it is, the above interpretation vaults over one important point. An omission was made in order to provide an analysis of the data as it might have been conducted by historians who have struggled to integrate their crime data into the broad themes of urbanization, industrialization, the rise of the middle class, the creation of state institutions for social control, and the development of a mass consumer society. It is worth noting again those complications with the data that stem from peculiarities in English-speaking jurisdictions. Throughout this family of societies, there was an evolution in the nineteenth century from prosecution by individuals to prosecution with the aid of the police. This fact could mean everything in terms of how we come to understand an apparent decline in the assault rate.

As with theft, the victim in earlier decades initiated action by coming to the police magistrate's office and requesting a summons to court or a warrant for an arrest. From the late 1870s and early 1880s onward, there is evidence of the police magistrate and police department giving a fair amount of advice to complainants and lobbying for the city to pay the court costs of the poor who prosecuted. When Mr Tinsley threw his wife out of their house, her father-in-law recommended that she prosecute. The magistrate advised her to go with a witness to her husband and demand support.[62] This case from 1884 suggests again that the use of the police court was part of the lore of city living and that the authorities counselled some complainants, though this was in the process of changing.

Part of the explanation for the fact that the victims brought actions in assaults lay in the lingering idea that, in the lowest court, individuals were to prosecute as plaintiffs or complainants. But another aspect of the explanation had to do with communications in the pedestrian and pre-electronic city. Unless there were a police constable close at hand on the beat, there was no direct way of securing police intervention, of catching the offender 'red handed.' Theft was a slightly different matter; stolen goods could trip up the offender. Assaults usually had to be dealt with after the fact, although there were a few arrests for fighting in the street. In the wake of a fight or of a wife beating, the injured male or the battered female might elect to bring a complaint to the court because there was little else to be done *via* the formal mechanisms of the criminal justice system.

A decision turned on many calculations. The male could take his lumps and remain silent, knowing that he might have to have dealings with the assailant again. Obviously, the injured or threatened wife or companion could fear a loss of support if the male were fined or sent to jail. To initiate a prosecution and appear in court to press the case entailed certain risks. In an indeterminate number of cases, however, the victim had enough and did request a summons. The assailant appeared in court; often the plaintiff then withdrew the charges. Representing what seems to have been a common pattern, Eliza Milligan on 10 August 1865 had the police prepare a summons for her husband Thomas. When the case was called the next day, the 'prosecutor did not appear.'[63] The idea may have been to scare the assailant into future decency. That an accused may have intimidated a complainant can be inferred from the phrasing of an entry for 13 June 1865. Sarah McElroy had a summons issued on Hugh Boyle for assault, but 'Complt would not appear.'[64] In a few cases, the court clerk noted in the margins of the ledger that an agreement had been reached. On 20 February 1859 John Pettigrew 'settled' with Leopold Wertheimer and Leopold dropped the charge.[65]

It is also apparent that violence begat violence and that the ease of access to the police magistrate's court in the mid-Victorian era often became an ingredient in calculations of vengeance. In his address to the court prior to his sentencing, convicted murderer Michael McConnell gave an astonishing account of how he, fellows in the same trade, and his neighbour used the court to inflict misery on one another. His brother butchers had given him a hard time. On one occasion, they got him drunk and then took him to the police cells where he was arrested. On an another, they assaulted him and he brought charges. One of these butchers retaliated later; McConnell made gestures at him and he had McConnell arrested for threatening. McConnell's neighbour allowed her cattle to stray into his yard. He rounded them up and started off with them to the city's animal pound with the aim of laying a charge against her, but he relented. However, she laid a complaint of assault against him, and Police Magistrate Cahill fined him for failing to drive the loose animals to the pound.[66] It is likely that in later years, the intervention of the law in circumstances such as these would have come through a request for action made to the police department.

Just as adults occasionally prosecuted children for theft, so they also took them to court for assault. Indeed, the cases themselves suggest that far from being a particularly violent epoch – a period when violence figured as a notable cultural trait – there was considerable attention devoted to punishing violence even among and from children. In February 1863 two boys were fined one dollar each for assaulting a 'small girl.' After some boys had their sport, throwing stones at him, the night watchman at the Great Western Railroad yards took after them and caught one, whom he prosecuted; the magistrate levied a one-dollar fine.[67] Even parents turned to the court. Exasperated by the misdeeds of her son Addie, Mrs Adcock prosecuted the lad for threatening. The reporter opined that 'like all bad boys Addie showed his cowardice by bawling and begging for mercy.' He was discharged to live with his father in Detroit and told to stay away from Hamilton until 'he had made up his mind to be a good boy.'[68] On occasion, children brought complaints. Thomas Owen, fourteen, charged Haley Lebundy with assault; Lebundy had slapped him, allegedly for using abusive language.[69] Workingmen also used the court. After Alex Lochart, a shop foreman, had punched him in the head 'for not working harder,' Thomas Cathcart prosecuted and had the satisfaction of seeing Lochart fined four dollars.[70]

The recourse to defence counsel, which appears to have become more and more common from the 1880s forward, added to the complexities of a decision to make a formal complaint. The costs of a defence, as well as court costs, and a fine may have made victims cautious, particularly if they assumed that they would continue to have some contact with the defendant. How far should a complainant go before pressing charges? It was the simplicity of the police court that made this question a little easier to answer in the nineteenth century. Nineteenth-century procedures for taking people to court – procedures that minimized obstacles between victims and the court and precluded police investigation – had the potential to generate a substantial record of incidents, a deceptive legacy to historians. In these circumstances, it is possible to think of court records as tantamount to what latter became known as occurrence reports, that is, a collection of complaints.

In the light of these reflections, the decline in the assault rates now appears as a measure of changing criminal justice practices, specifically the development of the common contemporary police chore of intervening in domestic disputes and other common forms of violence. To some extent, the argument relies upon speculation as to how the police and complainants interacted, but it also ties into institutional and technological innovations in policing in the late-Victorian era. The staffing and supervision of beats, the transportation of constables to the scene of a crime, and the diffusion of the telephone are factors to take into account.

Certainly from the late nineteenth century onward, the police were increasingly easy to contact and able to reach quickly the scenes of reported incidents. Beat patrols were reorganized and subjected to intense discipline in the mid-1880s. The police wagon, introduced in 1884, was believed to have cut down on response time to such a degree that the force could 'do the work of one [that was] a third larger'. Constable Harris, the driver who volunteered this estimate, had made six calls during the night in August 1887 when a reporter interviewed him. Harris enthused about the 'suddinness [*sic*] with which wrongdoers are dropped upon.'[71] Then there was the telephone, which came early to Hamilton and was well established by the 1890s. It was certainly being used in the late 1880s by businesses to report disturbances in their neighbourhoods.[72] During a street affray in 1892, 'Ed Wilson, of Nordheimer's, hurried in to telephone for the wagon.'[73] By the mid-1920s, a few motorcycle constables stayed in a dormitory with a telephone that connected them to headquarters. A sergeant made certain that members of the 'flying squad' did not snooze and miss a call.[74] Complainants got a swift response from the police, who restored order and spoke to the accused; often, that was all the complainant wanted or felt free to ask of the police. By the 1920s, the introduction of police cars and motorcycles had made the arrival of the police on the scene an even more immediate probability.

The improved ability of the police to respond to a complainant's call or to come when a third party reported something meant that more incidents could be handled at the scene. If the victim merely wished to intimidate someone who was abusing her or him – but not to alienate forever the other party – then the police would play the same role as the police court once had done. In fact, the police did not charge for their peacemaking service, whereas an action in court could have required the payment of court costs. As for the attitude of the constables, it seems that not all of them liked to make arrests after an occurrence. When a beloved and respected constable died in 1917, he was eulogized for having made few arrests. 'If Andy Price makes an arrest, he had to do it.'[75] It must be added here that the police in more recent times – certainly by the 1950s – have endeavoured to convince victims of domestic violence to prosecute their assailants.[76]

The draftsmen of the grand curves of crime rates have downgraded conventional 'major historical events' and replaced them with the artifacts of 'long-term trends.'[77] Yet 'minor' historical events cannot be dismissed if one is truly to understand the culture of a community or the nature of power and of deviance. Several obvious short-term swings in the Hamilton data, for example, are best interpreted by reflecting on developments within policing, or at least the interaction of policing practices with quite specific urban phenomena. These episodes are indicative of important phases in the history of the city and in the history of modern anxieties about crime and the related pursuit of order. The graph on assaults shows a dip around 1908; during this time the city was in the midst of a remarkable boom and the population estimates, which excluded the rapidly settled working-class suburbs, were well below the true population 'at risk.' In other words, a divisor based on population was too small and therefore the rate should have been even less than the 2 per thousand. Why was this? There are several explanations: a set of social causes and an institutional cause. Conditions of full employment, active house building and buying, and the family formation that accompany such trends may have kept an unusually large segment of the young male population – typically the population involved in assaults – tied down and away from taverns, unquestionably an environment where violence flourished. It is also possible that police department hiring, which was falling behind population growth in these years, simply could not maintain the level of arrests that it had in prior and less dynamic years.

Immediate social and institutional factors also explain the rise in the assault index that peaked dramatically in 1913. Unemployment, ethnic tensions, and gang violence and feuds in a newly created multicultural industrial district with dwindling jobs could well have affected the rate of violence. Intolerance combined with a collapsing economy undoubtedly made for social friction. At the same time, the police commission had authorized a great deal of hiring and the ratio of police to citizens was restored to its normal level of one per thousand. Moreover, deputy chief Whatley, hired in 1910, was a perfect martinet and a tenacious foe of crime, and the force opened its east-end station on Sherman Avenue in late 1911. In sum, significant social and institutional developments coincided with a rise in actions before the court.

TRENDS IN HOMICIDE

It was noted earlier in the chapter that historians and social scientists have proposed that homicide rates may serve as reliable indicators of the level of violence in a society. But a word of caution is in order here. Homicides are complicated matters; jealousy, domestic disputes, street and tavern affrays, assaults during robberies, and gang wars were among the more common causes of homicide in Hamilton from 1869 to 1970.

Despite the complexity of the crime, a number of researchers have argued that homicide rates fell from the mid-nineteenth century to the early twentieth and then started to rise. The 133 homicides committed in Hamilton from 1870 to 1970 capture this trend (Figure 5.8).[78] However, the unusual circumstance of three homicides in 1876 skews the graph.[79] In addition, relative to larger Canadian cities, Hamilton had a modest homicide rate and it certainly ran well below American urban rates, coroner's inquests established only twelve homicides for the period from 1869 to 1900. During most of this period, the coroner had the authority to investigate sudden deaths and indict suspects, making inquests a reasonably firm source for establishing the number and character of homicides, especially since court records obviously ignore murder-suicides.[80] Except for the year in which McConnell stabbed Nelson Mills, when there were three murders, the homicide rates for Victorian Hamilton were no higher than rates for several decades in the twentieth century. Homicide rates show no notable long-term drop.

Number per 100,000 inhabitants

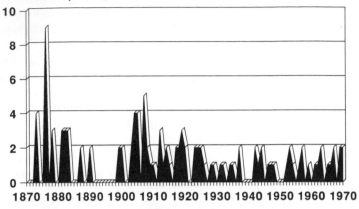

■ Homicides

Figure 5.8
Homicides in Hamilton, 1870–1970
Source: HPL, RG 10, Series A, *Annual Reports*; coroners' inquest books; assorted
newspaper scrapbooks on Hamilton murders.

Several short-term swings are apparent. In two depression eras, the
homicide rates stand out as remarkably low. In the 1890s, only the brutal beating of an old man by a neighbour in 1890 and the crazed act
of drunk who killed his parents in 1899 marred a perfect decade.
During the 1930s, as will be seen in more detail, domestic homicides
furnished the bulk of the grim reports. Each terrible crime had its own
circumstances, but it is plausible to suggest that economic distress put
troubled households under severe strain. This conjecture, of course,
leaves the problem of accounting for the sustained high homicide rates
during the years from 1905 to 1925, the period between depressions.

An explanation for the relatively high homicide rate across these
twenty years relates to the previous discussion of assaults. Homicides by
foreign-born men was notable, but the assailants had more in common
than birth abroad. These males were fairly young. The mean age for
male assailants was thirty-three and the most frequently cited age was
twenty-seven. The gender and age combination merits attention. Homicide rates vary from country to country, but one point in common
is worth citing: 'Killings are done by exactly the same proportions of
men, rather than women, and by the same proportions of different
age groups. The murder tendency peaks at twenty-five for all men
everywhere, then trails off at exactly the same rate – and always has.'[81]
The Hamilton data comes very close to confirming this generalization.
The young men who lived, worked, and took their recreation in the

predominately male environment of industrial boarding-house districts moved in an abrasive environment where, typical of their sex and age, they encountered situations that seemed in their eyes to challenge their manhood. They had much in common with James Owen and John Rooney, the men discussed in chapter 1, who were convicted for murdering a provocative and insulting drunk during a row near a tavern in Dundas on St Patrick's day, 1834.

Ten per cent of Hamilton's homicides occurred in boarding-houses, a fact that calls into question romantic assumptions about the role of such accommodation in fostering class or ethnic solidarity. They sometimes promoted jealousy and envy; they were the scenes for numerous petty thefts. The 1920s – a period of immigration, boarding-houses, and prohibition – was the only decade between 1870 and 1970 in which male brawls exceeded domestic violence as the principal cause of homicides. As well, the 1910s and the 1920s saw a higher ratio of male homicide deaths than female deaths than at any other time. Overall, the ratio was three to two, but in those decades it ran four to one.

Several cases give a sense of the homicides committed in these years by males against other males around boarding-houses. In 1907 someone poisoned Simon Buda at his boarding-house and Jake Tamillo killed a man and a women in a fit of jealousy.[82] A few years later 'a foreigner killed one of his boarders by striking him on the head with an axe.' The police suspected jealousy.[83] Yet more than jealousies ripened in boarding-houses; pride demanded that insults be answered. In 1924 an immigrant landlord went to collect his rent. The tenant grabbed him by his 'privates' and made rude remarks about the landlord's mother. The landlord then took a handgun from his hip pocket and killed the man.[84] The casualness of gun-play among immigrants in the 1920s is startling. Angelo Duca's declaration about the murder of a friend is a case in point. He and the deceased were walking along the street when they met two other Italians who started to swear at Duca. 'Then they both started to shoot at me.'[85] A few years later the police attempted to register the city's handguns and 'were surprised that so many citizens had business-like looking pistols of every description in their homes.' The report failed to indicate whether there were differences in ownership among the city's ethnic groups.[86]

National as well as personal honour had to be defended. A Ukrainian and a Polish immigrant had a dispute at a boarding-house in 1931 about Poland's boundaries; the Pole slapped the other man who retaliated by beating him to death.[87] In a 1965 incident, the reputation that Italians had for responding to certain insults and for defending family honour explained a charge of manslaughter instead of non-capital murder. The assailant's daughter had been beaten by her husband, who spat in the face of his father-in-law: an insult 'beyond comparison to an Italian.'[88] An ethnic pattern to homicides cannot be denied. In cases where males killed males, the parties involved almost always had known one another. Bulgarian killed Bulgarian; Pole killed Pole; Yugoslav killed Yugoslav; Russian killed Russian; Italian killed Italian; Anglo-Celt killed Anglo-Celt. Although it is difficult to be certain and precise about national origins, it appears that around 85 per cent of male homicides in Hamilton took place within the same ethnic group. Apart from the Ukrainian who beat the Pole to death, one of the few exceptions to fraternal homicide by an immigrant occurred when a Pole on death row attacked and killed an unwary member of his death watch in 1919. At the gallows, this sociopath threatened the hangman.

The violent killer executed in 1919 had worked with a ring of bootleggers. This fact did not make him unusual. Boom growth attracting newcomers, money for booze and the sporting life, and interest in the city by criminal entrepreneurs provided the ingredients for gang killings throughout the region. Several important additional factors had a bearing on these crimes. Prohibition in Ontario and the United States as well as Hamilton's location were connected to the slayings. The traffic in prohibited beverage alcohol fostered the growth of and rivalries among gangs that operated in Hamilton. As a port city close to the United States, the export of booze to the United States and the profits in the local trade attracted gangsters from south of the border.

Vice and rackets flourished in the boarding-house and immigrant district and at least some of the murders stemmed from bootlegging and protection. From 1918 to 1922, the police attributed a series of fatal shootings of Italians by Italians to the Black Hand or Cormorra, an old country criminal association that was heavily involved locally in protection, blackmail, and bootlegging since at least 1910.[89]

These mob killings and others like them in and around Hamilton in the 1920s were a part of a conflict that extended to Welland, Niagara Falls, and Buffalo. The Mediterranean tradition of settling the score by vendetta also played a role, compounding the initial shooting with others and making the crimes difficult to solve. 'Italian murders,' it was alleged, 'are the hardest kind to clear up, since even the victims will not talk.'[90] It was also a fact that Italians who committed homicide showed a marked preference for firearms. Two thirds of them used firearms; only a third of Anglo-Celts who committed homicide used a gun and killers from other ethnic groups likewise employed a variety of weapons: knives, blunt objects, and fists. Newcomers from some areas of Europe had different concepts about a citizen's relationship to the state and the means of achieving justice; they distrusted authority and settled grievances on their own. The gun conveyed personal authority, minimized risk, and inflicted quick vengeance. Astonished that the landlord who had killed his tenant in 1925 had toted a pistol in his pocket, the trial judge felt it necessary to issue a general warning. 'I want you and the others who come from southern Europe to not get the impression that they may carry revolvers or that they will not be punished if found guilty of crimes.'[91]

The wave of gang killings passed and the homicide rate stayed low from the late 1920s until the 1960s, with the exception of 1946 when the Evelyn Dick case was joined by several others. The rise in the rate in the 1960s did not stem from a renewal of gang slayings – though Hamilton by then had a reputation as a city with organized crime. Assaults by men against women – particularly within the family – now led the way in the homicide rate, as they had throughout the city's history.

Having established that the long-term trend in homicide must be interpreted in relation to specific episodes in the city's history, it is worth asking if there were patterns to homicide that cut across the decades. Where can we discern any evidence of continuity?

One of the tragic themes arising from the homicide data is the persistence of domestic violence culminating in homicide and sometimes a subsequent suicide. The tale of domestic violence in the region is at least as old as the 1828 death of Michael Vincent's wife. In the series of data used here, the story began in 1873 with the first murders reported in the city for at least four years. In an instance of 'Wilful and Deliberate Murder,' a father had slit the throats of his son and daughter.[92] Three years later, shortly after the trial of McConnell, Victoria Macrae 'came to her death from the effects of injuries inflicted on her by her husband.'[93] The next case of a wife killed by her husband happened in 1882 and it had features that recurred often throughout the period of the study. In this instance, the husband shot his wife and an innocent bystander and then committed suicide. The list of murder-suicides resumed in the early twentieth century. In 1902 Charles Vosper shot his wife and committed suicide; in 1905 Philander Burkholder slaughtered his wife and child with an axe and then cut his own throat.[94] Leaping ahead over an appalling set of similar tales and to the end of the period covered in this book, there was the case in 1967 of a church elder – 'the greatest guy on the block' – who used a shotgun on his wife, his children, and himself.[95] Out of 133 homicides, fourteen ended with the suicide of the assailant and in eleven instances the first victim had been a girlfriend or wife.

Altogether, out of 133 homicide cases in 100 years, thirty-three were instances where a man killed a woman; on twenty seven of those fatal occasions, the woman was a wife or companion. Several other cases involved jealous boyfriends. Citing Canadian data from the 1980s, criminologist Neil Boyd has observed that 'we are most likely to kill the ones we love.'[96] Hamilton cases support the conclusion. George King, who shot his seventeen-year-old girlfriend in 1922, said that he had 'heard stories from people that she was going out with other fellows. I turned the gun on myself and it jammed.'[97] In virtually every instance of the death of a spouse, witnesses reported a domestic dispute.

Separation failed to protect wives against a violent spouse. Forbes, the man who shot his wife in 1882, had been separated from her for several years. He had a 'heart filled with the demon of jealousy.'[98] The annual report of the police department in 1913 cited the case of a man who had shot his wife 'from whom he had been estranged for many years.'[99] Another man, in 1955, killed his wife and committed suicide shortly before a legal separation.[100] Several years later, another killer broke into the flat of his ex-common-law wife and shot her while she telephoned the police.[101] Rarely did the newspaper or official accounts comment on the criminal history of the assailants, but one of these murderers, Frank Truckle, who killed his wife in 1912 and then shot himself, had earlier appeared in magistrate's court for assaulting his wife. In 1969 an estranged husband stabbed his wife fifteen times on the verandah of her home.[102] Wife beating will be examined in chapter 6, but at this point it is important to note that homicide cases revealed the pattern of male violence against females. Given that so many homicides arose out of domestic violence and boarding-house disputes, it is not surprising that 60 per cent of Hamilton homicides occurred in a dwelling. The street proved the next most dangerous locale.

Three other homicides by males resulted in the death of a member of the family other than a spouse. In 1932 a father killed his son in a quarrel over the boy's girlfriend, and, in the same year, an estranged husband entered his father-in-law's house and shot him and a brother-in-law before turning his shotgun on himself.[103] Male rage out of all proportion to domestic situations that had gone terribly wrong led to a few other types of homicides. Jealous husbands or boy friends stormed in and took the lives of rivals. 'Where is my wife,' asked one man before he killed another in 1924.[104] A boarder who had made advances to his landlady suffered a fatal beating at the hands of an unremorseful husband. 'He was bothering my wife, so I wacked him and wacked him good.'[105]

The 1925 murder of Bud Taylor by his companion Lily White – an inversion of the usual pattern – affords glimpses into jealousy, passion, and irrationality. According to her confession, Lily had started to doubt Bud's affection for her the day she arrived at his place after her release from jail following a conviction for running a disorderly house. 'I found Bud there with three girls. One was a colored girl. One an Indian and the other a white girl.' Not long after that, just after dawn, they drove out to the race-track where Bud worked. They argued and he threw some money at her and told her to get lost. She stabbed him. She expressed no remorse. 'I would like to see him at the inquest and take another stab at him.' But she still loved him. 'I want him to be in Heaven and will always pray for him.' Lily knew best the origin of her plight. 'I killed him because he hurt my heart. I was a fool to stick around with him. Love is a funny thing isn't it.' She was convicted of manslaughter.[106]

On thirty occasions, homicides were committed by men against men with no apparent domestic connection to the victim, no motives of jealousy; these included gang murders, business- and work-related disputes, and tavern fights. Acts of robbery led to eleven homicides. In most instances, cash was the objective of the felony. John Barty entered a shoe store in 1926 and attempted to rob it. The clerk tried to stop him and he killed her with a hammer.[107] Because assailants and victims in robberies did not know one another, these homicides left more unsolved cases than any other group.

The Alameda, California, study discovered patterns similar to those reported here. The authors observed that 'homicide was not particularly common.'[108] Often it was a family affair and frequently it involved jealousy. 'Other murders exploded out of brawls.'[109] The combination of drinking, gambling, and quarrelling led to a substantial portion of fatal encounters. These findings suggest that, in addition to exploring change and its significance in historical data, students of crime in history should inquire about contextual continuities shared by related groups of offences over time and place.

CAVEATS AND CRIME

Neither the short- nor the long-term analysis of crime rates has sustained any proposition about social pathology; nor has either proven that the new power of the state in the late nineteenth century held crime down. What this discussion does demonstrate, however, is the importance of understanding the nexus between the public and the criminal justice system. More particularly, this chapter has underscored the transition from a court-based system of complaint to one in which the police handled public complaints. That transition, incidentally, may explain why the police court eventually lost its attraction as civic news and entertainment deserving coverage in daily newspaper columns. From the late nineteenth century on, police action filtered out cases and minimized the scenes for the daily morality play in a scruffy courtroom.

Finally the warnings of the pioneer Guerry ought to be recalled; for, although his tables and reasoning have flaws, he had the wit to realize how complex the issues were. He pointed out that, if observations even seemed to resolve into a simple conclusion, then that conclusion should be distrusted. Shaving square pegs to fit them into round holes produces the filling in of gaps by hypothesis, the supplying of 'facts' that really remain unknown, and a slide into an interminable series of errors.[110] The claims based on long-term crime trends ought to be exposed to Guerry's rules of thumb; at the very least there is a need for more curiosity and inquiry as to the meaning of 'crimes known to the police.' It is possible that events and practices in Hamilton were exceptional, but the possibility that other courts elsewhere also sought to unload their burdens argues for a reassessment of the late-nineteenth-century decline in the rates of crime.

6 The Enduring Circumstances of Violence and Theft

Shortly after midnight on 13 March 1954, a radio call instructed two constables on patrol in a police cruiser to respond to a telephone call for help that had just come into the station: a husband had stumbled home in a drunken stupor and struck his wife. The police arrived at the scene a few minutes later. They advised the woman to see the morality officer at the central station and then to lay an information of assault before the justice of the peace at the family court. The report concluded: 'We had answered a call to these premises for the same reason the previous night and gave the same advice which she did not take.'[1] The woman's husband had already been before family court three times.

Two weeks later, in the early evening of 26 March, two constables in a cruiser responded to a radio despatch and arrived at the scene of a domestic dispute. The husband had come home in a drunken state. As he came in the door, his wife struck him in the mouth with her fist. He struck back, cutting her above the left eye; her laceration required hospital treatment. Interviewed by the police, she complained of his habitual drinking. Economic survival was her chief anxiety, not her injury or the laying of charges – the husband operated a taxi and she worried that he might have an accident. The police recommended that she speak to a justice of the peace at the family court.[2]

These cases show that victims of crime still had to proceed through the time-honoured legal channels, even if the justices of the peace were no longer pivotal figures in the community. They also offer a very different perspective on crime and criminal justice in the city than that presented by the series of data on trends. Besides giving glimpses of context, they make tangible several practices described in earlier chapters. In the mid-twentieth century, victims came first to the police and not to the magistrate. Moreover, electronic communications, the automobile, and the attitude of officials toward assault had effected another alteration in the manner in which individuals interacted with criminal justice. Victims now could frequently get prompt intervention. Interestingly, the police by this time went beyond establishing order in a given situation by encouraging the victim to make a formal complaint.

Horror stories about the failure of the criminal justice system in relation to domestic violence are legion and protection for battered wives has been inadequate, but it cannot be said that the system has formally permitted men to beat their wives with impunity.[3] Public disapproval of wife beating was certainly evident in the late-nineteenth century. As noted earlier, whippings were administered to a number of wife beaters convicted by magistrate Jelfs, despite his distrust of women who forcefully insisted on prosecution. Furthermore, to judge from the Ontario-based *Canadian Law Journal*, Ontarians took pride in applying this form of punishment to men convicted of physically abusing women. Noting that some provinces had abolished the cat o' nine tails, an 1873 editorial stated tongue in cheek that 'probably cases of personal assault on women are not so common there!'[4] Later in the century, in 1889, a grand jury recommended that 'all tramps, drunkards, and wife-beaters be put on the stone heap and made to earn a living.'[5] It is possible that, by lumping such offenders together, these late Victorians were expressing the belief that the transgressions mentioned were related or even equivalent. Still, in Hamilton and Ontario generally, whippings seem to have been reserved for wife beaters. This fact alone suggests that wife beating was considered a very serious offence.

Of course, despite the system's awareness of the seriousness of wife abuse, the position of the battered woman was unenviable in the nineteenth century and has remained so in the twentieth. The male-dominated nature of the economy, female dependence on working husbands, and, until the late 1960s, the restrictive divorce laws have combined to make it extraordinarily difficult for women to escape abusive situations.[6] In recent times, such women have gained greater protection through tighter restrictions on the terms under which their assailants are released on recognizance. At the mid-century mark, however, it was a much different story. The two incidents recounted above underline how perilous the situation of these women was.

These incidents also point to common themes in the crime of wife beating. Specifically, wife beating occurred often within the same families; husbands, after appearing in family court and being released on their own recognizance, went home to commit the same crime; and alcohol triggered, or at least exacerbated, family violence. Drawing on episodes such as these, therefore, one may search for patterns in crime without accenting long-term trends. As noted in the last chapter, grand theories about changes in crime rates and culture should be viewed with scepticism; in the case of Hamilton, criminal justice data cannot prove the existence of either more or less theft and violence over the long term. Yet short-term movements in the data are another matter. Though they need to be interpreted carefully and with an eye to a multiplicity of factors, they still offer valuable information to the historical researcher.

Rather than notable changes, there may actually have been remarkable continuity, not in the putative rates of crime but in the etiology of crime – the actual circumstances that culminated in crimes, as well as in the motivations and lives of the criminals. Judith Fingard expressed the point eloquently in *The Dark Side of Life in Victorian Halifax.* For her, Victorian Halifax held lessons for 'our advanced capitalist society.' 'We still have,' she concluded, 'people who are delinquent before they reach maturity, people who drink and drug themselves to ruin and death, men who beat their wives or rape the girl next door, parents who batter their infants, adolescents who risk disease and violence to prostitute themselves in order to secure an adequate living or assert their independence, desperate people whose fate is prison, mental illness or suicide.'[7] The proposition of continuity in the history of crimes in Hamilton stems from an analysis of the commonplace crimes of theft and assault as well as the extremely rare crime of homicide. An analysis that takes into consideration the location of the crime, the concept of opportunity, the relationships of the parties involved, hints about motives, and – in the case of theft – the stolen articles themselves and their value strongly suggests many features of continuity.

Normally, the detailed reconstruction of specific crimes is not readily undertaken by historians in English-speaking societies because of the generally laconic quality of court records. Conversely, continental European historians have fewer series of court records, but what they do have is a rich supply of details collected by investigative courts and preserved by written depositions. However, the context of crime in Hamilton for more than one hundred years can be reconstructed. The proceedings of the police magistrate's court were frequently reported in useful detail from the 1850s to the mid-twentieth century. Rarely did the reporters charged with this beat include accounts of all the cases of the day, but they mentioned over half. Unquestionably, reporters delighted in writing longer accounts of cases which would titillate the public or register a moral point. Perhaps some cases and names were kept out of the papers. Nevertheless, the reports from 1860 to 1885 – the reports used in the following assessment – covered the gamut of offences, from violations of the snow removal by-law to rape. A further point in their favour as source material is that what they recounted bears an uncanny similarity to what is found in the far more detailed sources for the period from the 1930s to the 1960s. A broken set of police occurrence books has been examined for some of those years in order to shed light on crime in the mid-twentieth century.

If Hamilton's experience is any indication, historians of English-speaking societies may discover that occurrence reports can stimulate fresh discussions about the motives of law-breakers and the plights of their victims.

VIOLENCE IN LATE-VICTORIAN HAMILTON

Assaults prosecuted in the police court in late-Victorian Hamilton transpired most commonly in the tavern and the home. Alcohol intoxication almost always had a role. Clearly, then, alcohol abuse ought to be accepted as fact and not treated as the fancy of zealous temperance men among the police. After all, complainants brought the charges and both they and witnesses slipped in remarks about drunkenness as part of their accounts of events. Indeed, they occasionally stated that they also had too much to drink.

Saying that drink formed a part of the overwhelming majority of instances advances our understanding of violence only slightly, for drinking does not necessarily end in violence and, besides, drinking and violence derive from circumstances that are simply out of the sight of the court. There will always be serious argument about how to discern the ultimate cause of family violence. Nevertheless, the immediate surroundings of violence are clear enough.

Alcohol incites certain forms of behaviour and action, forms common to situations of drinking and violence or drinking by itself. In discussing the causes of wife beating in her pathbreaking study on family violence, Linda Gordon reviewed the anthropological literature on alcohol and violence and then reached the conclusion that 'liquor did and does not in itself cause aggressive behaviour or even loosen inhibition against it.'[8] In fact, drunken behaviour could itself be learned. Gordon argued further that 'the social relations involved in drinking escalated hostilities.'[9] Among the frequent manifestations – or learned behaviour related to drinking – are laughing, backslapping, kissing, showing off, and bragging. While good-natured and probably aspects of the subculture of the underclass, these impulsive actions can cross personal boundaries among strangers.[10] Recent applications of the 'selfish gene' theory – a view which posits that animals, including humans, behave essentially as if they were mere vehicles for the transmission of genes between generations – suggest that 'a young man's reputation as he tries to ascend a dominance hierarchy depends on a credible threat of violence.'[11] Alcohol loosens the tongues of young men and fosters pride; specifically, it elevates pride over prudence and promotes circumstances where threats of violence are tested.

Besides bringing together people who might normally want to have nothing to do with one another, taverns have historically attracted a great deal of unconventional market activity: the selling of stolen goods, money lending, and commercial sex. Hamilton's drinking establishments fit this pattern. Feuding relatives, irate neighbours, and individuals from different ethnic backgrounds mingled and then often tangled in the city's taverns. As a result tensions abounded there that did not exist in other places of entertainment. A patron would be wronged by someone's unflattering characterization; someone would step across a boundary because of the effects of alcohol. Yet the clash that ensued was guided, not by drink, but by cultural factors. Who was king of the turf?

Incidents from the daily reports of the police magistrate's court lack crucial information about the background of particular feuds or the levels of intoxication. Still, they imply that the mix of young males, alcohol, and the tavern setting served to produce a substantial proportion of the violent incidents in the city. The reasons cited above applied to many occurrences. Thus, in late 1862, the arrival of English soldiers in Hamilton spiced the social scene. A few young ladies fell for the uniform and that heightened tension between town lads and newcomers. There was also resentment of colonial status. For example, while one cannot be certain which complicating factor set off the tavern brawl that centred on Henry Hinds, a member of a visiting British rifle brigade, the episode suggested hostility between soldiers and civilians in certain venues. Depending on whose story was to believed, Hinds either arrived at a neighbourhood tavern stone sober or dead drunk. A farmer offered him a drink, which he refused. This insult – for such it often was construed – provoked the farmer to say something uncomplimentary about the Englishman. In a flash, a brawl erupted. The next day, Hind came to the police magistrate and brought charges against three men.[12] Four years later, in an almost identical episode, Joseph Kerns of the 16th Foot sought refreshment, company, and perhaps more at McMahon's tavern. Kerns claimed that he and the proprietor 'got into a conversation and he said I insulted him.' McMahon's friends supplied a different version, testifying that Kerns had entered the tavern drunk and boasted that he could 'whip any man the weight of ten stone ten.' The challenge was taken up. The truth of the claims and counter-claims are less significant than the fact that challenges, insults, male strangers, and alcohol were crucial elements in the altercation.[13]

While it is impossible to say whether or not wife beating was more prevalent in the late Victorian era than in periods before or since, it certainly was not a hidden evil. In her Boston-based study, Linda Gordon found that in the late nineteenth century 'wife-beating was not generally accepted as a head-of household's right, but was considered a disreputable, seamy practice, and was effectively illegal in most states of the United States by 1870.'[14] Many Hamilton victims sought help by making formal complaints. With certain qualifications, the authorities proved receptive and the newspapers printed names and details. The complainants came almost universally from the city's poor and working poor, a fact duplicated decades later in police occurrence reports. Élite and middle-class families did not use the police court or, later, the police. The exception that demonstrates the rule may have been William Stewart, a lawyer, who in 1879 charged his sons with assault. As it turned out, they had attacked him alright, but only after he had come home from a heavy drinking bout and threatened to harm their mother.[15] Neither Victorian newspaper coverage nor the later police occurrence books reported significant traces of domestic violence in middle-class homes.

The invisibility of middle-class domestic violence and the visibility of violence among the poorer people of the city presents a problem with no clear answer. Were restraint and self-control easier for middle-class males, whose culture valued restraint and moderation? Was such behaviour easier for men whose adequacy was measured by comfortable earnings rather than brawn? Or was the openness of the complaint system too visible and too seedy for status-conscious middle-class city dwellers? Remarks by the court reporter about the crowds of the unwashed embodied as well as broadcast the idea that the police court provided a distinctly lower-class place to resolve disputes. Thus, even though reporting on wife beating was very common and contrasts with the relative silence cast over the problem in the mid-twentieth century, the public airing had a class flavour that made it an imperfect medium for noting and exposing a broad class spectrum of violence – if it existed. With their emphasis on episodes in the lives of the poor and the working class, daily morality tales from the courtroom were not so much about men beating women as about misconduct among people who led disorderly lives. Court reporters for the city's newspapers simply did not discuss wife beating systematically as a serious matter.

Domestic violence entered into the discourse of social issues in connection with temperance crusades. Once again, the moralists who pointed to alcohol as a cause had fingered an important, if partial, truth. In a recent study of alcohol and violence in present-day Thunder Bay, Kai Pernanen observed a high level of alcohol use by offenders who had attacked female victims. This, he says, 'is not entirely unexpected, considering the links between problem drinking and domestic violence reported in the literature.'[16] The origins of problem drinking and the erosion of respect between partners are not to be blamed on the alcohol alone, but again it seems fair to say that it plays a role in the complex social histories of individual families.

The case of a Mrs Hiscox provides insights into brutality and the exercise of power within a family wherein civil conduct had collapsed. No details of the assault came before the court, for, like many other women who laid a charge against a spouse or companion, Mrs Hiscox subsequently dropped the complaint. Of course, the court could not compel a prosecution. When her case was called, she came forward and claimed that both she and her husband had been drunk when they had a disagreement. In fact, she now alleged that she had been more at fault and was still drunk when she came to the police office to make her complaint. More than that, she now insisted that he had not beaten her. A fall had caused the cut on her lip. No one in the court believed her new story, but the judge had no choice but to dismiss the case with costs. The unfortunate Mrs Hiscox could not pay the court costs awarded against her and she had to spend a term in jail.[17]

Not long after the Hiscox case, Hamilton's police chief in his annual report for 1879 proposed that the city set up a fund to aid the poor with their court costs. He recommended that a sum of money be retained for this purpose by the city chamberlain who would release sums on the recommendation of one of the police commissioners.[18] There is no record of this having been done. Amounting to the state paying someone for a prosecution, it would have violated common law notions about the state tampering with witnesses and complainants. The state's relationship with a complainant remains a tricky subject, particularly in cases of alleged domestic violence where the firm desire of the state to protect people runs into complex relationships between companions and encounters the duty of the legal profession to protect the rights of the accused.

Understandably, assaults that took place in houses involved people who knew one another. Although wives seem to have figured as the most frequent victims, they were not the only family members to be beaten. One unfortunate woman, thrown out of her house by her husband in March 1863, went to stay with her mother-in-law; her brother-in-law would have none of that and beat her.[19] Lost forever are the complete stories; no explanations accompanied the tale about John

Shield who broke into his cousin's house and assaulted him.[20] Certainly, family violence included child abuse. Bernard Fleming stood accused of beating his daughter, but she refused to press charges. The authorities found this act of violence more revolting than most other kinds. For his part, the magistrate, astonishingly enough, refused to dismiss the case; rather, he adjourned for the day, putting Fleming back in jail for at least another night. Fleming may not have relished this development, because the police had worked him over already. The reporter indicated that the police had handled him 'pretty roughly as this morning he appeared in the dock with his head tied up and his shirt front besmeared with gore.' [21]

These few cases not only illustrate domestic violence: they also show the eagerness of the authorities – acting within and outside the law – to deal with men who beat women and child abusers. They hint, too, at the existence of a chivalric code that inspires some men to dispense rough justice to other men. Rumours still circulate at the Hamilton central station about past episodes of rough justice on the part of police constables in matters of family violence.

VIOLATION OF THE PERSON IN THE MID-TWENTIETH CENTURY

It is a peculiar exercise to attempt to link two gross sets of variables – the dependent one of crime rates and the independent ones of socio-economic change and culture – in the absence of an understanding of what occurs or has occurred in the criminal act itself. If historical and contemporary social truths are to be spun out of narrative and analysis, then specific context is a crucial matter. When seen up close – or as close as reports permit – violence and harassment were concrete and ugly matters. Many are readily explained by old-fashioned concepts such as envy, lust, and anger.

The socio-economic and cultural factors favoured by social scientists and historians, using the big canvas of a century or more, is incapable of explaining what has happened in a specific incident. Yet the possible merit of some generalizations cannot be ignored nor can their reasonableness be denied. Violent crimes do appear to increase after wars; localized employment booms, which pack large numbers of men into confined areas, are notorious tinder for flare-ups of violence.

Two opposing and supportable views have surfaced from time to time. From the perspective of the authorities in the period under review, the criminal often acted out of uncontrolled passions, out of a simple lack of respect for others, and so the details of crime focused attention on the foibles of humanity. However, from the vantage-point of social reformers, crimes were to be understood in the context of society. To them, offenders were like motes blown about by the drafts of misfortune, piling up into the peaks and troughs of a crime rate. In recent times, the array of explanations has been broadened by the addition of genetic and bio-chemical theories. Since this study is one that often uses the police as a guide to features of life in the city, police perspectives and responses to crimes against persons provide the bias. The following fragments suggest a pattern that the city police have seen for many generations. It is a pattern that adds to the complexity of policing; indeed, it adds to their social-service functions.

Most of Hamilton's surviving occurrence books deal with theft, but several list only non-property crimes. Especially prominent in these volumes are assaults, indecent assaults, and varied forms of harassment, including telephone calls, and vandalism. The earliest of these books covers 1955, a year in which, according to the annual report, there were approximately 170 charges of common assault laid. The occurrence book lists roughly 500 reports of assault, suggesting a ratio of reports to charges laid of one to three. In many of the occurrence reports, the police encouraged the victim to lay charges. Thus, as in the mid-nineteenth century, court action on an assault usually required a complaint; the difference is that, by the mid-twentieth century, the plaintiff had initial access to the police before going to court. Mostly the police occurrence reports were made out in response to a telephone call by a victim or a neighbour. Two officers normally responded. Sometimes, however, a single officer on a beat stumbled onto an occurrence or was given information. One report on a domestic assault began: 'At 1:55 I was told by a passing motorist that a woman and a young girl was standing on King St.E.'[22]

The most impressive overall observation to emerge from the occurrence of crimes against persons – including vandalism – is the one most expected: women and men reported somewhat different sets of crimes and within even the same set they had distinctive experiences. For men, the most frequent complaints were of common assault (34.8 per cent) and vandalism and wilful damage (32.4). Dozens of other offences completed the number of reports. For women, assault figured prominently (20.0). Vandalism and wilful damage were not especially prominent (7.5), possibly reflecting a male assumption of responsibility for property and their greater ownership of autos and businesses. The balance of occurrences reported by women included complaints about harassment (8.4), threatening (6.3), indecent exposure (6.3), family disputes (5.3), indecent assault (4.2), molestation (4.2), and abusive language (3.2). In sum, women reported having had their person attacked in many more ways than men.

By 1955 the city was in the midst of postwar 'normalcy.' Men had displaced women from their wartime positions, and consequently family, house, and school were the principal concerns for many females. Therefore, it is not surprising that half of the reported incidents affecting women happened around the home, whether a house or an apartment. A quarter of the incidents transpired in public areas such as a street or park. That a residence was an exceptionally dangerous place is at odds with popular contemporary images of the happy home, but constables knew better. About a third of the occurrences reported by men took place around the house, although this total was raised by vandalism. Men also reported occurrences in a specific set of public places: taverns (6.8), streets and playgrounds (6.0), factories and factory yards (5.6), rooming-houses (3.4), and railway yards (2.2).

If the occurrences are sorted out into three main clusters – common assault, sexual offenses, and wilful damage which was indirectly aimed at an individual – the gender differences are more fully understood. Men assaulted men in ten different locales, half of which were public places. Six out of ten times the victim knew the assailant; indeed, family and neighbours made up roughly a quarter of the alleged assailants. Dangerous strangers rarely caused injury. But if strangers did inflict harm, it was more likely against men than women, for men had more contact with strangers through work, recreation, and even as drivers of cars, for some incidents arose out of friction on city streets. Women could identify assailants eight out of ten times; in almost four out of ten times they singled out the husband.

The occurrences reveal further patterns that offer some insights into root causes of violence. No simple argument can summarize the causes of violence; in Hamilton, they seem to have been brought about by cultural values with gender-based dimensions and by a narrowing of the cultural values through socio-economic deprivation. There is no dichotomy between culture and economics; rather, the interplay of the two makes the question of violence appear so difficult to explain and so intractable a social problem as to seem unresolvable. The following description and analysis considers the context for male-male violence, male-female violence, and female-female violence.

Assaults

Altercations between males commonly originated in four situations. There were others, but these cover many of the occurrences. In each of them there figures a very old cultural attitude: regardless of era or of culture, verbal insults or offensive gestures intended to bruise male pride have provoked retaliatory action in defence of what is felt to be an individual's self-respect. In modern North American urban areas – as in the Victorian cities – one locale stands out as a high-risk area for the trading of insults and the exchange of punches: the tavern. Reviled by reformers and much romanticized by a few historians of the working class, it is clearly an institution deserving assessment from another, perhaps more critical, perspective.[23] As we have seen in the discussion of theft and the sketches of Victorian violence, the tavern or hotel bar was not purely the convivial watering hole of fraternal labourers. Whatever the era, alcohol affects judgment and mood, and the tavern environment itself – a gathering place for those who usually do not have the resources to entertain at home – has accentuated risk. It has brought together strangers and known enemies. In sum, it has been a parlour into which friends, acquaintances, strangers, and enemies alike mingled. Here the defence of turf, the display of masculinity, is more important than in most other places precisely because of the entertaining of friends in such a dynamic and public environment. Canadian poet Al Purdy in 'At the Quinte Hotel' captures exactly the necessary pose when he describes the victor in a punch-up. 'He roosters over to the table.'[24]

Twenty-seven-year-old Tom Stark was lurching out of the Crown and Anchor Hotel when he accidentally bumped into twenty-five-year-old Ralph Jones. Words were exchanged. Jones struck Stark in the face, breaking his upper plate of false teeth in three places.[25] Quietly snacking on peanuts and drinking beer at the Kings Arms, Albert Wilson was disrupted when a stranger bumped his chair and 'made a remark he did not like.' He pushed this intruder away and in a flash was sitting on the floor with a broken nose.[26] It seems that a few very unhappy and disturbed men went into public places intending like some pathetic duellists or gunslingers to spew insults in order to provoke a confrontation. Such was the case of the aptly named 'Jumbo' who swaggered into more than one restaurant or tavern in 1955.[27] Sometimes the parties knew each other. Sometimes the sight of a person brought back memories of an old grudge. Carl Snider and his wife had been drinking at the Willingdon Hotel when, at around 10:30 p.m., his cousin approached and slapped him across the face. The police report noted that 'this incident was the result of a family dispute of long standing and was probably the result of too much drinking on the part of all involved.'[28]

Oddly enough, another frequently encountered situation where insults or slights about manhood could escalate into violence involved motor vehicles. By mid-century, driving prowess had attained an important role for some youths and adults yearning to test their competence and manhood. For younger and poorer residents of the city, the display of status by home-buying or occupation was not possible; the car thus became that much more important and displays of driving skill were related to the article itself. To call into question a man's driving ability, therefore, was not just an expression of fact. It was a insult.

A reckless driver nearly struck Pete Amberly as he walked across a street at an intersection. Pete shouted – it was winter and the car windows were closed – 'you are supposed to stop at the white lines.' The driver retorted, 'you mind your own business.' Later in the day, their paths crossed downtown and the driver attacked Pete.[29] A nearly identical episode happened to Dom Tambuello. A car almost ran over him. 'You'll kill somebody,' he shouted. The driver slammed on his brakes, burst out of the car, and punched Dom in the mouth.[30] In the winter twilight, Arno Fordychuk noticed that a truck at an intersection did not have its lights on. He told the driver. 'Words passed back and forth.' A brawl ensued.[31]

What John Adams did combined the bar insult and the touchy-driver scenarios. Drinking late at O'Brian's Tavern, he decided to take the bus home. He waited and waited. Finally, the bus arrived. With hands and feet cold from the November night air and his tongue oiled, John inquired, 'Where have you been sleeping?' The driver was silent; John was insulted by the driver's failure to acknowledge him. 'What did you do, get up on the wrong side of bed?' With this the driver stopped the bus, took off his hat, ejected John, and punched him in the mouth.[32]

Punching in the mouth may merely have been the instinctive way of doing the most damage, but it may also have been a symbolic blow to the source of an insult. By way of comparison, the slapping of a face could have been – like nineteenth-century beard-pulling – an expression of contempt, a means of inflicting an insult.

The third notable senario for an assault, like the previous two, involved insults. In these cases, the men were insulted through female family members and took action to defend honour – both that of the women and their own. Bill Woods beat up on two 'Italian boys' in front of the Raleigh Hotel; apparently, they had mistaken his wife for a 'street walker.'[33] The August heat brought Nelson MacDougall onto his porch. He was spotted there by a group of local youths in a car who decided to have some sport. 'Hi Governor, how about letting us use your daughter?' Nelson chased the car, throwing stones. He located it later and hurled a rock through the windshield. The youths then caught Nelson snoozing on the porch and beat him.[34] Finally, assaults occasionally arose from festering problems with neighbours. When the police went to Bill Copeline's house, for the second time in two weeks, they found that he had a gash inflicted by his neighbour who had attacked him with a fifteen-foot length of pipe.[35] The smearing of human filth onto the Herberts' front door by Harry Thomas had been occasioned by an old dispute. 'There has been trouble between the complainant and his neighbour over a mutual driveway.'[36]

Male-female violence, including a few instances of wives beating their husbands, usually took place in the home. There were other common denominators. While there had to have been a first time for a specific couple, the bulk of the reports came as occurrences in a series. 'Cruiser has responded to this home on similar complaints'; 'the police have been to this address several times on similar complaints'; 'three calls in the same week at the same place'; 'trouble has existed in this house for the past two months.'[37] With the exception of the last quote, the reports cited took place in late December; the occurrence book suggests that the festive season was a period abounding with family stress.

The roots of domestic violence ran deep and cannot often be recovered from the occurrence reports. What evidence there is points to jealousy, estrangement, moral conduct, and sexual conduct as the main motives. Arguments in the Tanguay household stemmed from Barbara's drinking and Bob's teetotalism; her frequent departures to parties while he stayed at home were also probable grounds for jealousy.[38] Alex Semiovitch was angry with his spouse because 'she spends the family grocery money on drink.' Both parties were taken to the police station where they were advised by Sergeant Croft.[39] These instances of male concern about the conduct of wives are cited to highlight a double standard: men felt they could display violent anger over their wives' conduct, but women could not react the same over their husbands' behaviour – on the contrary, when they dared to do that, they were commonly beaten. Clearly, what was sauce for the goose was not sauce for the gander. Men, moreover, believed that it was their right to make demands of women. When Helen Smith said no to her husband's demands for sex, he beat her. On being interviewed by the police, he volunteered the conclusion that as far as his wife was concerned 'I'm nothing.' The danger posed by males who defined themselves in terms of dominance in sexual relations is obvious. It is just as obvious that alcohol – which figured in every case of domestic assault examined – was no elixir for the good life. But a few cases simply defy explanation. One of the more repulsive assaults of 1955 was committed by a thirty-three-year-old man who beat his son – aged two and a half – for removing some articles from under the Christmas tree. He broke the child's hip and refused to take the crying infant to hospital.[40] Children as well as women fell victim to domestic violence.

The context for the attacks cannot help to explain the varied levels of violence. This uncertainty is what makes outbursts of domestic violence so very dangerous for the parties involved and for the police. A good many occurrences reported a sort of ritualized violence that stopped short of wife beating. The intoxicated husband began by arguing with his wife; next he would escalate to attacking furniture. Chairs and coffee-tables would be held aloft and flung to the floor; telephones would be ripped out to prevent calls to the police. By now, if there were children, they would be in hysterics. The next rung on the scale of violence would be reached when the husband would slap the wife's face; some wives would attempt self-defence, making up for a disadvantage in strength with the throwing of household articles or a quick move with a kitchen knife. On a few occasions, the build-up to physical violence would happen so quickly and terribly that, even if neighbours alerted the police, someone would require hospital care. Jack Stephensen had beaten his wife Jill so badly that she could not come to court to give testimony; a constable was authorized by the court to go to her hospital room, take down her statement, and report on her injuries.[41] Fortunately for Elizabeth Tucker, there was no gun in her home when her husband attacked her in late December. Jim Tucker was 'an alcoholic who several years ago shot a man.' He had threatened to shoot Elizabeth.[42]

On the few occasions when women assaulted women, the causes resembled male assaults on males. The violence was preceded by insults and long-standing disputes. A thirteen-year-old girl complained that a seventeen-year-old 'had assaulted her by slapping her face.' There was more to the case. The assailant defended her action, alleging that the other party had pushed her younger sister.[43] It was a hot July day when Mrs Balfour invited some ladies for tea; the heat drove them to the basement, the open window of which made them a tempting target for Mrs Rankin's garden hose. Furious, three wet ladies stormed up onto Mrs Rankin's porch, where they were met with another spray of water. Grabbing what first came to hand – flower pots – they counter-attacked, causing Mrs Rankin to fall while ducking floral missiles. The police reported dryly that 'it seems this trouble has been going on for some time.'[44]

Sexual Offences

It is quite a leap from the foolishness of a neighbourhood feud to the second group of crimes against person. As with assaults, children frequently were victims of sexual offences.

Indecent assaults on both girls and boys occurred more often than one might suppose. The vulnerable age group was from six to ten, and the principle locations for such crimes included cars (children were lured into them), parks, playgrounds, alleys, and the home. The mother of one victim reported to the police that 'neighbours had told her a gray car had been attempting to get young girls into it on several occasions.'[45] One boy was dragged into an alley while putting out garbage; he was saved by the appearance of two people.[46] There were instances of girls molested in the home by their fathers.[47]

Men indecently assaulted adult women on the streets, in streetcars, and in theatres. In fact, theatres were havens for sex offenders. Boys were attacked or propositioned in the washrooms; children were brought there by child molesters; and older men – pathetic gropers – moved around from seat to seat stalking a knee to grab. One groper in his mid-fifties was grabbed by his victim who held onto him while shouting for help. The man had nine children and the woman decided not to press charges, but the police – holding the accused in the theatre manager's office – brought in the man's eldest son and insisted that he see to it that his father received psychiatric treatment. It was usually older men who committed acts of indecent exposure, opening overcoats on buses, on sidewalks near schools, and even from the windows of their homes.[48] They were – like the groper – having 'problems.' The theatre groper had to come to the police station and report to an inspector on his treatment by a doctor.[49]

By 1955 at least, the police were trying to convince victims of crimes against person to lay charges or, failing that, to persuade the assailant to seek treatment. They usually gave advice to the victim about legal action, the family court, and the Children's Aid Society; they seem to have been trusted by victims – indeed by the public at large. One constable was walking on his beat when at 11:05 p.m. a mother approached him to complain about her daughter, who, at thirteen, was keeping the company of a man twenty-four. He had been warned to stay away, but refused. The constable alerted other constables who covered the beat and put out a description of the man's 1954 Oldsmobile. From a civil-libertarian point of view, this risked escalating into police harassment; but to a family afraid of a tough guy and concerned about their daughter's morals and reputation, the action was welcomed.

Wilful Damage

In the sense that wilful damage or vandalism is directed not just at an object but at an individual, it is a crime against a person. Vengeance was indeed the objective when the former employee of a restaurant smashed a pane of glass in the front door on Christmas day.[50] Vengeance and jealousy were likely the reason that Lucy Vanberg's telephone wires had been cut five times in two years. She told police that the attacks 'always came after her boy friend's wife finds out.'[51] Young male hooligans' peculiar sense of self-respect, likely tinged with more than a little racism, led to a vicious attack on a corner fish-and-chip shop owned by a Chinese Canadian. The shop owner had ejected several youths for disorderly conduct. They retaliated by throwing green paint on one side of the building; they also splashed coal oil over the front window which they tried to ignite.[52]

POLICE CONDUCT AND LAYING CHARGES

Upon sizing up an occurrence, the police had to make a decision about how persuasive they should be in convincing the victim to become a complainant and bring charges. From what can be gathered about assaults from the occurrence-book reports, well over half of the time the police recommended emphatically to the victim that charges should be laid. Sometimes they said nothing about charges, believing that the incident did not require a court action. Thus, in the case of the fracas involving the two teenage girls, 'both parties were warned to keep the peace, and stay away from each other.'[53] Interestingly, in cases where men were the victims, the laying of charges was a subject very often avoided. Perhaps, as in the case of a tavern brawl, the police assumed that all parties were culpable. Rarely did the police neglect to deal with the matter of charges in the cases where women were victims, but there were such occasions. In the instance of a domestic dispute where the wife had given out more than she had received – hitting her husband over the head with a plaster ornament – the constables simply 'advised them to settle differences when sober.' Both parties had been drinking and the woman bordered on complete drunkenness.'[54] On other occasions, constables advised the parties about charges; that is, they simply indicated how the law worked in these matters.

Officers attending to occurrences often recommended to women that they should lay charges. The statistics do not capture the officers' exasperation when they refused. A woman called the police to report that her common-law husband had slapped her in the face. The report ended with this comment: 'We have advised the complainant to lay an assault charge against her husband if she still felt the same way in the morning. We can recall in the past when we were called to settle a fight between the husband and wife. On each visit we have advised the wife what to do, but it appears that she does not want our advice.'[55] In some instances, the victims determined on a civil action. Mary South's husband came home intoxicated and smashed a table. The trouble had been going on for six months. She 'would not go to family or criminal court but would see a lawyer about divorce.'[56]

The rise of a middle class may have had some marginal influence on crime rates or at least on the rates of the reporting of crimes, for there are almost no middle-class addresses in the occurrence book on crimes against the person. Even allowing for the potential privacy of suburban houses as a barrier to the prying ears of neighbours, even taking into account the possibility that middle-class victims of wife beatings were loath to have a policeman approach their houses, the lack of occurrences is too complete to be explained just by a successful hiding of incidents or by a police bias in patrolling largely working-class areas. The explanation lies rather in the contrast between the lives of middle-class Hamiltonians and those of the poor. Because the urban poor possessed very little private space and few pride-building material goods, they were often pressured into determined defences of what they had or what they understand they had: their honour, their prowess. The result, in short, was a high level of crime among those who were most disadvantaged.

Occurrence records are not only vital criminal-history sources and criminological tools; they also affirm that the police as urban professionals have a complicated field of work. Which hat should the constable wear as he rounds the next corner? Should he act as the defender of the young and innocent, as the protector of the old-enough-to-know-better, or as legal counsellor? On 21 September 1955 a constable on the beat in Hamilton found himself in the role of social worker. The officer observed a woman collapse on the street. He carried her into a store where she recovered enough to tell him that she had not eaten in two days; her husband had been reduced to part-time work at Westinghouse. The constable took her home and found no food in the house; he reported the case to the morality department, which handled the liaison between the police and the city's public and voluntary social service agencies. No longer did the force operate its crude hostel, but constables remained alert to the welfare of city residents.

THEFT IN MID-VICTORIAN HAMILTON

Professional thieves or major thefts were rare in the city during the mid-nineteenth century. Burglaries were infrequent – only two to ten a year in the 1870s, robberies were only slightly more common, ranging from three to twenty a year. Repeat offenders generally committed larceny and, in a few instances, the act provided a desired ticket to winter quarters in the jail. No 'dangerous class' of serious habitual criminals stalked the streets of Hamilton. In fact, one of the earliest references to a smooth professional criminal concerned Charlotte Evans with her 'sweet looking innocent face.' Charlotte was a well-known pickpocket active around Hamilton in the early 1860s.[57]

In several annual reports in later years of the century, the police chief provided the total value of articles stolen. In 1879 the approximately 250 cases of larceny, fraud, robbery, and burglary had produced a loss of $1307, or an average of five dollars per occurrence. The chief noted that the articles taken in that year were of greater value than was usually the case; he cited jewellery, cutlery, meerschaum pipes, and clothing.[58] The value of articles taken by various means in 1891 was $2444, based on 204 occurrences and thus averaging twelve dollars each.[59] The average values are misleading because the bulk of thefts were petty larcenies; a few large losses raised the average, but the majority of thefts involved very small and cheap articles. The property of the local bourgeoisie was not in much danger from hardened criminals, or from anyone else.

One commonplace theft was the snatch-and-run perpetrated around the central business area by boys or young men. They stole newspapers, boots, pants, coats, shirts, and caps. The shops of the era were cluttered with goods and many had outdoor displays and items hanging from the doorways. So often did losses from the shop displays occur that in early 1875 the police chief reported that these crimes were 'to a certain extent invited by the carelessness of the victims.' This statement practically admitted that the police could really not do much to prevent crime, that shopowners had to take some actions of their own. Of course, at the same time the police proposed that if their number were increased they could do a much better job of protecting property. Interestingly enough, these virtually contradictory statements surfaced again in the 1930s. The continuity of the notion that the victim was an accomplice through carelessness also points towards the similarity in thefts across many decades.

In addition to lightly attended store goods, unattended wagons and sleighs offered easy pickings. The decision to steal, therefore, came often as an impulse based on opportunity. Morris Badgely noticed a pair of boots in a sleigh in mid-January 1865. There was no one about. He lifted them out and scurried away. On the surface, one might have surmised that he had taken the boots as a matter of necessity, of dire need made acute by the winter. In fact, Morris attempted to trade them in for a good time; he went to a local tavern, ordered drinks for himself and chums, and tried to pay for the spree with the boots. The tavern keeper was suspicious and reported the incident. It is possible, of course, that Badgely needed shelter and had resolved to bid adieu to the streets in style.[60]

Petty thieves such as Badgely – for whatever reason – did not act in especially clever ways and this circumstance rather than cunning detective work made their arrest fairly simple. In what seems a crime of necessity, William Duggan took a pair of mitts from a sleigh in February 1863 and he proceeded to wear them around the city market. The owner recognized them and reported Duggan. Raising three young children on his own, the unfortunate man gained the sympathy of the magistrate who released him after a stern warning.[61] In the 1930s, the theft of blankets and clothes from parked cars was a crime comparable to the removal of articles from earlier forms of transport.

Theft by servants had no exact counterpart by the 1930s, for domestic service had been replaced by appliances. During the nineteenth century, it had been fairly common for women to bring charges against their servants for stealing household articles such as silverware and linen. In late January 1873 Elizabeth Davis took three sheets from the house where she worked and, like Badgley, attempted to exchange them for a drink.[62] Another case, which revolved around a betrayal of trust by two 'nice young men' recently arrived from England, suggests how stealing by servants fits into a more general pattern of acts that embraces later decades. Former shoemakers, the pair had come to Canada to seek their fortune. They could only find work at a farm outside Hamilton. They had the run of the place. One day, they walked off with a watch, boots, and a jacket.[63] They had pilfered from the workplace. That would prove to be a persistent form of theft.

Besides the shop, the house, the vehicle, and the workplace, obvious places for thefts were boarding-houses, taverns, and brothels. In these places, strangers and opportunity mingled. One of the more bizarre cases of petty larceny involved a man who gave his name as Baptiste Irizik, allegedly an Italian vendor of plaster images. In 1863 he went to brothel and, while distracted, lost a statue and fifty cents.[64]

THEFT DURING THE GREAT DEPRESSION AND THE SECOND WORLD WAR

At 1:10 in the afternoon of 22 June 1934, on a west-end Hamilton street, three men sprang from an automobile and intercepted a pair of couriers conveying a leather bag with $4705.95 belonging to the Tuckett Tobacco Company. One of the hold-up men brandished a nickel-plated revolver.[65] The heist was one of several armed robberies in the city that summer; others occurred in a bank, a restaurant and two drugstores. With the exception of the bank robbery, the sums taken were under $100. In another case the same year, a young girl sent by her mother to buy twenty-five-cents worth of meat at the corner grocery returned home in tears. Two older girls – aged ten or twelve – had snatched the quarter.[66]

These incidents, representing two extremes on a scale of thefts, pose commonplace problems in criminology: what is a crime and who is a criminal? Indeed, they put a fine point on such questions because the occurrences were reported by the public. The report about the quarter, for example, denoted a popular perception rather than an institutional determination of what constituted a theft.

The episodes had little in common, except that they had been reported in detail to the police during the same summer and hence appear in a most interesting set of local records. The victims in these incidents had no hesitation in calling upon the authorities to deal with the loss of valuables, regardless of the sums involved. This belief in the efficacy of having the police assist with a great variety of problems was widespread in Hamilton, where the police long had been appealed to for assistance.[67]

If the reporting of crime by the public appears to be fairly comprehensive, then not only are the resulting records a valuable source but the acts of reporting are noteworthy in themselves because they temper class-based interpretations about the criminal justice system. The practice of keeping records on the public's reports of incidents began in Hamilton with an 1879 order from the police commission. 'All reports of Criminal occurrences made to any member of the Police force must as soon after they are received be reported to the Sergt Major at the police office City Hall to be entered in a book kept for that purpose.'[68] The bookkeeping may have lapsed, because the police commission issued another order in 1895: 'The Chief should in future cause all reports to be entered in a book kept for that purpose.'[69] Occurrence books survive for some months in the late 1920s and for various periods through to the mid-1940s.

There are grounds for believing that the Hamilton reports of theft must have encompassed a substantial amount of actual crime, despite the problematic nature of reporting noted in criminological studies. One common criticism of occurrence reports as a measure of crime has been the observation that patrolmen and communications officers have filtered out many minor incidents.[70] Yet the Hamilton set contains plenty of seemingly trivial episodes. It also might be argued that victims in certain instances would be too embarrassed by the circumstances of thefts to report them; however, some citizens fleeced in compromising situations were candid and their reports enliven the narrative portions of this chapter.

Many of the reporting victims were blue-collar and petty-bourgeois residents. Their reporting of crime to the police implies that they accepted the institution as an aid to them regardless of whether the police might have been seen by some people as an instrument of a capitalist élite. Conflict theorists have maintained that the law and its instruments have been created primarily by the ruling classes to serve their interests. Abundant events in the history of criminal justice and policing can be adduced to support conflict theory.[71] Indeed, as we have seen, the Hamilton police force had its roots in social turmoil and labour protest in the 1840s and 1850s.[72] It did pay special notice to the protection of the property of an élite.[73] Nevertheless, recruitment of constables from the working class and the force's performance of social-service functions had modified its original character. By the early 1900s, the Hamilton police were close to their public.[74]

The willingness of Hamilton residents to report occurrences of both a major and a relatively minor nature translated into the official recording of some 3900 incidents during twelve months from May 1934 to May 1935. This is equivalent to about one incident for every seven or eight households, a level of reporting that provides quite a different impression of crime in the city than one based upon statistics generated by the courts. A well-known problem faced by all historical inquiries into crime is that the most accessible sources – those consisting of the outcomes of court proceedings – represent only an unknown fraction of incidents. Records closest to the incident – namely initial reports of complaints brought forward to the authorities – rarely have been discovered, although some criminologists undertaking contemporary studies have had access to such reports.[75]

For the years 1900 to 1950, conviction rates in the annual reports were not cited by crime. Consequently, for Hamilton there is no short and simple route to seeing how reports on thefts were pared down to investigations and investigations into convictions. It would be safe to say, however, that no more than 5 per cent of theft occurrences led to convictions.[76] Complicating the picture is the fact that the Hamilton police chiefs had the annoying practice of mixing all manner of offences in the conviction statistics, including by-law infractions. By this device, the police may have been burying distressing information. In fairness to the police, however, the trifling quality of many thefts and the lack of clues precluded earnest investigation. Furthermore a very significant proportion of occurrences (Figure 6.1) included an element of doubt as to whether missing articles had been stolen or lost. In many cases, perception was important: when an article was left behind through carelessness and taken by another party, the incident

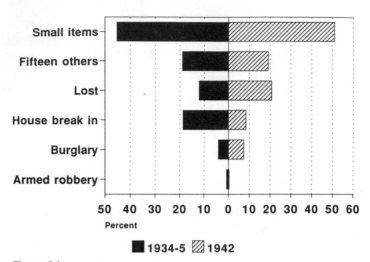

Figure 6.1
Major Groupings of Theft Occurrences, Hamilton, 1934–5 and 1942
Source: HPL, RG 10, Police Occurrence Books, Thefts, 1934–5; 1942.

could be viewed either as a crime or as an instance of negligence. This point reintroduces a methodological problem. If what the public considered a theft is of consequence, the police-generated records about offences and the court-generated ones about prosecutions are tainted sources and must be dealt with cautiously. There are many grey areas in criminal justice history.

Every set of data has limitations, for questions posed by researchers inevitably reach beyond the parameters imposed by sources. The most annoying limitation of the Hamilton occurrence books is their restricted time-span; no time-series analysis is possible using them alone, and yet such analysis is the bread and butter of historical work with criminal justice data. Nevertheless, other things can be accomplished. By adding several variables to those in the occurrence books, it has been possible to delve into the social contexts of theft in two different eras and, indeed, into the grey areas of how to define theft. Moreover, minor but revealing differences in the patterns of theft and in the tone of the reports underline the shortcomings of summary data ordinarily used in criminal justice history. Fortunately for this study, the chief constable in 1931 ordered an improvement in the quality of the reports upon which the occurrence books were based. Among other things, he insisted that theft reports should specify the item taken.[77]

To render the inquiry manageable, every tenth case of theft was drawn to compile a sample and notes were kept on the more richly detailed typical and atypical cases. The sample made it feasible to use city directories to establish the occupations of the victims, and to assign the address of the crime to one of twenty-nine neighbourhood planning districts, each of about thirty square blocks. Entered by longhand into notebooks, the occurrence reports did not adhere to a form. Yet, from the content of the reports, it is certain that the vast majority of reports came from victims.[78] The fairly terse accounts included the occasional aside. Virtually all contained the following information: the name of the victim; the address of the complainant; the article stolen; a description of the place from whence the article had been taken; the value of the article; whether the suspect could be identified or described; and a marginal notation – often in red – about the recovery of the missing article and arrests. The coding process required interpretation of some entries which were understandably vague about whether articles were missing or really stolen.

Studies of other North American cities during the Depression have not reached a consensus on what impact, if any, the economic collapse of the 1930s had on crime rates.[79] Problematic though they are, annual-report data on theft occurrences in Hamilton seem to confirm that the onset of the Depression may have been accompanied by a rise in thefts. However, the trend is weak (Figure 5.6) and qualitative evidence contradictory. In the 1932 report, the chief claimed that despite 'the exceptional crisis through which we have been passing ... there has been no serious increase in crime.'[80] In the 1934 and 1936 reports, he commented on unusually large numbers of breaking and entering incidents. And in 1936 he went so far as to claim it was an 'epidemic ... all over the country.'[81] But a similar assertion was made in 1944.[82] In sum, neither the data – somewhat suspect in any event – nor the qualitative evidence make a firm case for theft rising during the Depression. What is more, a notable rise in occurrences truly came with the return of prosperity and the booming wartime economy.[83] Keeping in mind this interesting reversal of the assumed association between economic depression and theft, we can turn to a detailed study of 1934–5 and 1942.

No compelling argument can be found for the notion that the rate of theft invariably increases in periods of economic distress, because opportunity is a significant variable and scarcity is a slippery concept. The merit of these caveats is evident when the data in the occurrence books is examined. The unique conditions of life during the Depression as well as during a period of wartime prosperity produced subtle differences in thefts as opportunity and scarcity shifted. However, significant similarities can also be detected. Motives and opportunities – insofar as we can tell – remained fairly consistent throughout *the mass* of thefts in the two periods. Given certain prevailing traits in the data for the two eras, it seems difficult to accept that crude rates of reported theft – consisting largely of minor items taken on impulse – could be tied to Depression conditions. But changing socio-economic conditions could affect marginally a list of items taken and the context – the place and related events – of these thefts. Annual rates alone, therefore, are not the ideal way to study relations between crime and socio-economic conditions.

Both the consistency and the variability in what was taken provide insight into human frailty across changing social circumstances. Similarity will be considered first. The pettiness of most thefts is striking (Figure 6.2). Once the handful of major hold-ups are removed from the samples, for they were large enough to skew the mean, the average value of stolen articles becomes $14 for both 1934–5 and 1942. With almost a quarter of all reported thefts in the 1934–5 sample valued from $1 to $5 and another 45 per cent having a value of less than 50 cents or no reported value at all (both coded as 0, for values were coded to the nearest dollar), the minor incident involving children that introduced this section seems closer to the norm than the armed robbery (Figure 6.1). Small losses – small at least to the distant observer – filled page after page in both periods and can help to explain why some reports were not treated as offences and why few complaints led to police investigations. In the case of many thefts, impulse and opportunity fashioned the deed and the articles taken were trivial.

The circumstances of most thefts imply the youth and inexperience of those committing the acts. Sophistication was rare; opportunity critical. Unlocked cars beckoned to be entered and the police chief chided careless drivers in 1936 for encouraging 'persons criminally inclined to commit crime.'[84] Open windows in the summer were a temptation, as were farmers' trucks parked on side streets on market day.[85] Particulars were unique and with the seasons came slight variations, but many thefts had common traits. What happened to Andrew Comfort[86] was both singular and commonplace. Andrew did not use an icebox in the winter but rather put food in a box on the back steps. On the night of 15 December 1934 he lost a roast of pork and a glass pie plate. He suspected children who lived in the neighbourhood.[87] His casualness had allowed an impulsive act.

The combination of opportunity, youth, and a low level of planning or skill may be an enduring trait of the bulk of urban theft.[88] In their study of residential burglary in Toronto in the early 1970s, Irvin Waller and Norman Okihiro found that about 40 per cent of entries were through unlocked doors.[89] Even in the Depression, many people displayed trust and left low-value articles exposed to young sticky fingers. Those with more to lose, as we shall witness, may have practised greater vigilance.

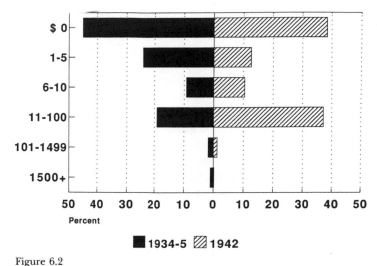

Figure 6.2
Values of Items Stolen, Hamilton, 1934–5 and 1942
Source: HPL, RG 10, Police Occurrence Books, Thefts, 1934–5; 1942.

In some cases it seems probable that thefts were the result of more deliberation, even though the takings were slight. Some small thefts hint at a *modus operandi*, an intentional and premeditated carrying out of many similar actions to yield a significant total of small sums. Purse snatchers who lurked behind their victims in cinemas and the person or persons unknown who took purses from the cars of widows visiting grave sites may have had slim pickings on each occasion but a healthy sum over a few weeks.[90] The party who broke into eight gasoline stations across the city in two nights in May 1942 by breaking glass in the front door got small sums in several and none in others, but for two nights' effort he had garnered about a week's pay.[91] Calculating criminals were not unknown: their presence leaps out from occurrence-book pages when a chain of like offences happened during the same night. Break-ins conducted the same way at four houses on Cedar Avenue on 18 July 1942 comprised a truly exceptional act, but there were other less dramatic examples of deliberate crimes.[92] Sometimes an arrest led to a confession of a string of break-ins. The sharp rise in these incidents in 1934, as reported by the chief, can partly be attributed to Steve Chesick, who was charged with fourteen counts of housebreaking and two of autos theft.[93]

In addition to the 'professional' criminals who picked pockets or broke into houses, there were a few short-change artists and safe crackers who turned up in the reports. Beginning in the 1930s, the latter appear to have been driven off the main streets and into smaller out-of-the-way establishments. Larger industries had guards and downtown stores had begun to place their safes near front doors where they could be seen by police and passers-by. There were risks to breaking into shops near where operators resided. With what the chief of detectives described as 'an effective display of butcher knives and choppers,' the Lapcewich brothers – corner grocers – sent two would-be-thieves to hospital in November 1935. The brothers had been shot during the confrontation.[94] And there were other reports of citizen pursuit. Out-of-way places – coal yards, auto wreckers, lumber yards, and warehouses – provided easier targets for thieves.[95]

In terms of the overall make-up of thefts in the sample years, there is no satisfactory way of determining which thefts were planned. It seems likely, however, that the majority of burglaries were undertaken without planning and directed against residences.[96]

AN ASSORTMENT OF MOTIVES

In addition to the complexity and elusiveness of fixing the level of spontaneity involved in crimes, there is the related matter of motives. Despite the self-evident challenge of dealing with these topics, the reports do help us to see an improvised side to theft. Irrational 'motives' stood behind many thefts; they were not all driven by necessity, alone or even primarily. Risk-taking, envy, impulsive gratification, and vengeance accounted for some thefts. The owner of a gas station broken into on the night of 23 December 1935 believed that it was 'spite work.'[97] Doubtless, the hundreds of bicycles stolen each year (perhaps as many as 500 in 1934–5 and 900 in 1942) included some that were coveted for parts and resale, but how many were stolen irrationally when an opportunity arose for a thrill or to inflict discomfort?

If we count bicycles and other small articles found around schools and playgrounds, irrational and impulsive conduct by children could have accounted for far more property crime than the perceived needs of adults. The prevalence of bicycle thefts prompted the introduction of licensing in 1945.[98] Beyond the list of selected articles in Figure 6.3, the complete data strings out modest items appearing two or three times in the sample: apples, bread, candy, radiator caps, hubcaps, skates, sleighs, and suitcases. The very small value of stolen articles is a reminder that the majority of thieves, if they really had planned to offset economic distress, likely came up disappointed. Both disappointment and stupidity are not to be dismissed, and they are compatible with the proposition that what many thieves had done was quite irrational and truly 'juvenile.' The prominence of money and purses among the stolen articles in both periods reinforces the assump-

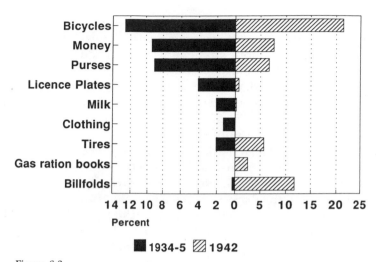

Figure 6.3
Articles Most Frequently Reported As Stolen, 1934–5 and 1942
Source: HPL, RG 10, Police Occurrence Books, Thefts, 1934–5; 1942.

tion that most thieves acted apart from any crime ring or without any elaborate scheming. Cash has the obvious quality of being immediately negotiable. It does not require the service of a 'fence' or other buyer.[99]

Not all small thefts were done for a thrill on impulse. Perceived need, even protest, and the host of motives arising from social frustration can be read into a few differences between the articles stolen in the Depression and those in the war years. A graph of occurrences or offences per thousand or hundred thousand residents – the routine measures of criminal justice history – could fluctuate but remain silent about precisely what was taken. Short of interviewing thieves, historians have thus been forced to speculate about motives and opportunity. While such speculation is inevitable, information about stolen articles allows us to draw closer to the nexus of crime and socio-economic conditions. Thefts are not only points on a graph but victims, places, and items. Articles of clothing and food were more prominent among the missing articles in 1934–5 than they were in 1942. So too were cigarettes, a low-cost pleasure item. There were also more break-ins, thefts of jewelry, and armed robberies. The latter came complete with the not-too original order 'stick 'em up!'[100] The Depression may not have affected the volume of crimes against property in Hamilton, still, its impact may have been expressed on the margins of what was being taken and how.

The occurrence data – as helpful as they are in dealing with items and context – are not free from problems. Though people apparently reported a great deal of small crime, the theft of milk – a plausible indicator of distress in the Depression data – often went unreported, or at least was not reported regularly. Thus, in addition to data, remarks recorded in the occurrence reports provide crucial evidence on the contrast between depression and wartime. These remarks show that some people, on not receiving their regular order of milk from the dairy, assumed that it was a case of negligence on the part of the deliveryman or waited until a second or third incident before calling a police station. A driver for City Dairies reported on 4 July 1934 that milk was being stolen 'routinely every morning in the vicinity of Roxborough, Frederick, Robins, Wexford, etc.' This was a working-class area and the driver suspected juveniles. Family need was the probable cause, for it is hard to imagine that youths pilfered milk for thrills at 6:00 a.m.[101] A few days earlier, Pete Domitro finally became annoyed enough to report having had 'milk stolen off rear steps for about two weeks.'[102] Edgar Smith complained on 6 December 1935 that milk had been stolen from him 'almost every morning.'[103] A similar delayed report had come in on 16 April 1935 from a driver for Hills Bakery; he complained about 'rolls' being 'stolen almost every morning from the Brass Rail Restaurant' where he left them on the doorstep.[104] When reporting the theft of two baskets of apples on 9 April 1935, grocer Art Black mentioned losses during the preceding weeks.[105] In the Depression, the theft of small food items spoke of need and opportunity; the aggregate data on investigations and convictions could never have disclosed this fact.

It is in the seemingly petty details of thefts or in the chief constable's daily orders to the men or in his annual reports that Depression circumstances are best revealed. For example, there were thefts of backyard poultry and reports about these were not postponed. What is particularly interesting about them is the fact that the complaints came from the city centre during the Depression. Chicken coops seem to have been pervasive even in the urban core in the 1930s. The stripping of clothes lines also brought immediate reports.[106] Just after dark on 23 March 1935, Mrs R. Potter saw a man 'who looked like a foreigner' enter her backyard and attempt to steal clothes from her line. 'He succeeded in getting a bath towel [sic].'[107] Another type of theft was common in Hamilton during the Depression. When houses were left vacant by tenants or defaulting buyers, their plumbing drew thieves who sold to scrap dealers.[108] But the most telling piece of evidence about hardship in this industrial city was the chief's order of 11 July 1935: 'Men on the beats and also those in the Patrol Cars are to pay particular attention to garbage pickers etc. who are around the city at nights. No doubt some of these men are stealing, frequently garden hose, children's tricycles, etc.'[109]

Finally, the Depression precipitated suspicions that never could have surfaced in criminal justice proceedings but did make their way into occurrence reports. Tramps and beggars asked for little as they went house to house requesting work or a meal. But a few aroused fear. 'A tough looking fellow' came to the home of the manager of the Eaton's department store and asked the price of a bed. The wife offered to call the Salvation Army. The man rejected this idea and went away, stopping to talk to a couple in a car before proceeding to knock on other doors. He may have been trying to 'cadge' silver from the couple, but the manager interpreted the episode as evidence of a burglary gang.[110] Fragments of hardship can be gleaned from the Depression era reports and they, perhaps more than any highly distilled criminal justice data, document the relationship of theft – and fear of theft – to economic collapse.

A comparison of wartime and Depression data underscores the importance of opportunity and changing elements of scarcity. The war created new forms of scarcity and a distinct set of valuable items that turned up often among public reports of theft: gasoline ration books, gasoline, and definitely auto tires.[111] In the 1930s an open car tempted the theft of a car blanket or possibly a radio, but in 1942 the object of attention was the ration book. It would be very difficult to prove that 'professional' criminals were involved often in these wartime thefts; however, rationing was a situation tailor-made for professional crime. When thieves broke into the Imperial Service Station on 28 August, they reaped a bonanza of 1212 ration coupons.[112] Thieves siphoned off gasoline from trucks at cartage company yards.[113] Some tire thefts were deliberate and well engineered. Imagine the shock to William Weir when he went out to start his 1937 Pontiac on the morning of 20 November 1942. Over night, parties unknown had jacked up his car, stolen all four tires, tubes, and wheels; thieves then had lowered the Pontiac onto bricks.[114] The problem of tire thefts, one of national proportions, forced a federal order-in-council banning the sale of used tires which had illegible serial numbers.[115]

THE SCENE OF THE CRIME

The data from the occurrences highlight change and continuity in articles stolen. Before demonstrating that there is much more social history to be garnered from unquantifiable asides in the reports themselves, it is worthwhile scanning the data for what had not changed. In the two periods, the playground and the house remained the principle settings for stealing. Indeed, continuity went deeper. In both periods, the five leading places remained the same and with only a minor switch in ranking. The five major articles included some slight changes, but they all remained similar in the sense of being portable and commonplace. If any practical lesson can be derived from the data, it would be the timeless one that prevention was the only sensible way of minimizing loss of small articles. The police recovery rate was, as we will explain, low. What the locations and the articles suggest – and this seems supported by the presence of many wives as complainants – is that a great deal of reported theft occurred because of front doors left unlocked when householders were in yards, out shopping, or away from vestibules where coats and purses lay vulnerable.

Losses from residences in 1942 were low relative to 1934–5 and the reason may have been that more people went out more often. However, there was a panic in 1942 about sneak thieves who stole from homes when people had gone to work, a more common situation in the war than during the Depression.[116] Just below the high-risk locations so common to both eras, a few others turned up with greater frequency in 1942. Restaurants, movie theatres, and hotels surfaced more routinely because Hamiltonians had the money and the leisure for commercial socializing. The morality squad, for example, stepped up its activities, 'visiting restaurants, dance halls, etc.', not to deal with theft but to avert 'tragedy to Hamilton homes.'[117] Moral strictures, it seems certain, had been relaxed and young people with money stepped out. When they did they also carried tempting billfolds and purses which, judging from the tenor of reports, a number handled carelessly. One might have assumed that the Depression years would have witnessed more incidents of stolen money, especially if hypotheses about Depression privation as a trigger to theft are valid. The flaw in these propositions is that, even if some of those with a desperate need thought of stealing cash, it was not found often dangling temptingly close at hand.

But in the setting of a heavy-industry city in the midst of full employment, boodle lay about and young men who had earned some of it put themselves in jeopardy during quests for 'a good time.' A great many reports were about 'missing' billfolds in 1942. Hamilton had recovered its vigorous night life, attracting factory workers, soldiers, and 'lonesome' travellers in town on business. On the night of 25 January 1942, Domenic Kovacs had been drinking heavily at the Grand Hotel. Two new bar chums asked him for a ride. Once in the parking lot, the pair stole his money and a watch.[118] With slight variations, this story was often repeated. On the night of 14 April, Mike Costain linked up with three strangers while drinking at the Grand Hotel – the same place where Kovacs had come to grief. The quartet left together for 'a place where they met some women.' Later the men robbed him.[119] The mix of women and substantial quantities of alcohol contrasts with Depres-

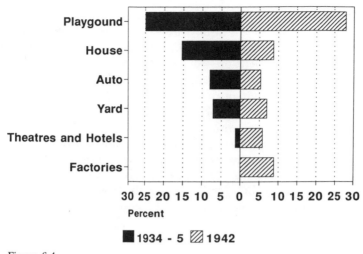

Figure 6.4
Most Frequently Cited Places for Thefts in Hamilton, 1934–5 and 1942
Source: HPL, RG 10, Police Occurrence Books, Thefts, 1934–5; 1942.

sion privation. Harry Baker from St Catharines settled into the King George Hotel on 30 May 1942 with Evelyn – a woman who 'came to his room.' Harry procured two bottles of whiskey and – not surprisingly – became intoxicated. Evelyn did not. Harry lost a wallet and a watch.[120] Earlier that year, at the upscale Connaught Hotel, Philip Pidgeon of Montreal invited a woman to his room where he had laid in a bottle of wine and a dozen bottles of beer. In the morning, the bottles were empty, the woman was gone, and so were a watch and lighter.[121]

Of course, it was not only men who found that risks accompanied prosperity, independence, and fleeting pleasures. An unidentified married woman brought home an airman for a week and he left with some of her jewelry.[122] Mrs Amelia Williams, whose husband was overseas, hosted a party on the night of 1 March 1942. One of the guests left with $70 from her purse.[123] Young ladies fell victim to a purse-snatching scam at Westminster Hall, often the site of wartime dances. In early October, a group of four girls turned over their purses to 'some chap who told them to check their purses.' Exactly one month later at the same hall, Gertrude Nelson had her purse stolen from the check room.[124] Roland's Restaurant, the site for many dances, was another risky spot, as Ellen Donegale found out at an air force dance on 11 April when money and rings were taken from her purse. A few weeks earlier, two people had reported having had their pockets picked there at a dance.[125]

In the 1942 sample, the reported thefts of money, billfolds, and purses amounted to 113; in other words, since the sample represents only one-tenth of the total number of cases, there easily could have been 1100 such incidents or about three a day. In contrast, in the Depression sample there were more than seventy such cases, or around 700 for the year and less than two a day. The 40 per cent difference far exceeded the city's population growth. Domenic Kovacs and others like him, flush as never before, found themselves in the company of strangers drawn to employment opportunities. Interesting as an aside about the contrast between Depression and wartime society, the contents of wallets and purses were somewhat different. Victims in the latter era reported the theft not only of money, but also of national service registration cards, medical discharge cards, and work passes to war industries. What was at once both a fairly affluent and free-wheeling society was also a regulated one. What remarkable and swift transformations had overtaken this community!

Similar to prior explosive growth periods in the city's history, the war brought into combination unattached young men, people from outside the city, ample drink, and money. The occurrence reports of the Depression period commented on suspicious people but they seldom went farther in their descriptions because the city's national or ethnic homogeneity had not yet been upset by newcomers. On the contrary, Hamilton lost people through migration. In 1942 strangers meant 'foreigners' and the French-Canadian industrial workers who flocked to Hamilton. As a result, ethnic stereotyping in the reports now became pronounced. A shop-breaker who had highly polished black shoes, nice clothes, a pasty complexion and black hair combed straight back 'looked like an Italian.'[126] How well a suspect spoke English or whether he spoke with a French-Canadian accent was noted, for the city had become polyglot.[127]

Labouring brothers possibly associated freely and generously – they certainly did at taverns. However, the occurrence reports – an admittedly biased source for commenting on brotherhood – imply that the anonymity of strangers also encouraged criminal acts. Happy hang-outs where strangers bent elbows were high-risk places. Besides the night spots, the very accommodations provided for wartime workers proved insecure. Fred Maychark returned to his rooming-house late one Saturday night to find his trunk forced open and a loss of $70 and three new shirts.[128] The Army Trades School staff house was the scene of many thefts; so was Bud Fischer's Hotel, which housed factory workers.[129] Workplaces, too, were not immune from theft. Stephen Golitza, for example, had his locker broken into at the Steel Company and there were other such cases there and at Dominion Foundries.[130]

Something else distinguishes the wartime pattern of opportunity – always a very important factor in theft – from that of the Depression. In 1934–5, the city's major corporations, though often enough stolen from, were not remarkably prominent in the occurrence books. Yet they figured quite prominently in 1942 when almost one in ten thefts was reported as taking place at a major establishment (Figure 6.4). Patriotic zeal, it seems, did not have a universal and constant grip on the minds of war-industry workers as tools, tool boxes, building materials, scrap metal, and gasoline went missing. It might have been thought that industries would have been major targets of theft in the Depression. Once again, however, the crucial factor was opportunity. War industries generated more possibilities than the depressed factories of the 1930s. During the Depression, meat packers, furriers, trucking companies, wholesalers, and railway express offices would have been tempting targets were it not for the fact that managers put in special requests to the police for protection at vulnerable times and places.[131] The frantic pace of work and production in the wartime city – the comings and goings from plants – precluded diligent scrutiny. In wartime England, according to Edward Smithies's study, the situation was much the same: in the dockyards and factories, virtually everything moveable was in danger of being stolen.[132]

THE VICTIMS OF THEFT

Social scientists since the 1940s often have reported on the existence of comparatively high crime regions within cities, and also on the congruence between these locations and poor housing and poverty. Plausible explanations abound: better preventive measures in wealthier areas; a weaker attachment to property in poor ones; the hopelessness of that portion of the city's population with no prospects of future reward within existing social relations; the poor's lack of privacy and security at home, and, in general, their disrupted and disorderly lives. The environmental approach, of course, may call attention to the reality of high-risk areas but does not explain why certain individuals living in such areas become criminals while others do not.

Environmental observations apply to Hamilton where, in 1934–5, 49 per cent of the reported incidents took place in the city's central districts. These districts contained a disproportionate share of the city's tenements and run-down houses. In comparison, the middle-class suburbs in the west end accounted for a scant 2 per cent of reports. The contrast in the number of reports by the two types of neighbourhood is important on many counts. Prejudice toward immigrant groups or a stereotyping of areas as prone to crime probably helped to skew the geography of incidents, for some areas were certainly more heavily patrolled than others. As late as 1953, for instance, the force acknowledged that it regarded James St North and Barton St East as 'favourite gathering places of persons of doubtful reputation.'[133] However, it is worth stressing again that citizens, not the police, were the originators of most of these reports. Citizens in poorer parts of the city actively reported losses to the police; they trusted the police and saw them as potentially helpful. What is tragic about the thefts reported from poor areas is that the poor could have comprised a disproportionately large share of the victims of theft in the Depression. Yet this assumption commits the environmental fallacy. Location is no proof of social attributes; the coding of occupations is a valuable but imperfect route to proving the victimization of the poor. Moreover, the real value to the spatial analysis is that it once again raises the theme of opportunity. The five central districts contained a substantial set of the city's retail streets, hotels, parking areas, and schools.

The proposition that the poor were victimized – that theft was not a Robin Hood endeavour during the Depression – receives additional support from a consideration of complainants' situations. Such information was not easily secured. Terse police reports almost never said anything about the state of the victim's circumstances. The single exception was Mrs Waincott, who lived in a fairly poor area of the city; she reported that her milk had been stolen the previous two mornings and volunteered the information that 'she is on City Relief.'[134] To obtain some insight into the circumstances of the victims, city directory information was coded.

Consider first the set of cases with missing information. Roughly 15 per cent of the people who reported a theft to the police in 1934–5 could not be found in the appropriate city directories, though they had given the police a city address. Perhaps they had moved or lived as boarders or relatives in households where they had not been listed separately. While not firm evidence for impoverished circumstances, the want of a directory listing during the Depression is suggestive of a lack of security and independence. Another 4 per cent who were listed cited no occupation in the city directory. It is difficult to say what this meant: retirement, or unemployment, or a wish for privacy. Similarly, it is not clear how we should interpret finding the surname at the address but not the complainant's name: Is this a child or an adult relative? And finally, what can we make of those who gave the police no address? They constituted a much larger group in 1934–5 than in 1942. Can we assume that many were without a fixed address? In spite of several unanswerable questions, it is not rash to propose that most reporting victims led a precarious existence in hard times.

About 20 per cent of the victims may be designated poor by virtue of missing information, and to this figure we can add half of the shopkeepers (full labels reveal them to be petty operators: barbers; confectionists; newsagents; tobacconists; grocers); half of the skilled and semi-skilled labourers; half of the widows; and all of the labourers. By such a fair estimate, it seems that around 40 per cent of the victims were poor by definition of occupation and without taking into account that many skilled labourers in the building trades and industry were hard hit by the Depression. In contrast, well-to-do victims likely constituted only around 15 per cent of the complainants, and that is a high estimate because white-collar occupations included clerks and stenographers. All in all, it seems safe to say that half the reported thefts in the Depression were committed against fairly poor folk. The fact that so many reported losses transpired around houses and apartments during the 1930s, rather than in places of recreation and work, suggests too that crime in the lean years of the Depression struck hard at those least able to sustain the losses.

Three other clusters of victims should be considered. One of the most numerous set of complainants (8.5 per cent) consisted of wives – the householders who noted missing articles or were at home when someone was seen dashing off a porch. Teachers and students produced a cluster of around 5 per cent. Next came the out-of-town victims (4.4 per cent). Does their surprising presence stem from a vulnerability common to all travellers? Hotel rooms and restaurants are not as secure as a house and, as Cecil Fleming discovered, not every house is a home. Cecil drove in from RR2 Hamilton on the evening of 2 September 1934, looking for a good time. Around 11:00 p.m. he picked up a woman and went to a nearby house where they spent the night. He left at 7:00 a.m. and discovered soon that he was missing $120. He did not press charges.[135] Hotels figured prominently not only as places in which thefts occurred but as locales in and around which crimes developed. Toronto salesman Melville Potash stopped for the night of 5 December 1935 at the Commercial Hotel. Sometime between 9:00 and 11:00 five dresses were stolen from his car.[136] It does not seem improbable that serious thieves watched hotels and nearby parking spots and that the carelessness of victims offered tempting targets. These are propositions supported by recent research.[137]

Overall, the list of parties reporting crimes is heterogeneous, containing a good number of householders, petty-bourgeois proprietors, and working men. Additionally, there is the substantial number of reports concerning the theft of goods of relatively small values. The fact that perhaps 1450 people called the police to complain about the loss of items with no reported value or with values worth less than $5 says something about their circumstances and their trust in the police. Given the paltry pickings, it is probable that the relatively poor were notably victimized – and probably by other individuals who were also poor.

Regrettably, the occurrence books say nothing about suspects that would permit a description of their social status, though the term juvenile does turn up from time to time. In any case, the reported incidents rarely provided clues on identity to the police. Victims could supply the name of a suspect, a description of the suspect, or some relevant evidence in anywhere from 12 to 20 per cent of the cases. That is, the police had the foundation for an investigation in just about the same number of cases as they reported investigating in their annual reports. In about 20 per cent of the reported cases it seemed that the incident was complicated by the likelihood of the article having been lost or missing prior to being 'stolen.' The trail here had to have been weak. In over 60 per cent of the cases, the party reporting provided no description or other help to the police.[138]

One lesson to be learned from anthropologists and historians researching the centuries before the modern era is that insights about the commonplace must be extracted from whatever slender and even indirect sources survive. Casually mentioned contexts for medieval or early-modern crime and death have provided important glimpses into the realities of work, family, and play. To a degree, occurrence books can perform a similar function.

Children rode everywhere on their bicycles, dropping them at the edge of playgrounds, and they routinely forgot their coats at school; occasionally, both items were taken by others. Housewives went about their daily chores with doors unlocked. Unless the thefts or the startling appearance of tramps caused them to reconsider, few doubted that they lived in a safe world. We can imagine widows walking from their cars to a graveside and people in the midst of new-found wartime prosperity going out to a restaurant and a movie. Apparently, there was much trust in this urban society as well as neighbourhood convenience. Corner grocery stores and home delivery were prevalent. Early morning summer sounds, now lost, can be heard again: the urban roosters crowing and the clink of milk bottles. We can visualize farmers' produce trucks crowding streets around the market square. Something of the texture of urban life can be rediscovered in laconic reports by police constables who more than anyone else dealt with urban society on a daily basis.

Accounts of crime and criminal justice from the past often have been confined out of necessity to studying prosecution and conviction data; that is, they have been forced to manipulate and analyse data from truncated sources. Therefore, the first conclusion is an obvious one: now that we have had a glimpse into the type of records which provide a full or almost full account of incidents, the deficiencies of court and jail records as gauges of crime over time are reconfirmed. Secondly, the status of occurrence data in annual reports, and of the original occurrences from which they are derived, depend upon what *guess* we are willing to venture regarding the consistency of incident reporting over time. For the 1930s and 1940s, there appear to have been high levels of public reporting. But had it been so in the 1920s or the 1900s? Time-series analysis must be treated warily owing to the likelihood of differences in public reactions. Thirdly, as the occurrence books themselves have disclosed, the changing attributes of opportunity and scarcity are neither simple nor to be extracted readily from aggregate data. Depression and war created circumstances affecting thefts that are understood only when looked at closely; correlations of occurrences with economic indicators, therefore, cannot adequately supply connections between crime and social climate. Finally, details about the minor articles taken or missing ought to rattle any trust in the capacity of crude summary-occurrence data cited in the annual reports to provide material for a crime index. Indeed, the original reports force us to ask what theft in fact is, and more important, what it is not. Answers to these questions trail off into a conundrum.

Studies in the history of crime and criminal justice commonly emphasize that moral order matters are those which demonstrate that an uncertain number of offences are generated by policy and police responses to it. To a certain extent the same pertains for theft, where, especially given the number of reports, there had to be latitude for police discretion. Some cases were surely disposed of as 'borderline'. The catechism of the Church of England's Book of Common Prayer lists duties to neighbours. My duty to my neighbour, it instructs at one point, is 'to keep my hands from picking and stealing.' The division of theft into two deeds has merit. Picking – that is, detaching and removing with the fingers – describes much of what the citizens of Hamilton reported: articles were set down, possibly neglected, and picked by unseen others. Stealing, in contrast, has a deliberate and serious ring. That the police should exercise discretion and not investigate many episodes of picking is understandable.

But what were the police to do about reports of very petty losses that indicated a public trust in them? For some Hamilton mothers during the Great Depression, a child's loss of a quarter was a meaningful incident. It is improbable that the misery depicted in Vittorio de Sica's *Bicycle Thieves* was equalled in any of the hundreds of Hamilton households which had bicycles picked or stolen during 1934–5 or in 1942. But can we afford to be so dismissive when the victims were not? And is it correct to assume that adults did not ride bicycles to work in urban Canada? Alex Dzwolkic, a worker at Dominion Glass Works, and Sergeant MacGuinn, the caretaker of the Armouries, certainly would have disputed the point as victims of bicycle theft in 1942.[139] We can assume little. In the end, we are left wondering whether police officers were perplexed too: What was a 'real' crime; What deserved investigation? What was not a crime? Did policemen agonize over their ineffectual standing as crime solvers? Did they find it distressing or curious that they could do so little while the public expected so much? Even in the modern era, the police exercise discretion, determining whether or not to use the old and new techniques of detection. In the mid-twentieth century, the fundamental dilemma of the police with respect to reports of thefts were not all that different from similar reports made by victims to justices of the peace and police magistrates a century earlier.

In his influential study of American policing, Eric Monkkonen examined his data on arrest trends and wondered 'why increased policing [should] have produced fewer arrests.'[140] The complete answer is surely complex, but one aspect must be that the complainants in property crimes could seldom provide the police with a suspect or even a description of one. Of course, as chapter 5 argued, securing an arrest in alleged cases of theft or in cases of assault may not have been the primary goal of complainants; they may have found that a visit from the police served their purposes. The attitude of the courts adds a further dimension to an explanation of Monkkonen's apparent paradox of more police but fewer arrests. Another consideration is that the police had to ration their resources, resources that were stretched by the automobile revolution.

Conclusion

History confirms facts and renders accounts. Occasionally, however, history involves more than these already taxing objectives by discussing issues in the light of current affairs. As if this is not challenging enough, it is necessary for historians in certain areas to learn from other disciplines. Historians of crime and criminal justice, for example, cannot ignore contemporary issues, criminology, and commentaries on the law. As a result, they often perceive past and present as inseparable. By looking for patterns in events and then proposing explanations for these patterns, histories of criminal justice in the modern era distinguish their craft from antiquarian or purely narrative accounts. And yet, difficulties abound. The conclusions are far from simple.

The risks of introducing explanations and arguments from scholarship based in, and focused on, present-day concerns are plain to see. Organizing concepts drawn from the controversies of today can, in a few words written in haste, carry history away from the caution that serves as its hallmark into a reckless fabrication of intentions and motives. Thus, national and ideological myths, the politically correct ideas of a particular moment, raw contemporary questions applied to historical documents, and sheer carelessness can blemish historical analysis. The creative cycle for the historical specialist – analysis, criticism, and synthesis – will usually catch the errors and safeguard the integrity of historical inquiry. Craft standards and competition will dot the 'i's' and cross the 't's.' But few may notice. Historiographic debates and indepth discussion on research methods throw wet blankets on public enthusiasm for history. Ideally, works on modern history should try to balance description with analysis, popular narrative with academic rigour, contemporary concerns with respect for the characteristics of the past.

Such balances have been pursued – with difficulty – in the writing of this book. It was written in the belief that research into the past ought to pay attention to current debates and be accessible to more than just specialists. It should inform a community about the wisdom and folly revealed in the story of its development; it should include saints and sinners. Serious responsibilities press on anyone writing about the recent history of crime and criminal justice, because any mention of crime, law enforcement, trial, and punishment can ignite fiery rows. Moreover, today criminal justice processes come under nearly continuous review in Ontario and its cities. Historical research in the area of criminal justice can bring perspective and warnings both to popular debates and formal reviews.

The previous chapters have occasionally touched on modern controversies about law and order, crime and the criminal justice system. They have discussed the reputation of the police in different eras and in various situations, and their conclusion has been that the allegations of critics and the claims of supporters of the police sometimes lack resounding confirmation in historical experience. Recognizing that political, judicial, and journalistic accounts of crime often assert that crime rates in fact prove something, chapter 5 argued that long-term crime rates should be read with a good knowledge of how and why the data was collected. Considerable scepticism may be in order when there is talk about trends in criminal occurrences. Other chapters have insisted on the value of a firm maintenance of the rights of the accused; here and there, the book also traces the advances in humanitarian reform leading to the abolition of capital punishment. The historical discussion can prompt an awareness of the reasons for strict rules of evidence and statements which laypersons all too commonly believe coddle the guilty. Other portions of the book have emphasized something about which there can be no debate, namely the fact that most violence is committed by males.

Such examples of how this book interacts with recent concerns about crime and criminal justice affirm its purpose. The goal has been to focus on selective events covering a century and a half in the Hamilton region and to use them to help educate contemporary society on issues of law and order, to make it more familiar with criminal justice institutions, and to promote critical thinking about crime. One aspect of this objective was simply to describe the origins of various official positions, their powers, and their practices. The task was not so simple nor the results so complete as originally envisioned. In even one provincial jurisdiction, the legislative trail is often tedious, long and winding, and periodically obscure. Other aims of this book were to encourage academics to extend beyond a particular topic or era and to help non-specialists get past sensationalism. In keeping with the books instructional goals, it is worth reporting that – behind its outward structure of chapters and subsections – the analysis is comprised of basic facts outlining developments in law and order, arguments about the meaning of these developments, and a number of ironies. A review of these components is in order, beginning with the facts, proceeding to the arguments that connect them, and concluding with ironies and paradoxes.

It was proposed in the introduction that the British system of maintaining law and order encapsulated particular notions of sovereignty. In the beginning, institutions introduced into Upper Canada expressed the eighteenth-century English constitutional compromise between crown and local aristocracy. In Upper Canada, representatives of the crown and district or county magnates reproduced the tension between centre and periphery evident in the English constitution. The crown commissioned its justices of the peace and routinely despatched its judges – of the King's or Queen's Bench – to different parts of the province; the justices, sheriff, and juries provided the local machinery. On those extreme and rare occasions in colonial times when an accused was hanged, the symbolism emphatically asserted the old authority of the English monarch. Yet the parallel between Upper Canada and England was far from exact. The colony lacked the home country's material resources, its established country élite, and its flourishing and sophisticated bar. As happened often in later eras too, authorities tailored the criminal justice system to fit their budgets; the limits to resources helped shape criminal justice and punishment. Upper Canada's governing élite improvised with the rudiments of the old regime: finding men to act as justices of the peace who might not have been deemed suitable in England; banishing prisoners to the United States; and getting by with poorly prosecuted cases at the quarter sessions. The élite also restrained innovation. On questions such as the list of capital offences or the right of a defence counsel to address the court on behalf of the defendant, members of the élite prevented English practice from entering the colony, not because of circumspection but because of their insecure grasp of the law and their satisfaction with a harsh order.

Backed by a relatively weak state apparatus, the old regime relied upon local amateurs, impressively staged judicial events, and an arsenal of public punishments – ranging from shaming at the stocks to the open-air theatre of the public execution. A fierce criminal code –

which could serve up 'examples' when required – was mitigated in practice by petitions for mercy. Personal character, the facts of the case, background, reputation, loyalty, and deferential attitude could – and often did – help in the petitioning process. To work properly, the entire system – whether in England or the colony – had to promote voluntary service and rely to a good degree upon knowledge of personal relations and reputations. It was a system well suited to fairly stable communities and a ruling class keen about ruling. Population growth, urbanization, and the industrial revolution imposed critical stresses on the system in England.

By and by, mighty ripples from the industrial and demographic revolutions of the old country reached Upper Canada. Urban growth, public works, and the vast movements of immigrants and migrants rocked both the social order and the sense of security of colonial élites. The immigration flow and the rise of state-supported capitalism in Upper Canada contributed to exploitation. And that provoked protest. The social forces of a market-based economic expansion promoted anonymity and thereby undercut the effectiveness of shaming punishments; the massive movement of labour introduced small cities to the plentiful rounds of rowdy conduct by young and unattached males. All the while, news and opinion concerning European social and political upheavals primed the anxieties of colonial élites as they faced localized disturbances. A new generation of leaders – pragmatic reformers – responded by modifying the criminal justice system of the old regime, although mild ideological differences among them inspired a few debates about the details of this reformation: for example, should the provincial government or municipal ones command the police? Having marshalled a battery of criminal justice reforms to confront similar social disruptions, England and the American states provided examples of institutional remedies that attracted the attention of colonial legislators. Upper Canadians certainly embraced American measures and material: the reform penitentiary, the municipal police, technology and equipment, and the idea of a state or public prosecutor – the county crown attorney.

The name given the prosecutor suggests that in this colonial society a utilitarian reform adapted from a republican nation may have benefitted from a royal association. Even as it learned from the United States, the colonial criminal justice system polished and further exalted monarchical symbols. More recently, however, such symbols have suffered blows. In 1991 a recommendation by the New Democratic Party government in Ontario that police officers no longer had to pledge allegiance to the crown upset law enforcement agencies and certain members of the public. An earlier provincial government had abolished the naming of new queen's counsels. A few traditions involving the crown still persist – though greatly weakened – in the criminal justice system. Ontario continues to wrestle with the task of reconciling the tradition-bound reality of the criminal justice system with the reality of a fluid cultural identity.

Not only was the preservation of tradition considered important by the judges, court officials, and the legal profession, but in the mid-twentieth century they cooperated to foster traditions new to the region. In September 1958 they attended a 'red mass' held by the Roman Catholic Church to mark the opening of the fall assize. Originally held in Catholic counties of Europe to mark the opening of higher courts where the judges wore red robes, the church introduced the mass into the United States in 1928.[1] Hamilton's Protestant churches responded in 1963 with a special church service to open the winter assize held in January.[2] There may have been church services for the opening of Upper Canadian assizes in the nineteenth century, but none have come to light in Hamilton. In any event, the mutual embrace by clergy and the legal profession at ceremonies marking an important judicial event provided both with a public occasion to invoke the name of God, tradition, and justice.

'Members of the legal profession, like members of the church, respect tradition,' intoned a priest at the 1970 'red mass.' Young people, he proceeded to lecture, should be taught to respect tradition. This truism, however, left unanswered abundant questions about tradition. Whose traditions were to be taught? Which traditions should be conveyed to young people: the rich and complicated traditions of the common law; the tradition of order and respect for law enforcement; the tradition of civil liberties which calls for safeguards against the overzealous as well as the despotic? The implication of the address at the 'red mass' – a European tradition, not an English one – was that the survival of civilization depended on the cooperation of state and church. Since it seems unlikely that either church or state will sponsor lectures on the lessons of the Evelyn Dick case, it might be worthwhile for educators to stress the lesson that the history of liberty has often been a history of the struggle to secure procedural safeguards in the criminal justice system.

The special services introduced by churches at the end of the period studied stocked the press with items conveying a broad yet subtle message subscribed to by many people who worked in the law and order system and in organized religion. This message was that the preservation of order depended on more than just a knowledge of the law and the exercise of its sanctions. It rested on moral instruction by the institutions of faith. In his own cranky way, Hamilton magistrate Jelfs had preached the same message in his turn-of-the century tracts and lectures on religion and morality. The city's police magistrate had argued that the churches ought to minimize the teaching of doctrine and focus on paths to good conduct. As for Ontario residents more generally, they may have disputed which denominations did or did not merit support, but many had little difficulty accepting the general proposition that church and state had a mutual interest in teaching 'right from wrong' and, therefore, they should not be entirely separated. Of course, the degree to which the state accepted the position of the churches on moral order issues was always subject to compromise. Yet, in a vague general way, agencies of the state such as the school system, relief departments, and child welfare bodies believed that churches helped maintain the social order. The original British constitution of the colony of Upper Canada and the political compromises worked out for its principal denominations assured that Ontario would have less difficulty than American jurisdictions in accepting the mingling of church and state.

Despite the persistence of tradition, the invention of tradition, and instances of a local backwardness – for example the overdue appearance of women as constables and jurors – the criminal justice system also made progress in a few areas. Progress will always be an abused and loaded term. Admittedly, too, the idea of progress flattens historical analysis. During the 1970s and 1980s, the work of Michel Foucault, Michael Ignatieff, Robert Storch, David Philips, and others led to an effective questioning of a prior consensus in criminal justice history. The consensus view proposed that the extensive set of criminal justice reforms in the English-speaking world in the nineteenth century heralded a new age of enlightenment, humanitarianism, and improvement in law and order. This view truly ignored the many darker aspects of reform. The aim of the penitentiary, for example, was not simply to reduce the inhumane treatment of prisoners but to manipulate them toward approved conduct. As for the police, they were not greeted as a welcome innovation everywhere; indeed, in some locales they often acted on the side of employers in disputes with employees. At other times they zealously enforced a particular idea of morality. Revisionists now question the need of replacing the amateur constables in rural England with uniformed and paid constabularies. In Hamilton and vicinity, the picture was not clear. Nevertheless, the insights of the revisionist school have informed the study of this Canadian community. The revisionists put discussions about criminal justice on a higher, more sophisticated plane and issued a pertinent warning about the repressive potential of state-led reforms.

Key innovations in the criminal justice system may have given civil libertarians just cause to challenge the idea of progress. Certainly many of the innovations chronicled in this book strengthened the state and embodied the state's fascination with efficiency and uniformity. The local community lost much of its original role and significance in the criminal justice system, though it must be said that old-regime localism had concentrated power and influence in the hands of men of substance. During the nineteenth and twentieth centuries, the state remade the justice of the peace. In steps extending over many decades, they ceased being crown agents at the very centre of the law and order apparatus, and outwardly they ceased being drawn from local political notables. Instead, they became useful but virtually anonymous functionaries. Legislators had effected some of this transformation by marginalizing justices of the peace, creating police magistrates, and eliminating the quarter sessions. Additionally, the grand jury – the ancient means by which communities and central court judges informed one another – was nudged repeatedly towards oblivion. The advent of policing and the creation of the office of crown attorney were important innovations, coincidentally conceived in the mid-nineteenth century and fashioned initially as local institutions.

The great social changes of the mid-nineteenth century induced reforms that attacked amateurism and voluntarism. Bumbling was by no means confined to the old regime's amateurs. It persisted in so-called 'professional agencies,' but a corner had been turned and local voluntarism receded as a principal virtue in civil society. Strikes, riots, immigration, and migration had frightened the élites of the colony. They reacted by legislating the lineaments of the modern state, a state increasingly free from the local community. Initially, the alterations established local institutions, for localism was a strong current in Upper Canadian liberal reform and it served the interests of financially cautious provincial governments, but there also was pressure for uniformity and centralized control.

The assault on localism advanced in many ways. The Hamilton police commission, for example, was torn between the politically desirable practice of hiring hometown lads and the opposing belief that outsiders could best enforce the law. It often favoured hiring senior men from other forces and this represented a departure from the historic practice of the courts of quarter sessions appointing local men to act as constables. It is true that as a result of a crucial parliamentary debate in 1856 the police remained a municipal institution. However, this point – like the claim that the police in English-speaking countries have not been like military bodies – crumbles under critical scrutiny.

Police departments cooperated across many jurisdictions, sending members through common training programs. There were also official measures to further centralization. Municipal police forces were subject to provincial oversight beginning in the late 1940s.[3] Beyond the period under study, the establishment of a regional government for Hamilton and Wentworth County forced an amalgamation of departments in 1974. More interestingly, police constables from forces throughout the province achieved an intense comraderie; occasionally they staged remarkable displays of solidarity, such as impressive funeral parades for fallen comrades. In the fall of 1992, many Ontario departments supported 'a blue ribbon campaign,' a different show of solidarity; it indicated support for a protest by constables in Toronto who had been ordered to file reports every time they drew their handguns. The local police have a complex identity; however, they likely perceive of themselves as police rather than the police of a particular municipality.

Meanwhile, centralization progressed on other fronts. Starting in 1967, crown attorneys became agents of the attorney general for purposes of the Criminal Code of Canada, thus effectively ceasing to be purely county officials.[4] The province also assumed full financial responsibility for the county jails in 1968.[5] With ample resources and a will to overhaul many of its institutions, the province from the late 1940s to the late 1960s financed rationalizations to the criminal justice system in the name of uniformity of service and improved standards. The city and county withered as integral parts of the criminal justice system. In very recent times and again in the name of efficiency, the reform of the court system has allowed for the movement of judges around the province, thereby ending the strong identification of judges with communities which had hitherto prevailed at the intermediate level of criminal courts. Because of training and government-imposed qualifications, individuals staffing the criminal justice system have become interchangeable. That is a far cry from the localism intrinsic to the old regime's reliance on justices of the peace and other non-professionals. Unquestionably, demands for greater economy and efficiency in the criminal justice system will lead to greater centralization and homogeneity.

In another area, that of criminal detection, the justice system proceeded along the same path to modernization. Throughout the period under study, popular opinion represented crime as a universal phenomenon and criminals as a mobile group. One response by the police to the problem of identity in a transient world was to build up lore, lore about the recognition of well-known street characters and lore amounting to a stereotyping of 'criminal types.' Originally this approach focused on clothing and physical appearances, but it soon embraced racial stereotyping as well. Toward the end of the nineteenth century, the police began systematically to seek, collect, and distribute information about suspects and fugitives. They experimented with new technologies and by the First World War had settled on fingerprinting and photography. Policing, in short, adjusted to a modern world of mobility and strangers. Without abandoning old-style street wisdom on the beat, the police at the headquarters today have kept abreast of information technology, fashioning local information bureaucracies and joining international information networks.

Some of the changes in the criminal justice system truly provided the basis for a more humane and just system. The elimination of public executions and the eventual abolition of capital punishment came as improvements; abolition extinguished one rarely exercised but dreadful form of state power that had required – in the classic form of old regime – local administration to satisfy royal authority. While legislation struck down capital punishment, several of the more important advances in human rights in criminal justice came through the evolution of case law. Owing to the widespread – though not universal – reflex to celebrate the history of English common law and its differences from continental inquisitorial procedures, case law gradually established strict safeguards for the taking of statements by the accused and for the identification of accused parties by witnesses. The police may not have observed these rules scrupulously, possibly far from it where minor offences have been concerned. Nevertheless, the principles could not be and cannot be effaced. There has also been the development of specialized courts in Hamilton to deal with juveniles and family problems including domestic violence. Finally, the greater gender and ethnic inclusiveness found today in police forces and courts came as long overdue advancements. The history of criminal justice in the jurisdiction under consideration is not a history of increasing oppression, though it is a history of growing centralization, regulation, and professionalization. To put it another way, as police powers have grown so have citizens' rights; as centralization of criminal justice has increased, so has citizen access to participation and help. At least in Ontario, and in Hamilton in particular, the history of criminal justice holds many such paradoxes.

The topic of gender relations has surfaced often in this book. For a remarkably long time, the criminal justice system in Hamilton operated as an entirely male enterprise. It was not until the middle of the twentieth century that the police commission began to hire women as constables or that the sheriff placed women on jury panels. Other centres had acted earlier and Hamilton's delay seems inexplicable. Male domination of the system extended to more than staffing. In the late nineteenth century, the police force ensconced muscular masculinity and chivalry as values central to its self-image. The male realm of policing was not just a product of an all-male force; most of the police's work focused on males. Certain transgressions that they dealt with arose from the more dangerous aspects of a youthful male culture. Males were overwhelmingly the parties arrested, for alcohol, when mixed with hormones and stirred by a socialization process for young working-class males that encouraged them to be 'tough,' could produce small and jealous minds that had something to prove. The mix frequently led to violence.

The vast majority of violent offenders were men. If the popular press is any indication, society seemed to accept this condition – without condoning the deeds – as being the order of things. Wife murderers or murder-suicides carried out by males attracted some local attention as 'crimes of passion,' but when Evelyn Dick stood charged with murdering her husband, she was excoriated as an immoral curiosity and her trials attracted the attention of the press throughout Canada and in many American states. Women simply did not murder men! That was almost an indisputable fact, but, in the circumstances of how the police behaved and how the attorney general's office tenaciously prosecuted the Dick case, it also resembled an official statement about moral depravity.

The few women who came before the courts generally stood accused of violating the moral order codes and were charged mainly with drunk and disorderly conduct and to a lesser extent with prostitution or vagrancy. In general, after the stormy years of the mid-nineteenth century, the Hamilton police merely kept an eye on prostitution and did not attempt to eliminate it. Periodic anti-vice crusades highlighted the hypocrisy of punishing women but not the male clients. Further evidence of the inequality of men and women before the law was provided by Jelfs – the long-serving police magistrate – who went on record as favouring men in domestic disputes if the female complainant adamantly insisted on prosecuting. That said, a prevailing chivalric code implied that males obviously guilty of treating women badly ought to receive very punitive treatment by the court – as well as an occasional bruising in transit to jail or court. On the whole, the conduct of magistrates and constables confirms that in fundamental respects the criminal justice system treated men and women differently. But a lesson to be derived from this fact is that the outcomes of such separate treatment were not entirely predictable and some women received the 'benefits' of a sense of chivalry. The complex meanings of a chivalric code have been explored by Canadian legal historian Carolyn Strange. She has pointed out that such a code perpetuated male and female stereotypes: male heroism and female frailty. The code obfuscated the abuse of women when the subject was exposed to public view through cases involving women as complainants or defendants.[6]

It should be said too that, while women were not always victimized by a criminal justice system that treated them differently at least well into the 1950s, they certainly were far more likely to be victimized by the broader social and economic circumstances that made them dependent on men. The recent changes in the area of family courts are beyond the compass of this study, but it is worth quoting Dorothy Chunn's statement that 'much of the family-welfare legislation administered by domestic-relations courts improved the position of married women in the family.'[7]

A review of crime and criminal justice in one community from its origins to recent times has provided lessons, although perhaps not the ones expected by a reader seeking firm answers or confirmation of assumptions. This analysis of crime and criminal justice concludes that serious complications arise with every important generalization. Historical inquiry maintains a sinuous up-hill course to wisdom; it does not offer ultimate truths. For example, whether the long-term rate of crime has been rising or falling is a tangled issue.

Irony and paradox surround some of the findings of this inquiry and emphasize the need for caution before pronouncing on tricky points. Now and then, irony serves the conclusions well because it describes outcomes other than what might have been expected. For instance, irony arises in the unexpected findings about theft in the Depression and wartime; similarly, a host of seemingly simple claims about the police also falter in a morass of evidence about a complicated occupation. It is possible to exaggerate the municipal police's effectiveness both as crime fighters and as alleged agents of social control. They have experienced less success than they and their friends have claimed and have exercised less power than their critics have believed. It is impossible to measure either their social-service activities or the subtle coercion posed by size, uniform, and manner. Their helpfulness and usefulness have been undervalued by critics and their menacing traits underestimated by their champions.

While the force has been profoundly affected by technology, the basic work today resembles that of the amateur colonial constables and early professional police; there are warrants to be served, disputes to still, streets to be made safe, and people to help. And yet, to compare the late-twentieth-century police officer with the village constable of the early nineteenth century would be to dismiss the struggle to implant professional standards, to forget the impact of technology on police work, and to ignore the social-service demands placed on the police by city governments. By the mid-twentieth century policing brought together the roughneck and the lab technician, the interrogator and the safety officer, the stereotyping of suspects and the adoption of ever improving techniques of identification. The modern police force is a different organization altogether in comparison with its predecessor, though many of the patrol officer's tasks are fundamentally like those of earlier constables.

The chapter on crime rates proposed another paradox. Instead of assuming, as several pathbreaking studies have, that the nineteenth-century innovation of policing intensified prosecutorial pressures throughout the criminal justice system, it pointed out that another set of significant innovations and attitudes may actually have deflected cases from the courts. While the state's power increased and while it tried to impose professional standards, it simultaneously discouraged complainants' use of the courts, which is another way of saying that the state sought to minimize the direct use of courts by individuals. This practice in turn encouraged the more frequent resolution of conflict through the police practice of 'taking charge.' In effect, to reduce the volume of cases in the courts, the state relied on informal resolution by constables. Oddly enough, therefore, the Hamilton police increased the non-judicial clearing of incidents. For the same reason, the growth of the police force – in this city at least – probably reduced prosecutions. Through a series of adjustments in the criminal justice system, the state has shifted conflict resolution onto the police force. In this respect, one of the most notable features of the progression from the old regime to the present has been the evolution of the village constabulary into the city police. Once a paid force was created, politicians heaped new duties onto it; the community's rising and diverse expectations for it made the police the city's most visible institution.

Clive Emsley has astutely observed that 'the English system of criminal prosecutions and trials entered the twentieth century shot through with paradoxes though few contemporaries appear to have been aware, or, at least much concerned.'[8] With respect to prosecutions, Ontario and England shared a major paradox. In the public's estimation and in the eyes of many jurists, trial by jury remained a noble ancient institution and a foundation for democracy. Yet a substantial number of crimes could be brought before a police magistrate who sat without a jury, and many serious crimes could be tried by a judge without a jury at the intermediate level of courts if the accused agreed.

Ontario also created a paradox of its own by establishing the office of crown attorney, an official originally assigned a triple role: watchdog of malicious prosecutions, prosecutor, and advisor to the bench.

After more than a century, an Ontario law reform commission finally deemed the combining of the later two functions into one office as inappropriate. The presence of a judge sitting on city police commissions likewise seems suspect and certainly at odds with the English common law concept of state, court, and prosecution working as separate entities. Resorting to expedients, Victorian legislators in Ontario created paradoxes which did not trouble them (or various jurists); at least at the two lower levels of courts, they simply may not have cared about such supposedly sacred institutions and principles. They legislated many other expedients, including longer lists of summary offences and speedy trials without juries.

Some scrupulous and learned jurists cared about principles; by landmark decisions and law reform commissions, they managed to sustain the principles of the common law. But it is troubling to read the 1975 comments of an Ontario crown attorney written as a defence of appeal against acquittal. To oppose this innovation of 1892, the crown attorney alleged, is tantamount to believing that an accused is 'entitled to escape from the consequences of his crime by illegal means.' One of Ontario's nineteenth-century expedients had defended another in an alarming way; a crown attorney – a colonial invention – defended another recent invention – the appeal against acquittal. The outrageous attack on the presumption of innocence – indeed on a finding of innocence – is shocking but not surprising. Ontario is a jurisdiction where expediency has long undermined the jury. It would be interesting to know if any American jurisdictions have come close to Ontario in reducing the numbers of trials by jury. They have not condoned appeal against acquittal.

This conclusion opened with a declaration that modern history cannot escape references to and involvement with contemporary issues. Of course, in and of themselves, the historian's findings cannot settle today's controversies or provide solutions to its ills. The best that historical inquiry can do is to promote questioning. It is hoped that this historical account of crime and criminal justice in one community will alert interested citizens to the folly of uninformed opinion and to the persistent tensions existing between civil liberties and law and order in an open society.

From an international perspective, the conduct of the criminal justice system and the modest number of serious crimes have given this young society a relatively remarkable degree of freedom both from fear of state oppression and from grave losses at the hands of criminals. No system, of course, is free of error and biases. It has not been too difficult to ascertain abuse in the criminal justice system of Ontario where legislators, jurists, and constables sometimes acted rashly to combat occasional outrages or mere perceived threats. However, it is important to remind ourselves that the discovery and criticism of abuse have occurred because the law has espoused a commitment to open inquiry. Within an imperfect world, the struggles for justice and law and order in Hamilton have – well – progressed.

Yet a critical and sceptical attitude informed by history remains an essential asset for any society which treasures civil liberties. Judging from the past, Ontario is a jurisdiction where the criminal justice system's impact on civil liberties must be watched very closely. Since the mid-nineteenth century, the governments of Ontario have pursued efficiency at the expense of the jury, established and retained considerable powers for the prosecution, and sought centralization in policing.[9] Sometimes the reforms were checked and delayed, as in the defeat of a plan for a provincial gendarmerie in 1856 and the postponement of the elimination of the grand jury. Nevertheless, politicians – consciously or unconsciously, it matters little – have largely succeeded in centralizing, rationalizing, and professionalizing the criminal justice system. These are mixed blessings.

Notes

ABBREVIATIONS

AO   Archives of Ontario
AR   *Annual Reports,* Hamilton Police Department
DHB   Dictionary of Hamilton Biography
HPL   Hamilton Public Library
OB   Occurrence Books
MTPL   Metro Toronto Public Library
NA   National Archives
RSO   Revised Statutes of Ontario
SO   Statutes of Ontario
UCKB   Upper Canada Court of King's Bench

INTRODUCTION

1 This influence extended even to the penal colony of New South Wales.
See David Neal, *The Rule of Law in a Penal Colony: Law and Power in
Early New South Wales* (Melbourne: Cambridge University Press 1991).
2 Paul Romney, *Mr Attorney: The Attorney General for Ontario in Court, Cabinet,
and Legislature, 1791–1899* (Toronto: Published for the Osgoode
Society by the University of Toronto Press, 1986), 222.
3 Timothy Curtis, 'Explaining Crime in Early Modern England,' *Criminal
Justice History,* 1 (1980), 117–21.
4 Dorothy Chunn, *From Punishment to Doing Good: Family Courts and Socialized
Justice in Ontario, 1880–1940* (Toronto: University of Toronto Press
1992).

5 For background, see John Weaver, *Hamilton: An Illustrated History* (Toronto: James Lorimer 1982); Michael Doucet and John Weaver, *Housing the North American City* (Montreal: McGill-Queen's University Press 1991).

6 Desmond H. Brown, *The Genesis of the Canadian Criminal Code of 1892* (Toronto: Published for the Osgoode Society by the University of Toronto Press 1989), 68.

7 *Hamilton Spectator*, 30 September 1950.

8 Michael S. Cross, '"The Shiners' War": Social Violence in the Ottawa Valley in the 1830s,' *Canadian Historical Review*, vol.54 (1973), 1–26.

9 Pieter Spierenburg, *The Spectacle of Suffering: Executions and the Evolution of Repression from a Preindustrial Metropolis to the European Experience* (Cambridge: Cambridge University Press 1984), 203–5.

10 *Stanton* v. *Andrews* (1836) 5 UCKB (Old Series) 211. I am grateful to Phillip Sworden for this reference.

11 I appreciate the contributions made to this book by Greg Marquis, who read it in manuscript and added many useful ideas. He emphasized that the old regime was repressive but the state was weak.

12 Allan Greer and Ian Radforth, 'Introduction,' *Colonial Leviathan: State Formation and Mid-Nineteenth Century Canada*, Greer and Radforth, eds. (Toronto: University of Toronto Press 1992), 9–11.

13 E.P. Thompson, *Whigs and Hunters: The Origins of the Black Act* (London: Allen and Lane 1975), 265.

14 Originally, I had accented the contrast between the United Kingdom and Canada, but Greg Marquis questioned whether the British system was all that centralized in practice.

15 Clive Emsley, *Policing and Its Context, 1750–1870* (London: Macmillan 1983), 69–82.

16 I am grateful to Greg Marquis for the observation that the New York reform may have influenced that in Canada West.

17 Lawrence Friedman and Robert Percival, *The Roots of Justice: Crime and Punishment in Alameda County, California, 1870–1910* (Chapel Hill: University of North Carolina Press 1981).

18 *Hamilton Spectator*, 7 June 1958.

19 Gene Howard Homel, 'Denison's Law: Criminal Justice and the Police Court in Toronto,' *Ontario History*, vol.73 (September 1981), 183.

20 Joseph L. Tropea, 'Situationally Negotiated Transactions and Domination: From Tribe to Rational-Legal Order in the Anglo-American Legal Tradition,' *Criminal Justice History*, vol.12 (1991), 1–13.

CHAPTER ONE

1 For a fine account of this case, see Robert L. Fraser, 'Michael Vincent,' in DHB, vol.1, Patricia Filer, John Weaver, Robert Fraser, eds.

(Hamilton: Dictionary of Hamilton Biography 1981), 203–6. Also, see F.W. Fearman, 'Fifty Years Ago,' *Hamilton and Its Industries* (Hamilton: *Hamilton Spectator* 1884), 14–17. The first recollection appeared in a letter to the editor of the *Hamilton Spectator*, 6 October 1880. The author wished to correct errors in a previous article.

2 AO, RG 22, Series 134, vol.5, Assize Minutebook, Criminal, 1809–19.

3 RG 22, Series 134, vols. 6, 7, 9, Assize Minutebooks, Criminal, 1820–48.

4 6 Vic. c.3 s.1–2. An Act Respecting the Qualifications of Justices of the Peace.

5 Ontario Law Reform Commission, *Report on the Coroner System in Ontario* (Toronto: Department of Justice 1971), 10.

6 Robert Fraser, 'Michael Vincent.'

7 W.C. Keele, *The Provincial Justice or Magistrate's Manual, Being a Complete Digest of the Criminal Law and a Compendious and General View of the Provincial Law; with Practical Forms for the Use of the Magistracy of Upper Canada* (Toronto: *Upper Canada Gazette* 1835), 125–7.

8 J.A. Sharpe, *Crime in Early Modern England, 1550–1750* (New York: Longman 1984), 30.

9 Canada, Law Reform Commission, Working Paper 59, *Toward a Unified Court* (Ottawa: Law Reform Commission 1989), 4.

10 4 Wm. IV c.iv. An Act to Provide for the Summary Punishment of Petty Tresspass and Other Offences (1834).

11 4 Wm. IV c.iv s.xiv.

12 'On the Duties of Magistrates,' *Upper Canada Law Journal*, vol.1 (January 1855), 5–7.

13 The quarter sessions were not well attended. See James K. Wilson, *The Court of General Sessions of the Peace: Local Administration in Pre-Municipal Upper Canada* (MA thesis, McMaster University 1989), 108–10.

14 3 Wm. IV c.iii. An Act Relating to the Bailing and Commitment, Removal and Trial of Prisoners in Certain Cases (1833).

15 7 Wm. IV c.iv. An Act to Abolish the Distinction between Grand and Petit Larceny (1837).

16 16 Vic. c.178. An Act to Facilitate the Performance of the Duties of Justices of the Peace, Out of Sessions, in Upper Canada, with Respect to Summary Convictions and Orders (1853); 16 Vic. c. 179. An Act to Facilitate the Performance of the Duties of the Justices of the Peace ... with Respect to Persons Charged with Indictable Offences (1853).

17 'On the Duties of Magistrates,' *Upper Canada Law Journal*, vol.1 (October 1855), 182–3.

18 Hilda Neatby, *The Administration of Justice under the Quebec Act* (Minneapolis: University of Minnesota Press 1937), 298–305.

19 Wilson, *The Court of General Sessions of the Peace*, 108–110.

20 Canada, Law Reform Commission, Working Paper 62, *Controlling Criminal*

Prosecutions: The Attorney General and the Crown Prosecutor (Ottawa: Law Reform Commission 1990), 4.

21 7 Wm. IV c.iv s.I, II, V. An Act to Abolish the Distinction between Grand Larceny and Petit Larceny (1837).

22 34 Geo. III c.2. An Act to Establish a Superior Court of Civil and Criminal Jurisdiction, and to Regulate the Court of Appeal (1794).

23 34 Geo. III c.2. An Act for the Regulation of Juries (1794).

24 19 Vic. c.43. An Act to Amend, Repeal and Consolidate the Provision of Certain Acts therein Mentioned, and to Simplify and Expedite the Proceedings in the Court of Queen's Bench and Common Pleas in Upper Canada (1856).

25 James Edmund Jones, *Pioneer Crimes and Punishments in the Toronto and the Home District* (Toronto: George N. Morang 1924), 131.

26 This term was used several times in the Hamilton press in the twentieth century. See *Hamilton Spectator*, 15 July 1926, 12 January 1953.

27 Jones, *Pioneer Crimes and Punishments*, 131.

28 A very brief but sound account of the history of the grand jury was prepared in 1973 by an Ontario inquiry into the administration of the courts. One of the recommendations of the report was that the grand jury be abolished. See Ministry of the Attorney General, *Report of the Administration of Ontario Courts: Ontario Law Reform Commission*, part 1 (Toronto 1973), 351–2.

29 William Holdsworth, *A History of English Law*, vol.3 (London: Methuen 1935), 617–19.

30 RG 22, Series 390, Supreme Court of Ontario, Judges' Benchbooks, J.B. Macaulay, box 19, Miscellaneous, 'Notebook on Indictments.'

31 Patrick Brode, 'Grand Jury Addresses of the Early Canadian Judges in an Age of Reform,' *The Law Society of Upper Canada Gazette*, vol.23 (June 1989), 136.

32 RG 22, Series 390, box 2, envelope 5, J.B. Macaulay, Charges to Juries, September 1832.

33 NA, RG 5, A1, 39295–6, William Campbell to Major Hillier, 19 September 1825.

34 For a factual and interpretative account of the jury, see Thomas Andrew Green, *Verdict According to Conscience: Perspectives on the English Criminal Trial Jury, 1200–1800* (Chicago: University of Chicago Press 1985).

35 34 Geo. III c.1.

36 Paul Romney, 'From Constitutionalism to Legalism: Trial by Jury, Responsible Government, and the Rule of Law in Canadian Political Culture,' *Law and History Review*, vol.7 (Spring 1989), 132–8. See also 13, 14 Vic. c.55. An Act for the Consolidation and Amendment of the Laws Relative to Jurors, Juries and Inquests in that Part of this Province Called Upper Canada (1850).

37 RG 22, Assize Minutebook, Criminal, 1819–32, Gore District Assize, September 1828.

38 Although Hamilton records are among the best in Ontario for a history of law and order, the quarter sessions records are negligible. The best sets exist for Brockville, York-Toronto, London, and Sandwich-Windsor.

39 J.K. Johnson, *Becoming Prominent: Regional Leadership in Upper Canada, 1791–1841* (Kingston and Montreal: McGill-Queen's University Press 1989), 61–8.

40 Keele, *The Provincial Justice*, 259–60.

41 An Act for the Relief of William Conway Keele, 6 Wm. IV c.xxv.

42 Ruth Paley, '"An Imperfect, Inadequate and Wretched System?" Policing London Before Peel,' *Criminal Justice History*, vol.10 (1989), 99.

43 RG 5, A1, 12813–14, Hatt to Lieutenant Colonel D. Cameron, 15 May 1816.

44 RG 5, A1, 30043–4, Matthew Crooks to Major Hillier, 18 October 1822.

45 Arthur Walker Wright, *Pioneer Days in Nichol* (Mount Forest, Ont.: 1932), 156.

46 Keele, *The Provincial Justice*, introduction.

47 RG 5, A1, 22756–7, Titus Simons to Major Hillier, 9 February 1820.

48 RG 5, A1, 12014, Petition from Mount Pleasant to Lieutenant Governor Sir Francis Gore, 20 February 1816.

49 RG 5, A1, 13249–54, Court of Quarter Sessions to Lieutenant Governor Francis Gore, 11 July 1816.

50 Donald R. Beer, *Sir Allan Napier MacNab* (Hamilton: Dictionary of Hamilton Biography 1984), 22–5.

51 Ibid., 23.

52 RG 5, A1, 49969–76, Affidavit of John Binkley, 19 September 1828.

53 RG 5, A1, 48971–2, The Representation of the Magistrates of the Gore District in the Adjourned Sessions, 10 May 1828.

54 Leo Johnson, 'The Gore District "Outrages," 1826–1829: A Case Study of Violence, Justice, and Political Propaganda,' *Ontario History*, 83 (June 1991), 115.

55 RG 5, A1, 49969–76, Affidavit of John Binkley, 19 September 1828; RG 5, A1, 2174–88, Petition, 9 May 1829.

56 HPL, Ferrie Family Papers, Letterbooks of Cases Tried before Robert Ferrie in the County of Waterloo, 1850–7.

57 4 Wm. IV c.4. An Act to Provide for the Summary Punishment of Petty Trespass, and Other Offences (1834); 7 Wm. IV c.4. An Act to Abolish the Distinction between Grand and Petty Larceny (1837).

58 9 Vic. c.73 s.45. An Act to Alter and Amend the Act Incorporating the Town of Hamilton, and to Erect the Same into a City (1846).

59 DHB, 13–14.

60 RG 5, A1, George Armstrong to Captain Higginson, 17 April 1844.

61 RG 5, A1, 6658, George Armstrong to D. Daly, 1 November 1843.

62 RG 5, C1, vol.195, 15960, List of Applicants for the Office of Stipendiary Magistrate in Hamilton, 5 February 1847.

63 HPL, 'Report of the Police Committee: Re City Officers and Employees,' Hamilton City Council Minutes, 14 March 1849.

64 RG 5, C1, vol.202, 16784, *The Report of the Grand Jury of the Gore District,* 7 May 1847.

65 See, for example, the following description of the stripping of the countryside around the Welland Canal by navvies and their women and children in 1843: RG 5, C1, vol.122, 7057, Petition from Residents near Welland Canal, n.d. [1843].

66 For evidence of the relatively modest enforcement of moral order, see NA, RG 5, B29, Clerks of the Peace, Extracts of Fines, 1811–33, file on the Gore District. On the widespread use of alcohol, see John Young, *Reminiscences of the Early History of Galt and the Settlement of Dumfries in the Province of Ontario* (Toronto: Hunter, Rose 1880), 68.

67 RG 5, C1, vol.269, 1515, Report on the Case of *Queen* v. *Hugh W. McCulloch,* 9 May 1843.

68 Young, *Reminiscences,* 101.

69 McMaster University, Mills Memorial Library, Marjorie Freeman Campbell Collection, typescript of Hamilton Police Village Minutes, 27 July 1837.

70 NA, RG 11, A2, Board of Public Works, vol.94, Correspondence Book, Canals, 1839–46, William Shaw, 'Report on Grog Shop,' 30 April 1845.

71 McMaster University, Mills Memorial Library, Marjorie Freeman Campbell Collection, typescript of Hamilton Police Village Minutes, 11 August 1835; 1 September 1835; 6 August 1838; 5 October 1840; 6 October 1840; 5 January 1844.

72 F.W. Fearman, 'Fifty Years Ago,' *Hamilton and Its Industries* (Hamilton: *Hamilton Spectator* 1884), 17–18.

73 RG 7, G14, vol.9, Ebenezer Griffin to James Hopkirk, 18 March 1842.

74 *Christian Guardian,* 5 December 1829; William Gregg, *History of the Presbyterian Church in the Dominion of Canada* (Toronto: Presbyterian Printing and Publishing Company 1885), 535; MTPL, Baldwin Room, *The Second Report of the Upper Canada Religious Tract and Book Society* (Toronto: *Christian Guardian,* 1834).

75 RG 5, C1, vol.250, Cartwright Thomas to Sir George Arthur, 16 December 1840.

76 RG 5, C1, vol.6017, 6124, Sheriff Cartwright-Thomas to Provincial Secretary, 7 July 1843.

77 RG 5, C1, vol.6017, 6137, Petition of the Catholic Inhabitants of the Town and Vicinity of Brantford, 19 July 1843; 6124, John Wetenhall to Civil Secretary, 2 August 1843.

78 Carolyn Steedman, *Policing the Victorian Community: The Formation of English Provincial Police Forces, 1856–80*, London: Routledge and Kegan Paul, 1984), 56.

79 Maximilian Ivan Reichard, *The Origins of the Urban Police: Freedom and Order in Antebellum St. Louis* (Washington University: PHD thesis, 1975), 77–85.

80 McMaster University, Mills Memorial Library, Marjorie Freeman Campbell Collection, typescript of Hamilton Police Village Minutes, 9 October 1837; 25 May 1840; 21 September 1840; 19 September 1842. The vagrancy by-law was passed on 29 July 1843.

81 Noah Webster, *An American Dictionary of the English Language*, vol.2 (New York and London: Johnson Reprint Corporation 1970; reprint of 1828 edition).

82 *OED.*

83 Greg Marquis, 'The Contours of Canadian Urban Justice, 1830–1875', *Urban History Review* (February 1987), 270–1.

84 Clive Emsley, *Crime and Society in England, 1750–1900* (New York: Longman 1987), 183–5.

85 RG 5, C1, vol.317, 284, Petition from the Inhabitants of the City of Hamilton in Public Meeting, 12 February 1851.

86 RG 5, C1, vol.317, 284, Extract from a Report of a Committee of the Executive Council, 17 February 1851; Mayor Holden to Provincial Secretary, 24 April 1851; vol.389, 1050, C.L. Brydges to Provincial Secretary, 30 June 1853.

87 HPL, *Times Scrapbook* vol.O1, part 1, obituary of John Carruthers, 13 January 1913.

88 For a full account of the gender aspects see John Weaver, 'Crime, Public Order, and Repression: The Gore District in Upheaval, 1832–1851,' *Ontario History*, 78 (September 1986), 193–5.

89 This quote and the preceding account come from the judge's bench book. AO, RG 22, bench books of J.B. Macaulay, box 2, envelope 10, 'Notes 1834: Gore, London, Niagara,' *King* v. *John Rooney*.

90 John M. Beattie, *Attitudes towards Crime and Punishment in Upper Canada, 1830–1850* (Toronto: University of Toronto Centre of Criminology 1977), 1.

91 Weaver, 'Crime, Public Order, and Repression,' 196–8.

92 *Hamilton Spectator*, 11 April 1863.

93 *Hamilton Spectator*, 12 November 1921.

94 40 Geo. III c.1 s.III (1800). An Act for the Further Introduction of the Criminal Law of England into this Province, and for the More Effectual Punishment of Certain Offenders (1800).

95 Ibid.

96 Jones, *Pioneer Crimes and Punishments*, 16–19.

97 *Hamilton Spectator*, 29 June 1910.

98 4 Wm. IV c.37. An Act to Provide for the Maintenance and Government of the Provincial Penitentiary (1834).

99 40 Geo. III, c.1 s.V. An Act for the Further Introduction of the Criminal Law of England into this Province, and for the More Effectual Punishment of Certain Offenders (1800). 3 Wm. IV c.iv s. xxv. An Act to Reduce the Number of Cases in which Capital Punishment May Be Inflicted (1833).

100 RG 22, Series 134, Assize Minutebook, Criminal, 1819–32.

101 RG 22, Series 390, box 1 (1–2), J.B. Macaulay Benchbook, Gore Assize, 1827, 91.

102 Louis Masur, *Rites of Execution: Capital Punishment and the Transformation of American Culture, 1776–1886* (New York: Oxford University Press 1989), passim.

103 7 Geo. IV c.3 s.I. An Act to Dispense with the Necessity of Actually Pronouncing Sentence of Death in Certain Cases of Capital Conviction (1826).

104 Weaver, 'Crime, Public Order, and Repression,' 203.

105 12 Vic. c.63. An Act to Make Further Provision for the Administration of Justice ... and also a Court of Error and Appeal (1849). 20 Vic. c.61. An Act to Extend the Right of Appeal in Criminal Cases in Upper Canada (1857).

CHAPTER TWO

1 Pieter Spierenburg, *The Spectacle of Suffering: Executions and the Evolution of Repression: From a Preindustrial Metropolis to the European Experience* (Cambridge: Cambridge University Press 1984), 183–99.

2 DHB, vol.1: 55.

3 AO, RG 22, Series 390, box 19, Judges Benchbooks, Judge C. Patterson, April 1875–May 1876 (Assize/Criminal).

4 C.G. Stogdill, 'Joseph Workman, M.D., 1805–1894: Alienist and Medical Teacher,' *Canadian Medical Association Journal* (reprint of article from 29 October 1966), 1–4.

5 In 1843 a man named McNaghten was found innocent by reason of insanity of killing the prime minister's secretary. The unpopular verdict produced the McNaghten rules. See E.G. Thompson, 'Proof in a Criminal Case: Reasonable Doubt, Insanity, and Drunkenness,' *Special Lectures of the Law Society of Upper Canada, 1955: Evidence* (Toronto: Richard De Boo 1955), 83.

6 *Hamilton Spectator*, 31 January, 1 and 2 February 1876.

7 Ibid., 12 February 1876.

8 9 Vic. c.73 s.45.

9   12 Vic. c.81 s.70. An Act to Provide ... for the Erection of Municipal Corporations (1849).

10 14 and 15 Vic. c.96 s.21. An Act to Facilitate the Performance of the Duties of Justices of the Peace, Out of Sessions, with Respect to Persons Charged with Indictable Offences (1851).

11 By a reorganization of jurisdictions in Ontario courts in 1984, justices of the peace were able to try cases in the provincial offences court. That is, they could deal with traffic violations.

12 *Hamilton Spectator*, 12 March 1883.

13 Ibid., 14 December 1901.

14 Ibid.

15 George T. Denison, *Recollections of a Police Magistrate* (Toronto: Musson, 1920), 6.

16 Gene Homel, 'Denison's Law: Criminal Justice and the Police Court in Toronto,' *Ontario History*, vol.73 (September 1981), 174. Also see Joan Sangster, '"Pardon Tales" from Magistrate's Court: Women, Crime, and the Court in Peterborough County, 1920–50,' *Canadian Historical Review*, 74 (June 1993), 161–97.

17 12 Geo. VI c.59 s.10. An Act to Amend the Municipal Act (1948).

18 HPL, clipping from *Hamilton Times*, 26 August 1912, *Times Scrapbook*, vol.P3, Police Court.

19 *Hamilton Spectator*, 14 December 1901.

20 Paul Craven, 'Law and Ideology: The Toronto Police Court, 1850–80,' in David Flaherty, ed., vol.2, *Essays in the History of Canadian Law* (Toronto: Published for the Osgoode Society by the University of Toronto Press 1983), 265.

21 *Hamilton Spectator*, 8 September 1927.

22 Ibid., 11 January 1881.

23 HPL, clipping from *Hamilton Times*, 9 December 1910, *Times* Scrapbook, vol. P3, Police Court.

24 HPL, clipping from *Hamilton Times*, 19 May 1910, *Times Scrapbook*, vol. P3, Police Court.

25 Denison, *Recollections of a Police Magistrate*, 9.

26 *Hamilton Spectator*, 14 December 1901.

27 Ontario, Commission on Best Mode of Selecting, Appointing, and Recommending Sheriffs, etc., *Interim Report Respecting Police Magistrates* (Toronto: King's Printer 1921), 16–29.

28 Stuart Ryan and F.B. Sussman, 'The Adult Court,' in W.T. McGrath, ed., *Crime and Its Treatment in Canada: Second Edition* (Toronto: Macmillan 1976), 195.

29 Michael Katz, Michael Doucet, and Mark Stern, *The Social Organization of Early Industrial Capitalism* (Cambridge, Mass.: Harvard University Press 1982), 240.

30 *Hamilton Spectator*, 14 December 1901.

31 The *Hamilton Spectator* editorialized that Montreal needed a whipping post to deal with wife beaters, an assertion motivated by prejudice as much as by any concern for the women. *Hamilton Spectator*, 5 January 1905.

32 Lawrence Friedman and Robert Percival, *The Roots of Justice: Crime and Punishment in Alameda County, California, 1870–1910* (Chapel Hill: University of North Carolina Press 1981), 133.

33 Craven, 'Toronto Police Court, 1850–80,' 267–8.

34 *Hamilton Spectator*, 28 March 1873. The loss of a tavern licence was a serious matter and so were fines for infractions of the liquor laws of the province or for permitting gambling.

35 *Hamilton Spectator*, 1 February 1882.

36 HPL, clipping, *Hamilton Times*, 18 July 1893, *Victorian History Scrapbooks*, vol.11: 49.

37 Denison, *Recollections of a Police Magistrate*, 6.

38 HPL, clippings from *Hamilton Times*, 27 November 1924, 18 December 1924, *Times* Scrapbook, vol.P3, Police Court. It should be added that he was critical of the Ontario Temperance Act at a time when the Government of Ontario worked feverishly to enforce this measure.

39 HPL, clipping, *Hamilton Times*, 25 May 1910, *Times Scrapbook*, vol.P3, Police Court.

40 Homel, 'Denison's Law,' 180.

41 *Hamilton Herald*, 11 July 1913.

42 *Hamilton Spectator*, 28 November 1930, 27 July 1939.

43 32–33 Vic. c.32. An Act Respecting the Prompt and Summary Adminstration of Criminal Justice in Certain Cases (1869).

44 Bill Stoll, 'The Nature of Crime and Characteristics of Offenders in Hamilton, Ontario, 1886' (McMaster University, unpublished geography research paper, 1976); John Fierheller, 'Social Disorder within a City: An Analysis of Criminal Behaviour in Hamilton during the 1890s' (McMaster University, unpublished history research paper, n.d.). Both papers are in the possession of the author.

45 Katz, Doucet, and Stern, *The Social Organization of Early Industrial Capitalism*, 228.

46 Ibid., 228.

47 HPL, clipping from *Hamilton Times*, 18 August 1910, *Times Scrapbook*, vol.P3, Police Court.

48 HPL, clipping from *Hamilton Times*, 18 March 1921, *Times Scrapbook*, vol.P3, Police Court.

49 8 Vic c.13. s.III. An Act to Amend, Consolidate, and Reduce into One Act, the Several Laws Now in Force, Establishing or Regulating the Practice of District Courts in the Several Districts of that Part of the Province Formerly Upper Canada (1845).

50 36 Vic. c.8 s.56. An Act for the Better Administration of Justice in the Courts of Ontario (1873).

51 *Canadian Law Journal*, vol.8 (May 1862), 115.

52 12 Vic. c.81 s.xciii. An Act to Provide ... for the Erection of Municipal Corporations (1849); 32 Vic. c.6. s.10. The Law Reform Act of 1868.

53 12 Vic. c.81 s.93–s.105. Law Reform Act of 1868.

54 32 Vic. c.6. s.6–s.16.

55 32–33 Vic. c.36. An Act Respecting the Criminal Law, and to Repeal Certain Enactments Therein Mentioned (1869).

56 *Canadian Law Journal*, vol.5 (November 1869), 285–6.

57 36 Vic. c.8 s.57.

58 *Canadian Law Journal*, vol.13 (September 1877), 265.

59 The data appears in the annual reports of the Inspector of Legal Offices published in the Ontario *Sessional Papers.*

60 *Upper Canada Law Journal*, vol.3 (March 1857), 57.

61 Paul Romney, *Mr Attorney: The Attorney General for Ontario in Court, Cabinet, and Legislature, 1791–1899* (Toronto: Published for the Osgoode Society by the University of Toronto Press, 1986), 218–19.

62 Quoted in Philip C. Stenning, *Appearing for the Crown: A Legal and Historical Review of Criminal Prosecutorial Authority in Canada* (Cowansville, Quebec: Brown Legal Publications Limited 1986), 110.

63 Ontario, *Report of the Commissioners Appointed to Inquire Concerning the Method of Appointing and Remunerating Certain Provincial Officials Now Paid by Fees and the Extent of the Remuneration They Should Receive* (Toronto: Warwick Bros. and Rutter 1896), 38. There is a fine account of the establishment of the office in Romney, *Mr Attorney*, 217–28.

64 James Kains, *'How Say You?': A Review of the Grand Jury Question* (St Thomas: The Journal 1893), 23–7. Romney, *Mr Attorney*, 224–5. 20 Vic. c.59. An Act for the Appointment of County Attorneys, and for Other Purposes, in Relation to the Local Administration of Justice in Upper Canada (1857).

65 *Upper Canada Law Journal*, vol.3 (March 1857), 57.

66 Romney, *Mr Attorney*, 225.

67 I am indebted to Greg Marquis for pointing out this distinction in citing cases.

68 Romney, *Mr Attorney*, 222.

69 Quoted in Romney, *Mr Attorney*, 223.

70 *Hamilton Spectator*, 20 July 1893.

71 Ibid., 24 January 1895.

72 *Upper Canada Law Journal*, vol.3 (March 1857), 57.

73 *Hamilton Spectator*, 30 October 1888.

74 Ministry of the Attorney General, *Report on the Administration of Ontario Courts; Ontario Law Reform Commission*, part 1, (Toronto 1973), 88.

75 RSO 1877 c.78 s.9.

76 *Hamilton Spectator*, 23 June 1893.

77 *The Daily Spectator and Journal of Commerce*, 18 February 1856.

78 Allan Greer, 'The Birth of the Police in Canada,' in *Colonial Leviathan: State Formation and Mid-Nineteenth Century Canada*, Greer and Ian Radforth, eds. (Toronto: University of Toronto Press 1992), 16–49.

79 Canada, *Journals of the Assembly for the Province of Canada, 1854–1855. Report of the Commissioners Appointed to Inquire into the Riot at Chalmers Church, Quebec, on the Occasion of Gavazzi's Lecture* (appendix G).

80 *Montreal Gazette*, 29 March 1856.

81 *Toronto Daily Globe*, 31 March 1856.

82 Greg Marquis has called my attention to similar debates in New Brunswick and Prince Edward Island.

83 Carolyn Steedman, *Policing the Victorian Community: The Formation of English Provincial Police Forces* (London: Routledge and Kegan Paul 1984), 27–32.

84 These ideas about distinctiveness and similarity were suggested by David Sugarman, 'Law, Economy and the State in England, 1750–1914: Some Major Issues,' in *Legality, Ideology and the State*, David Sugarman, ed. (New York: Academic Press 1983), 239.

85 22 Vic. c.99 s.374.

86 Wilbur Miller, *Cops and Bobbies: Police Authority in New York and London, 1830–1870* (Chicago: University of Chicago Press 1977), 17–18.

87 Maximilian Ivan Reichard, *The Origins of Urban Police: Freedom and Order in Antebellum St. Louis* (Washington University: PhD thesis, 1975), 300.

88 Roger Lane, *Policing the City: Boston, 1822–1885* (New York: Atheneum 1971), 184–98.

89 Gene E. Carte and Elaine Carte, *Police Reform in the United States: The Era of August Vollmer, 1905–1932* (Berkeley: University of California Press 1975), ix.

90 In fairness to the Cartes, their book does suggest some of the problems for policing that have stemmed from professionalism as an occupational model.

91 Carte and Carte, *Policing Reform in the United States*, ix.

92 HPL, *Hamilton Police Commission Minutebooks*, 6 February 1875.

93 *Hamilton Spectator*, 11 January 1878.

94 Ibid., 11 October 1880.

95 Ibid., 13 October 1881.

96 Ibid.

97 Ibid., 25 March 1881.

98 Ibid., 30 November 1883.

99 Ibid., 14 March 1887.

100 Ibid.

101 Denison, *Recollections of a Police Magistrte*, 35–6.

102 *Hamilton Spectator*, 28 January 1876, 28 August 1881.

103 This claim is based on a loose-leaf note in the book of application forms. It is from a psychologist and reports on the alleged mental age of several applicants.

104 Clive Emsley, *Policing and Its Context, 1750–1870* (London: Macmillan 1983), 3–4.

105 Albert J. Reiss, Jr and David Bordua, 'Environment and Organization: A Perspective on the Police,' *The Police: Six Sociological Essays* (New York: John Wiley and Sons 1967), 47.

106 *Hamilton Spectator*, 28 August 1874.

107 Ibid., 4 September 1874.

108 Ibid., 28 December 1877.

109 Ibid., 2 January 1878.

110 Ibid.

111 Ibid., 5 January 1888.

112 Ibid., 7 September 1887.

113 Ibid., 15 September 1887.

114 Ibid., 7 September 1887.

115 Ibid., 20 September 1904.

116 Ibid., 29 November 1877.

117 Ibid., 9 January 1879.

118 Ibid., 13 June 1881.

119 HPL, *Minutebook*, 24 June 1875.

120 *Hamilton Spectator*, 27 August 1881.

121 Ibid., 27 December, 1884.

122 Ibid., 5 September 1881.

123 Ibid.

124 Ibid., 16 August 1883.

125 Ibid., 13 October 1881.

126 Ibid., 10 December 1880.

127 Ibid., 9 May 1881.

128 Ibid., 12 May 1881.

129 Lane, *Policing the City*, 146.

130 Wilbur Miller, *Cops and Bobbies*, 37.

131 HPL, *Minutebook*, 21 May 1875.

132 *Hamilton Spectator*, 2 September 1881.

133 Ibid., 3 September 1881.

134 Ibid., 3 June 1881.

135 Ibid., 25 October 1881.

136 Gordon V. Torrance, 'The History of Law Enforcement in Hamilton from 1833 to 1967,' *Wentworth Bygones* (1967), 74.

137 *Hamilton Spectator*, 5 June 1885. Desmond Morton, 'Introduction,' *The Queen v. Louis Riel*, Desmond Morton, ed. (Toronto: University of Toronto Press 1974), xi.

138 *Hamilton Spectator*, 8 October 1885.

139 HPL, *A Centennial Profile of the Hamilton Police Force: The Hamilton Police Department, Past and Present: The History of Law Enforcement in Hamilton, 1833–1967.*
140 *Hamilton Spectator,* 5 March 1887.
141 Ibid., 5 March 1887,
142 Ibid.
143 Ibid., 13 November 1880.
144 Ibid., 16 April 1883.
145 Ibid., 30 November 1883.
146 *Manual of the Police Department of the City of Hamilton* (Hamilton: Spectator Printing 1889), rule 21.
147 Ibid., rule 22.
148 Ibid., rule 19.
149 Ibid., rule 24.
150 *Hamilton Spectator,* 1 September 1884.
151 Ibid., 25 January 1879.
152 Ibid.
153 Ibid., 18 July 1883.
154 Ibid., 30 November 1883.
155 HPL, *Minutebook,* 4 July 1887.
156 HPL, *Minutebook,* 6 March 1875.
157 HPL, *Minutebook,* 22 October 1895.
158 HPL, *Minutebook,* 16 December 1896; 16 February 1897.
159 *Hamilton Spectator,* 21 April 1883.
160 Ibid., 4 May 1883.
161 Denison, *Recollections of a Police Magistrate,* 36.
162 *Hamilton Spectator,* 15 August 1887.
163 Ibid.
164 HPL, *Minutebook,* 18 February 1888, 6 March 1888.

CHAPTER THREE

1 *Hamilton Herald,* 9, 10 January, 1895; *Hamilton Spectator,* 12, 19 January 1895.
2 *Hamilton Spectator,* 19 January 1895.
3 Ibid., 12 January 1895.
4 Ibid., 18 January 1895.
5 22 Vic. c.54. s.374. An Act Respecting the Municipal Institutions of Upper Canada (1858). The Hamilton commission met for the first time on 8 December 1858. See *Spectator,* 9 December 1858.
6 Eric Monkkonen, *Police in Urban America, 1860–1930* (Cambridge: Cambridge University Press 1981), 136–47.
7 Helen Boritch and John Hagan, 'Crime and the Changing Forms of Class

Control: Policing Public Order in "Toronto the Good,"' *Social Forces*, vol.66 (1987), 329.

8 Ibid., 314.

9 HPL, Special Collections, Records of the Hamilton Police Department, Police Commission Minutebooks 1872–1913 (hereafter cited as minutebook), 11 April 1896.

10 The reports were misleading in the sense that they listed by category the offences investigated by the police and then they listed the number of people found guilty, fined, sent to jail, found innocent, and so forth. The problem is that the two series were not cross-tabulated. The chief's report failed to note how many of those convicted were convicted for vagrancy and how many were convicted for theft. The conviction rates were surely quite different.

11 Minutebook, 14 January 1895. First names were never cited in the minutebooks and this convention of referring to individuals by rank and surname is followed throughout this chapter. In many cases the names were not clearly written. Therefore a few names may not be correct.

12 *Hamilton Spectator*, 16 April 1878.

13 Ibid., 2 November 1912.

14 David Philips, '"A New Engine of Power and Authority": The Institution of Law Enforcement in England, 1780–1830,' in *Crime and the Law: The Social History of Crime in Western Europe since 1500*, V.A.C. Gatrell, Bruce Lenman, and Geoffrey Parker, eds. (London: Europa Publications 1980), 187–9. Also, see Robert Storch, 'The Plague of the Blue Locusts: Police Reform and the Popular Resistance in Northern England, 1840–57,' *International Review of Social History* vol.20 (1975), 87–107.

15 See especially James F. Richardson, *The New York Police: Colonial Times to 1901* (New York: Oxford University Press 1970); Monkkonen, *Police in Urban America* (Cambridge: Cambridge University Press 1981).

16 There are some splendid exceptions. See for example W.J. Lowe, 'The Lancashire Constabulary, 1845–1870: The Social and Occupational Function of A Victorian Police Force,' *Criminal Justice History, An International Annual*, vol.4 (1984), 41–58. The ongoing work of Greg Marquis on Canadian police forces is notable as well.

17 The controversy over the relationship of the police to working-class culture and more particularly to the effectiveness of police reformers and the departments in establishing a separate police culture is well presented in two important Canadian works. See Nicholas Rogers, 'Serving Toronto the Good: The Development of the City Police Force, 1834–1884,' in *Forging a Consensus: Historical Essays on Toronto*, Victor Russell, ed. (Toronto: University of Toronto Press 1985), chapter 11; Greg Marquis, 'Working Men in Uniform: The Early Twentieth-century Toronto Police,' *Histoire sociale/Social History*, vol.20 (November 1987),

259–77. To a degree, these articles concern the sources of police conduct or misconduct that have disturbed liberal observers. Rogers focuses on the 'apartness' of the police, on the notion of the police as a distinct group whose professional identity and social associations could promote intolerance or dangerous misunderstanding. Marquis calls attention to the working-class roots of the police and to the ways in which constables were a part of the crude and rough urban culture of their class. The nuances in interpretation are worth considerable attention, because they are pertinent to contemporary reviews of police work, recruitment, and training. For a recent and insightful study of policing and the enforcement of moral order laws in London, see Stefan Petrow, *Policing Morals: The Metropolitan Police and the Home Office, 1870–1914* (Oxford: Clarendon Press 1994).

18 Minutebook, 4 October 1909.
19 For a petition for protection of private property, see Minutebook, 6 November 1901.
20 Ibid., 25 July 1901.
21 Ibid., 2 October 1912.
22 Desmond Morton, *Mayor Howland: The Citizens' Candidate* (Toronto: Hakkert 1973), 37.
23 Minutebook, 26 January, 5 February 1884.
24 Ibid., 3 December 1885.
25 Ibid., 5 November 1895, 16 November 1896.
26 Ibid., 4 February 1903.
27 *Hamilton Times*, 18 April 1910.
28 *Hamilton Herald*, 25 June 1907.
29 Ibid., 22 July 1907.
30 Minutebook, 13 November 1908, 31 March 1909.
31 For an account of the anti-white slavery movement in Canada, see Angus McLaren, 'White Slavers: The Reform of Canada's Prostitution Laws and Patterns of Enforcement,' *Criminal Justice History*, vol.8 (1987), 53–119. *Hamilton Spectator*, 15 February, 13 November 1908; *Hamilton Herald*, 12 November 1908.
32 *Hamilton Spectator*, 14 December 1901.
33 Ibid., 13 November 1908.
34 Tom Irwin, 'Moral Order Crime in Hamilton: 1907–1912' (McMaster University, unpublished graduate research paper, August 1990), 34. The paper was based on a study of the police court records and newspaper reports.
35 Minutebook, 2 October 1912.
36 Joseph L. Tropea, 'Situationally Negotiated Transactions and Domination: From Tribe to Rational-Legal Order in the Anglo-American Legal Tradition,' *Criminal Justice History*, vol.12 (1991), 11.

37 *Hamilton Herald,* 17 September 1912.

38 Ibid., 25 September 1912.

39 Ibid., 9 November 1912.

40 Ibid., 23 March 1914.

41 Ibid., 9 November 1912.

42 Irwin, 'Moral Order Crime,' 37, 42, 44.

43 HPL, clipping, *Hamilton Times,* 23 August 1912, *Times Scrapbook,* vol.P3, Police Court.

44 John Weaver, 'Crime, Public Order, and Repression: The Gore District in Upheaval, 1832–1851,' *Ontario History,* vol.78 (September 1986), 193–4. The article is reprinted in R.C. Macleod, *Lawful Authority: Readings on the History of Criminal Justice in Canada* (Toronto: Copp Clark Pitman 1988).

45 Judith Fingard claims that, in late-Victorian Halifax, the frequent arrest of black prostitutes was a case of 'racial persecution.' See *The Dark Side of Victorian Halifax* (Porters Lake, Nova Scotia: Pottersfield Press 1989), 105.

46 *Hamilton Spectator,* 28 June 1909.

47 *Hamilton Herald,* 17 May 1916.

48 HPL, *Hamilton Times Scrapbook,* 22 April 1915, quoted in Rachael Janecka, 'The Hamilton Police and Moral Order: 1905–1925,' (McMaster University, unpublished undergraduate paper, 3 March 1993).

49 *Hamilton Times,* 18 December 1917.

50 Bryne Hope Sanders, *Emily Murphy, Crusader* (Toronto: Macmillan 1945), 206–12.

51 *Hamilton Times,* 16 March, 21 March, 18 June 1914.

52 *Times,* 12 January 1912; Minutebook, 22 January 1912; personnel records.

53 Lawrence Friedman and Robert Percival, *The Roots of Justice: Crime and Punishment in Alameda County, California, 1870–1910* (Chapel Hill: University of North Carolina Press 1981), 75.

54 *Hamilton Times,* 16 February 1912.

55 Minutebook, 7 December 1899, 31 January 1901.

56 *Hamilton Spectator,* 8 February 1872.

57 McMaster University, Mills Memorial Library, Special Collections, Robert L. Fraser, '"We Walk": The Story of the Hamilton Street Railway Strike of 1906,' (McMaster University, unpublished undergraduate research paper, 1970), 24–8. This remarkable, thesis-length essay anticipated much subsequent labour and social history and explored the connections between Methodism, the social gospel, and labourism.

58 Fraser, '"We Walk,"' 72–94.

59 Ibid., 101, 140.

60 I am indebted to Carolyn Gray for this information. She has worked on the Cataract Power and Traction Company records at the Ontario

Hydro Archives in connection with her biographical study of John Gibson.

61 Dahn Higley, *O.P.P.: The History of the Ontario Provincial Police Force* (Toronto: The Queen's Printer 1984), passim.

62 *Hamilton Spectator*, 20 July 1914.

63 The city council voted on the budget recommendations of the commission. It occasionally tried to use the police for municipal chores. In 1905 the council wanted the force to conduct a local census; the chief rejected the request and the commission supported him. Minutebook, 6 December 1905.

64 Minutebook, 6, 7 November 1901.

65 Ibid., 4 November 1908.

66 Ibid., 29 January 1908.

67 *Hamilton Spectator*, 29 October 1888.

68 See HPL, *Hamilton Times* Scrapbooks, vol.P4, *Hamilton Times*, 12 March 1910, 6 September 1912, 12 June 1913.

69 *Hamilton Times*, 4 February 1892.

70 Ibid., 12 March 1910.

71 Ibid., 2 September 1914.

72 Minutebook, 6 November 1901.

73 Ibid., 7 February 1912.

74 Ibid., 11 April 1913.

75 Ibid., 5 1905.

76 Ibid., 9 June, 25 August 1902.

77 Ibid., 27 June 1913.

78 Ibid., 10 December 1910.

79 Unidentified newspaper clipping in the Minutebook, 6 March 1907.

80 *Hamilton Spectator*, 1 November 1907.

81 Ibid., 17 May 1876.

82 Ibid., 3 November 1884.

83 Minutebook, 3 February 1904.

84 *Hamilton Spectator*, 28 February 1881, 28 December 1883.

85 Ibid., 3 November 1884.

86 This is the conclusion of Clive Emsley, who has compared the unknown or unreported instances of police violence to the likewise unknown amount of crime. In both cases, there is a 'dark figure' that cannot be captured in the existing data. Clive Emsley, '"The Thumping of Wood on A Swede Turnip": Police Violence in Nineteenth-Century England,' *Criminal Justice History*, vol.6 (1985), 143.

87 Minutebook, 29 January 1909.

88 Minutebook, 27 July 1898.

89 These propositions are presented in an interesting book which proposes that policemen have picked up most of their crime-fighting and sur-

vival techniques by learning from criminals, acting on impulse informed by lore, and 'reading' clothes and behaviour. In effect, the book concludes that the police have continued to secure some of their most effective practices from sources other than professional training and have attitudes which would legitimately upset liberal reformers. See David R. Johnson, *Policing the Urban Underworld: The Impact of Crime on the Development of American Policing, 1800–1887* (Philadelphia: Temple University Press 1979), 122–46.

90 Minutebook, 30 January 1907.

91 Minutebook, 21 February 1911; 2, 17 October 1912; 24 December 1913.

92 Ibid., 21 February 1911.

93 *Hamilton Times*, 11 December 1912.

94 Minutebook, 1 April 1900.

95 Ibid., 7 September 1910.

96 Greg Marquis, "Working Men in Uniform: The Early Twentieth-Century Toronto Police," *Histoire sociale/Social History*, vol.20 (November 1987), 261.

97 On wages, see Minutebook, 8 February 1905, 13 January 1906, 22 January 1912.

98 *Hamilton Spectator*, 13 January 1912.

99 Ibid., 17 February 1913.

100 Ibid., 3 March 1913.

101 Minutebook 10 July 1900, 25 July 1901, 7 July 1909.

102 Ibid., 24 June 1896.

103 Ibid., 28 August 1905.

104 Ibid., 4 July 1907, 29 January 1909.

105 Ibid., 8 July 1905, 10 December 1909, 28 November 1912.

106 *Hamilton Spectator*, 4 March 1913.

107 The data on hiring comes from the application forms and oath books of the department deposited with the Hamilton Public Library. These were linked with personnel records in the same collection.

108 *Hamilton Spectator*, 27 January 1915.

109 *Hamilton Times*, 4 February 1892.

110 John C. Weaver, *Hamilton: An Illustrated History* (Toronto: Lorimer 1982), Table VIII, 199.

111 Minutebook, 22 February 1879; also, see 31 July 1906.

112 Marquis, 'Working Men in Uniform,' 273–7.

113 George T. Denison, *Recollections of a Police Magistrate* (Toronto: Musson 1920) 31.

114 *Hamilton Spectator*, 2 August 1880.

115 *Hamilton Times*, 5 June 1915.

116 *Manual of the Police Department of the City of Hamilton* (Hamilton: Spectator Printing 1889). See the section entitled 'catechism for probationers.'

117 *Hamilton Herald*, 19 July, 17 September 1918.

118 Ibid., 19 July 1918.

119 SO, Ontario 1946 c.72.

120 Minutebook, 10 April, 5 November 1895.

121 *Hamilton Spectator*, 6 January 1912.

122 Ibid., 19 November 1874.

123 Ibid., 5 October 1905.

124 Ibid., 22 January 1872.

125 Ibid., 22 May 1957. The cornerstone of station number 2 was discovered in 1957 and an amateur historian with the police force found someone on the force who could recall the building and describe it for an artist.

126 *Hamilton Spectator*, 21 June, 5 August 1873.

127 Ibid., 7 February 1872, 30 April 1873.

128 Ibid., 20 March 1909; *Hamilton Herald*, 5 March and 25 November 1909.

129 HPL, clipping from the *Hamilton Times*, 28 March 1910, vol.P3, Police Court.

130 *Hamilton Spectator*, 28 September 1925.

131 *Hamilton Times*, 19 November 1910.

132 *Hamilton Spectator*, 6 April 1878.

133 Eric Monkkonen, *Police in Urban America*, 10.

134 *Hamilton Spectator*, 19 November 1874.

135 Ibid., 11 February 1876.

136 Ibid., 11 February 1874.

137 Ibid., 6 April 1878.

138 Ibid., 11 February 1876.

139 HPL, *Hamilton Times* clipping file, 17 November 1910. I am indebted to Cathy Giudice of the Hamilton and Wentworth Regional Police Force for this reference.

140 Judith Fingard, 'The Winter's Tale: The Seasonal Contours of Pre-industrial Poverty in British North America, 1815–1850,' *The Canadian Historical Association, Historical Papers 1974*, ed. Peter Gillis (Ottawa: CHA, 1974), 67–72.

141 *Hamilton Spectator*, 2 March 1872.

142 *Hamilton Times*, 19 November 1910.

143 *Hamilton Spectator*, 20 November 1877.

144 Ibid., 13 March 1876. For a systematic examination of tramps in Ontario around this time, see Richard Anderson, '"The Irrepressible Stampede": Tramps in Ontario, 1870–1880,' *Ontario History*, vol.54 (March 1992), 33–56. Anderson concludes that the tramps were part of the reserve army of unemployed labour.

145 Ibid., 24 January 1920.
146 Ibid., 24 October 1873.
147 Ibid., 23 June 1884.
148 *Hamilton Times*, 19 November 1910.
149 Ibid., 21 November 1910.
150 *Hamilton Spectator*, 11 February 1876.
151 Ibid., 27 November 1914.
152 *Hamilton Times*, 21 December 1914.
153 *Hamilton Spectator*, 22 January 1914.
154 Ibid., 22 May 1957.
155 HPL, Hamilton Police Department Records, RG 10, Series C, Deputy Chief's Order Book, 1932–6, 1 October 1932.
156 Gene E. Carte and Elaine Carte, *Policing Reform in the United States: The Era of August Vollmer, 1905–1932* (Berkeley: University of California Press 1975), 7–8.
157 *Hamilton Times*, 19 April 1911, 10 April 1913.
158 *Hamilton Spectator*, 12 March 1884.
159 Ibid.
160 *Hamilton Times*, 19 April 1911.
161 *Hamilton Spectator*, 3 June, 20 October 1884.
162 James Q. Wilson, 'Police Morale, Reform, and Citizen Respect: The Chicago Case,' *The Police: Six Sociological Studies*, ed. David J. Bordua (New York: John Wiley and Sons 1967), 141.
163 *Hamilton Times*, 4 January 1910.
164 *Hamilton Spectator*, 14 April 1924.
165 Ibid., 17 October 1910.
166 *Hamilton Herald*, 14 April 1924.
167 *Hamilton Times*, 17 October 1910.
168 Ibid., 7 January 1911.
169 Ibid., 21 November 1910.
170 Ibid., 22 November 1910.
171 Ibid., 29 December 1910, 15 March 1911.
172 Ibid., 24 April 1912.
173 Ibid., 28 August, 14 November 1912.
174 Ibid., 5 August 1912.
175 *Hamilton Herald*, 15 August 1913.
176 *Hamilton Spectator*, 22 March 1912.
177 HPL, RG10 Hamilton Police Department Records, Series C Chief's Order Book, 1912–26, 20 November 1920.
178 Ibid., 31 March 1917.
179 Ibid., 16 August 1913.
180 Marquis, 'Working Men in Uniform,' 270.
181 Minutebook, 28 November 1912.

182 Marquis, 'Working Men in Uniform,' 261.
183 Marquis, 'Working Men in Uniform,' 270.
184 Minutebook, 13 November 1908. A number of hotel keepers made a practice of giving liquor to constables. Minutebook, 4 October 1909.
185 Ibid., 10 November 1909.
186 *Hamilton Spectator*, 22 May 1913.
187 Minutebook, 20 December 1912.
188 Ibid., 22 October 1904.
189 Ibid., 16 November 1900.
190 Ibid., 25 July 1901.
191 Ibid., 15 October 1913.
192 *Hamilton Times*, 20 December 1913.
193 Ibid., 9 May 1910.
194 Ibid., 21 September 1910, 13 January 1913.
195 Ibid., 25 April 1910.
196 Ibid., 3 June 1910.
197 Ibid., 14 February 1913.
198 Ibid., 9 November 1912.
199 Ibid., 20 December 1913.
200 Ibid., 28 June 1911.
201 Ibid., 21 September 1910.
202 Friedman and Percival, *The Roots of Justice*, 97.
203 *Hamilton Times*, 14 October 1912.
204 Ibid., 21 September 1910.
205 Wilbur Miller, *Cops and Bobbies: Police Authority in New York and London, 1830–1879* (Chicago: University of Chicago Press 1977), 16.

CHAPTER FOUR

1 See *Hamilton Spectator*, 5, 16 October 1946.
2 Ibid., 21 September 1948.
3 Ibid., 24 October 1953.
4 Ibid., 4 September 1958. The reason for the lack of criminal work at the general sessions of the peace held by the county was simply that a number of accused had elected to be tried without benefit of jury before the county judge or the police magistrate.
5 *Hamilton Spectator*, 9 October 1946.
6 Ibid., 5 October 1926.
7 Ibid., 24 February 1947.
8 Ibid., 17 October 1946.
9 Ibid., 3 April 1947.
10 Ibid., 24 February 1947.
11 AO, RG 22, box 185, Dinietto murder, 1921, note from S.F. Washington, n.d.

12 John Honsberger, 'The Power of Arrest and the Duties and Rights of Citizens and Police,' *Special Lectures of the Law Society of Upper Canada, 1963: Part IV, Representing an Arrested Client and Police Interrogation* (Toronto: Richard De Boo Limited 1963), 24. Honsberger cites the Dick case.

13 *Hamilton Spectator*, 23 March 1946.

14 HPL, clippings from the *Hamilton Herald*, 24 February 1914, 20 August 1917, 15 March 1918, 24 November 1919, *Hamilton Herald Scrapbooks*, vol.M4.1, Murders. In each of these cases, the suspects were arrested and held on a charge of vagrancy.

15 *Hamilton News*, 16 February 1951.

16 Judge Felix Frankfurter in *Culombe* v. *Connecticut*, quoted in Ronald Joseph Delisle and Don Stuart, *Learning Canadian Criminal Procedure* (Toronto: Carswell 1986), 267.

17 For comment on the public feeling against Evelyn Dick, see Jack Batten, *Robinette: The Dean of Canadian Lawyers* (Toronto: Macmillan 1984), 162.

18 The Dick case, following *Gach* v. *The King*, significantly weakened the value of statements made in the absence of a warning, but in a 1949 ruling, *Boudreau* v. *The King*, the absence or presence of a warning was not to be taken as the sole determining factor in deciding whether a statement would be accepted or rejected. Batten, *Robinette*, 94–5.

19 Honsberger, 'The Power of Arrest and the Duties and Rights of Citizens and Police,' 11.

20 HPL, RG10, Hamilton Police Department Records, Series C, Chief's Order Book, 1926–36, 2 December 1932.

21 *Hamilton Spectator*, 3 October 1935.

22 *Globe and Mail*, 15 October 1946.

23 *Hamilton Spectator*, 10 January 1947.

24 Edward Peters, *Torture* (London: Basil Blackwell 1985), 40–73.

25 Norman Borins, 'Police Investigation and the Rights of an Accused,' *Special Lectures of the Law Society of Upper Canada, 1963*, 62.

26 *Hamilton Spectator*, 10 January 1947.

27 R.S.M. Woods, *Police Interrogation* (Toronto: Carswell 1990), 165.

28 AO, RG 22, box 185, Maranga murder, 1920, statement by Giovanni Maranga, 26 December 1920. The phrasing of the statement is odd. It probably meant that Maranga was warned in the usual way, though the statement did not spell out the terms. Were these his words?

29 Hamilton-Wentworth Regional Police Department, 'Statement of [name deleted] regarding the death of [name deleted],' Hamilton Wanted Persons, 1924–26. This material was obtained under freedom of information and privacy legislation; a research agreement was signed and all reference to individuals has been eliminated from research notes.

30 Ontario Low Reform Commission, *Report of the Coroner System in Ontario* (Toronto: Department of Justice 1971), 11.

31 Hamilton-Wentworth Regional Police, historical records, coroner's inquest books, volume marked 1939, 11 May 1939.

32 Hamilton-Wentworth Regional Police, historical records, coroner's inquest books, see entries for 10 November 1938, 23 April 1939, 29 December 1942, 18 February 1954.

33 Coroner's inquest books, see entries for 2 September 1954, 28 April 1955.

34 E. Richard Lovekin, 'Magistrates' Courts,' *The Criminal Law Quarterly*, vol.1 (February 1959), 385–6.

35 T.G. Zuber, *Report of the Ontario Courts Inquiry* (Toronto: Queen's Printer 1987), 23–4.

36 *Hamilton Spectator*, 11 January 1947.

37 Ibid., 12 April 1947.

38 Delisle and Stuart, *Learning Canadian Criminal Procedure*, 267.

39 *Hamilton Spectator*, 24, 25 April 1947; *Globe and Mail*, 17 July, 24 July, 9 August 1947.

40 Batten, *Robinette*, 95.

41 An unidentified 1952 clipping about police methods stated in part: 'Statements are typed as dictated, but only after the suspect has been warned and advised that anything he says may be used in evidence.' HPL, Hamilton Police Department Scrapbook of Clippings, 1952–1957, vol.1, part 2.

42 32–33 Vic. c.31 s.91.

43 Canada, *Documents in Reference to the Abolition of the Grand Jury System* (Ottawa: Queen's Printer 1891), 21, 36.

44 42 Vic. c.14. An Act to Amend the Jurors' Act (1879).

45 55 Vic. c.12. An Act Reducing the Number of Grand Jurors (1892).

46 *Hamilton Spectator*, 11 January 1961.

47 Ibid., 12 January 1953.

48 Constance Backhouse, *Petticoats and Prejudice: Women and Law in Nineteenth-Century Canada* (Toronto: Published for the Osgoode Society by Women's Press 1991), 337.

49 Arthur Maloney, 'Sex Offences and Corroboration,' *Special Lectures of the Law Society of Upper Canada, 1959: Jury Trials* (Toronto: Richard De Boo Limited 1959), 82–3.

50 *Canadian Law Journal*, vol.12 (February 1876), 30–1.

51 John A. Kains, *'How Say You?': A Review of the Grand Jury Question* (St Thomas: *The Journal* 1893), 5–14.

52 Canada, *Documents in Reference to the Abolition of the Grand Jury System*, 8, 21.

53 Ibid., 15.

54 *Hamilton Spectator*, 22 November 1886.

55 G. Blaine Baker, 'Legal Education in Upper Canada, 1785–1889: The Law Society as Educator,' *Essays in the History of Canadian Law*, vol.2,

ed. by David Flaherty (Toronto: University of Toronto Press, 1983), 49–142.

56 *Hamilton Spectator*, 15 January 1920.

57 For examples of reports on institutions, see *Hamilton Spectator*, 12 January, 4 and 19 September 1958, 12 January 1961. For an example of the grand jury altering the charge, see *Hamilton Spectator*, 23 September 1952.

58 *Hamilton Spectator*, 12 April 1969.

59 Ibid., 10 January 1940.

60 Ontario Law Reform Commission, *Report on Administration of Ontario Courts*, part 1 (Toronto: Ministry of the Attorney General 1973), 356–7.

61 Roger Salhany, *Canadian Criminal Procedure* (second edition, Agincourt: Canada Law Book Limited 1972), 97.

62 Paul Romney, 'From Constitutionalism to Legalism: Trial by Jury, Responsible Government, and the Rule of Law in Canadian Political Culture, ' *Law and History Review*, vol.7 (Spring 1989), 141.

63 Revisions to the code in 1923 had accidentally repealed the 1892 measure. In 1975 a revision limited the power of the Court of Appeal to order a new trial. Romney, 'Trial by Jury,' 141.

64 Ontario, Commission on Best Mode of Selecting, Appointing and Recommending Sheriffs, etc., *Interim Report Respecting Police Magistrates* (Toronto: King's Printer 1921), 13.

65 Dieter Hoehne, *Legal Aid in Canada* (Lewiston: Edwin Mellen Press 1989), 19–24.

66 *Hamilton Spectator*, 18 March 1953; *Hamilton Daily News*, 2 January 1955.

67 Hoehne, *Legal Aid in Canada*, 59–60.

68 William Robinson, 'Murder at Crowhurst: A Case Study in Early Tudor Law Enforcement,' *Criminal Justice History*, vol.9 (1988), 44.

69 Hamilton-Wentworth Regional Police Department, Information for Search Warrants, 1928–9. This material was released under freedom of information legislation, but has been transferred to the Hamilton Public Library.

70 Leon Radzinowicz, *A History of English Criminal Law and Its Administration from 1750*, vol.4 (London: Stevens and Sons 1968), 200–1.

71 HPL, Hamilton Police Department Records, *Annual Report for 1949*. Hereafter, these reports will be cited as *AR*.

72 *AR*, 1920.

73 *AR*, 1920.

74 *AR*, 1921.

75 *AR*, 1935.

76 *AR*, 1939.

77 *AR*, 1945.

78 Kerrie Adkins, 'Wanted Posters: A Reflection of Social and Policing Issues in the Early Twentieth Century' (McMaster University, unpublished

undergraduate paper, 1993). The posters are part of the records of the Hamilton police force now located in the Special Collections of the Hamilton Public Library and described as Departmental Notification Registers. Printed on cheap paper, they have deteriorated to such an extent that they may not be used again.

79 Hamilton-Wentworth Police Department, Wanted Book. This volume is the only one found.

80 John Berry, 'The History and Development of Fingerprinting,' in *Advances in Fingerprint Technology*, Henry Lee and R.E. Gaensslen eds. (New York: Elsevier 1991), 22.

81 *AR*, 1915.

82 *AR*, 1925.

83 The system involved assigning numerical values to odd and even fingers on the basis of whether or not they had whorls.

84 Berry, 'The History and Development of Fingerprinting,' *33*.

85 Gordon V. Torrance, 'The History of Law Enforcement in Hamilton from 1833 to 1967', *Wentworth Bygones* 1967), 75.

86 *AR*, 1917.

87 *Hamilton Spectator*, 25 October 1951.

88 *Hamilton Review*, 3 December 1953.

89 HPL, clipping file on Leonard Lawrence, unidentified clipping.

90 *AR*, 1961. In April 1961 the Hamilton force hosted a conference dealing with the exchange of information.

91 *AR*, 1961, 1962.

92 *Hamilton Spectator*, 28 March 1952.

93 SO, 1949 c.72 s.61.

94 *Hamilton Spectator*, 2 June, 7 June 1944.

95 HPL, unidentified clipping, Hamilton Police Department, Scrapbook of Clippings, 1952–7 , vol.1, part 2, 375.

96 Ibid.

97 Quoted in Woods, *Police Interrogation*, ix.

98 *AR*, 1929.

99 *Hamilton Spectator*, 14 January 1955.

100 Ibid., 7 June 1958.

101 This claim is based on the fact that in the early 1900s the preliminary hearings reported on in the press or extant in the criminal assize records appear quite long and are filled with detailed questions that look as if they were meant to help the defence prepare for a jury trial.

102 Lawrence Friedman and Robert Percival, *The Roots of Justice: Crime and Punishment in Alameda County, California, 1870–1910* (Chapel Hill: University of North Carolina Press 1981), 79.

103 *Hamilton Spectator*, 5 December 1883.

104 *AR*, 1940.

105 *AR*, 1944.

106 *AR*, 1959.

107 *AR*, 1955, 1959.

108 Honsberger, 'The Power of Arrest and the Duties and Rights of Citizens and Police,' 3. Honsberger was quoting an unidentified English home secretary.

109 Dahn D. Higley, *O.P.P.: The History of the Ontario Provincial Police Force* (Toronto: The Queen's Printer 1984), 322.

110 Hamilton, *Revised By-Laws of the City of Hamilton* (Hamilton: Spectator Printing 1910), 82–96. Stephen Davies, *Ontario and the Automobile, 1900–1930* (McMaster University, PhD thesis, 1987), 64,

111 Dorothy Chunn, *From Punishment to Doing Good: Family Courts and Socialized Justice in Ontario, 1880–1940* (Toronto: University of Toronto Press 1992), 13.

112 *Hamilton Herald*, 4 April 1918.

113 I am indebted to the research of Rachael Janecka as presented in 'The Hamilton Police and Moral Order: 1905–1925' (Unpublished McMaster University undergraduate paper, 4 March 1993). Magistrate Jelfs was a critic of the OTA. *Hamilton Herald*, 19 May and 15 December 1924.

114 Torrance, 'The History of Law Enforcement in Hamilton,' 77.

115 *AR*, 1924.

116 *AR*, 1929.

117 *AR*, 1936.

118 *Hamilton Times*, 21 September 1910.

119 *Hamilton Spectator*, 5 April 1929.

120 David R. Johnson, *Policing the Urban Underworld: The Impact of Crime on the Development of American Policing: 1800–1887* (Philadelphia: Temple University Press 1979), 143.

121 *AR*, 1959.

122 *Hamilton News*, 5 June 1953.

123 *Globe and Mail*, 8 October 1963.

124 *Hamilton News*, 5 June 1953.

125 The introduction of real training and its displacement of or uneasy coexistence with old habits and attitudes will be a challenging new area for research on the development of policing in Canada.

126 *Hamilton Spectator*, 29 January 1952.

127 Ibid., 11 March 1960.

128 *Hamilton Herald*, 30 August 1924.

129 *AR*, 1936.

130 *AR*, 1937.

131 *AR*, 1944.

132 *Hamilton Spectator*, 7 April 1951.

133 Ibid., 2 February, 7 April 1951.

134 Ibid., 3 August 1951.

135 Ibid., 1 January 1954; 22 June 1956.

136 Ibid., 5 October 1957.

137 Ibid., 10 May 1894.

138 Ibid., 22 December 1950.

139 *Fifty Years of Activity, 1893–1943: Commemorating the Golden Anniversary of Hamilton Local Council of Women* (Hamilton: Hamilton Printing Service 1944), 87–8.

140 *Hamilton Spectator*, 24 January 1944.

141 *Hamilton News*, 30 May 1952.

142 *Hamilton Spectator*, 22 November 1958.

143 Ontario, *Report of the Commissioners Appointed to Enquire into the Prison and Reformatory System of Ontario, 1891* (Toronto: Warwick and Sons 1891), 121.

144 Ibid., 129.

145 Ibid., 246.

146 Ibid., 247.

147 Ibid., 253.

148 Paul W. Bennett, ' "Turning Bad Boys into Good Citizens": The Reforming Impulse of Toronto's Industrial Schools Movement, 1883 to the 1920s,' *Ontario History*, vol.78 (September 1986), 227.

149 Andrew Jones, ' "Closing Penetanguishene Reformatory": An Attempt to Deinstitutionalize Treatment of Juvenile Offenders in Early Twentieth Century Ontario,' *Ontario History*, vol.70 (1978) 227–44.

150 HPL, RG 10, Series O, Police Court Register with section for juvenile court proceedings from 1923 to 1928.

151 Elsie Gregory MacGill, *My Mother the Judge: A Biography of Judge Helen Gregory MacGill* (Toronto: The Ryerson Press 1955), 166.

152 Brian Raychaba, 'The Hamilton Children's Aid Society, 1894–1914: A Social and Institutional History' (McMaster University, MA paper, 1992).

153 See NA, MG 28, I 10, Charlotte Whitton Papers, vol.45, Robert E. Mills, Charlotte Whitton, and Elizabeth King, *Report Re: The Children's Aid Society of Hamilton, Ontario, Made by A Special Committee of the Children's Aid Society of Hamilton* (December 1929). I am indebted to Brain Raychaba for this reference. For an excellent account of child protection in a city, see Raychaba, 'The Hamilton Children's Aid Society.'

154 Dorothy Chunn, *From Punishment to Doing Good*, 99.

155 *AR*, 1946, 1960.

156 Frank W. Anderson, *A Concise History of Capital Punishment in Canada* (Calgary: Frontier Publications 1973), 39–40.

157 Ibid., 41.

158 Ibid., 50.
159 Helen McKenzie, 'Capital Punishment in Canada,' *Current Issue Review, Library of Parliament* (19 November 1979; revised 10 July 1987), 10; Neil Boyd, *The Last Dance: Murder in Canada* (Scarborough: Prentice-Hall 1988), 30–2.
160 Ibid., 57–73.
161 Anthony Mardiros, *William Irvine: The Life of a Prairie Radical* (Toronto: James Lorimer 1979), 129.
162 It may have been fewer than eight, because the outcomes of requests for leniency were difficult to locate in the press.
163 Helen McKenzie, 'Capital Punishment in Canada,' 10–14; Boyd, *The Last Dance*, 42–4.
164 Torrance, 'The History of Law Enforcement in Hamilton,' 78.

CHAPTER FIVE

1 *Hamilton Herald*, 27 December 1920; 23 February 1921.
2 Ibid., 27 December 1920.
3 Ibid., 7 October 1921.
4 Jennifer Davis, 'A Poor Man's System of Justice: The London Police Courts in the Second Half of the Nineteenth Century,' *The Historical Journal*, vol.27, no.2 (1984) 397–426; 'Prosecutors and Their Context: The Uses of the Criminal law in Later Nineteenth-Century London,' *Policing and Prosecution in Britain, 1750–1850*, Douglas Hay and Francis Snyder, eds. (Oxford: Clarendon Press 1989).
5 For an account of the underlying general systems of thought relating to penal reforms in England, see William James Forsyth, *The Reform of Prisoners, 1830–1900* (New York: St Martins 1987). Though not as penetrating as works on the origins of the penitentiary by Foucault and Ignatieff, it does cover a longer period and changes in thinking about treating deviant behaviour.
6 A.M. Guerry, *Essai sur la statistique morale de la France* (Paris: Crochard 1833), 43, 51.
7 On the role of romanticism in promoting an anti-urbanism in American culture, see Morton and Lucia White, *The Intellectual versus the City: From Thomas Jefferson to Frank Lloyd Wright* (New York: Mentor Books 1964), 233.
8 Paul Boyer, *Urban Masses and Moral Order in America, 1820–1920* (Cambridge, Mass.: Harvard University Press 1978), 68–70, 125–7.
9 Josiah Strong, *The Challenge of the City* (New York: Young People's Missionary Movement 1907), 51.
10 J.S. Woodsworth, *Strangers within Our Gates or Coming Canadians* (Toronto: The Missionary Society of the Methodist Church 1911), 251.

11 Boyer, *Urban Masses and Moral Order*, 286.
12 Theodore Ferdinand, 'The Criminal Patterns of Boston since 1849,' *The American Journal of Sociology*, 73 (July 1967), 98.
13 Ibid., 93.
14 Roger Lane, 'Crime and Criminal Statistics in Nineteenth Century Massachusetts,' *Journal of Social History*, vol.2 (December 1968), 158–9.
15 Roger Lane, 'Urbanization and Criminal Violence in the 19th Century: Massachusetts as a Test Case,' *The History of Violence in America: the Historical and Comparative Perspectives*, Hugh Davis Graham, ed. (New York: Frederick A. Praeger 1969), 471.
16 Ibid., 480.
17 Ferdinand, 'The Criminal Patterns of Boston since 1849,' 98.
18 Roger Lane, 'On the Social Meaning of Homicide Trends in America,' in *Violence in America*, Ted Robert Gurr, ed. (Sage Publications 1989; previously published in 1979).
19 Roger Lane, *Violent Death in the City: Suicide, Accident, and Murder in Nineteenth-Century Philadelphia* (Cambridge, Mass.: Harvard University Press 1979), 121–5.
20 Lane, 'On the Social Meaning of Homicide Trends,' 76.
21 Eric Monkkonen, '"Crime and Poverty in a Nineteenth-Century City: The Dangerous Class" of Columbus, Ohio, 1859–1885,'(University of Minnesota, PhD thesis, 1973), 68, 71–2, 222.
22 Helen Boritch and John Hagan, 'Crime and the Changing Forms of Class Control: Policing Public Order in "Toronto the Good,"' *Social Forces*, vol.66 (1987), 316–17.
23 Theodore Hershberg, Alan N. Burstein, Eugene P. Ericksen, Stephanie W. Greenberg, and William L. Yancey, *Work, Space, Family, and Group Experience in the 19th Century*, Theodore Herschberg, ed. (Toronto: University of Oxford Press 1981), 482–5.
24 Gunther Barth, *City People: The Rise of Modern City Culture in Nineteenth-Century America* (New York: Oxford University Press 1980), 5.
25 Eric Monkkonen, *America Becomes Urban: The Development of U.S. Cities and Towns, 1780–1980* (Berkeley: University of California Press 1988), 97.
26 Howard Zehr, 'The Modernization of Crime in Germany and France, 1830–1913,' *The Journal of Social History*, vol.8 (Summer 1975), 132.
27 Ted Robert Gurr, 'Historical Trends in Violent Crime: Europe and the United States,' in *Violence in America*, 33.
28 Gurr had first published his table in 1981. See Gurr, 'Historical Trends in Violent Crime: A Critical review of the Evidence,' *Crime and Justice*, vol.3 (1981). Lawrence Stone, 'Interpersonal Violence in English Society, 1300–1980,' *Past and Present*, no.101, (November 1983), 32–3.

29 J.S. Cockburn, 'Patterns of Violence in English Society: Homicide in Kent, 1560–1985,' *Past and Present*, no.130 (February 1991). Cockburn's article includes many more quibbles.

30 Gurr, 'Historical Trends,' 23–4.

31 Lane, 'On the Social Meaning of Homicide Trends in America,' 58–9.

32 Cockburn, 'Patterns of Violence,' 106.

33 V.A.C. Gatrell, 'The Decline of Theft and Violence in Victorian and Edwardian England,' *Crime and the Law: The Social History of Crime in Western Europe since 1500*, V.A.C. Gatrell, Bruce Lenman, and Geoffrey Parker, eds. (Europa Publications Limited 1980), 334.

34 Ibid., 238.

35 Ibid., 335.

36 Clive Elmsley, *Crime and Society in England, 1750–1900* (New York: Longman 1987), 27.

37 The police reports are only available from 1906; however, the newspapers published the annual reports for many years in the late nineteenth century. A check of newspaper statistics against cases in the police court yields the same figures. On that basis, manual counts of police court cases were used to fill in data where newspaper accounts were missing.

38 Gatrell, 'The Decline of Theft and Violence,' 249.

39 4, 5 Vic. c.25 s.55.

40 *Hamilton Spectator*, 17 November 1857.

41 Ibid., 23 November 1857.

42 Ibid., 7 July 1863.

43 ibid., 17 April 1873.

44 I am indebted to Wolfgang Ziegler for calling these sayings to my attention.

45 *Hamilton Spectator*, 22 January 1873.

46 Ibid., 12 March 1883.

47 Lawrence Friedman and Robert Percival, *The Roots of Justice: Crime and Punishment in Alameda County, California, 1870–1910* (Chapel Hill: University of North Carolina Press 1981), 125.

48 Douglas Hay and Francis Snyder, 'Using the Criminal Law, 1750–1850: Policing, Private Prosecution, and the State,' in *Policing and Prosecution*, 31.

49 *Hamilton Spectator*, 30 October 1888.

50 Ibid., 31 May 1893.

51 HPL, clipping for the *Hamilton Times*, 2 April 1892, *Victorian History Scrapbook*, vol.10, part 5: 5.

52 HPL, clipping *Hamilton Herald*, 30 March 1914, *Hamilton Herald Scrapbook*, vol.P3, Police Court.

53 *Hamilton Spectator*, 23 June 1893.

54 *Hamilton Times*, 14 December 1901.

55 HPL, clipping, *Hamilton Times*, 13 July 1912, *Times Scrapbook*, vol.P3., Police Court.

56 Zehr, 'The Modernization of Crime,' 131.

57 *Hamilton Spectator*, 19 December 1862.

58 Ibid., 4 August 1863.

59 Ibid., 2 February 1863.

60 Ibid., 3 January 1871.

61 Ontario, *Report of the Commissioners Appointed to Enquire into the Prison and Reformatory System of Ontario* (Toronto: Warwick and Sons 1891), 111.

62 *Hamilton Spectator*, 6 February 1884.

63 HPL, Special Collections, Police Department Records, Police Court Journals, 11 August 1865.

64 Ibid., 13 June 1865.

65 Ibid., 22 February 1859.

66 *Hamilton Spectator*, 2 February 1876.

67 Ibid., 24 February 1874.

68 Ibid., 18 January 1883.

69 Ibid., 20 January 1882.

70 Ibid., 6 January 1875.

71 Ibid., 9 August 1887.

72 Ibid., 28 March 1887.

73 Ibid., 12 October 1892.

74 Ibid., 27 May 1926.

75 *Hamilton Herald*, 18 April 1917.

76 See chapter 6.

77 Lane, 'On the Social Meaning of Homicide,' 75.

78 The following discussion is based on 133 cases of homicide reported in the coroner's reports (1869–99; 1934–46; 1953–6), the annual reports of the police department (1906–70, with some gaps), Hamilton Public Library newspaper clipping files on famous murders, and the coverage of the assizes by the *Hamilton Spectator*. A data file was created that included information on the victims and assailants, the context of the crime, the weapon, the charges laid, and the outcome of trials.

79 Homicide is the term used here rather than murder, because the cases collected included murder, manslaughter that had involved an assault, and death owing to aggravated assault. The rule observed in the research was that a homicide was an act that involved a loss of life resulting from some altercation or intention to do harm. The figures differ from the police annual reports in several instances. In 1944 an act of arson killed ten people; the police department annual report for that year cites each death as a homicide. Only one homicide was counted for this project. The police reported the official charge of aggravated assault in several cases

that ended in a death, but for this research the cases were entered
as homicides.

80 A thorough reading of newspapers failed to turn up more homicides than
those in the coroner's inquest book.

81 *The Economist*, 4 April 1992, 107.

82 *AR*, 1907.

83 *AR*, 1913.

84 Hamilton-Wentworth Regional Police Department, 'Statement Made by
X Regarding the Murder of Y,' Hamilton Wanted Persons, 1924–6.
This information was secured under freedom of information legislation
and, as part of a research agreement, the names have not been
recorded.

85 AO, RG 22, box 185, Merenga murder file, statement by Angelo Duca,
26 December 1920.

86 *Hamilton Spectator*, 31 December 1931.

87 Ibid., 18 February 1931.

88 Ibid., 14 January 1965.

89 HPL, clippings from *Hamilton Herald*, 20 May 1922, 22 September 1922,
Hamilton Herald Scrapbooks, vol.M4.1, part 2, murders. On the Black
Hand, see *Hamilton Spectator*, 21 July 1924. Editorial comment in Hamilton
stereotyped Italians as dangerous and prone to violence. The particular conduct of a very few contributed to this stereotyping. The origins
of the idea that Italians were especially violent needs to be seen not
only in association with racism, but in relation to different subsets of criminal acts. The use of handguns, for example, may have been unusual
enough to help brand Italians as violent. For a discussion of stereotyping,
see Karen Dubinsky and Franca Iacovetta, 'Murder, Womanly Virtue,
and Motherhood: The Case of Angela Napolitano, 1911–1922,' *Canadian
Historical Review*, vol.72 (December 1991), 518–19.

90 HPL, clipping from *Hamilton Herald*, 20 May 1922, ibid.

91 *Hamilton Spectator*, 15 January 1926.

92 HPL, RG 10, Series W, Coroner's Inquest Book, 1869–1899, 12 June 1873.

93 Ibid., 13 May 1876.

94 HPL, clipping from *Hamilton Times*, 6 March 1909, *Famous Murders in
Hamilton*, vol.1.

95 *Hamilton Spectator*, 24 May 1967.

96 Neil Boyd, *The Last Dance: Murder in Canada* (Scarborough: Prentice-Hall
1988), 77. Margo Wilson and Martin Daly have found regional variations in spousal homicide for Canada. Yet they have also discovered several common risk factors over the period 1974–92. For all of Canada,
during these years, a woman was nine times as likely to be killed by her
spouse as by a stranger. See Margo Wilson and Martin Daly, 'Spousal

Homicide,' *Jurist*, vol.18, no.8, 1–12; 'Uxoricide in Canada: Demographic Risk Patterns,' *Canadian Journal of Criminology*, Vol.35 (July 1993), 263–91.

97 *Hamilton Spectator*, 17 August 1922.

98 Ibid., 22 June 1882.

99 *AR*, 1913.

100 *Hamilton Spectator*, 7 December 1955.

101 Ibid., 27 February 1957.

102 *AR*, 1969.

103 *AR*, 1932.

104 HPL, clipping from *Hamilton Herald*, 21 July 1924, *Herald Scrapbooks*, vol.4.1, Murder.

105 *AR*, 1942.

106 Hamilton-Wentworth Regional Police, historical records in storage, ledger marked '1924 Hamilton Wanted Persons,' statement of Lily White, 8 July 1925.

107 *AR*, 1926.

108 Friedman and Percival, *The Roots of Justice*, 137.

109 Ibid., 138.

110 Guerry, *Essai*, 41, 69.

CHAPTER SIX

1 HPL, RG 10, Series U, Police Occurrence Book, 13 March 1954. Henceforth cited as OB.

2 OB, 26 March 1954.

3 Rumours still circulate among constables about the old days when wife beaters were dealt with on the scene.

4 *Canadian Law Journal*, vol.9 (January 1873), 1.

5 *Hamilton Spectator*, 18 December 1889.

6 Del Martin, 'The Historical Roots of Domestic Violence,' *Domestic Violence on Trial: Psychological and Legal Dimensions of Family Violence*, Daniel Jay Sonkin, ed. (New York: Springer Publishing Company 1987).

7 Judith Fingard, *The Dark Side of Victorian Halifax* (Porters Lake, Nova Scotia: Pottersfield Press 1989), 189.

8 Linda Gordon, *Heroes of Their Own Lives: The Politics and History of Family Violence, Boston, 1880–1960* (New York: Viking 1988) 264.

9 Gordon, *Heroes of Their Own Lives*, 265.

10 Fingard, *The Dark Side*, 191.

11 *The Economist*, 4 April 1992, 107.

12 *Hamilton Spectator*, 27 November 1862.

13 Ibid., 8 January 1867.

14 Gordon, *Heroes of Their Own Lives*, 255.

15 *Hamilton Spectator*, 21 January 1879.
16 Kai Pernanen, *Alcohol in Human Violence* (New York: Guilford Press 1991), 101–2.
17 *Hamilton Spectator*, 13 January 1880.
18 Ibid., 24 January 1880.
19 Ibid., 7 March 1863.
20 Ibid., 3 April 1863.
21 Ibid., 30 January 1882.
22 OB, 28 July 1955.
23 For the romanticized version based on one case study, see Peter De Lottinville, 'Joe Beef of Montreal: Working Class Culture and the Tavern, 1869–1889,' *Labour/Le Travailleur* vols.8–9 (Autumn/Spring 1981/82), 9–40. Bryan Palmer refers to Joe Beef in *Working-Class Experience: The Rise and Reconstitution of Canadian Labour, 1800–1980* (Toronto: Butterworth 1983), 85–9.
24 Al Purdy, *The Collected Poems of Al Purdy*, Russell Brown, ed. (Toronto: McClelland and Stewart 1986), 109.
25 OB, 30 December 1955.
26 Ibid., 25 June 1955.
27 Ibid., 13 November 1955.
28 Ibid., 30 May 1955.
29 Ibid., 12 January 1955.
30 Ibid., 29 December 1955.
31 Ibid., 15 December 1955.
32 Ibid., 9 November 1955.
33 Ibid., 16 December 1955.
34 Ibid., 13 August 1955.
35 Ibid., 16 December 1955.
36 Ibid., 26 November, 1955.
37 Ibid., 18, 30 December 1955; 10 August 1955.
38 OB, 26 November 1955.
39 Ibid., 13 December 1955.
40 Ibid., 29 December 1955.
41 Ibid., 24 November 1955.
42 Ibid., 29 December 1955.
43 Ibid.
44 Ibid., 26 July 1955.
45 Ibid., 30 December 1955.
46 Ibid., 31 December 1955.
47 Ibid., 10 December 1955.
48 Ibid., 28 November, 24 December 1955.
49 Ibid., 12 November 1955.
50 Ibid., 25 December 1955.

51 Ibid., 20 February 1955.
52 Ibid., 13 November 1955.
53 Ibid., 29 December 1955.
54 Ibid., 31 December 1955.
55 Ibid., 26 November 1955.
56 Ibid., 31 December 1955.
57 *Hamilton Spectator*, 18 August 1863.
58 Ibid., 24 January 1880.
59 Ibid., 16 February 1892.
60 Ibid., 17 January 1865.
61 Ibid., 16 February 1863.
62 Ibid., 25 January 1873.
63 Ibid., 14 March 1873.
64 Ibid., 27 January 1863.
65 OB, 22 June 1934.
66 Ibid., 3 August 1934.
67 The duties of the Hamilton police as detailed in the police commissions minutebooks are well summarized by the phrase 'aid business,' which is employed by Clive Emsley in *Policing and its Context, 1750–1870* (London: Macmillan 1983), 4.
68 HPL, Minutebook, 21 June 1879.
69 Ibid., 5 November 1895.
70 Robert J. Silverman and James J. Teevan Jr, *Crime in Canadian Society* (Toronto: Butterworths 1980), 65.
71 Ibid., 6–7.
72 John Weaver, 'Crime, Public Order, and Repression: The Gore District in Upheaval, 1832–1851,' *Ontario History*, 78 (September 1986), 175–207.
73 There are several examples of services for the middle class and the élite. The police maintained a special vacant-house patrol in the Depression for families away at their summer homes. During the many major strikes of 1946, the force attempted and failed to clear picket lines for the entry of men and material, especially at the Steel Company of Canada. There are indications that the force did not relish this last function. The annual report for 1946 noted that the labour disputes had received more attention from the police and publicity about the police than they deserved when compared to the death toll from auto accidents, which had climbed to about twenty a year.
74 I have hypothesized a high degree of reporting, but a 1976 United States study estimated that only 53 per cent of personal robberies were reported to the police. Charles H. McCaghy, *Crime in American Society* (New York: Macmillan 1980), 138.

75 Irvin Waller and Norman Okihiro, 'Residential Burglary in Toronto,' in Silverman and Teevan Jr, *Crime in Canadian Society*, 307–16.

76 This is based on the marginal notes in red ink which denoted an arrest in the case reported.

77 HPL, RG10, Hamilton Police Department Records, Series C, Chief's Order Book, 1926–36, 3 December 1931.

78 One American study done in the mid-1960s estimated that 86 per cent of crimes reported to the police are citizen-discovered and the remaining 14 per cent are police discovered. Silverman and Teevan Jr, *Crime in Canadian Society*, 64.

79 For an excellent review of the literature on the Depression and crime, see James Huzel, 'The Incidence of Crime in Vancouver during the Great Depression,' *B.C. Studies* (Spring/Summer 1986), 361–81. Huzel has faith in the serial data for Vancouver and employs it with economic indicators to achieve sophisticated evidence for a rise in theft during the initial years of the Depression. For an old but valuable account of the methodological problems arising from assorted studies of crime and the Depression, see Johan Thorsten Sellin, *Research Memorandum on Crime in the Depression*, (New York: Arno Press 1972), 31–62.

80 *AR*, 1932, 2.

81 *AR*, 1936, 7.

82 *AR*, 1945, 8.

83 In his study of wartime crime in England, Edward Smithies noted that 'the war saw a marked quickening in pace' of crime. Edward Smithies, *Crime in Wartime: A Social History of Crime in World War II* (London 1982), 2.

84 *AR*, 1936, 8.

85 OB, 17 November 1934, 19 August 1935.

86 All names have been changed.

87 OB, 15 December 1935.

88 British and Scandinavian studies conducted from the 1960s to the 1980s have arrived at similar conclusions. Juvenile burglars may be responsible for about half of burglaries. Mike Maguire and Trevor Bennett, *Burglary in a Dwelling: The Offence, the Offender, and the Victim* (London: Heinemann 1982), 24–5. George Rengert and John Wasilchick, *Suburban Burglary: A Time and a Place for Everything*, (Springfield, Illinois: Charles C. Thomas 1985), 77.

89 Waller and Okihiro, 'Residential Burglary in Toronto,' 309–10; Maguire and Bennett, *Burglary in a Dwelling*, 166.

90 OB, 31 August 1935.

91 Ibid., 4–5 May 1942.

92 OB, 18 July 1942.

93 *AR*, 1934, 23.

94 *AR*, 1935, 27.

95 OB, 1 December 1934. The report listed Family Packers, Dominion Metal, and the CPR express office as requesting special attention; Loblaws reported that it had moved its safe to the front of the store. For the reports on more remote places, see OB, 18 June, 3 September 1934.

96 The residential nature of burglary has been noted in contemporary studies done in the United States. McCaghy, *Crime in American Society*, 148–9.

97 OB, 23 December, 1935.

98 *AR*, 1945, 7.

99 This observation is commonplace in criminological studies. See Maguire and Bennett, *Burglary in a Dwelling*, 18.

100 OB, 27 March 1935.

101 Ibid., 4 July 1935.

102 Ibid., 30 June 1935.

103 Ibid., 6 December 1935.

104 Ibid., 16 April 1935.

105 OB, 9 April 1935.

106 Ibid., 14, 15 June 1934. The same woman had shirts and socks taken two days in a row.

107 OB, 23 March 1935.

108 Ibid., 26 March 1935.

109 Chief's Order Book, 1926–1935, 11 July 1935.

110 OB, 17 April 1935.

111 'Theft of automobile tires and gasoline ration books has given this Department considerable trouble during the past year.' *AR*, 1942, 29.

112 OB, 28 August 1942.

113 Ibid., 28 March 1942.

114 Ibid., 20 November 1942.

115 This was recorded in OB, 23 February 1942.

116 *Hamilton Spectator*, 14 October 1942.

117 *AR*, 1944, 18.

118 OB, 25 January 1942.

119 Ibid., 14 April 1942.

120 Ibid., 30 May 1942.

121 Ibid., 24 February 1942.

122 Ibid., 5 January 1942.

123 Ibid., 1 March 1942.

124 Ibid., 4 October, 4 November 1942.

125 Ibid., 2 March, 11 April 1942.

126 Ibid., 6 March 1942.

127 Ibid., 14, 21 February 1942.

128 Ibid., 22 November 1942.
129 Ibid., 10, 20 December 1942; 10 May 1942.
130 Ibid., 18 July 1942.
131 Chief's Order Book, 1926–1935, 31 January 1931.
132 Smithies, *Crime in Wartime*, 34.
133 *Hamilton News*, 5 June 1953.
134 OB, 5 June 1935.
135 Ibid., 11 September 1934.
136 Ibid., 5 December 1935.
137 The opportunity-based crimes associated with licensed hotels has been remarked upon by Peter A. Engstad, who used 1968 data for Edmonton. 'Environmental Opportunities and the Ecology of Crimes,' in Silverman and Teevan Jr, *Crime in Canadian Society*, 203–19.
138 A study of recovery of property stolen in burglaries in the Thames valley in 1975 showed that only 12 per cent of victims saw any of the lost property again. Maguire and Bennett, *Burglary in a Dwelling*, 18. Canadian researchers Waller and Okihiro (1978) and Engstad and Evans (1980) 'were beginning to suggest that the investigation of burglary should be given lower priority ... partly because efforts to solve cases were not proving cost effective.' Ibid., 144.
139 OB, 29 November, 8 December 1942.
140 Eric Monkkonen, *Police in Urban America* (New York: Cambridge University Press 1981), 130.

CONCLUSION

1 *Hamilton Spectator*, 13 September 1965.
2 Ibid., 13 January 1964.
3 SO, Ontario 1946 c.72; SO, Ontario 1949 c.72. The Police Act.
4 SO, Ontario 1967 c.18. An Act to Amend the Crown Attorney Act. See also Paul Romney, *Mr Attorney: The Attorney General for Ontario in Court, Cabinet and Legislature, 1791–1899* (Toronto: Published for the Osgoode Society by the University of Toronto Press, 1986), 231.
5 SO, Ontario 1968, c.28. An Act to Amend the County Courts Act.
6 Carolyn Strange, 'Wounded Womanhood and Dead Men: Chivalry and the Trials of Clara Ford and Carrie Davies,' in *Gender Conflicts: New Essays in Women's History*, Franca Iacovetta and Mariana Valverde, eds. (Toronto: University of Toronto Press 1992), 152.
7 Dorothy Chunn, *From Punishment to Doing Good: Family Courts and Socialized Justice in Ontario, 1880–1940* (Toronto: University of Toronto Press 1992), 195. Also see Karen Dubinsky and Franca Iacovetta, 'Murder, Womanly Virtue, and Motherhood: The Case of Angelina Napolitano, 1911–1922,' *Canadian Historical Review*, vol.72 (December 1991), 527–9.

8 Clive Emsley, *Crime and Society in England, 1550–1900* (New York: Longman 1987), 162.
9 The demise of the jury is covered by Paul Romney, 'From Constitutionalism to Legalism: Trial by Jury, Responsible Government, and the Rule of Law in Canadian Political Culture,' *Law and History Review*, vol.7 (Spring 1989), 121–65. The article is a bold interpretation of constitutionalism in Canada that traces the origins of several assaults on civil rights to responsible government.

Index

The italicized letters 't' and 'f' after page numbers indicate that the information cited is in a table or figure, respectively.

accused: identification, 170–1, 271; interrogation, 152–3, 155
Adams, John, 236
Adcock, Addie, 214
Aitken (constable), 114
alcohol. *See* bootlegging; drunk and disorderly charges; police misconduct
Alderman, Bucklin, 57
Alexandra Industrial School for Girls, Scarborough, 184
Amberly, Pete, 236
ambulance service, 138–9, 177
Andrew Mercer Reformatory, Toronto, 183–4
Anglin (chief justice), 170
appeals, 62, 161–2
Armstrong, George, 42–3, 52, 69, 74
arson, 169
artists, 170
assault (*see also* violence; wife beating): mid-

1900s, 234–8; rates, 192, 193*f*, 195*f*, 211–17; reporting, 199, 201, 203, 213, 215–16, 225–6
Assize of Clarendon (1166), 35–6
assizes (*see also* superior courts): 26, 32, 35
automobile accidents: 1870–1970, 176–7, 177*f*; drunk driving, 177–8; speeding, 177–8
automobile offences, 145–6, 175–8
automobiles: and assaults, 235–6; offences, 172, 175; police use, 145–6, 164–5, 178
Aylen, Peter, 10

Badgely, Morris, 242–3
Bagot, Sir Charles, 42
bailiffs, 28
Bainbridge (constable, later sergeant), 102, 144

Baker, Harry, 255
Baldwin, Robert, 36, 42, 82
Balfour (Mrs), 238
banishment (punishment), 60–1
Barty, John, 223
Beasley, Richard, 41*t*
Beatty (constable), 101
benevolent fund, 106, 127
Bennett (constable), 200
Bennett, Dennis, 124
Bertillon, Alphonse, 166
Bertillon system, 110, 166–7
Black, Art, 252
blackmail, 220
Bleakley (constable), 117
blue ribbon campaigns, 270
bootlegging, 116–17, 163, 220
Boyle, Hugh, 214
branding (punishment), 58
Bread Act, 172
break and enter. *See* theft
breathalyser, 177
Brown, Bob, 91

Buda, Simon, 219
burglary. *See* theft
Burkholder, Philander, 221
Burton (mayor), 178
Buttenham, Russell, 180

Cable (constable), 101
Cahill, James, 69, 74, 214
Campaign (constable),
   123–4
Campbell, Alexander, 89,
   102
Campbell (doctor), 66
Campbell, Donald, 103
Campbell, John, 95
Campbell, William, 36
capital punishment (*see also*
   hanging): 61–2, 271
Carr, Leeming, 145
Cartwright-Thomas (sher-
   iff), 48
Case, Alfred, 136
Case, Joe, 47
Cathcart, Thomas, 215
centralization, 269–71, 276
charges. *See* reporting
   methods
charity: police relief fund,
   137–8; police shelter,
   132–8, 177, 179
Chesick, Steve, 249
Chief Constables'
   Association of Canada,
   95
chief of police: role, 100;
   training, 168
chiefs of police: Lawrence,
   Leonard, 168, 181;
   McKinnon, Hugh,
   98–100, 108–10;
   Smith, Alexander, 115,
   121, 129, 138–42;
   Stewart, Alexander D.,
   93–8, 106, 123,
   138–40; Torrance,
   Gordon, 168; Whatley,
   William, 130, 141–2,
   144, 207
children: criminals, 84,
   183–4, 205–6, 214,
   243, 248, 252; victims,
   232, 237–9

Children's Aid Society, 184,
   239
Childrens' Protection Act,
   172
church. *See* religion
cities: as crime reducers,
   191–4, 196, 198; as
   crime sources, 189–91,
   197–8
city recorder, 80
Civic Improvement
   Association, 118
Clancey, Catherine, 206
Clark, John, 143
class differences, crime
   rates, 211–12, 216–17,
   230–1, 241, 245,
   257–60
clerks of the peace, 38–40
Collins, Francis, 36–7
Combs, George, 206
common law, origins, 25–6
Common Law Procedure
   Act (1856), 32
confessions, 153
constable: ethnicity, 129,
   181–2; gender, 164,
   181–2, 268, 271; historical overview, 6, 16–18;
   locals *vs.* outsiders, 269;
   pensions, 103–6; re-
   cruitment: 1800s, 52,
   88–90; 1900s, 121–6,
   125*f*, 125, 127*f*, 128,
   130–1, 180–1; role:
   1800s, 28, 71, 90–1, 171,
   206; 1900s, 126–7,
   144–6, 164, 171–5,
   178–80; training,
   99–100, 168, 180–1;
   wages, 103, 126*f*, 126–7
Contagious Diseases Act,
   172
Coombs (constable), 142
Copeline, Bill, 236
coroner: 1800s, 27, 34, 66,
   154; 1900s, 154, 176
Costain, Mike, 254
Coulter (constable, later
   detective), 101, 144
County Attorneys Act
   (1857), 82

County and Borough Police
   Act (1856), 51
County Judge's Criminal
   Court, 66, 81–3
court of appeals, 62
Court of King's Bench,
   32
Court of Oyer and
   Terminer and General
   Gaol Delivery, 30*f*, 32
court system: evolution, 29,
   30*f*, 199–200; gender
   bias, 230–2, 272–3; historical overview, 10–12,
   265–6
Creen (constable), 114
Crerar, John, 66–7, 84
criers, 33
crime rate: 1800s, 37–8,
   43–4, 47–8, 56–7;
   1900s, 173*f*; assault, 192,
   193*f*, 195*f*, 211–17;
   class differences,
   211–12, 216–17,
   230–1, 241, 245,
   257–60; conclusions,
   223–4, 274; domestic violence, 227; gender differences, 75*t*, 233;
   homicide, 55–6, 189,
   192, 195–6, 217–23,
   218*f*; relation to cities,
   189–94, 196–8; theft,
   192, 194*f*, 196, 198,
   204–10, 205*f*, 210*f*,
   247–8; 'waves,' 188–9
crime reports. *See* reporting
   methods
crime research: analysis
   methods, 189–98;
   sources (*see also* reporting
   methods), 244, 246–7,
   260; statistical biases,
   20–1, 189–98, 223–4,
   227–8, 246–7
crime-solving rate, 119–20
crime types: early 1900s,
   75*t*, 76–7, 131–2, 132*t*,
   175; late 1800s, 74–5,
   75*t*, 76–8, 78*t*, 175;
   mid-1800s, 37, 40,
   43–50, 55

Criminal Code (1892), 154, 160–2
criminals: definition, 198, 261–2; ethnicity, 53–5, 57–8; gender, 54–5, 272; identifying, 110, 166–7, 170–1
Croft (sergeant), 237
Crooks, Matthew, 38
crown attorney: position created, 67, 82, 202, 269; role, 19, 83–5, 149–51, 154, 159–61, 270, 274–5; training, 162
crown attorneys, role, 33

Davis, Elizabeth, 243
Davis, George, 74
Davison (constable), 93
Deardon, Catherine, 84
defence attorney: costs, 215; role, 33, 156–7, 161
Denison, George T., 19, 70, 73, 75, 77, 128
detective: role, 66, 71, 95–7, 169–70, 201; training, 98, 100, 167–8
DeWilloughby, Percy, 167
Dick, Evelyn, 147–58, 163, 169–70, 221, 267, 272
Dick, John, 149
Domitro, Pete, 252
Donegale, Ellen, 255
drug trafficking, 116
drunk and disorderly charges, 150, 175, 200
Duca, Angelo, 219
Duggan, William, 243
Duncan (constable), 120, 123
Durand, Charles, 46
Dzwolkic, Alex, 262

Edward VII, King of Great Britain and Ireland, 72
Egg Grading Act, 172
electric chair, 186
Ellis, Arthur (second hangman), 186

Ellis, Arthur (third hangman), 186
Ellis, Jane, 54, 63
ethnicity (see also immigrants): homicides, 219–20; jail population, 53–5, 57–8; police bias, 115–17, 141–2, 166, 174, 208, 271; of police force, 129, 181–2; public bias, 116–17, 188, 239–40, 256
Evans, Charlotte, 241–2
evidence, 96–7, 152, 155, 171

family court, 184–5, 271, 273
Farewell, J.M., 124
Federal Bureau of Investigation, U.S., 167
felonies: procedures, 29, 31, 34–6; rates, 68
Fennessy, John, 57
Fenton (constable), 101, 105–6
Ferrie, Colin, 40, 41t
Ferrie, Robert, 40
Ferrier (early JP), 38
Ferris, Peter, 91, 104–5
fines, 58–9, 77, 79t
fingerprinting, 110, 167–8
firearms: criminal-owned, 188, 219–21; police-owned, 90, 118, 122–3
Fleming, Bernard, 232
Fleming, Cecil, 259
Food and Drug Act, 172
Forbes (murderer), 222
Fordychuk, Arno, 236
fraud. See theft
funeral parades, police officers, 270

Gage, Nathan, 41t
gambling, 112–13, 116, 140, 163
Game and Fisheries Act, 172
gang violence, 217, 221
Garrick Club, 67
Gas Company Act, 172

gender: court system, 230–2, 272–3; crime rates, 75t, 218–19, 233–40; jail population, 54–5; police force, 164, 181–2, 268, 271
general sessions, 30f, 80
Gibbs (constable), 143
Gibson (Mrs John), 113
Gigg (constable), 103
Ginerick, John, 40
Gold and Silver Marketing Act, 172
Golitza, Stephen, 256
Gore District, defined, 43
Gorman, Daniel, 55
Gould (Mrs Tommy), 108–9
Gould, Tommy, 108
Gowan, James R., 158–9
grand jury: abolition, 157–62, 269; role, 31–4
Griffin, Ebinezer, 48
Guerry, A.M., 190, 224
guns. See firearms

Hagerman, Christopher, 24, 32, 36–7
Hall, James, 55
Halliday, Elizabeth, 136
Hallisey (constable), 91
Hamilton, history, 7–8, 10, 13–14
Hamilton Citizens League, 113
Hamilton Law Association, 160, 162
Hamilton Local Council of Women, 182
Hamilton Police Association, 130, 179
Hamilton Reform Association, 69
Hamilton Street Railway, 118–19
Hamilton-Wentworth Regional Detention Centre, 3–4
hanging (see also capital punishment): of McConnell, 64; and pun-

ishment reform, 61–2;
of Vincent, 23–5, 37, 65
hangmen, 185–6
Harbour Commissioners'
Bylaws, 172
Harris (constable), 102,
215
Hatt, Richard, 38
Haycock, John, 57
Henderson, Nora Frances,
182
Herbert family, 237
Hickman, Jesse, 55
high courts. See superior
courts
Hinds, Henry, 229
Hiscox (Mrs), 231
homicide: age of assailant,
218; crown plea, 27;
gender of assailant,
218–19, 221–3; gen-
der of victim, 219,
221–3; rates, 55–6, 68,
176, 177f, 189, 192,
195–6, 217–23, 218f
Hotel Registrations Act,
172
housebreaking. See theft
Howland, William, 112

identification: Bertillon
system, 110, 166–7;
line-ups, 170–1
immigrants (see also
ethnicity): bias against,
15–16, 116–17, 144,
167, 174, 188, 192,
208; and crime types, 43,
48–9; economic oppor-
tunity, 194, 207, 266;
homicides, 219–21
indecent assaults, 238–9
insanity (criminal), 67–8,
183–4
intermediate courts, 29,
30f, 79–85
International Association of
Chiefs of Police, 168
international connections,
165–8
interrogation techniques,

152–3, 156, 163,
169–70
investigation techniques,
169–71, 200–1, 270–1
Irizik, Baptiste, 243
Iron and Steel Company,
111–12
Irvine, William, 186

jail committals, 1800s,
43–7, 44–45f, 47f, 49,
77
jail conditions, 59–60,
182–3
jailer, 28
Jeffrey, Nicholas, 152, 154
Jelfs, George: day in the
life, 70–2; interpreta-
tion of law, 73–4, 85,
115, 130, 203, 205,
267, 272; investigates
McKinnon, 108–9; ju-
venile court judge, 76,
84, 184; stiff sentences,
74, 78–9, 84, 226; train-
ing, 69
Johnson, Thomas, 89
Johnston, Ada, 75
Jones, Ralph, 235
judges (see also police magistrate): assizes, 32–3,
35; county, 80; district,
80; training, 6, 162
jurors, 32, 36–7, 81–2,
157–8, 161
justice of the peace: ap-
pointments, 38–40; his-
torical overview, 269;
role, 28–9, 31, 33–4,
40–1, 69, 80, 154, 163,
185, 200; training, 27,
31
justices. See judges
juvenile court, 30f, 184–5,
271
juvenile delinquency,
182–4

Kavanagh (sergeant
major), 72, 104–5
Keele, William Conway, 38

Kennedy, Jennie, 101
Kern, Thomas, 206
Kerns, Joseph, 229
King, George, 222
Kingston penitentiary,
60–2
Kinrade, Ethel, 134
Kovacs, Domenic, 254, 256

labourers: strikes, 118–19,
133–4; unemployed,
136–7
Lapcewich brothers, 250
larceny: charges, 200; defi-
nitions, 31; rates, 35,
192f, 192, 204
Lavill, Mary, 47
Law Reform Commission,
5, 161
Lawrence, Leonard, 168,
181
lawyers: role, 75–6, 80;
training, 160, 162
Layton, Charles, 124
Lebundy, Haley, 214–15
legal aid, 162–3, 231
Levy, Joseph, 146
Lewis (constable), 182
Lily, May, 47
line-ups, 170–1
Littlehales (constable), 102
Local Council of Women,
113
localism, 49, 269–71
Lochart, Alex, 215
Lord's Day Act, 112
Lottery Act, 172
Lowery, John, 122
Luckey (Mr and Mrs), 47
Lyle (Mrs Samuel), 113

Macaulay, James Buchanan,
32, 34–5, 56
McConnell, Michael, 64–9,
81, 84, 214, 217
Macdonald, John A., 86–7
MacDougall, Nelson, 236
McElroy, Sarah, 214
McGee, D'Arcy, 65
MacGill, Helen, 184
MacGuinn (sergeant), 262

McKenzie (constable), 102
McKinnon, Hugh, 98–100, 108–10
McMahon (tavern owner), 229
McMenemy, Alexander, 129
MacNab, Sir Allan, 42
Macrae, Victoria, 221
magistrate, role, 155
magistrate's courts, 155
Mahon, John, 206
Mallet, James, 75
Maloney, Arthur, 158
manslaughter. *See* homicide
Maranga, Giovanni, 153
Markle, James, 26
Martin, Dora, 136
Marwood, William, 185
Masiah, Henry, 54
Mason, Charles, 135
Masonic lodge, 128–9
Maychark, Fred, 256
mayors' court, 30*f*
medicine, 67–8
Meharg, Wilfred, 188–9
men: and alcohol, 229; criminals, 54–5, 75*f*, 221–3, 234–9, 272; victims, 233–7
Merritt (constable), 143
Mewburn, S.C., 120
Meyers (constable), 122
militarism, 93–4, 97, 109, 174
Milligan, Eliza, 213
Milligan, Thomas, 213
Mills, Nelson, 65–6, 69, 217
misdemeanours, 29
Moore (constable), 101
morality: early 1900s, 113–18, 140; late 1800s, 110–12
motorcycles, 156, 164–5
Motor Vehicle Act, 172, 175
Moving Pictures Act, 172
murder. *See* homicide
Myers (constable), 127
Myers, Eliza, 206

Nelson, Gertrude, 255
New Democratic Party, 266
non-support cases, 74, 78
North-West Mounted Police (*see also* Royal Canadian Mounted Police): 14, 87

Ogilvie, James, 183
O'Heir (attorney), 202
Ontario law, historical overview, 4–7, 9–19
Ontario Police College, 168
Ontario Provincial Police (OPP): link to municipal force, 164–5, 168, 175; women on force, 182
Ontario Temperance Act, 163
Orange lodge, 128–9
O'Reilly (major), 124
Osler, B.B., 66
Owen, James, 56, 219
Owen, Thomas, 214

Patterson (judge), 67
Pawnbrokers Act, 172
Penetanguishene Reformatory, 183
Perry, Gideon, 121
petit jury, 32, 35–6
Pettigrew, John, 214
petty sessions, 29, 30*f*, 68–9
photographs: scene, 167; suspect, 166–7
pickpocketing. *See* theft
Pidgeon, Philip, 255
pillory, 23, 58
Pinch (sergeant), 102
Pinch, Bill, 167
Pinch, John, 184
Piper (constable), 124
Police Act (1949), 168
police artists, 170
police clerk, 72
police commissions, 76
police magistrate: historical overview, 19–20; position created, 41–2, 269; provincial commission

of 1921, 73; role, 68–79, 81, 154–5, 200–3, 206; training, 69, 162
police magistrate's court, 30*f*, 68–9, 71–5, 77–8, 83–5, 184–5
police misconduct: early 1900s, 123–4, 140, 142–4; late 1800s, 100–3
police relief fund, 137–8
police shelter, 132–8, 177, 179
police unions, 130
policing: changing attitude toward, 186–7; conclusions, 273–4; historical overview, 17–18, 21–2, 269; international connections, 165–8; and moral order, 110–18; origins, 50–3, 85–7; professionalization, 88–98, 109, 178–9; size of force, 165, 166*f*
Potash, Melville, 259
Potter, R., 252
Power Commission Act, 172
preliminary hearing, 9, 34, 171
Price, Andy, 216
Pritich, Budimir, 76
prosecuting attorney. *See* crown attorney
prostitution, 47, 112–13, 115, 140, 272
protectionism, 220
provincial court, 30*f*, 155
provincial district court, 30*f*
provincial offences court, 30*f*
Pryer (constable), 165
Public Health Act, 172
public prosecutor. *See* crown attorney
punishment. *See* specific types
punishment reform: late 1800s to mid-1900s, 182–7; mid-1800s, 58–63

quarter sessions, 29, 30f, 80
Quinn, Archibald, 200

Rabies Act, 172
Racey, Thomas, 41t
Radclive, John Robert, 185–6
radios (patrol cars), 165
Rankin (Mrs), 238
rape (see also sex offences): 192
Ravelle, Marianne, 47
RCMP. See Royal Canadian Mounted Police (RCMP)
recorder's court, 30f, 80
recruitment: early 1900s, 121, 124–6, 125f, 127f, 128, 130–1; ethnic minorities, 117, 129, 181–2; late 1800s, 88–90; mid-1900s, 180–1
red mass, 267
Reed, James, 56
reformatories, 183–4
religion: of constabulary, 128–9; moral instruction, 267–8; and policing, 48, 112–13, 267
repeat offenders, 54, 56
reporting methods: assault, 199, 201, 203, 211, 213, 215–16, 225–6; and statistical analysis, 198–9, 223–4, 227–8; theft, 199–201, 204–6, 209, 210f
Riel, Louis, 97
robbery. See theft
Robinette, John J., 155–6
Robinson (constable), 90
Robinson, John Beverley, 11, 31, 66
Rolph, George, 39–40
Rooney, James, 56, 219
Rooney, John, 56
Rowe, William, 104–5
Roxborough, Alex, 41t
Royal Canadian Mounted Police (RCMP) (see also North-West Mounted Police): fingerprint bu-

reau, 167; link to municipal force, 164, 168, 174
Ryan, Mary, 158

Salvation Army, 115
School Act, 172
Semiovitch, Alex, 237
sex offences, 158, 238–9
Sharp (constable), 143
shelter, police-run, 132–8, 177, 179
sheriff, 28, 32, 36, 185
Shield, John, 231–2
shoplifting. See theft
Simons, Titus, 39
Sinclair (judge), 89, 92, 103, 138
Smith (constable), 90
Smith, Alexander, 115, 121, 129, 138–42
Smith, Charlie, 121
Smith, Edgar, 252
Smith, George, 201
Smith, Helen, 237
Snider, Carl, 235
social workers, 6–7
South, Mary, 240
'speedy trial' act of 1869, 81
Spence (constable), 90
Springer (constable), 122, 143
Standish, John, 61
Stark, Tom, 235
statements: importance, 151; obtaining, 152–3, 164, 169–70; safeguards, 153–6, 271
statistics. See crime research
Stelco, 174
Stephensen, Jack, 238
Stephensen, Jill, 238
Stewart, Alexander D., 93–8, 106, 123, 138–40
Stewart, William, 230
stocks (punishment), 23, 58
strikes, 118–19, 133–4, 174–5
Sturgeon, James, 206
summary courts, 29, 30f

superior courts (see also assizes): 29, 30f
Supreme Court of Judicature of Ontario, 30f
suspects, identifying, 110, 166–7, 170–1
Sutherland (constable), 101
Swayze, Caleb, 55

Tambuello, Dom, 236
Tamillo, Jake, 219
Tanguay, Barbara, 237
Tanguay, Bob, 237
Taylor (translator), 153
Taylor, Bud, 222–3
Taylor, Charles, 206
technology: and automobile accidents, 177–8; early 1900s, 145; late 1800s, 106–7, 110, 188; mid-1900s, 164–5, 168, 180, 188
temperance movement, 48, 112
theft: dollar value, 248, 249f; locations, 253–7; mid-1800s, 241–3; mid-1900s, 243–50; motives, 250–3; rates, 192, 194f, 196, 198, 204–10, 205f, 210f; reporting methods, 199–201, 204–6, 209, 210f; victims, 257–62
Thomas, Harry, 237
Tolliver, Daniel, 47
Toronto, Hamilton, and Buffalo (TH&B) Railway, 15–16
Torrance, Gordon, 168
Townsend, John, 84
Trades and Labour Council, 119, 130
traffic court, 30f, 178
translators, 76
treason, 32–3
trial practices, 157
trials by jury, 31, 274–5
Truckle, Frank, 222
Tuck (constable), 143

Tucker, Elizabeth, 238
Tucker, Jim, 238
Tucker, William, 99
Tuckett, George C., 145
Tuckett Tobacco Company, 243

unions: police, 130; police action against, 118–19, 133–4, 174–5

vagrancy: 1800s, 48–9, 74, 78*f*; 1900s, 78*f*, 132–5, 137
Vagrancy Act (1824), 48
vagrancy charges, 150
Vanberg, Lucy, 239
vandalism, 239–40
Vanotter (sergeant), 143
Van Patten, Henry, 56
vice, 113, 114*f*, 131–2, 140, 220
Victoria Industrial School for Boys, Mimico, 184
Vincent, Michael, 24–8, 31–4, 36–7, 55, 62–3, 65, 221
violence (*see also* assault; homicide; wife beating): and alcohol, 228–31, 235, 237; do-

mestic, 185, 217, 221–2, 225–7; laying charges, 240–1; locations, 234; male predominance, 272; precipitating factors, 228–30, 232–3, 235–40; rates, 196, 198, 217, 228–40
Vosper, Charles, 221

Waincott (Mrs), 258
Wallace (constable), 145
war veterans' association, 174
Washington, S.F., 150
weaponry (*see also* firearms): 90–1, 118
Weights and Measures Act, 172
Weir, William, 253
Wertheimer, Leopold, 214
West (constable), 200
Whatley, William, 115, 119, 130, 139–42, 144, 207
whippings, 23, 58–9, 74, 226
White, Lily, 222–3
White, Thomas, 66
Whitworth, T.J., 188–9
wife beating (*see also* assault): and alcohol,

225, 227–8; homicides, 222; laying charges, 74, 201, 203, 213–14; serious offence, 74, 226, 230
Williams, Amelia, 255
Willis, John Walpole, 62
Wilson, Albert, 235
Wilson, Andrew, 124
Wilson, Ed, 215
Wilson, James, 24, 32
witnesses, 33, 156, 169
women, battered (*see* also wife beating): criminals, 54–5, 75*t*, 221–3, 238, 272; jurors, 158, 268, 271; lawyers, 158; police, 164, 181–2, 268, 271; victims, 233–4, 237–9
Women's Christian Temperance Union, 181–2
Woods, Bill, 236
Woodsworth, J.S., 191
Workman, Joseph, 67–8

Young, George, 61
Young Women's Christian Association (YWCA), 115